The Making of Britain 2

Front cover. From Plate 1.

Back cover. *Cockfighting.* From the 1759 engraving, 'Pit Ticket for the Royal Sport', by William Hogarth. This bears out well von Uffenbach's description of the 'sport' in Anne's reign (see pp. 254-5). It shows the cocks with their steel spurs fighting on the small, mat-covered arena, separated by a ledge from the spectators. It shows, too, the mixture of social classes who followed this diversion – with a blind nobleman as its central figure, placing his bets among the shouting crowd. And the shadow of a defaulting debtor, imprisoned in a basket lifted to the ceiling, is shown upon the table-top dangling a watch as a pledge for his debts.

Front endpaper. *The Riding from the Tower.* From a watercolour copy (1785) by S. H. Grimm of an original (c. 1547) painting destroyed in 1793. It shows the coronation procession of Edward VI passing through Cheapside on its way from the Tower to Westminster Abbey. On the left is the Tower with its moat and the entry to it from the river; and, slightly to its right, the church of St. Mary-le-Bow with the water-conduit column, known as the 'Standard', beside it. In the centre is Cheap Cross (one of the 'Eleanor Crosses', of which Charing Cross originally was another) and, to the right, old St. Paul's with its soaring spire. London Bridge is shown, built over with houses, and the church of St. Mary Overy (now Southwark Cathedral), a little to the right of its far end.

Back endpaper. *John Ogilby's Road Book.* A section of one of the hundred plates in the first volume of Ogilby's *Britannia* (1675) – the first survey of English and Welsh roads, part of whose importance was the displacement of the old British mile of 2,428 yards by the statute one of 1,760 yards. The wheel by which the survey was made is shown at the top left – easily operated by one man. The maps are all one-inch, as the marked distances from London show, and indicate the main crossing roads together with street maps to the same scale of the most important towns (here Oxford). Considerable detail is given: e.g. roads bounded by black lines are hedged while pricked ones are open; and ascents on the outward route are shown as formalized hills and descents by hills upturned. By the end of the century the maps were being printed in a pocket octavo edition and so must have added greatly to the convenience of travel at the time. (Cf. text p. 204.)

BOOKS IN THIS SERIES

By T. K. Derry and M. G. Blakeway

(1) The Making of Britain: Life and Work to the Close of the Middle Ages

(2) The Making of Britain: Life and Work between the Renaissance and the Industrial Revolution

By T. K. Derry and T. L. Jarman

(3) The Making of Modern Britain: Life and Work from George III to Elizabeth II

T. K. Derry
MA DPhil (Oxon.)

M. G. Blakeway
MA (Cantab.)

The Making of Britain 2

LIFE AND WORK BETWEEN THE RENAISSANCE AND THE INDUSTRIAL REVOLUTION

John Murray · London

Printed in Great Britain by
Cox and Wyman Limited, London, Fakenham and Reading
Library edition 7195 1833 4
Students' edition 7195 1834 2

PREFACE

THIS is the second of two volumes on earlier British history, which follow the same general plan as *The Making of Modern Britain*, laying the main emphasis on social and economic development rather than on the details of politics and diplomacy. But it is hoped that sufficient space has been given to the political outline to show the stages by which the inhabitants of our island became united. The point of view is not that of the government but of the people themselves, as their history slowly shaped them for the great age of industrial and imperial expansion which lay ahead.

The book is designed for use in outline courses, or as an introduction to more advanced studies. The text includes a good many quotations from contemporary sources, which may help to give life and authenticity to the narrative for those who find separate collections of documents unpalatable; there is also an appendix recording the impressions of foreign visitors to the island from the reign of Henry VII onwards. The Table of Events is intended to enable the reader to fix the general chronological framework in his mind, so that the material in successive chapters, which is often grouped by subject rather than by date, may fall more readily into place. The Book List suggests books at about the same level of difficulty as our own, where particular topics are treated in greater detail, as well as standard authorities recommended for more advanced work. The student will find his way to accessible contemporary writings through the Appendix of References; this shows where every such item quoted in the book is to be found, usually in its full context.

The authors wish to acknowledge their deep indebtedness to Mr M. St. John Parker of King's School, Canterbury, for many helpful suggestions; to Mr W. F. Spinks, Senior Science Master, St Marylebone Grammar School, for his guidance on scientific matters; and to the staff of Messrs John Murray for the care which they have lavished upon the illustrations.

T.K.D.
M.G.B.

ACKNOWLEDGEMENTS

Thanks are due to the following who have kindly permitted the reproduction of copyright illustrations:

Plate 1 (photograph by Edwin Smith, copyright Gordon Fraser Gallery Ltd.); 2 (Trinity College, Cambridge); 3 (National Gallery); 4 (Country Life); 5 (Bodleian Library, Oxford); 6, 7, 9, 12, 13, 14, 15, 23 (Trustees of the British Museum); 8 (Wigtown County Library); 10, 16, 20, 21, 25 (Mansell Collection); 11 (International Wool Secretariat); 17 (Clerk of Records, House of Lords); 18 (City Art Gallery, Bristol); 19 (Crown copyright. By permission of the Controller, H.M. Stationery Office. Photograph: National Monuments Record of Scotland); 22 (Trustees of the London Museum); 24 (National Monuments Record); 26 (Worcester College Library, Oxford); endpapers, front (Trustees of the London Museum), back (Map Room, British Museum); covers, front (as for plate 1), back (Trustees of the London Museum).

CONTENTS

The Tudor Period

The Stuart Century

Early Hanoverian Britain

PLATES

MAPS

THE TUDOR PERIOD

I

INTRODUCTORY

> The whole country of Britain is divided into four parts, whereof the one is inhabited by Englishmen, the other of Scots, the third of Welshmen, the fourth of Cornish people . . . which all differ among themselves either in tongue, either in manners, or else in laws and ordinances.

So wrote the naturalized Italian cleric, Polydore Vergil, in a history of England which he composed at the request of the first Tudor king, Henry VII. In the present volume we shall try to trace the process by which these peoples were welded together to form the Britain of the mid-eighteenth century, whose name the youthful George III was to glory in.[1] Eight generations lie between the first Tudor and the third Hanoverian sovereign, generations of which it is hardly too much to say that each of them left a distinctive mark upon the making of the British people. But the marks left by the Tudor period were perhaps the deepest of all, for during these one hundred and eighteen years the British peoples were being reshaped, not only by the flow of events within their own island, but to an exceptional extent by greater movements which were transforming the life of the whole of western Europe.

[1] See p. 323.

Three European Movements

Medieval Christendom and the system of ideas for which it stood, after governing men's thoughts and actions for many centuries, were now disappearing into the past – just as long-accepted ideas of Britain's place as a world power or of a world civilization centred upon Europe have been disappearing in our own time. Then as now, men lived in a ferment of change. In particular, we may notice the effects of three great movements, which did not indeed originate among the British but which in the long run affected their fortunes as fully as the lands of origin.

The Renaissance or revival of art and letters under the influence of classical models had its first home in Italy in the fifteenth century and even earlier. Literature, painting, sculpture, and architecture all derived new inspiration from direct contact with the writings and other remains of ancient Greek culture and, to a lesser extent, from an accompanying revaluation of the works of ancient Rome. In the medieval world everything centred upon God; man was thought of as a forlorn creature hurrying through this vale of tears, which God had created to test him in preparation for the future life. All knowledge was supposed to serve a religious purpose: even the reading of a pagan Latin poet such as Vergil had to be justified by the belief that he had prophesied the coming of the Messiah. How different was that ancient Greek world which had now been rediscovered! Its gods had been shadowy figures; man had been at the centre of everything, with a prescriptive right to use, enjoy, and seek to understand whatever the universe had to offer. The Italians shook off the limitations of medieval thought, and through the medium of their artistic achievement transmitted a new freedom to other lands.

Renaissance ideas spread across the Alps into Germany, France, and the Low Countries, from which they were passed on to England, Scotland, and eventually Scandinavia. In England they found their supreme expression at the close of the sixteenth century in the genius of William Shakespeare, but long before his time Italian verse-forms, music, and architecture, German portrait painting, and Netherlands scholarship each played a part in the life of the Tudor age. So did new ideas regarding the supreme authority of the secular state over its subjects, preached by the Florentine, Machiavelli, in *The Prince* and practised by such ministers as Thomas Cromwell, in accordance with the general trend of European thought, long before the book itself became known outside Italy.

But the belief in the nation state as entitled to an absolute loyalty from its subjects, with which even the obligations of religion must be made to conform, derived its chief impetus from the splitting up of the medieval Church by the Reformation movement. It was in 1517 that the Augustinian friar, Martin Luther, challenged the authority of the papacy in the Saxon university city of Wittenberg. His was not the first, but the first effective, challenge to a spiritual power of which the origins are hidden in the first Christian centuries and the astonishing vitality remains to our own day. When Luther died in 1546, half the rulers of Germany and both their Scandinavian neighbours had set up reformed Churches based on repudiation of the pope and of much Catholic doctrine, especially that of transubstantiation, the miraculous changing of bread and wine into Christ's body and blood in the service of the Mass; the use of a new liturgy and Bible in the native tongue; and the confiscation of the accumulated wealth of monasteries and other Catholic institutions.

For England, however, and still more for Scotland, what may be called the second wave of the Reformation was more important, when Switzerland became the first home of the more strongly anti-Catholic theologies of Ulrich Zwingli of Zurich and the French exile, John Calvin. The presbyterian Church which Calvin presided over in Geneva based its theology on predestination, the strange but inspiring belief that salvation is restricted to a tiny minority of saints, whose identity is known in advance to God and to God alone. But it is better remembered for its moral standards, which were of superhuman strictness, and for the relatively democratic political outlook implied in its replacement of bishops by church assemblies of ministers and lay elders. The Dutch, the French Huguenots, the Scots, some German princes, and most of the English Puritans came to look to Calvin as their main religious teacher.

In the second half of the sixteenth century, however, the further spread of both these main forms of Protestantism was severely checked by the effective re-organization of the Catholic Church under the auspices of reforming popes. One of its long-term consequences was to be the outbreak in 1618 of the Thirty Years War in Germany. But the feature of this Counter-Reformation movement which had most effect on Britain was the spread of the new priestly Order of Jesus, many of whose members were secretly recruited in Protestant states, very thoroughly trained and indoctrinated at Jesuit colleges in Rome and elsewhere, and then smuggled back to work as missionaries for the conversion of their home countries.

Meanwhile the states of western Europe were also being transformed in another way, through the voyages of discovery which brought Africa south of the Sahara, America, and the eastern half of Asia into effective contact for the first time with our own diminutive continent. Portugal for a short period enjoyed the fabulous profits of the spice trade in the Far East. Supreme in the western hemisphere, Spain had her Golden Century. But the intrusions of the Dutch East Indiamen into the oceanic trades, which papal decisions of 1494 and 1529 had reserved exclusively for Spain and Portugal, enabled the Protestant Netherlands to maintain their independence from their former Spanish masters. In a rather similar way her advantageous position on the edge of the new ocean trade routes helped England, as we shall see, to build up the strength which defeated the Spanish Armada.

Impact of Printing

In our island, as elsewhere, the impact of all these great continental movements was felt much more immediately and widely than the events of past centuries had been, because printing had given wings to men's thoughts. Without it, the knowledge of Greek texts would have taken generations to become widespread; there could have been no worthwhile diffusion of the first tentative advances in mathematics and science, which led the way to greater things; the sixteenth-century translations of the Bible would have had only the same limited success as Wyclif's; and such opinion-forming works as Foxe's *Book of Martyrs* and Hakluyt's

Voyages would have had their influence restricted to a small circle of well-to-do persons who could afford to buy manuscript copies.

Latin was still the language of the learned world, in which most major political and religious writing was done. When Calvin published 'a prospectus of the Church militant on earth, a handbook for Christian warriors',[1] it made its first appearance as the *Christianae Religionis Institutio*, and the 3,000 surviving letters of Dutch Erasmus are likewise all in Latin. But translations were common, and in the course of the sixteenth century more and more books of all kinds came to be written in Italian, French, English, and other vernaculars. In printing, though not in the growth of its language, England had lagged behind the continent. But from the first year of the new century there was a King's Printer, and before 1558 the existence of at least 91 different stationers in London can be proved from their signs. Many of the books they sold were still imported from abroad in sheet form; Elizabethan printers, however, though restricted by order of the Council to London and one press in each university, made nearly all the black-letter folios which we associate with the great writers of the age. They even produced the copper-plate engravings for such a masterpiece as Saxton's *Atlas of England and Wales*, the first of all national atlases.

One consequence of the growth of printing in this age was that every kind of controversy was, for the first time in history, left on record in great detail for the study of later generations. This may often be misleading. The growth of national feeling, which the historian traces in so many states at this time, may appear more sudden and decisive a phenomenon than it really was, simply because rhapsodies about one's own country and denunciations of the depravity and sinister intentions of foreign powers survived in quantity through being committed to print. It was also easier for social and economic difficulties to leave a permanent impression. Such difficulties figure prominently in the history of Tudor England, for instance. But in their case it is possible for us to trace important disturbing influences which are common to most parts of sixteenth-century Europe.

[1] E. G. Rupp in *New Cambridge Modern History*, Vol. II, p. 117.

The Growth of Population

The fall in population, which had been very marked for a century or more after the Black Death, gave place at this time to a fairly rapid rise. The reasons are not known, though it is possible that plague, which had been so great a killer, was becoming more local in its incidence. "They have some little plague in England every year," writes the Venetian ambassador in 1554, "for which they are not accustomed to make sanitary provisions, as it does not usually make great progress." Other factors may have been earlier marriages, a more nourishing average dietary, and better arrangements made by many governments to secure supplies of grain in the event of famine. But whatever the reasons, the fact is clear:[1] Tudor England shared in an upswing of population which can be traced as far afield as the Balkans and which doubled the numbers of our Dutch neighbours, for example, in the course of a century.

In spite of the institution of parish registers in 1538 and the preservation of many which have been actually entered up from the accession of Elizabeth, no precise vital calculations are feasible for any part of her kingdom. But it seems likely that the population began to increase slowly about 1450, was rather less than 4 million at the turn of the century, rose to about 4½ million by 1558, and may have topped 5 million at the time of the Queen's death, in spite of a final decade of stagnation. London certainly grew at an altogether disproportionate speed, perhaps doubling in size during the single reign of Elizabeth, when some authorities believe that it may even have reached 300,000, which might be the equivalent of the whole of Wales.

The military manpower estimates for Armada year, which we may suppose were diligently prepared, indicate that Gloucester, Somerset, Kent, and Devon (in that order) were the most populous counties of southern England. But Norfolk, which may well have been the most crowded county of all, is excluded from this enumer-

[1] "The population of Europe was growing at a secular rate sufficient to yield substantial increments in all countries over the level of 1450." (K. F. Helleiner in *Cambridge Economic History of Europe,* Vol. IV, p. 72.)

ation. For the towns of the provinces we have even less to go upon. Norwich and Bristol undoubtedly stood first, but were completely dwarfed by London: they may have had between 12,000 and 15,000 citizens apiece. Next came Newcastle and York in the north, Exeter and Gloucester in the south, with populations of about 8,000 or less. Scotland, whose total population may have reached 850,000 by 1600, had even smaller towns: Edinburgh was probably little bigger than Newcastle, and only half a dozen other burghs are believed to have contained as many as 2,000 inhabitants.

The Rise of Prices

The main result of population pressure was a rise in the price of food and in the value of the land on which it was grown, which meant wealth for some people and destitution for others. A German chronicler writes in 1538:

> Landed property and rents for dwellings be become so very dear that they can hardly go higher.

A generation later, an Englishman puts the same problem more forcibly:

> The people are increased and ground for ploughs doth want, corn and all other victual is scant. People would labour if they knew whereon; the husbandman would be glad to have ground to set his plough to work – if he knew where.

Thus the Tudors had to grapple with a problem of more mouths calling out for more food, which was not made easier by the fact that it faced many other governments as well.

But the rise in prices was made much steeper and more prolonged by other influences, which combined to produce effects on the whole life of Europe which, at the time at least, were comparable in importance to the better-known changes in politics and ways of thought. Neither the extent of the rise nor the relative weight of its different causes is clearly defined by contemporary outcries. In broad outline, however, it may be said that an upward turn in prices began during the last decades of the fifteenth century, when the increasing demands of trade caused the German and Bohemian silver mines, from which medieval Europe derived most additional supplies of precious metals, to be more efficiently exploited. Early in the new century a further supply of both gold and silver began to reach Europe from the Spanish conquests in Mexico and other parts of the New World. Then in 1545 the Spaniards began to exploit a seemingly inexhaustible mountain of silver at Potosi in Peru, with the result that by the end of the century the annual flow of treasure into Spanish harbours was equivalent to almost 300 tons of silver. After this date there was some falling off, and the figure was not exceeded until about 1750.

Thus in about a hundred years Europe experienced an addition of perhaps 50 per cent to her total supply of the very durable precious metals, which had been slowly accumulated there in the two and a half millennia since the Athenians first exploited their silver mines at Laurium. Moreover, the effect of this increased supply in raising prices was intensified by the speed with which each annual arrival of new bullion at Seville made itself felt all over Europe, through the quick settlement of innumerable outstanding trade debts. "Whether as coins or bills of exchange," declares a recent study, "money cascaded from person to person and money market to money market."[1] Finally, it must be noticed that, when minted into coin, the precious metal increased its nominal value – and therefore its effect on prices – because in the course of this period the silver content of the standard currencies used for trade was almost everywhere reduced, though other debasements were less reckless than those of Henry VIII in Tudor England.

Prices rose at different speeds in different countries. In Spain, for example, they rose in the course of the sixteenth century by 500 per cent, in France by only 250 per cent. English prices had approximately doubled before the accession of Elizabeth, rose during her reign by a further 60 per cent, and by the outbreak of the Civil War were about three times as high as in 1500; then they at last began to fall, in company with those of the Dutch. But everywhere the result was in varying degrees to bring about economic

[1] F. P. Braudel and F. Spooner in *Cambridge Economic History of Europe*, Vol. IV, p. 448.

and social changes and to confront governments with new problems which they might solve or shirk.

Effects Abroad and at Home

Fortunes are more easily made on a rising market, so there was a stimulus given to mobility and enterprise. The quick-witted and adaptable members of every social class had much more chance of bettering their position than in the more stable medieval world. The main advantage lay, however, with landowners and others who had secure possession of land or other forms of property which were in wide demand: their incomes would almost inevitably rise faster than the general level of prices. Whoever had a fixed income was correspondingly unfortunate. So were all those people who depended on the land for a living and had to pay whatever was demanded of them for the right to occupy it, or else become landless labourers – or wander like the gipsies, who had appeared in western Europe in the previous century. In the towns, too, the labouring class (as distinct from highly skilled artisans with some savings to fall back on) suffered because uprooted country people increased the competition for too slowly rising wages. And in town and country alike, sickness, accident, or the ravages of war imposed special handicaps which reduced some unfortunates to utter destitution.

In the absence of statistics of prices, wages, rates of unemployment, and so forth, all this has to be stated in very general terms. For England, however, one detailed illustration of the course of events has now been made available.[1] The wages of workers in the building trades over a period of seven centuries have been traced from many different sources, and then compared with the cost of food, drink, fuel, lighting, and textiles – the items which would roughly make up the worker's household expenditure. The result is to prove that, for this representative type of worker, the wages of 1571 could buy only two-thirds as much as the wages of a century before, and that this fall in his standard of

[1] By E. H. Phelps Brown and Sheila Hopkins in a series of articles in *Economica*, 1955–61. The results are summarized in graph form by Braudel and Spooner, from whom the two quotations are also taken, in *Cambridge Economic History of Europe,* Vol. IV, pp. 483, 428, and 429.

living continued for another forty years. This disastrous era then gave place to a century and a half of 'slow, modest, but constant improvement', during which England, as fairly represented by its building operatives, was more fortunate than most of the nations of the continent, where "until well into the beginning of the eighteenth century the standard of living progressively declined".

The Trend Towards a United Britain

The Tudor period, in which the British peoples shared, for better and worse, in so many great changes that swept over the Continent, was also one of widespread trends towards national unity. To a great extent the English were already a united people, held together by such forces as a legal system based on the common law; a central government which was accustomed to consult from time to time with elected representatives of shire and borough; the nation-wide ramifications of the woollen industry; and a patriotic tradition fed on the memories of the bowmen of Creçy and Agincourt. But geographical compactness and an insular position gave the English some special advantage as they continued the long process by which, in one European state after another, local were being compelled to give place to national loyalties.

No foreign power was in a position to thwart the assimilation of Cornwall, where the community of race and language had formerly created many popular links with Brittany. By 1602 Cornish was everywhere on the retreat: "the English speech doth still encroach upon it and hath driven the same into the uttermost skirts of the shire." In Wales the language indeed survived, but in all other respects the institutions which Henry VIII imposed took root among a people who were separated by the whole width of England from any possibility of intervention from abroad. The northern counties of England, lying closer to Scotland than to the more populous and wealthy of the English shires, continued to be treated in many respects as a remote outlier of the kingdom: even Elizabeth, so fond of royal progresses, never went farther north then Derby. But from 1536 onwards a special council, with its seat at York, was gradually weaning the northerners from their feudal loyalty to earl and abbot, while the rapid growth of London strengthened their economic and social ties with the centre of government.

As for Scotland, it took exactly a hundred years and the accident of three childless sovereigns of England in succession to convert the marriage alliance, by which Henry VII's daughter became queen consort of Scotland, into the union of crowns. But it was increasingly obvious that the two nations occupied complementary parts of a small island, separated by no more than a sparsely populated moorland border. The Reformation brought them together, for its triumph in Scotland resulted directly from the help which Elizabeth gave in 1560 towards the expulsion of the Catholic French influence from Edinburgh. In consequence, her long reign was one of the very few which were not marred by any war between the two monarchies, and in the crisis of the Spanish Armada the Scots gave wholehearted support to the foreign policy of their southern neighbours.

Ireland

How different was the situation with regard to Ireland! Henry VII brought its legislature under complete control. Henry VIII, who assumed the title of King of Ireland, set to work to complete the piecemeal conquest made in the Middle Ages. Elizabeth attempted both conquest and settlement, with the result that a particularly barbarous series of wars did not end until the year of her death. The Irish people had then for the first time been fairly thoroughly subdued, but the history of the next three and a half centuries was to show that they were not in process of being made into a constituent part of 'the British people'. In comparison with the Scots, they were separated from the English by the emotionally more significant barrier of the sea, and they also differed more in racial origins, language, and level of civilization. But perhaps the biggest difference of all resulted from their determined adherence to the old faith – the first Jesuits were welcomed into Ireland within ten years of Henry VIII's breach with Rome – which embittered the whole course of Anglo-Irish relations. Whatever the reasons for this striking historical difference, it means that Irish history must in principle be passed over very briefly in a book of this scope.

The Tudor Dynasty

If the geographical factors facilitated the hammering of the peoples of the island, though not of the British Isles, into a single whole, it was a line of strong rulers which at this time wielded the hammer. Throughout western Europe monarchy was on the upgrade, but England was peculiarly fortunate in having a dynasty whose high level of talent was sustained through three generations.

Westminster Abbey contains no better-known memorial than the tomb of Henry VII with its noble effigy; but the personality of the king who rests there is familiar only through the long series of prudent, carefully considered, and self-controlled actions by which he restored the power and prestige of the monarchy. Looking back on his work after the lapse of a century, the philosopher Francis Bacon summed up the first Tudor in a memorable phrase: "What he minded, he compassed." Henry VIII, on the other hand, is pictured only too easily as a supreme egoist, whose matrimonial infidelities are for ever entangled in the story of the Breach with Rome, the most important act of state in the whole century. But there are many other aspects to this dominant and domineering figure – the popular Renaissance prince who, when tired of jousting, dabbled in scholarship and music; the gouty tyrant, before whom at least one of his subjects fell dead in fright; and above all the unwearying ruler, who steered the ship of state purposefully through very troubled seas.

At his death Henry VIII left a kingdom strong enough to hold together through nearly twelve years (January 1547–November 1558) of religious upheaval and social crisis. Both Edward VI and Mary inherited some part of their father's determined character. But the former was a child-king, and although he began to sit in Council at the age of 13, the royal powers were exercised in turn by the Protector Somerset and the duke of Northumberland. As for Mary, she easily suppressed Northumberland's attempt to substitute his daughter-in-law, Lady Jane Grey, upon the throne, but then dissipated her strength and popularity in a papal and Spanish policy which offended national sentiment. Even today we recall with reluctance the fact that her cousin, Philip of Spain, became titular King of England through his marriage with Mary.

Mary was the only Tudor whose mother was a foreign princess. With the accession of Elizabeth the dynasty became 'mere English' again, and reached its climax at its close. The glory of the Virgin Queen became a legend in her lifetime, a legend which has never wholly faded and, what is far more important, one that injected a new degree of patriotic fervour into the make-up of her people. "Politics," writes one of our most eminent twentieth-century historians, "were for a few decades simplified into service paid to a woman, who was to her subjects the symbol of their unity, prosperity and freedom."[1]

Growth of Parliament and of Sea Power

Politics cannot stay simplified for long. In the Tudor period the throne, with its succession of masterful occupants, far outshone the parliaments, summoned occasionally to vote money for wars or other royal activities which could not be financed without special taxation in an age of rising prices. Henry VIII, however, under the influence of his minister, Thomas Cromwell, led the way in giving parliament a more important role, as the instrument through which he carried out his religious changes and demonstrated that they had wide support. Elizabeth likewise employed it as an instrument in carrying out her religious and social policies. But in her later years especially, parliament-men were no longer content to be employed as an instrument. As they began to raise their voices in religious, legal, and financial controversy with the sovereign, the long struggle for representative government gradually took shape. Thus the reign of Elizabeth, in spite of the extreme loyalty by which it was marked, set the stage for the controversies which produced the Civil War, the English Revolution, and the eventual triumph of parliament over Crown.

Lastly, we may notice that the Tudor sovereigns helped in a more direct way to make the British a maritime people. Henry VII, who "could not endure to see trade sick" and found one remedy in shipbuilding for overseas commerce; Henry VIII, who

[1] G. M. Trevelyan, *English Social History*, c. VI, p. 139.

ended his reign with a Royal Navy containing fifty-three seaworthy vessels of various sizes; and even Edward VI and Mary, during whose troubled reigns English adventurers sailed into the unknown in search of the North-East Passage – all made their contribution. But it was through the exploits of the Elizabethan seamen that the English became fully inspired with the ambition to turn their island position to advantage as giving access to new wealth in the world beyond the seas. The story continues through the colonial enterprises and trade wars of the Stuart era until, in the first half of the eighteenth century, we find a united British people in apparently secure possession of a rich oceanic commerce and potentially the most valuable of all oceanic empires.

In the next chapter the Tudor State will be considered in more detail, as exercising a predominant influence on the lives of all its subjects, in cottage and manor house, church and college, market-place and quayside alike. But it may also be borne in mind that the most English of English dynasties, in moulding that state, helped to shape the lives of later generations as well.

2

THE TUDOR STATE

To the sixteenth-century Englishman the body appeared a natural image of the State, for the human head, arms, and legs pictured very well the institutions that made up government and also the relationship between them. With a little modification, we may find this picture instructive.

In this human image the head portrays the king, for it controls the rest of the body just as the Tudor king controlled the organs of government. The two arms of a man represent the King's Council and Parliament, both taking their orders from the throne and moving at the royal command. And his feet, more lowly than head and arms, are a pattern of the king's government at the local level – the Justices of the Peace in the countryside, as remote from the king perhaps as feet from head but (the irreverent modern might add) just as useful for kicking.

The New Monarchy

When we look at the head in this image, we see that the features are mature and dignified, marking the transformation from the weak kings of the middle part of the fifteenth century, unable to enforce justice and involved in wars with over-mighty subjects, to a line of monarchs who were feared, respected, and different in kind from the greatest of other men. A portrait of Henry VIII by Hans Eworth at Trinity College, Cambridge, shows him with feet astride, firm in his power. Of Elizabeth we have many word-pictures. At the beginning of her reign:

> If ever any person had either the gift or the style to win the hearts of people, it was this queen . . . in coupling mildness with majesty as she did . . . None knew better the hardest art of all others, that is, of commanding men, nor could more use themselves to those cares without which the royal dignity could not be supported.

We glimpse her again at the height of the Armada crisis, when

> full of princely resolution and more than feminine courage . . . she passed like some Amazonian empress through all her army.

And near the end of her life, the high view of monarchy which the great queen embodied, and which the Tudor age as a whole implicitly accepted, finds expression in Shakespeare's lines:

> *Not all the water in the rough rude sea*
> *Can wash the balm from an anointed king;*
> *The breath of worldly men cannot depose*
> *The deputy elected by the Lord.*

The Achievement of Henry VII

Though a new pattern of kingship was emerging at this time in other countries – in Scotland, for example, the strong reign of James IV began only three years after that of Henry VII in England – the English Tudors stand out, as we have already noticed, as a succession of particularly strong rulers. Modern English history begins, accordingly, with the foundations which Henry VII laid for others to build upon. By reviving the ancient strength of the English monarchy and systematically assembling its resources old and new, he enabled it to function with a new vigour which he himself personified. In more detailed terms, he did three things: he raised kingship above the nobility to an altogether loftier status; he deliberately weakened the power of the nobles; and he enriched the Crown so that in economic weight and even in outward show it should have no rival.

Much of the baronial unrest and plotting in the fifteenth century had been due to dynastic conditions: for many of the leading families were related in one way or another to the descendants of Edward III. Traces of royal blood went to their heads – given the weakness of the Crown and their own power, they thought of themselves less as subjects than as king-makers and potentially kings themselves. It was necessary for Henry Tudor to raise himself above this dynastic tangle. Within six months of his victory at Bosworth, he carried out his long-stated intention of marrying Elizabeth of York, daughter of Edward IV. Later on, the marriages of their children still further elevated the new royal house above its subjects. Arthur, Prince of Wales, and after his death the younger son, Henry, were married to a Spanish princess, Catherine of Aragon. Their elder daughter became queen of Scotland; the younger, Mary, was betrothed to the future emperor Charles V and was married (in the next reign) to the king of France instead.

Henry VII dated his accession from the day before the Battle of Bosworth and required his first parliament to accept him as king without any clear statement of his hereditary claim to the throne: the Act confirming his position merely declared that the inheritance should remain with 'our now sovereign lord King Harry the VIIth and the heirs of his body lawfully come'. More important were his measures to reduce over-mighty subjects. Liveried retainers were forbidden under penalty of £5 per head per month. The use of strong-arm men to influence sheriffs and juries, to intimidate witnesses, and to organize riotous mobs was to be prevented by the activities of a special tribunal, dating from 1487 and later merged with the regular sittings of the Council in the 'Star Chamber'. This special tribunal, which lasted at least until the time of Wolsey, employed no jury, could proceed against any person on information laid before the Chancellor, and reached quick, informal, and drastic decisions. In future, people like the Pastons[1] could no longer be robbed of their land or otherwise ill-used by any lord, however great. Moreover, the process of taming the noble class simultaneously impoverished it, through the confiscation of the estates of defeated Yorkists and the fines flowing

[1] See *The Making of Britain: Life and Work to the Close of the Middle Ages*, c. 14.

into the Exchequer for infringements of new laws. They could no longer afford to compete with the up-to-date artillery which Henry was accumulating in the Tower of London.

For the monarchy was becoming richer, as it supplemented fines with forced 'loans' and outright gifts from the nobility. The king became a merchant, building his own ships which he hired out to merchants for a share in the profits. A series of prudent treaties helped to produce a rise of 30 per cent in customs receipts. Even foreign policy yielded a profit to Henry VII, who secured parliamentary grants for a war against France and French bribes for changing his mind at the treaty of Etaples. The king who laboriously initialled his treasurer's accounts, page by page, left his successor a fortune of at least £1,000,000 with which to maintain the power of the dynasty.

The elevation of the Crown became all the more marked with the depression of the nobles. The king deliberately excluded them from advising him; instead, he relied on men of lower birth who distinguished themselves by their efficiency and loyalty. In Henry VII's Council such men as Richard Empson and Edmund Dudley, his notorious finance ministers, and Edward Poynings, the lord deputy by whose 'laws' the Irish parliament was brought completely under English control, show the type. Empson was a lawyer and had been Speaker of the House of Commons; Dudley was only distantly related to a baronial family of the same name; and Poynings was descended on his mother's side from the middle-class Pastons of the *Paston Letters*. Such men did not crowd the steps of the throne by right, and could be driven off them again at the royal discretion. The gentry were becoming a more important class in English society, and the Tudors could rely on its support.

Failure of Rebellions

Rebellion as a noble pastime was crushed by statecraft more than generalship, for the Tudors had no standing army beyond a few score yeomen of the guard. Yet Henry VII dealt successfully with two Yorkist Pretenders (Simnel and Warbeck) as well as with a disruptive movement in Cornwall, whose men marched as far as

Blackheath in support of a refusal to pay taxation for a war on the Scottish border. In the following reigns rebellion became altogether exceptional. In 1549, indeed, the enclosure movement – which we shall examine in due course – caused a social disturbance in Norfolk under Ket; the landlord class predominant in Edward VI's Council employed German mercenaries to suppress it at the cost of about three thousand peasant lives. The other rebellions were all primarily religious – the Pilgrimage of Grace against Henry VIII's dissolution of the monasteries; the outbreak in Devon and Cornwall against Edward VI's First Prayer Book; Wyatt's rebellion in Kent against Mary's Spanish marriage; and the Rising of the Northern Earls in 1569 to upset the Elizabethan religious settlement and release Mary Queen of Scots from her captivity. Although a religious cause made the maximum appeal to the emotions, the significant fact is that in each case public opinion rallied strongly to the support of the Tudor sovereign.

Henry VIII Supreme in Church and State

It was the achievement of Henry VIII to broaden still further the idea of monarchy, until it demanded from every subject that total allegiance which it had hitherto shared with the Church. He claimed to be equally supreme in Church and State, denying the right of the Pope to intervene between him and his people. This (as we shall see later) fitted in well with the rising national sentiment which regarded the Pope as a meddlesome foreigner. But the king's natural love of power was also stimulated by the example of the great minister, Cardinal Wolsey, who in the first two decades of his reign relieved the king of the heavier burdens of administration. The popular young sovereign, who routed the French at the Battle of the Spurs, who "from the moment of his accession devoted himself to the increase of his naval might",[1] and made diplomacy romantic with the empty splendours of the meeting of kings on the Field of the Cloth of Gold (June 1520), enjoyed a multitude of diversions. Meanwhile, ecclesiastical and lay authority accumulated to an unprecedented extent in one man's hands.

[1] J. D. Mackie, *The Earlier Tudors,* p. 268.

Wolsey had the powers and revenues – though he never attempted to discharge the duties – of the archbishopric of York, of four English and one French bishoprics, and of the abbacy of St. Albans. These offices gave him an income of about £50,000 a year, with which he built Hampton Court and three other palaces. But his position in the Church was crowned by his being legate for life, the permanent viceroy of the Pope in England. In secular affairs this was matched by his position as lord chancellor and undisputed head of the royal council. Long after his master's downfall George Cavendish, who had been his gentleman usher, recalled the scene when Wolsey made his entry as chancellor into the lawcourts at Westminster Hall. He was

> apparelled all in red, in the habit of a cardinal; which was either of fine scarlet or else of crimson satin, taffeta, damask, or caffa,[1] the best that he could get for money; and upon his head a round pillion,[2] with a neck of black velvet set to the same in the inner side. He had also a tippet of fine sables about his neck. Holding in his hand a very fair orange, whereof the meat or substance within was taken out and filled up again with the part of a sponge wherein was vinegar and other confections against the pestilent airs; the which he most commonly smelt unto, passing amongst the press, or else when he was pestered with many suitors.
>
> There was also borne before him, first the great seal of England, and then his cardinal's hat. . . .
>
> Thus passing forth with two great crosses of silver borne before him, with also two great pillars of silver. . . . and a great mace of silver-gilt. . . . thus passed he down from his chamber through the hall.

When Henry VIII for mixed reasons of passion and policy, having tired of his ageing wife (whose surviving child was a daughter, Mary) and needing to provide his kingdom with a male heir, demanded the annulment of his marriage, the stage was set for a greater assumption of power than Wolsey's. Since the Pope was in the power of Spain, he could not annul the marriage of a Span-

[1] A rich silk cloth (*O.E.D.*)

[2] A clerical head-gear (*O.E.D.*)

ish princess. Wolsey having failed his royal master in this matter died in disgrace, and parliament was brought into a new prominence as a willing instrument in the king's battle against what he and it denounced as the intrusion into English affairs of the foreign power of the Pope. Henry became free to marry whom he would: his second wife, Anne Boleyn, bore him a daughter, the later queen Elizabeth, and was executed on a charge of unfaithfulness; the third died a natural death within a week of bearing him the long desired son, the future Edward VI; a fourth was divorced; a fifth sent to the scaffold. But far more important than his domestic tyranny was the exaltation of the monarchy which grew out of the conflict with the Pope, as resolutely handled by Henry's new minister, Thomas Cromwell. In 1533, the Act of Appeals, designed to prevent such a case as Queen Catherine's from being brought before the Pope, declared in its preamble that "This realm of England is an empire, governed by one Supreme Head and King, unto whom a body politic, compact of all sorts and degrees of people, owe next to God a natural and humble obedience." One year later, the Act of Supremacy removed the last trammels of the external authority which had made its entrance to the island behind the cross of Augustine in 597:

> The King our Sovereign Lord, his heirs and successors kings of this realm, shall be taken, accepted, and reputed the only supreme head in earth of the Church of England called *Anglicana Ecclesia* . . . and shall have full power and authority to amend all errors, whatsoever they be.

Because his conscience forbade him to accept this sweeping transfer of spiritual authority, the saintly Sir Thomas More, the friend of Henry's youth and Wolsey's successor in the chancellorship, was executed as a traitor. As the duke of Norfolk warned him, "The wrath of the prince is death." The desire to rout out elements favourable to Rome precipitated the dissolution of the monasteries, and the struggle against the papal power likewise led on to the first official moves in the Protestant direction, such as the placing of an English version of the Bible in parish churches. But these matters carry us beyond our present theme of the growth of the royal power as such.

The Role of Elizabeth I

Henry VII, then, made the Crown independent of the nobility and Henry VIII declared its independence of the authority of the Pope. It remained for Elizabeth I to assert its independence of the greatest secular power of sixteenth-century Europe, namely the power of Spain. And Elizabeth added another dimension to the new monarchy: whereas her father and grandfather had been respected and feared, she became the object of her subjects' love. She was served by councillors of unusual wisdom, especially the secretary of state and (later) lord treasurer, William Cecil, but the queen herself was directly responsible in the view of the public for every benefit enjoyed in her reign. In 1584, after the assassination of the Dutch Protestant leader, William the Silent, by a Catholic emissary, a remarkable Bond of Association was signed by thousands of Englishmen, pledging them to pursue to the death any person by whom, or on behalf of whom, an attempt might be made on the queen's life. Nor was the devotion all on one side, witness the famous scene at the close of her last parliament, when a deputation from the Commons was assured:

> Though God hath raised me high, yet this I count the glory of my crown, that I have reigned with your loves... Though you have had and may have many mightier and wiser princes sitting on this seat, yet you never had nor shall have any that will love you better.

The Royal Council

It is time now to return to our human image for the state, transferring our attention from the head to the arms. The more continually active right arm will represent the King's Council, the left the Parliament.

The royal Council was the group of persons chosen by the king to advise him, when asked to do so, and to give effect to his will by making proclamations and ordinances, by drafting bills to be laid before parliament, and by issuing instructions to the justices of the peace. Down to the time of Elizabeth its membership might be as high as forty, including bishops, lay peers, and a good many officials of humble origins. In the north, where the influence of the aristocracy was still strong, this last feature caused a resentment which found expression in the complaint at the Pilgrimage of Grace that the king "takes of his Council and has about him persons of low birth and small reputation". In 1540, however, it was reorganized with its own clerk and minute book and the intention that the large Council, which met at Westminster and during law terms only, should be replaced by a much smaller body, meeting wherever and whenever the needs of government required.

This Privy Council became fully established under Elizabeth, whose policies were framed and executed under her direction by a body of twelve or so members, headed by the treasurer and secretary. Towards the end of her reign it often met twice daily, Sundays included, for this was the power centre of the state, "a body outside of which a man's influence on affairs barely existed."[1] Its activities were all-pervasive, ranging from matters of political and religious principle to the consideration of petitions from individuals, and from the issue of orders which read very much like laws to the interrogation of a single person, especially one suspected of treason, in which case it often inflicted torture.

Nevertheless, the Privy Council itself did not function as a law court. The king's councillors always exercised some judicial authority on behalf of the king: in the early part of Henry VIII's reign, indeed, so much of the political work was taken over by Cardinal Wolsey that the councillors acted mainly as judges. But this was a separate activity which, unlike the Council, an inner ring of whose members might move with the king and hold meetings anywhere, was located at Westminster and more specifically in the Star Chamber. Thus the only contemporary account of the Elizabethan constitution explains:

> In the term time . . . on Fridays and Wednesdays . . . the lord chancellor and the lords and other of the Privy Council, so many as will . . . from nine of the clock till it be eleven do sit in a

[1] G. R. Elton, *The Tudor Constitution,* p. 92.

place which is called the Star Chamber, either because it is full of windows or because at the first all the roof thereof was decked with images of stars gilded. There is plaints heard of riots.

Besides riots, which could be stretched to include any threatened breach of the peace, the Star Chamber concerned itself with the enforcement of royal proclamations and the protection of the ordinary law courts against abuse. With the help of the two chief justices, who sat with the privy councillors, it tried offenders by quick, commonsense methods without any jury. Though it could not take life or property, the Star Chamber imposed enormous fines (often reduced after the victim had been duly frightened), imprisonment, and humiliating physical punishments such as pillorying and cropping of ears. Its main business was of course to enforce the law in the interests of the Crown, but it also tended to support the poor and weak against the rich and powerful. This class was also helped by another court, which started as a Council committee in the time of Henry VII but came to have its separate professional judges: this was the Court of Requests 'for poor men's causes', sitting in the White Hall of the Palace of Westminster.

Regional Councils

The power which the Council and the Court of Star Chamber exercised at the centre was to some extent duplicated through the establishment of two great regional councils, to bring Wales and the troubled North into line with the rest of the king's dominions.

Plate 1. *Vaulting – Henry VII Chapel, Westminster Abbey.* This chapel, together with King's Cambridge and St. George's Windsor, represents the climax of English Gothic architecture. It was built between 1503 and c. 1512 and became the resting-place for the body of Henry VII (d. 1509) – a chantry chapel where masses could be said for the king's soul. The vaulting, only 3½ inches thick, is the most intricate in England, combining the ideas of the groined and the fan vaults with sugary pendants added (for a diagram of the system see p. 139 in Kidson, Murray and Thompson, *A History of English Architecture* (Pelican)). (Cf. text p. 12.)

Plate 2. *Henry VIII.* From the painting by Hans Eworth at Trinity College, Cambridge – copied from a picture in the old Whitehall Palace, burned in 1698. The original cartoon for this Whitehall painting is in the National Portrait Gallery and, since it carries Holbein's signature, the Eworth portrait is described as 'after Holbein'. More than one date appears on the picture, but if the year 1546 (below the Latin inscription at the bottom centre) is accepted, then the King is shown in his 55th year – one year before his death. (Cf. text p. 15.)

Plate 1

MAGNIFICE CVM TER DENOS REGNASSET
ANNOS QVIS MAIOR REGEM LABOR VLTIMVS ORNET
EX DONO ROBERTI BEAVMONT SACRE THEOLOGIE PROFESSORIS ET HVIVS COLLEGII MAGISTRI Aº1567

Plate 2

In Henry's VII's time Wales still consisted of two distinct parts – the half-dozen counties of Edward I's Principality and an equally large area of Marcher Lordships, though a great many of these were now estates of the Tudor Crown. In 1493 a Council was set up at Ludlow to act on behalf of Arthur, who was the first Prince of Wales to receive a British name. But it was not until 1534 that Henry VIII gave it full powers and extended its jurisdiction to cover the 137 surviving Lordships. The new president, a bishop, is supposed to have hanged 5,000 criminals in the first five years, and the court became a very strong instrument for reducing both Wales and the border counties to order. Its work came under the general supervision of the Privy Council, as may be illustrated from an item in the records of the latter body in 1571:

> A letter to the Vice-President and Council in the Marches of Wales, understanding lately of a great riot and assault made in the town of Bromyard upon the Bishop of Hereford's officers and servants, and that the offenders therein be of such insolency as the Bishop is afraid to seek redress and . . . dare not well without a great guard travel from his dwelling-house . . . They are required to give order that the principal offenders be apprehended and committed to prison . . . and to proceed with all due severity and by corporal punishment and fines, according to the quality of their offence.

In the North, too, regional councils had an earlier history; but the important event was the action of Henry VIII in 1536, immediately after the suppression of the Pilgrimage of Grace. A body of administrators and judges, with headquarters at York, was given wide authority over Yorkshire and the turbulent counties stretching to the Scottish border. A generation later, the Rising of the Northern Earls showed that the great feudal lords of the north still dared to defy the Crown. But the Puritan earl of Huntingdon then held the presidency of the council for nearly a quarter of a century, during which the wild northern counties were largely tamed.

The Tudor Parliament

We must look now at the left arm of our image, namely Parliament, observing at the outset that the action of the two arms was less separate than in the human body. For Council and Parliament had much else in common besides their close dependence upon the royal pleasure. The King's Councillors themselves attended parliament, where they had a right to sit (but not to vote) in the Lords, while an increasing proportion preferred to seek election to the Commons instead. In either house, Councillors played a very important part as exponents of the royal policies, defending them against criticism and marshalling for them parliamentary support.

Yet the parliament of Tudor times was not an organ with any continuous, day-to-day functions, much less with any prescribed right to supervise the actions of government. In 1566 Elizabeth told the French ambassador that she had held sufficient parliaments and would summon no more, and it comes as something of a shock to realize that in the whole of her long reign there were only thirteen sessions of parliament with a total length of 140 weeks. Under three years of parliamentary activity in a reign 45 years long! Yet in the Tudor period, and especially under Henry VIII, parliament moved up towards its present position in the governmental framework. For the Tudors chose to deal with the most important issues of their time – the questions of the Church and the succession – not through Council ordinances, as they might well have done, but through Acts of Parliament.

What was this parliament to which the Tudors gave so unexpectedly a new importance in the State? It had begun as a law court – the 'High Court of Parliament' – dealing mainly with petitions that came before it, but sometimes issuing general pronouncements – statutes – which had the force of law. During the Tudor period it was this aspect which was developed, as Parliament moved away from merely deciding the law in the particular cases that came before it to declaring it in general terms, which applied to all the subjects of the Crown. Parliament became, in fact, a legislative body which, because it in some sense represented the people, was useful to the Crown as a demonstration to the hostile powers of Catholic Europe that the people were on its side.

In Parliament, the peers had lost the overwhelming importance they had possessed during the Middle Ages. This was partly due to the disfavour into which the aristocracy fell with Henry VII, but also to the shock to the structure of the Upper House which accompanied the dissolution of the monasteries under Henry VIII. All the thirty-one abbots then disappeared from the Lords, and their loss was hardly compensated for by the creation of five new bishoprics whose holders took their seats there. The disappearance of the King's Councillors, apart from those who belonged to the peerage, also lessened its authority.

But the importance of the Commons grew fairly steadily. For instance, by 1549 they had acquired St. Stephen's Chapel as their own fixed meeting-place within the Palace of Westminster. By the end of the century, too, their procedure was coming to resemble its present-day form, with each Bill read three times and examined in detail by a committee, often a 'committee of the whole house'. There was also a tremendous increase in the number of members, from 296 to 467 in the course of the century. Wales was represented for the first time in 1536, together with the city and county of Chester, but the main factor was the grant of borough status to additional towns in southern England. In the four decades between 1547 and 1586, no fewer than 121 new borough MPs made their first appearance, half of them under Elizabeth. In some cases boroughs owed their representation to a genuine growth in civic wealth and importance, but many of them – in Cornwall, for instance – were mere villages. Some of them may have provided seats for persons whose entry to parliament the Crown particularly desired, but the main factor appears to have been local pressure, especially from country gentlemen with political ambitions.

It is relevant at this point to consider who were the voters at elections. In the counties, by an act of 1430, they were those men who owned land valued at 40*s*. a year: even then not a large sum, so that county elections engaged a fairly large number of people. In the towns, on the other hand, it was no longer true, as it had once been, that all free burgesses had the right to vote, for the privilege had been in most places confined to the richest of them – the heads of town government and the like. In the new Tudor boroughs it was restricted to them from the start.

The men whom these county and borough voters returned to parliament had both social position and property. In the counties they were the 'knights of the shire', who probably in fact were knights or at the least country gentlemen, landowners as a matter of course. And by Tudor times the same sort of member was returned by the towns too, largely because by the middle of the sixteenth century MPs no longer had to live within the borough which returned them, nor were they paid by their constituents. Country gentlemen, therefore, who lived outside the borough but influenced voters within it, who made useful spokesmen for its interests in London, and who could pay their own way during parliamentary sessions, came to represent all except the largest boroughs in place of the natural local leaders among their own traders and craftsmen.

Its Control by the Crown

This, then, was the parliament of the Tudor state, the child of the Crown, which in the next century was to grow to such unnatural strength that it would turn on its begetter. Even by the end of Elizabeth's reign it was claiming a right to debate those matters – the succession, church government, foreign policy and trade – which the Queen declared to be 'matters of state', the province of the Crown alone. Nevertheless, for the most part the freedom of action enjoyed by Tudor parliaments was severely limited. So infrequently were they summoned, and so short their sessions that there was little chance for them to develop an independence of the Crown. In any case the Speaker of the Commons was the servant of the monarch and bound to direct proceedings as the king wished – and in this he was helped by the members of the Council sitting in the House. Whereas other members of the Commons changed at election time, the Councillors did not (since it was unthinkable that they should lose an election) and so they acquired a parliamentary experience that most ordinary members lacked. And elections themselves could be influenced by the Crown, whether directly through instructions to sheriffs (who organized the county elections) or indirectly through the creation of new boroughs designed to return to parliament supporters of royal policy. The Crown, furthermore, had the right to reject any measure which parliament might put forward. Elizabeth stated the position fairly when she said, "It is in my power to call parliaments; it is in my power to end and determine the same; it is in my power to assent or dissent to anything done in parliaments." In the parliamentary pack most of the cards were Court cards.

Justices of the Peace

So at last we may turn our attention to the feet in our human image of the Tudor State. Far removed from the head, they represent royal rule in the localities – largely through the medium of the Justices of the Peace. These officials were not created by the Tudors – they were in fact fully established by the fourteenth century – but in the fifteenth century local government had withered, mainly because of the growth of the power of the great nobles who overawed all local juries and officials. But the energy of the Tudor sovereigns, flowing through all departments of the State, gave new life to the office of justice of the peace. Once the claws of the nobles had been clipped, the country gentry could be expected to play a larger part in the government of their shires, as was made clear in 1489 by 'an act for justices of the peace, for the due execution of their commissions'. One or two justices could deal with minor offences, but their main court was the quarter sessions for the whole county, at which all the justices were supposed to meet four times a year to try any crime short of treason – though the most serious were usually passed on to the assize judges. If the justices failed to hold this court or failed to conduct it properly, they were to incur penalties laid down in the Act.

These legal responsibilities were imposed upon about forty of the gentry of each county, picked by the Crown and quite unpaid: indeed, it became common for the sons of such families to go to the expense of a legal training at the Inns of Court in anticipation of the honour of appointment. And it was not only for judicial tasks that the Crown relied on the JPs: they became the civil servants charged with duties arising from most of the Tudor laws, such as the licensing of alehouses, supervision of wage-rates, poor relief, apprenticeship, and even the examination of weights and measures. For military matters, the Tudors about the middle of the sixteenth century introduced a new official at the head of the shire, the lord lieutenant, a great dignitary whose deputy lieutenants organized the local militia under his command. But even so we read that "The justices of the peace do meet by commandment of the Prince upon suspicion of war, to take order for the safety of the shire, sometimes to take musters of harness and able men . . ."

At the end of Elizabeth's reign a writer found that no fewer than 176 Tudor laws bore upon the duties of the justices, and suggested that there was a limit to the 'stacks of statutes' which their backs could bear without breaking. Here, from the point of view of the Crown, was the weakness of the system. Everything had been made to depend upon the loyalty and goodwill of voluntary groups of country squires, together with a small proportion of merchants and professional lawyers. If this class should turn against the Crown, as it did under the Stuarts, the royal system of government was bound to collapse. In the end, perhaps, it was not so much the head as the feet which controlled the 'body politic' and ensured its healthy functioning.

Incorporation of Wales

That healthy functioning was considerably promoted by the action of the second Tudor when he incorporated Wales with England. Since Henry VII had emerged from Wales to triumph under its emblem of the red dragon at Bosworth Field, both he and his successors could count on an increased measure of loyalty among the Welsh people from whom they sprang. William Cecil's grandfather, for instance, had founded his family's fortunes by following Henry Tudor from South Wales to London to become a yeoman of the guard. His master never forgot the Welsh: he freed the bondmen in the Crown lordships and the Principality, and gave Welsh burgesses full rights in the towns. In return the Welsh bards mourned for his death:

The Boar is cold in his grave.
The world is still and envenomed feuds are asleep.

Two great statutes of 1536 and 1543 were designed to unite Wales with England by three main changes. Firstly, after some parts of the Marches had been included in England (which had the incidental effect of blurring the border line, since there were some Welsh-speaking people on either side of it, especially in Herefordshire) the rest was carved up into new Welsh counties and the nominally English county of Monmouth. These were given the English system of local government through justices of the peace and sheriffs. Secondly, all the twelve counties of Wales and all but one of its county towns (the exception was Merioneth) were allocated one seat in Parliament – a not very generous provision, since the county and town of Monmouth each received two MPs. Thirdly, the people of Wales were expressly deprived of all special laws and customs, and appeals from local courts were to go either to the Council at Ludlow or to the English courts at Westminster. This meant the final triumph of the English system of landholding and the substitution of primogeniture for the ancient custom of 'gavelkind', under which property was divided up among all the male heirs.

In all these ways, the government and life of Wales were brought closer to the English form. Henry VIII may have been influenced mainly by his determination to keep every part of his dominions in line with the royal policy over the breach with Rome. But, whether this is so or not, there can be no doubt that these measures were in close harmony with all those Tudor statutes which brought each aspect of their subjects' affairs under the close control of the Crown as 'a body politic compact of all sorts and degrees of people'.[1]

Power of the Scottish Crown

From the growing power of the English monarchy in the south and west of the island, we may turn to the fortunes of the House of Stuart in the north. In Scotland the mountains and inlets fostered disunity as a fact of nature, and there were still many lords, such as the head of the great Clan Donald in the islands of the Hebrides, who took local loyalties more seriously than national ones. MacDonalds and MacKenzies, Homes and Hamiltons, each with their followers obedient and eager for spoils, made state-building almost impossible. Even more dangerous, because of

[1] See p. 21.

their wealth and royal connections, were the Black and Red Douglases, who held respectively the earldoms of Douglas and Angus with control over much of southern and eastern Scotland. These were the very type of the overmighty subject, dominating lesser men – 'None durst strive against a Douglas nor yet a Douglas man,' so it was said – and placing the Crown itself in peril. Anarchy almost overwhelmed the monarchy. Two fifteenth-century kings were murdered, one of them at the direct instigation of an earl. When a regency was set up in 1525, it was agreed that the young king, James V, should be held in their power by a succession of chief nobles acting in turn for three months at a time. The Crown was, so to speak, put into rotation.

Nevertheless the Scottish Crown was not entirely impotent, and in the fifteenth and sixteenth centuries it was fighting to assert its authority and to concentrate the resources of the throne. To invite the Earl of Douglas to Stirling Castle – as did James II in 1452 – and there to slaughter him was not, perhaps, the most civilized way of dealing with the problem. More sensible was it to confiscate the wide Douglas lands and annex them to the Crown. This was done before long and the same fate, at the hands of James V, befell those of the Red Douglas in 1528. For the power of the baronage depended on their lands and the tenants who lived on them.

James V (1513–42) asserted his authority not only in the lands of the Earls of Angus but to the extremities of the kingdom. To the wild southern border, where the lords proclaimed themselves independent of both Scotland and England, he took an army and hanged John Armstrong of Liddesdale together with forty of his followers. In 1540 he sailed north from the Firth of Forth and encompassed Scotland, reminding the lords of the north-west and the islands that there was a king in Edinburgh and taking hostages to make sure that they remembered it.

The unsecured border was a constant disadvantage to the weaker northern power. Disloyalty received encouragement: earls of Douglas and Angus alike made offers of allegiance so as to play off the English against the Scottish king. Though the English had their three protective Marches, based on Berwick, Alnwick, and Carlisle, the Scots rode in as readily as the English rode out. The lawless no-man's land – where the term 'blackmail' was first used for protection-money – lay so near the heart of Scotland that its barbarism tended always to affect the life of the country at large. Moreover, the existence of such a frontier provoked both nations easily to open war, by which the Scots were bound to suffer.

In 1513, when the youthful Henry VIII was busy winning his Battle of the Spurs against the French, his brother-in-law James IV succumbed to the temptation to invade England. But he was lured from a strong position at Flodden Edge by the veteran Earl of Surrey, and perished with 10,000 of 'the flowers of the forest' in the greatest defeat of Scottish history. The reign of his son, James V, likewise ended with an unsuccessful Scottish advance across the Border, the sick king dying of shame at the news of the mass surrender at Solway Moss. The Scots were thereupon driven to accept a marriage treaty for their infant queen, Mary, which would have made Edward VI in due course king of both countries. To compel them to carry it out, Henry VIII burnt Edinburgh (1544) and Protector Somerset advanced into Scotland, mowed down the Scots at Pinkie (partly with Italian mercenary musketeers), and swept up to the gates of the capital. The only political result was the sending of Mary Queen of Scots to begin her life's adventures as the prospective bride of the Dauphin of France.

Nevertheless, under these disadvantageous conditions the successive Scottish sovereigns strove to assert their authority by four types of long-term measures: reforms in government, the enrichment of the revenue, the expansion of the forces and the increase of the prestige of the Crown.

As regards governmental reform, the King's, or Privy, Council began, as in England, to be drawn from a wider social range. Although the great nobles remained, other middle-class members, usually with legal training, were brought in by James IV to provide a leaven of loyalty among the councillors, Again, James IV called nine parliaments between 1488 and 1496 – and two more in his later years – though the representatives of burghs and shires were still much outweighed by the two higher estates of the prelates and nobility. And it was under James IV that a special court to deal with the pleas of poor men (similar to the English Court of Requests) was set up in Edinburgh, where by this time the supreme royal courts were permanently fixed. The administration of justice was taken further by James V, for in his reign there was also set up in Edinburgh a civil court (with many clergy upon the Bench) whose judges were paid and therefore the less open to influence. This was building on older foundations, but in its use of paid professional judges the court was new.

In the reign of James IV the total annual revenue was probably no more than £11,000 sterling. With such slender resources it was not possible for the Crown to cut a figure in the new world of strong monarchs, and means had to be found to widen them. An important part of the revenue came from the Crown lands and there was therefore an obvious incentive, above that of simply weakening the nobility, for the king to take over the lands of rebellious lords. We have already seen how the estates of both branches of the Douglas line were forfeited to the Crown and the same fate befell the head of the Clan Donald, the 'Lord of the Isles', in the north-west. And, increasingly, the Crown insisted on money rents rather than those in produce or personal service. Customs duties, too, went to swell the royal Treasury, and so did fines from the law courts. The King's justices travelled the country and in the interests both of law and the pocket of the king raised fines as large as the cases brought before them would bear. One such unwelcome visit to Jedburgh raised £2,455.

Where the wild beasts prowl it is important to be strong, and the Scottish throne began in the fifteenth and sixteenth centuries to look to its arms. The old provision of the feudal host coming to the defence of the king at call could no longer be relied on, though it came to its final terrible test at Flodden, where almost every noble family was represented at the king's side. Before this, however, the Crown had begun to recruit troops for wages. This was expensive, as were the new weapons – the bombards or siege guns (such as 'Mons Meg' at Edinburgh Castle) and other artillery. Yet these the Crown had to have, for by reason of their expense they were the monopoly of monarchy – the status-symbol of the time.

The commencement of a royal fleet, with its dockyards at Newhaven and the Pool of Airth on the Forth, was another way in which James IV strove to emulate the achievements of other monarchs. So poor a country could not provide anything comparable to the splendours of the French or Spanish or even of the

English court. He did what he could, however, disporting himself at his marriage to Margaret Tudor in a fur-lined gown of cloth-of-gold which had cost £650, and starting to build the Palace of Holyroodhouse for himself and his bride. The appearance and home of a king must express his majesty.

By the middle of the sixteenth century the Scottish Crown had gone far in exalting its holder at the expense of the nobility. Yet the Highland mountains enfolding the restless inlets of the sea and the general lack of communications were obstacles to centralization too great to be overcome with the resources hitherto available. Moreover, the nobility were soon to find a new occasion for disrupting the kingdom, in religious strife. The Reformation was to shake the throne and to put up for auction the spoils of the Church, for which the nobles scrambled and fought. An English report in Elizabeth's reign wrote concerning the king of Scots:

> Feuds in every corner of his realm be such that he cannot bring a thousand men to field without a thousand particular quarrels.

3

RENAISSANCE AND REFORMATION

Tudor rulers were at pains to emphasize that they ruled over a self-contained state, one which owed nothing to any foreign power and was able for all purposes, including those of religion, to look after its own affairs. Was not England separated from the Continent by the Dover strait? Yet these straits had in fact been the path by which the main forces influencing English life had made their appearance. The best view of the Channel dividing England from Europe is to be obtained at the cliffs of Dover, from which the line of the French coast can also be picked out. This cliff-top view, which discloses both the separateness and the nearness of England and the continent, needs to be remembered.

The Renaissance

In Tudor times a great part of these continental influences reached back to very ancient sources beyond the Christian Middle Ages, in the classical Greek world. As has already been pointed out, lands farther south preceded England in experiencing an intellectual rebirth or 'renaissance' through fresh understanding of an ancient civilization which had hitherto been known only dimly and indirectly through Latin writings, such as translations from Arabic versions of Greek texts of Aristotle. But when Henry VII ascended the throne, England was already the home of at least a handful of Greek and Italian scholars. Thus, when Thomas Linacre and William Grocyn set off for Italy in 1486 and 1488 respectively, they probably knew a little Greek already and were well aware that a whole new world of ideas was to be discovered beyond the Channel and the Alps.

On their return the two men shared the honour of introducing the study of ancient Greek at Oxford. Grocyn later applied the new learning to the dangerous task of exposing the origins of some of the false documents of which the Middle Ages had blindly accepted the authority. Linacre, who became one of Henry VIII's doctors, translated parts of Galen's works from Greek to Latin, thus sharing in the renaissance of medicine, which sprang from the revived knowledge of the ideas of the greatest physician of antiquity. In both cases they were helping to revive the attitude which the Greeks had had, and which the world had so long forgotten.

Such Renaissance scholars are known as 'humanists' because they raised the human being to a more central position in the scheme of things. In doing so they were bound to make religion less of an all-absorbing interest and less of an all-comprehending study: but it was not at all their intention to shake the structure of the Christian faith. The men who brought the study of Greek and so the revival of learning to England in Henry VII's reign included Colet, a future Dean of St Paul's, who lectured at Oxford on the text of St Paul's Epistles, and the Dutchman Erasmus (a frequent visitor and for a time the holder of a Cambridge professorship), who published the first New Testament in Greek. The only layman among them was Thomas More, whose *Utopia*[1] shows how the Renaissance released the imagination to speculate freely: yet he was to die a martyr for the Catholic faith.

Nevertheless, this rediscovery of the ancient world was used for the benefit of another circle than the narrowly religious. The learning which had been largely the preserve of the monasteries became more especially that of the universities, where the curriculum was slowly made wider and more attractive to others besides the clergy. Not a single new monastery was established in the thirty years preceding the accession of Henry VIII; instead of cloisters the new vogue was for building college quadrangles. A royal example was set by Lady Margaret Beaufort, the mother of Henry VII, to whom Cambridge is indebted for two of its colleges; and her chaplain, Bishop Oldham, himself the founder of Manchester Grammar School, stated the case with uncourtly bluntness:

> Shall we build houses and provide livelihoods for a company of buzzing monks, whose end and fall we ourselves may live to

[1] See p. 39.

see? No, no: it is meet to provide for the increase of learning and for such as by learning shall do good to church and commonwealth.

The largest foundations in either of the ancient universities, namely Trinity, Cambridge, and Christ Church, Oxford, are associated with the reign and name of Henry VIII, the despoiler of monasteries.

Scientists and Artists

It was in accordance with the spirit of the age for wealth to be applied to educational purposes, since the Renaissance gave a great impetus to the natural human love of inquiry, which medieval religious teaching had largely suppressed. When a fourteenth-century Lincolnshire monk, for example, produced the map of the world which still hangs in Hereford cathedral, Jerusalem was located in the centre, not because scientific observation suggested it but because a central geographical position would fit in with its central position in religion. But now mankind was returning to the methods of observation and experiment which had belonged to classical science. One of the first fellows of Henry VIII's Cambridge foundation was a Welsh mathematician and geographer, John Dee, who did much to bring the scientific knowledge springing up on the Continent across to England. His reputation as a scientist is impaired in modern eyes by the fact that he was also official astrologer to Queen Elizabeth; but by the end of her reign Francis Bacon's teaching of the importance of experiment, induction, and the study of natural law fell on attentive ears. England was then making valuable contributions to mathematics, astronomy, and botany, and in 1600 the *De Magnete* of William Gilbert of Colchester laid the foundation for the later study of electro-magnetism.[1]

This objective view of nature affected the arts, especially painting. Medieval art had developed under the patronage of the Church: both the subject and its treatment were usually religious. Realism in representation was therefore of minor importance. People were often portrayed, not as men and women but as

[1] See p. 226.

saints and angels with golden wings and haloes and with smooth faces almost untouched by shadow or relief. And size came to indicate first and foremost importance – as, for instance, in the ancient sculptured slab at Chichester Cathedral, where Christ and his disciples dwarf the other figures at the gate of Bethany.

Renaissance artists, however, like the scientists, tried to see things as they were, and the Italian discovery of the principles of perspective in the fifteenth century was an essential step towards realizing this. Perspective brought the new dimension of depth to painting, so that it became possible not merely to look at, but into, a picture. The rediscovery, too, of the elements of anatomy made the painting of real men rather than smooth saints possible, and a new demand for portraits sprang up. In Henry VIII's reign it was met by the German Hans Holbein, who painted merchants and courtiers with sometimes unflattering exactness and in that of Elizabeth by Nicholas Hilliard, who painted miniatures of the society of the time.

Political and Historical Studies

The Renaissance revived, as we have seen, an interest in man. It was likely that it would also revive an interest in politics – the activity of man in society. In the ancient world there had been Plato's 'Republic' and the 'Politics' of Aristotle: as the starting point for all later thought they inspired such Renaissance writings as Thomas More's *Utopia* and Richard Hooker's *Of the Laws of Ecclesiastical Polity*. In the second book of his *Utopia* – written in 1515 while the author was on an embassy for Henry VIII to the Netherlands – More speculated about the conditions of society on an imaginary transoceanic island of 'No-place,' which was governed by pure reason. Its citizens hold all goods in common; they practise religious toleration; both sexes enjoy the benefits of education, including adult education, at the public expense; and universal military training for necessary wars is strikingly combined with anti-militarist principles. Hooker, an influential country rector in the later decades of the reign of Elizabeth I, concerned himself more directly with the government of state and church and the ways in which each was bound by moral law. He made the first reasoned defence of the independent Church of England, expressed with a moderation far more congenial than the writings of the Puritans which he controverts. As he claims prophetically in his preface:

> There will come a time when three words uttered with charity and meekness will receive a far more blessed reward than three thousand volumes written with disdainful sharpness of wit.

History was also important to the Renaissance mind, as the record of human endeavour. The Elizabethans showed it a special respect because their worship of the Queen gave them an enhanced interest in the sovereigns of earlier times. Thus Marlowe's tragedy of *Edward II* prepared the way for the many Shakespearean historical plays. As for directly historical writing, a *History of Richard III* is attributed to More and mention has already been made of Cavendish's *Wolsey*, written in the time of Mary. But again the main flow is Elizabethan – the *Chronicles* of Raphael Holinshed, freely drawn on by Shakespeare; Hayward's work on Henry IV, for which he was imprisoned by the Queen; the Anglo-Saxon studies of her first archbishop, Matthew Parker; and the Latin annals of her own reign by William Camden.

Camden, as we shall see in a later chapter[1], was one of the most successful writers of a type of survey which combined topography with antiquities. Many of these were local, such as the *Survey of Cornwall* published by Richard Carew in 1602, when its special character was fast disappearing, or William Lambarde's *Perambulation of Kent*. There was also John Stow[1], who "attempted the discovery of London, my native soil and country." But what is most significant is the expansion of interest from the local to the national theme, which began with the collection of materials for a great work by John Leland at the time of the dissolution of the monasteries. Though his *Itinerary* was not published before the eighteenth century, Leland inspired a series of patriotic Elizabethan studies of the country as a single whole, supplemented by the production of many improved maps: those of John Norden, for instance, were the first to show the roads.

[1]See p. 107.

Prose Literature

An interest in man as man was bound to find expression in literature, whose very basis is reflection upon the human condition. In England the Renaissance reached its climax in the literary achievements of the Elizabethan age, which are far too rich to be examined or even catalogued here. The prose writing may be briefly mentioned first, if only because it lagged behind the verse. Indeed, much of it was so artificial and sugary as to hide all meaning. Consider this example – a description of a woman sewing:

> The needle itself would have been loth to have gone fromward such a mistress but that it hoped to return thitherward very quickly again, the cloth looking with many eyes upon her and lovingly embracing the wounds she gave.

This highflown style, hailed as 'a new English' on its first appearance in the pages of John Lyly's *Euphues: The Anatomy of Wit*, fortunately made little appeal to writers with a serious intellectual purpose, such as Hooker or Bacon, and in the nature of things could not greatly influence the work of translators, such as North, whose rendering of Plutarch's 'Lives' provided Shakespeare with much of his classical knowledge. But by far the most influential translation was that of the Bible, accomplished mainly by William Tyndale and made accessible in parish churches in 1538, two years after he had been done to death as a Lutheran heretic at Louvain. This was substantially the version read by the Elizabethans, which (though inferior to the Authorized King James's Bible of 1611) had its effect on literary style as well as on the national character. With the Bible we may list also the effect of Cranmer's Prayer Book, much of it translated from the Latin, with its sonorous cadences.

Lyrical Poetry

The lyric poetry of the age included much writing which owed little to renaissance influences from abroad. These lines by Ralegh may serve as an example:

As you came from the holy land
Of Walsingham,
Met you not with my true love
By the way you came?

How shall I know your true love
That have met many one
As I went to the holy land,
That have come, that have gone?

* * * * *

Know that Love is a careless child
And forgets promise past;
He is blind; he is deaf when he list,
And in faith never fast!

* * * * *

But true love is a durable fire,
In the mind ever burning,
Never sick, never old, never dead,
From itself never turning.

Native inspiration, however, was wedded to new metrical forms to produce an unmatched lyrical perfection. The sonnet had been introduced from the Italian Petrarch – and modified – by Sir Thomas Wyatt, father of the rebel against Mary; blank verse was first used by Henry Howard, Earl of Surrey, who was the son of the general at Flodden. A major poet still more closely concerned with these changes was Edmund Spenser; he employed a stanza of his own invention for the 'Faerie Queene' and, with the youthful Sir Philip Sidney and two others, formed a society for popularizing classical metres.

In the 1590s the Elizabethan sonnet reached astonishing heights of beauty, many of the loveliest of them being among the 154 which sprang from Shakespeare's prolific pen. But in that decade when such varied geniuses as Thomas Campion and Ben Jonson, the Jesuit martyr Robert Southwell, and John Donne the future Dean of St Paul's, were all active, it is unnecessary to underline the excellence of the English lyric. It is, however, worth noticing that much of the impulse for the lighter forms, including the many anonymous songs which are still in use from this period, came from the vogue for Italian music, with its inventions of the madrigal and aria.

Music

Secular music flourished in England as seemingly never before. Its popularity at Court led to the institution of the Men of the King's Musick and the Chapel Royal, and in the humblest provincial town this was the age of the municipal Waits. But Thomas Tallis and William Byrd, the greatest composers of this great epoch, live on mainly through their magnificent settings for Church services. Though secret Catholics, in 1575 they were rewarded in a manner characteristic of the age, by a monopoly for the sale of printed music, for which they imported the type from Nuremburg.

The Drama

In the case of the drama, we have space only to sketch the story of its sudden ascent. At the start of Tudor times it had not advanced appreciably beyond the form of the religious play of the Middle Ages[1]. Development came largely through the interest roused by the Latin comedies of Plautus and Terence, which were commonly performed in schools as part of the revival of classical enthusiasms. Soon Latin plays in the same style were being written by English authors, and about 1553 the head master of Westminster School wrote *Ralph Roister Doister*, an English-language comedy in the Latin style, which is believed to have been performed by his pupils. A more wholly English comedy, *Gammer Gurton's Needle*, was acted in Cambridge in 1566. This was written in rhyming doggerel verse, but had plenty of action, unlike the rather earlier production of *Gorboduc* in the Inner Temple, which was important for its use of blank verse but must have been somewhat marred by the fact that none of the events in this drama from early British history took place on stage.

[1] See *The Making of Britain: Life and Work to the Close of the Middle Ages*, p. 178.

At this critical point in its development, the Court became an assiduous patron of the movement, and companies of actors were taken under the wing of leading figures about the Queen. Almost immediately, theatres began to appear in London and, literally, the stage was set for the Elizabethan drama. The 'Theatre' was built in Shoreditch in 1576, which was quickly followed by the 'Curtain' and then by the famous 'Globe' and two others on the South Bank. Modelled upon the inn-yards where 'groundlings' stood around the cart which served as a stage, while guests watched the performance from corridor-galleries above, these theatres were constructed 'in the round'; they were open to the sky, and accommodated their audience on every side of the projecting stage except the rear. But there were also some private theatres more like our own, where the stage was at one end of the covered rectangular hall of a college in the university or one of the Inns of Court or some country mansion.

These long-vanished theatres once echoed to the still living plays of Marlowe, Jonson, and Shakespeare himself. Like responded to like: to an England which had its real-life heroes the stage offered others of the same sort. The dramatic quality of Elizabethan life, its nobility and greed, its rough jollity and underlying tensions, were all mirrored in the stage drama of the age. But we are not belittling that age if we also reflect that the creations of Shakespeare's genius, like the Attic drama, have a timeless quality which may entitle them to outlast every other aspect of a period which we recall with such pride.

The Reformation in its National Aspect

The plays of Shakespeare embody every aspect of the many-sided Renaissance life, including the vivid sense of nationality which was helped by the study of history and political development and the example of the ancients. The generation which had defeated the Spanish Armada would be very ready to applaud John of Gaunt's famous reference to

England, bound in with the triumphant sea.

But when he also called it

> *This fortress, built by Nature for herself*
> *Against infection and the hand of war*

some at least of the audience would think of 'infection' by a foreign religious creed. For the national feeling which the Renaissance had helped to stimulate had become closely entangled with the changes in religious belief and practice which we call the Reformation.

In its earliest stages the English Reformation was primarily a nationalist movement, and its doctrinal debt to Luther and Calvin and other Continental reformers never deprived it of a strongly national character. When Henry VIII refused to accept the authority of the Pope and took his place as 'the only supreme head in earth of the Church of England', his reasons were personal and nationalist, not doctrinal: indeed, he had been made 'Defender of the Faith' by the Papacy for writing a book against Luther. As we have already seen, the annulment of his marriage to Catherine of Aragon offered the only chance of his begetting a legitimate male heir, without which the dynasty might collapse at his death and the nation with it. Nor was it at all impracticable for a sovereign to arrange for such an annulment on grounds of political necessity: but the Pope was at the mercy of a secular ruler more powerful than Henry – the emperor Charles V, who was Catherine's nephew. England therefore was separated from Rome so that Henry VIII might be separated from his wife.

Between 1529 and 1536, accordingly, a series of laws broke the ties which for so many centuries had connected England with the Papal See. But it is significant that the changes were made by statute law – by no fewer than thirty-two acts of the seven-year-long 'Reformation Parliament', leading up to the removal of the right of appeal to Rome from the English Church courts, the formulation of the new royal title and the extension of the law of treason to enforce its acceptance, and the first measure for dissolving the monasteries. Thus the king's anti-papal programme had the support of the people as represented in Parliament, and it is noteworthy that Thomas Cromwell, the masterful minister who had charge of the programme, himself had a seat in the House of Commons.

Dislike for the clergy as a class seems to have been widely prevalent in the days of Chaucer, though the parish priest may have been largely exempt from the feeling directed against the upper clergy, the rich abbeys, and especially the emissaries and money collectors of the Papacy. In the sixteenth century the growth of national feeling caused veneration for the Pope as a spiritual father of the faithful to be largely lost in crude resentment of him as a predatory and meddlesome foreigner, for ever imposing financial burdens on the people of England. The monks and friars, who were envied for their wealth and, perhaps, for their supposed idleness, belonged to Orders under papal authority which stood aside from the general life of the nation. The attacks of the humanists helped to increase their unpopularity. They were among the many objects of Erasmus's satire in his *Praise of Folly*, which was written at More's home in London; there they are described as "observing with punctilious scrupulosity a lot of silly ceremonies and paltry traditional rules" and as "gorging the carcase to the point of bursting".

Dissolution of the Monasteries

This national element in the slowly growing movement towards a reorganization of the Church joined forces with a social and an intellectual urge towards change. The social motive was the desire to appropriate Church lands to secular uses. By Acts of Parliament of 1536 and 1539 and through so-called voluntary surrenders, the Crown acquired possession of huge estates all over England and Wales, which had formerly been owned by about 600 monasteries and friaries. Thomas Cromwell, the vicar-general through whom Henry exercised his powers over the Church, had sent round commissioners in the year before the first Act, who made suitably unfavourable reports on the worldliness and alleged immorality of the monks' way of life. Monastic treasure passed directly into the hands of the King; but the estates, with the exception of about eighty gifts to persons in the royal favour, were rapidly disposed of to about a thousand grantees. They paid some £780,000 for lands which had an annual value of about £90,000, so it is clear that the King could have made more by slower sales or by keeping the ownership. But his urgent need of ready money for his French and Scottish wars (made more expensive by rising prices) compelled him to sell quickly on what was therefore a buyers' market.

In the following reign it was the turn of the chantries, whose business was to sing mass for the souls of the dead. The priest who sang the masses was usually paid from an endowment of land, which came either from the will of some wealthy individual or from a corporate organization such as a gild. When the land was taken under an act of 1547, it was not only the services in the chantry chapels which suffered; the chantry priests had also in many cases functioned as schoolmasters. Since episcopal estates were also reduced considerably in the early years of Elizabeth, it is safe to conclude that altogether one-fifth of the land changed owners. The result was to establish a large body of gentry who had the strongest material reasons for upholding the Reformation settlement. Some came from the class of court officials, some from the ranks of thriving merchants, many from among the younger sons of existing landed families. As a whole, they were probably more interested than the old-established gentry in the full economic exploitation of their property.

The First Wave of Protestantism

The intellectual urge towards change made rather fitful advances during the reign of Henry VIII, whose subjects were required to accept those elements in Lutheran teaching, and only those, which the king might temporarily adopt as part of his unceasing battle against the papacy. They were liable to the death penalty both for the denial of the Catholic doctrine of transubstantiation and for the denial of the Henrician doctrine of England's independence of the papacy. But by the time of his death the logic of events was driving Henry, and consequently his subjects, to side with Luther against the old order. As regards their learning to think independently, however, the only effective change was the official encouragement of Bible-reading. Cromwell's Injunctions to the clergy, issued in October 1538, ordered them to provide

> on this side the Feast of Easter next coming, one book of the whole Bible of the largest volume in English, and the same set up in some convenient place within the church that you have cure of, whereas your parishioners may most commodiously resort to the same and read it.

That the Bible penetrated like yeast to create a ferment in the minds of the people is made clear by the corrective legislation passed in 1543, when the right to read the Bible was restricted to noblemen and gentlemen, who might read to their families, and to substantial merchants and gentlewomen, who might read only for themselves.

In the reign of the boy-king Edward VI, whom enthusiastic preachers hailed as 'the young Josiah', the Protector Somerset and Archbishop Cranmer changed the official religion of England from anti-papal to Protestant. In 1549 and 1552 Cranmer produced two prayer books, the second and more strongly Protestant of which was enforced upon the laity as well as the clergy. Both books were compiled entirely in English and drew freely upon the ideas of the Continental reformers, especially Zwingli, but they preserved much of the forms of prayer and order of service from the liturgy of the Roman Church. The doctrine of transubstantiation was no longer accepted and a new stress was laid on the necessity of individual faith to procure salvation; but the shepherds of the bewildered flock still retained the ancient orders of bishop, priest, and deacon.

The Critical Decade, 1553–63

The most critical decade in the history of the English Reformation opened in 1553, with the death of Edward and the fiasco of the attempt to usurp the throne for Lady Jane Grey, a devoutly Protestant girl of sixteen with no ambition to be queen, albeit a grand-niece of Henry VIII. The years which followed under Mary were marked by reconciliation to Rome, but also by the refusal of Parliament to restore the monasteries (though an exception was made for Westminster Abbey), by her intensely unpopular marriage with her Spanish cousin Philip, and above all by the public burning of some 300 obdurate Protestants, mainly in London and the home counties. Although there had been some upper-class laymen among the 500 'gospellers' who fled abroad at Mary's accession, the 200 of the laity who suffered the extreme penalty for their faith included no one of aristocratic birth, but many artisans and no fewer than 60 women. Among the 100 clergy Bishop Latimer, a yeoman's son, gave a heroic and far-sighted lead. "Be of good comfort, Master Ridley, and play the man," he cried to his fellow-bishop as they were led to the stake. "We shall this day light such a candle by God's grace in England, as (I trust) shall never be put out."

That candle soon burnt steadily. Mary's early death, by bringing her politic half-sister Elizabeth to the throne, led quickly to the establishment of the *via media anglicana*, that English religious compromise which stood the test of time. The new sovereign repudiated the authority of Rome, and was styled by statute the 'Supreme Governor' of her Church. In the same year, 1559, Cranmer's second Prayer Book was reimposed, with modifications and ambiguities which made it a little easier for a Catholic to suspend judgment and accept it; about four-fifths of the Marian clergy apparently fell into line.[1] Similar encouragement was offered by the Thirty-Nine Articles of religion, promulgated by Convocation in 1563 (and enacted in 1571); for the body of doctrine which they prescribed preserved many of the Catholic concepts. Only John Foxe's *Acts and Monuments of these latter and perilous Days,* first issued in English in 1563, focused popular feelings against the principles and practices of Rome.

The Book of Martyrs, as it was popularly called, which highlights the martyrdoms suffered in the cause of English Protestantism, ran through five editions before the end of the Queen's reign. It went round the world with Drake, and on official orders was placed in every cathedral and in the houses of the great for the benefit of servants and visitors. But there needed no orders for its admission to the homes of ordinary people, where it long held a position of

[1] Cf. G. R. Elton, *The Tudor Constitution*, p. 389: "The number deprived has been much disputed but was probably between 200 and 400 in a total of over 2,000."

authority second only to the Bible itself. Many Englishmen therefore followed Foxe in linking the Pope with Antichrist and the English with God's Chosen People. "The living God is only the English God," declares John Lyly, and is echoed by John Davis the explorer, who exclaims: "Are not we only set upon Mount Zion to give light to all the rest of the world?"

The Catholic Recusants

Nevertheless, the Elizabethan religious settlement was attacked by two minority movements, a fact of great importance for the development of individual opinion. Though the younger generation of Catholics by degrees became conformers with the new order, some adhered firmly to the old faith. The excommunication of the Queen in 1570 meant that in Catholic eyes she was no longer sovereign, and the conflict was further exacerbated by the mission, first of secular priests trained at Douai, and later of Jesuits, who travelled the country in disguise, fortifying the faith of their co-religionists. The Rising of the Northern Earls, already mentioned,[1] was accordingly followed by three other Catholic plots on Mary's behalf. By laws passed in 1581 and 1585 it was made treasonable to 'withdraw the Queen's subjects from the religion now established to the Romish religion' and for English priests trained abroad to re-enter the country for any purpose: about 200 Catholics were executed, and another 50 died in prison, in some instances after torture which was applied to extract confessions and betrayals. The Act of 1581 also increased the fine for non-attendance at church from a shilling a Sunday to £20 a month. But after the execution of Mary Queen of Scots, the Catholic candidate for the throne, and the defeat of the Spanish Armada, intended as a crusade for the reconversion of England, this minority movement was somewhat less formidable in reality than it appeared in the imagination of a people who were so familiar with the facts of the Marian persecution.[2]

[1] See p. 19.

[2] Near the end of Elizabeth's reign there were 31 Jesuits in England, of whom 7 were in prison (letter from the Jesuit Superior to the General, May 5th, 1602, quoted in P. Caraman: *Henry Garnet*, p. 296).

The Puritans

The other minority movement was clearly important because of its continued growth. The Puritans criticized the religious settlement from the opposite point of view, as failing to purify the Church completely from every taint of Rome. They began by attacking whatever was left of ecclesiastical ritual – the use of vestments, the practice of kneeling, the wedding-ring, and the sign of the cross in baptism. But by 1570 many Puritans demanded the replacement of episcopacy by the more democratic presbyterian system of governing the church through ministers and lay elders, as practised by Calvin at Geneva. "Take away the lordship, the loitering, the pomp, the idleness, the livings of bishops," cried Thomas Cartwright, whom they had driven from his Cambridge professorship of theology. And ten years later some Puritans went even further, proposing that every congregation of Christian people should be free to choose its own form of worship. These early Congregationalists were severely persecuted, banishment and death being prescribed as penalties for their withdrawal from the lawful church.

But the Puritans as a whole were an increasing force in the universities, in Parliament, and presumably in the country at large, where they exercised a great influence beyond their own ranks through the encouragement they gave to the study of the Bible as the only source of authority in religion. The so-called Geneva version, the first to be divided into verses and equipped with 'most profitable annotations upon all the hard places', appeared in a handy octavo edition in 1579 and was reprinted biennially. The Puritans often laid themselves open to charges of hypocrisy and meddlesomeness and there seems to have been a lull in their general activities during the last years of the reign. But their readiness to raise questions of ethical standards and to argue from their texts gave them great driving-force – and was a valuable stimulus to intellectual activity in other spheres.

Education

One of these was education, which broadly speaking had been on the up-grade since the middle of the fifteenth century. There was gain as well as loss at the dissolution of the monasteries, for though the monks ceased to provide education for their novices and, at the humbler level, choristers, Henry VIII sought to put the cathedral schools on a stronger basis than before. Even in the time of Edward VI close examination seems to show that education registered some advance, in spite of the upheaval caused by the Chantries Act.[1] The grammar schools established by letters patent (and known later by the boy-king's name) were intended to serve as a model for many more, but the Marian religious reaction demanded no more Latin for the young than that "they may be able to answer the priest at Mass, and help the priest to Mass as hath been accustomed". In the reign of Elizabeth, however, godliness and good learning were believed to be interdependent.

Harrow, Repton, Rugby, and Uppingham were among the well-known provincial schools which opened their doors then. London added Merchant Taylors' to Dean Colet's re-foundation of St Paul's. Even far-off Wales, which had had no grammar schools at all before the Tudor period, acquired at least four, founded by a lawyer, a churchman, a peer, and a draper. In the course of the reign private benefactors gave £140,000 (the equivalent of several millions today) to schools and universities, of which more than one-half was for the grammar schools. Many of them were extremely small, but even so a school to about every 13,000 of population was no mean provision.

Very little is known about the state of primary education at this time. A pupil was normally required to be able to read and write his own language before he could be admitted to the Latin grammar class at the bottom of the grammar school; many other children needed to be able at least to read before starting on their apprenticeship, to say nothing of the demand in every kind of family for the reading of the Bible. Sometimes the grammar school had a 'petty school' attached to it, or there was a 'free school' of lower

[1] See J. Simon, *Education and Society in Tudor England,* cc. VIII–XI.

status, as at Worcester and Southwark, while at Blackburn Grammar School and Archbishop Holgate's School, York, we find the interesting provision that the art of reading was to be taught where necessary by the older pupils to the younger. No doubt there were many tiny schools kept by private persons, like what were later called 'dame's schools', and the more earnest among the clergy certainly helped the children of their parishes. Girls seem to have shared more commonly in the facilities for primary than in those for secondary education, which according to surviving records were reserved almost entirely for boys. This is an astonishing fact about an age when private tutors could educate a queen like Elizabeth, highly accomplished and with a lifelong interest in ancient and modern learning. It was the age, too, of other highly intelligent Renaissance ladies such as Lady Jane Grey (the 'nine days' queen') whom at the age of sixteen Roger Ascham "found in her chamber, reading *Phaedon Platonis* in Greek, and that with as much delight as some gentlemen would read a merry tale in Boccaccio".

There was not much reading of 'merry tales' in the grammar schools, where the boy of 7–15 was put through a rigorous course of Latin authors and Latin composition and (in theory at least) even conversed in Latin with his schoolfellows. The better schools also taught Greek and more occasionally Hebrew, as an aid to the universal study of the Scriptures. The pupils learnt incidentally to speak and write their own language more correctly. One landmark in the move towards standard English was a book in Henry VIII's reign, which demanded that children should be taught to "speak no English but that which is clean, polite, perfectly and articulately pronounced"; another, a work by the first head master of Merchant Taylors', on 'the right writing of our English tongue'.

The Universities

In the universities, to which the ambitious resorted in increasing numbers to prepare themselves for careers in State as well as Church, the Latin laboriously acquired at school provided the basis for the further study of classics and theology, mathematics, and the philosophy and medicine of the ancients. Graduates often went on to study the common law in the freer atmosphere of the Inns of Court in London, where a notable attempt was also made to establish a third university, at Gresham's College: this was to provide lectures in the liberal sciences, which were to be delivered in English instead of Latin and from notes instead of being read out 'after the manner of the universities'. But the religious conflicts of the day dominated the life of both the ancient universities, so much so that for the first time all students were required to be under the control of a college. This did not prevent Oxford from suffering a decline, with several of its leading scholars disappearing to the Catholic seminaries abroad. Cambridge, however, flourished greatly, with William Cecil as Chancellor and two new colleges (Emmanuel and Sidney Sussex) founded to strengthen its Puritan connections. In the last decades of the century the sermons of one Puritan divine exercised such an influence there that they make up almost one-quarter of the 200 publications of the University Press over a period of 28 years.

Change in the Parish

In that way Cambridge might be regarded as a rather extreme example of the influence of the Elizabethan religious settlement as it was worked out at the level of the parish. What practical difference did the Reformation make here? For the uncritical, not very much at the outset, at least if we accept the recollections of David Baker, who in James's reign became a Benedictine monk:

> At the first . . . the greatest part even of those who in their judgments and affections had before been Catholicks did not well discern any great fault, novelty, or difference from the former religion . . . in this new set up by Queen Elizabeth, save only change of language . . . And so easily accommodated themselves thereto.

But even the unobservant must have noticed the disappearance of the images and some of the stained glass, the obliteration of many wall-paintings with whitewash, and the replacement of the stone altar by a table placed in the body of the church. There was a Bible available for public reading, and a new type of service which slowly sank in because attendance was compulsory for everybody who could not afford to disregard strong social pressures and the risk of a fine.

The Roman service books – Missal, Breviary, and Ordinal - had been replaced, as for a previous short period in Edward's reign, by an English Prayer Book, in which the numerous Roman services had been reduced to three – Holy Communion, Matins, and Evensong. Slowly the English forms of prayer, which Cranmer had phrased with haunting beauty, would become familiar to the ear, would gather associations, would become sacrosanct. There was no intoning of prayers and the congregation entered more fully into the service than formerly: Luther, though not Calvin, had encouraged hymn-singing, and there was a rhymed English metrical version of the Psalms. Congregations were immensely appreciative of sermons, sometimes constraining a preacher to continue for a third hour and often organizing extra weekday sermons; the Puritans criticized as 'dumb dogs' those less energetic clergy who used the ready-made sermons of the official Book of Homilies. Except for the surplice the elaborate mass vestments of the priest had also gone, and outside church he looked like any other man. Last but by no means least, the parson was now usually a married man, whose wife and family played an increasingly large part in the life of the parish and eventually of the nation.

Wales

In Wales, as in England, it might be claimed that the importance of the Reformation can be seen most clearly at the level of the parish. As we have already suggested,[1] Henry VIII seems to have feared a Papal counter-attack by way of Wales. Yet the Catholic religion was not particularly strong there: the bishops were Englishmen who rarely entered the Principality, and the fifty monasteries were small and their resources easily plundered. But the Elizabethan régime, besides appointing Welshmen to the bishoprics, sought to insure the triumph of the new Church settlement by ordering them to translate both the Bible and the Prayer Book into Welsh. The New Testament and the Prayer Book were

[1]See p. 31.

completed in the prescribed period of four years and the whole Bible by the time of the Armada. Though no portable edition was available for another half-century, the Welsh Bible was henceforth accessible in every parish church, being placed alongside an English Bible to encourage the learning of English. Instead, a new impetus was given to Welsh literature: even one of Drake's sea-dogs translated the Psalms into Welsh verse. Although Puritanism did not get the same hold in Wales as in England during Elizabeth's reign, Puritan writers later produced at least one major Welsh classic and kept the Welsh Bible alive in the parishes by teaching the people to read it, together with their own religious tracts. Henry VIII's Act of 1536 had included the Welsh language as one of the separate customs to be eliminated: the Bible in the parish churches helped to defeat his purpose.

The Reformation in Scotland

The history of the Reformation in Scotland, a determining force in its development, remains to be considered. This is complicated by the interaction of its three main causes: the abuses within the Church, the spread of Protestant ideas, and the increasing vigour of Scottish nationalism.

Plate 3' '*The Ambassadors*' (*Hans Holbein*). This picture, painted in 1533 and now in the National Gallery, shows well some of the dominant Renaissance ideas – its interest in men and human activity and in the possibilities of perspective. The two figures are French diplomats – both for the moment in England – and they are backed by a miscellaneous collection of Tudor objects: on the upper shelf, upon a Turkey carpet, a celestial globe; two sundials flanking a quadrant; and, on the right, a 'torquetum' for determining the position of the stars. On the lower shelf are a terrestrial globe, two books (the open one showing a Luther hymn), a lute and some flutes. The object rising from the floor in the foreground is a skull as in a distorting mirror (a variant of the perspective technique). Detail is everything – even the floor is almost an exact copy of one still existing in Westminster Abbey. (Cf. text p. 39.)

Plate 4. *Falkland Palace, South Range.* A superb Scottish example of early Renaissance architecture, this façade was added to the earlier palace by James V between 1537 and 1541 with the help of French masons, though the architect was the King's cousin, Sir James Hamilton of Finnart. The buttress columns and the medallions between them are typical of the early Renaissance in France – the paired medallions themselves illustrating the Renaissance love of classical themes in their portrayal of mythological heroes and heroines.

Plate 5. *The Burning of Bishop Hooper.* John Hooper, Bishop of Gloucester and Worcester, was tried for heresy and burned at Gloucester in 1555 – one of the Protestant martyrs whom Foxe commemorated in his 'Book of Martyrs' from which this illustration comes. (Cf. text p. 49.)

Plate 3

Plate 4

Plate 5

As in many other countries, conditions in the Church were open to attack. Its income was far larger than that of the Crown itself, and lay mostly in the hands of the higher clergy and the monastic orders. Many monasteries, for instance, had taken over parochial benefices, putting in curates to do the work at low rates of pay. This abuse led to others, for these curates were forced to extort money from their parishes to relieve their own poverty. Such men were often ill-educated and in this were not different from the mass of the lower clergy. When a Scots catechism was issued in 1552, clergy intending to read it to their people were advised to practise first, so as not to 'stammer or stumble' in public. As Wolsey was in England, so in Scotland was Cardinal Beaton (1494–1546) the supreme example of wealth and power. He was archbishop of St Andrews, papal legate, Bishop of Mirepoix in France, Abbot of Arbroath and Chancellor of Scotland. As he had at least eight children, his private life too was something of a scandal.

Reforming influences seeped in slowly from abroad. Wyclif's ideas[1] survived in Scotland, where the papacy was under attack in 1494 by the 'Lollards of Kyle'. In the following century a ban on the importation of Lutheran writings did not prevent them from becoming known through such men as Patrick Hamilton, burnt as a heretic at St Andrews in 1528. "The reek of Master Hamilton," said a contemporary, "has infected as many as it blew upon." But by far the most important source of Protestant teaching was John Knox. Born about 1505, he was the son of what was probably a prosperous Lothian peasant family, and was certainly a Catholic priest before he emerges into the light of history in 1546, already a militant reformer. His hatred of Catholicism was sharpened by some two years of servitude in French galleys and his Protestant convictions took final shape in the England of Edward VI, where he refused a bishopric, and more especially under Calvin at Geneva. On his final return to his native land in 1559, the stern logic of his preaching led directly to riots at Perth and St Andrews, in which monasteries were plundered by what he himself called 'the rascal multitude'. But Knox was equally formidable as an organizer: within a year he had drafted his *First Book of Discipline*, a

[1] See *The Making of Britain: Life and Work to the Close of the Middle Ages*, p. 163.

blueprint for a new Church with a project for a system of national education thrown in.

The development of Scottish nationalism was, however, the determining factor. This had grown up in reaction to English aggression and had found in France its most natural protector. Now the situation was reversed – aggression came from France and protection from England. This was the long-term result of the marriage of James V and a widowed French duchess, Mary of Lorraine. Their daughter Mary, as already mentioned,[1] having become queen in infancy, was sent to the French court to marry the Dauphin instead of Edward VI, with the result that in 1554 her mother became Regent of Scotland. Frenchmen were put in charge of the Great Seal and of the Scottish finances; the French ambassador was given entry to the Privy Council; French garrisons were installed in Scottish towns; and in 1559, when the husband of the younger Mary became king of France, he also became in virtue of his marriage king of Scots.

Thus a body of Protestant nobles who, with one eye on the monastic lands, had set themselves up as the 'Congregation of Christ', received national backing when they rose, at first unsuccessfully, against the Regent and her French troops. The Lords of the Congregation then requested help from Elizabeth, to whom French power in Scotland was almost as great a danger as to the Scottish people themselves. Money, a fleet, and a force of 6,500 men from the counties north of the Trent turned the balance against the French, who withdrew from Scotland in the summer of 1560. The Scottish Parliament abolished both the Mass and the authority of the Pope, acting under the theological leadership of Knox and the protection of the Lords of the Congregation, who shared out much Church land.

But the settlement was far from secure. Her husband having died a year after his accession to the throne of France, Mary Queen of Scots returned home from her long stay in one of the most Catholic courts of Europe. For Knox her unlooked-for return even spoiled the summer weather:

The very face of heaven the time of her arrival did manifestly

[1] See p. 33.

> speak what comfort was brought unto this country with her, to wit, sorrow, dolour, darkness, and all impiety. For, in the memory of man, that day of the year was never seen a more dolorous face of the heaven than was at her arrival . . . The sun was not seen to shine two days before nor two days after.

For a time she played a waiting game with regard to the new Church, though the violent hostility of Knox helped to make her reckless. However, her involvement in the murder of her second husband, Lord Darnley, by Bothwell, who subsequently became her third husband, delivered her into the hands of her Protestant enemies. After her forced abdication, her infant son by Darnley was crowned king as James VI in her stead, and in 1568 Mary fled across the Border.

In England Mary, whose direct descent from Henry VII made her the obvious heir to the throne, became (as we have already seen[1]) the centre of ineffectual plots against Elizabeth; these ended only with her execution in 1587. During those nineteen years Scotland suffered many of the evils common during a royal minority, and when James was declared of age at fifteen, he was promptly kidnapped. It is easy to understand that, when his position became stronger, he sought to establish a royal supremacy over the Scottish Church, supported by a hierarchy of bishops But before the death of John Knox in 1572 a mainly presbyterian system had been set up, with the final authority placed in the hands of an annual General Assembly of the Kirk; and Knox's ideas on church government were ultimately to prevail. The English had helped the Scottish people to found a Church which, in a later generation, was to give powerful help in its turn to the cause of Puritanism and parliamentarism in England.

[1]See p. 50.

4

THE SEAFARERS

In the Hereford World Map of the thirteenth century, whose centre, as we have seen[1], is placed at Jerusalem, Britain is as far from that point as possible. She lies in the narrow band of ocean surrounding the single land-mass of the world, as insignificant as any one part of the decoration round a plate. Very different, however, is her situation on Mercator's Chart of the World (1569). Here she is almost in the exact centre of the flat projection of the globe, Europe lying to the east of her and America to the west.

The Impact of the Discoveries on England

The new maps were based on new knowledge. Columbus, sailing west from Spain in 1492, reached the West Indies and believed that he had touched the fabled east and so proved the roundness of the world. Vasco da Gama, setting out from Portugal in 1497, passed the Cape of Good Hope and reached India. From the Tagus in 1519 went Magellan's expedition, returning to Seville three years later after having sailed around the world, out by the Magellan Straits and back by what became the Cape of Good Hope. These discoveries revealed a round world containing two great land-masses – Asia with Africa and Europe, and North and South America – separated by the Atlantic and Pacific oceans. Between these two land-masses, on the edge of the overflowing life of Europe, lay the British Isles.

Yet in the early sixteenth century England was a small Power with little sea tradition, and was unable to make use of the trade opportunities that geography revealed to her. Newly united Spain and even the kingdom of Portugal, the mother countries of the early sea explorers, were then stronger than England, and their monopoly in the practice of discovery was underlined by the

[1]See p. 38.

Pope. In 1493 Pope Alexander VI divided the world between the two rivals, drawing a line down the Atlantic through the Azores (later shifted to the 40th meridian west) and partitioning the undiscovered areas of the world between Spain, to the west of the line, and Portugal, to the east.

The developing energies of England, therefore, were in theory shut out from sharing in the newly opened trading opportunities of east and west. To the east lay the fabulous Spice Islands of the Malay Archipelago, whose centre was the Moluccas. Here were the luxuries that Europe longed for – the cloves, nutmeg, pepper and mace which could make palatable the too-long-preserved meat of the autumn slaughterings; the silks, pearls and peacock plumes to brighten the eyes and the persons of northern ladies. And here was the rice that the very seamen who traded in it could use to vary their diet through the long months afloat. A portion of these things had always reached Europe through the Levant ports – those harbours in the eastern Mediterranean which were the ends of the overland route to China. But the caravan trains travelling the high mountain passes and arid deserts of the trade routes, and constantly faced by the threat of brigands, could never supply enough to meet the demands of Europe.

The west, too, soon proved to be rich, as into Spanish harbours there sailed ships heavy with silver from Peruvian mines. Nevertheless the eastern lure was stronger and the difficulties of getting there the more resented. Yet these difficulties might be overcome: the Spaniards and Portuguese confined themselves to warm southern latitudes and, whatever theory might say, could not in practice develop the whole of the vast empires granted to them by the Pope. In North America there was room enough for English exploration without clashes with Spanish activity. In 1497, therefore, Henry VII gave his approval to a voyage led by the Italian John Cabot, on condition that he should keep clear of previous European settlements. This really barred every direction but the west. Cabot sailed to Newfoundland, where he discovered seas rich in cod and believed, like Columbus, that he had touched the coast of Asia and was near to greater riches than fish could supply. The next year he went again and never came back.

At last it became clear that America was not the Far East and

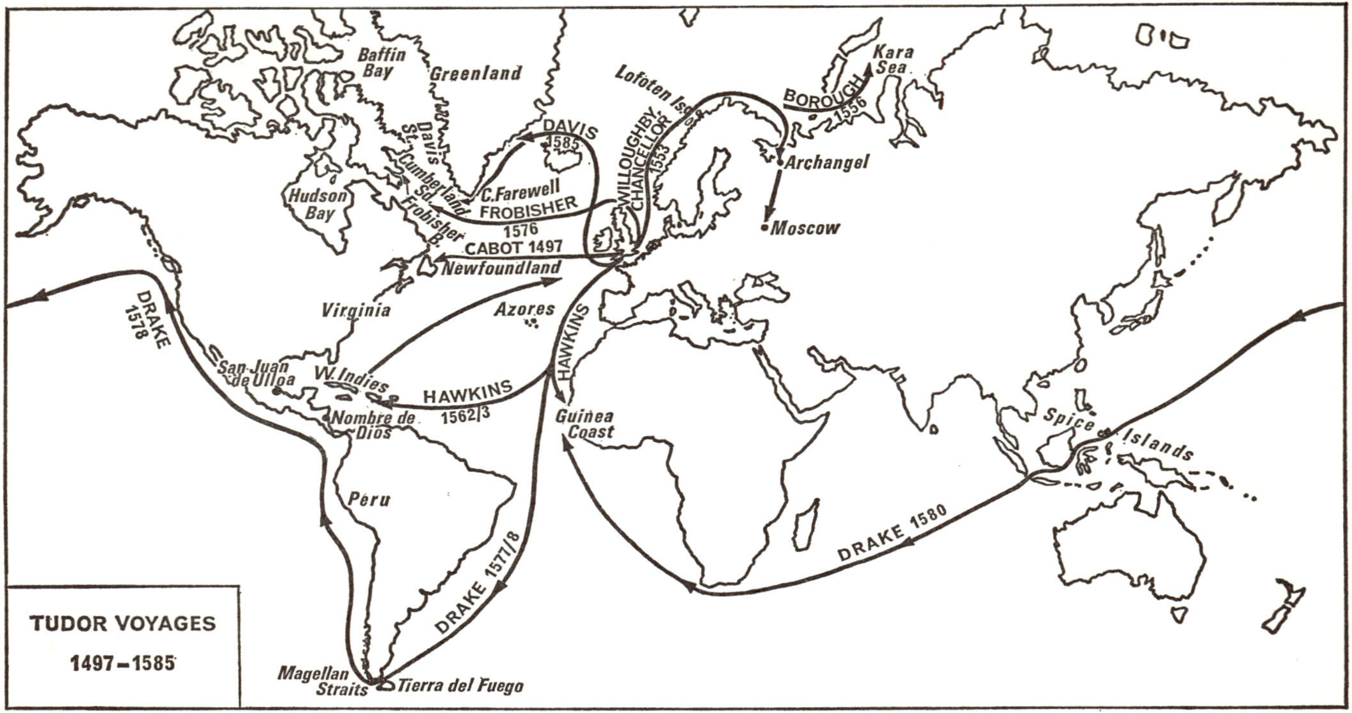
TUDOR VOYAGES
1497–1585
Baffin Bay
Greenland
Davis St.
DAVIS 1585
Cumberland Sd.
Frobisher B.
C.Farewell
FROBISHER 1576
CABOT 1497
Hudson Bay
Newfoundland
Virginia
Azores
Lofoten Is.
WILLOUGHBY, CHANCELLOR 1553
BOROUGH 1556
Kara Sea
Archangel
Moscow
HAWKINS
HAWKINS 1562/3
W. Indies
San Juan de Ulloa
Nombre de Dios
Guinea Coast
Peru
DRAKE 1578
DRAKE 1577/8
DRAKE 1580
Magellan Straits
Tierra del Fuego
Spice Islands

that a whole new continent separated English explorers from the pearl-bright waters of the Moluccas. A new world pattern was built up, in which the two land-masses faced each other from their two halves of the globe. The land to the south of these continents (at the Straits of Magellan and the Cape of Good Hope) tapered away so that it could be rounded by sea. For no good reason, save that the world's land pattern appeared symmetrical, it became a popular English belief that the land to the north must taper away too. If this were true, then without much danger from distant Spaniards and Portuguese, ships could reach the East Indies by sailing west round the north of America or east round that of Russia. The obsession with the North-West and the North-East Passages was born, and it dominated the minds of English seamen till the early seventeenth century.

Search for the North-West Passage

Each of these Passages had its own supporters. For the North-West there were Sebastian Cabot (son of John Cabot) and Humphrey Gilbert, who wrote in 1566 the *Discourse for a Discovery for a New Passage to Cathay* (China). The North-East was backed by the Cambridge savant, John Dee. Where these men pointed, others followed. Yet the flow of such followers was not constant: after the first wave of interest at the start of the sixteenth century had died down, there was little enthusiasm till declining trade in the 1550s forced men to think of new markets. Then the vision of Cathay danced again before their eyes and led men to follow it across unknown seas.

The great period of the north-west search began with Martin Frobisher. His first expedition (1576) with three small ships received £850 in backing from merchants, and discovered the 'straits' which Frobisher took to be the eastern entrance to the Passage and to which he gave his name. These were, however, no more than a deep inlet, which today is called Frobisher Bay. More important to his merchant supporters were the samples of 'gold ore' which Frobisher brought back and which were declared genuine by optimistic tests. Therefore more supporters were easily found, who put up £5,150 to fit out another expedition to explore the area of the so-called 'straits'. This sailed in 1577, and the next year Frobisher led another voyage with fifteen ships on the same business. No important discoveries were made and, although the strait leading into Hudson Bay was found, it was not seriously followed through. And the speculative backers of the expedition were disappointed by the 1,300 tons of ore brought back, which turned out to be worthless. Yet if little was done to dissolve the mystery of the passage to the east, the difficulties awaiting such northern voyagers were made clear enough. They were, for instance, described in *A True Discourse of the Late Voyages of Discovery* (1578):

> Some, even withoutboard on the ice, and some withinboard upon the sides of their ships, having poles, pikes, pieces of timber and oars in their hands, stood almost day and night without any rest, bearing off the force and breaking the sway of the ice with such incredible pain and peril that it was wonderful to behold.

In 1585 John Davis made the first of his three voyages to find the North-West Passage – the most single-minded English explorer in the whole of the century. Having obtained the support of courtiers, such as Ralegh, and of a well-to-do London merchant, he sailed to the east coast of Greenland. Thence he turned south and rounded Cape Farewell, only to become entangled in Cumberland Sound on Baffin Island, while he still believed that he was charting a 'course for China'. But he avoided this dead-end in his expeditions of the two following years, when he sailed through the straits now named after him deep into Baffin Bay. On the last occasion he was in ice-free waters at 73° N. and believed that he had found the Passage, but was stopped by contrary winds and dwindling provisions.

The North-East Passage

The navigators who attempted the North-East Passage were few. Easily the most important were Hugh Willoughby and Richard Chancellor, who in 1553 led an expedition there. It was powerfully backed by Northumberland himself and by 240 Londoners – officials, traders, and navigators – who provided the money to put it to sea. It was probably because of this rich backing that the ships of the expedition were the first to be metal-sheathed against barnacles. Willoughby and Chancellor, however, were separated by storms at the Lofoten Islands, and Willoughby and his men died while trying to winter aboard ship on the Murmansk coast. But Chancellor went on across the White Sea to the river-mouth where Archangel now stands. He then travelled by sledge to Moscow, where Tsar Ivan the Terrible offered trading privileges to English merchants. These were what the backers of the expedition had hoped for, and the result was the formation of the Muscovy Company. In 1556 the Company sent to the north-east Stephen Borough, who had sailed with Chancellor, and he was successful in pushing farther across the roof of the world than Chancellor had done. He reached the Kara Sea and discovered the islands on its western side. Finally, in 1580 the Muscovy Company sent another expedition to penetrate as far to the east as possible and to settle the existence of a passage to China. Its leaders were Arthur Pett and Charles Jackman who, reaching no farther than Borough had done and pressed by the groaning ice, were forced to turn back. In the east as in the west, the attempt on a passage to Cathay and the Spice Islands proved fruitless.

Organization of Trading Companies

Whether they failed or succeeded, the financing of all these voyages involved risk, which their backers tried to spread by organizing in Companies and acquiring a royal charter to give them a monopoly of the trade to be opened up. Often before the first sailings on a new project, when the dangers of total loss appeared great, merchants would organize on a 'joint-stock' basis. They would themselves take a large or small share in the enterprise and invite anybody else with spare capital to do the same. From the money raised they would hire or buy ships; at the end of the voyage the original contributions would be repaid and the profits shared out in proportion to the amounts originally risked. The company would then be dissolved or perhaps continued with a new investment in another voyage. In this way the risks were both spread widely and limited to a particular enterprise. However, if a monopoly of any trade opened up were granted under its charter, the company might wish to take advantage of this by organizing on a more permanent basis. It might, in fact, develop into the other main sort of company at this time – the 'Regulated Company'. This was altogether a more settled affair. Like a Joint Stock Company, it existed by right of a royal charter which gave it monopoly trading rights. But its members were merchants who traded for themselves in the area of the monopoly, either hiring space in company ships for their exports or trading in their own ships with company protection. There was something chancy about the joint stock company: it might or might not pay off and, if it did not, there was total loss of the investment. The regulated company was more certain: it provided opportunities for regular trade by members who might profit or not according to their own skill.

The most important of the Elizabethan joint stock companies were the Muscovy Company (founded 1555), the Turkey Company (1581) and the East India Company (1600); and of the regulated companies, the Eastland Company (1579) and the Levant Company (1592 – regulated in 1605). Perhaps the most interesting of them in this early period is the first. The Muscovy Company specialized in trading cloth into Russia along the route that Richard Chancellor pioneered by Archangel and Moscow. One of its greatest representatives was Anthony Jenkinson, who never lost sight of the original goal of all this eastern trading exploration, the wealth of the Far East. Across the high lands of southern Asia came the old 'silk route' from China – by Samarkand and Baghdad to Aleppo and Damascus, where the traders of the Levant (then not English) awaited it. Jenkinson believed that part of the trade might be diverted up the Volga towards Moscow and the White Sea, so becoming the prize of the Muscovy Company. This plan never came off, but Jenkinson did manage for about ten years to keep open a profitable trade from Persia, using waterways for the most part: from the Caspian Sea to the Volga River, up the North Dvina to Archangel and the northern seas. Profitable, that is, until the Turks overran Persia in about 1580 and closed down the trade.

The other companies must be dealt with more briefly. The Turkey Company tapped the same eastern trades as the Muscovy Company, for they were still accessible at the Turkish ports of Smyrna and Aleppo. Its ships had to be heavily armed for the precarious Mediterranean voyage, but the resulting cargoes of silks, sweet wines, currants, and carpets were very valuable. In 1592 it was reorganized as the better-known Levant Company, of which the East India Company was virtually an offshoot, attracting many of the same merchants. This started as a tentative joint-stock venture to Sumatra and Java, based on the special privilege of taking £30,000 out of the country in gold and silver to supplement its export wares. At first the stock was returned to its owners together with the profits after each voyage, and the most ardent patriot could not have guessed that the Company would become proprietors of an empire. The Eastland Company supported the effort of the oldest regulated company, the Merchant Adventurers,[1] by exporting cloth to the Scandinavian and Baltic countries, from which it brought home naval stores for the shipyards.

The Slave Trade

So far we have dealt mainly with voyages to the north-east and north-west. Farther south there were the Spaniards and Portuguese, insisting on their rights by Papal decree to reap for themselves the rich trading harvests of the world. To oppose them would not be possible, but there might be a chance of giving help and so gaining a small share in the gleanings. In this way the English slave trade to the West Indies began. In 1562 John Hawkins, the son of a prosperous Plymouth merchant, sailed to the African Guinea coast; there he bargained with tribal rulers for Negro slaves, exchanging them for English manufactures. The north-east trade winds took him to the Spanish island colonies in the Caribbean Sea, where he bartered his slaves for pearls, hides and sugar which, taken back to England, brought him a rich profit. It was the start of the triangular trade, whose three points were England, West Africa and the West Indies and whose lines were drawn by English manufactures, West African slaves and West

[1] See p. 94.

Indian sugar. Judged by modern ideas of the rights of men the trade was of course infamous, but the Elizabethan world was not awake to such considerations and asked no moral questions. Nor did the colonial Spaniards resent the English intrusion: the native population in the islands and along the Main (the north coast of South America) was declining fast and they needed the labour. The expedition was a success and in 1564 Hawkins went again. He thought that the authorities who allowed no foreign trade in the empire without licence, might agree to accept English help in putting down pirates in the Caribbean and give him a licence to trade. Spain, however, insisted on her trading monopoly and repulsed foreigners, so that in the event the hopes of Hawkins appeared vain dreams. Nevertheless, on his first and second voyages he and his backers had done well and might reasonably expect to continue to do so.

These backers, though they never formed themselves into a formal company, did in fact act on a joint-stock principle. The Queen herself was among them, together with Privy Councillors, officials of the Navy Board and substantial London merchants. On the second voyage the Queen contributed one of her own ships, the *Jesus of Lubeck*, and allowed Hawkins to fly the royal standard. Cecil, later Lord Treasurer, and the Lord High Admiral both took shares in the venture and must have been satisfied at its profit of 60 per cent.

Attempts at Colonization

Peaceful trade with Spain was to end with Hawkins's second voyage but, before we consider the emerging conflict, we must notice the earliest beginnings of the English colonial empire. The appeal of colonization was first felt among the gentry class and, in particular, among a close-knit group of Devonshire gentlemen – Humphrey Gilbert, his half-brother Walter Ralegh, and their cousin Richard Grenville. The energetic John Dee, ever ready with maps to reinforce his ideas, Sir Philip Sidney, and the Catholic Sir George Peckham (anxious to provide a refuge for his co-religionists) supported the Devon group, which was also in favour with the Queen and Court.

The colonizing idea gained the support of such patrons because there seemed good reasons for it. First, there were the poor. It was thought by some that the poverty and unemployment of the times were caused by too fast an increase in the population. Colonies could skim off the surplus population and so confer a social benefit. The precious metals, which it was felt north America must contain, would also enrich England; and it would be useful to have bases on the west of the Atlantic from which to search for the North-West Passage. To make settlements in America should not be difficult, since it was possible to establish them in the same latitudes as those in England: virtually nothing was known of the influence of ocean currents and other such factors upon climate.

In 1578 the charter, long hoped for by Humphrey Gilbert, the propagandist for the North-West Passage, was granted. In North America he was allowed to discover and occupy such 'heathen lands not actually possessed of any Christian prince or people, as should seem good to him'. What appealed to him was Newfoundland, and in 1583 he took an expedition of 260 men and claimed possession of St John's. He then sailed south with the probable aim of landing settlers in Nova Scotia. But, when a ship was lost off Cape Breton, fortune deserted him. Gilbert still had two ships – the *Squirrel* (10 tons) and the *Golden Hind* (40 tons) – and decided to make for England, he himself sailing in the tiny 'frigate' the *Squirrel.* When a storm hit the ships off the Azores, the little boat went down and Gilbert with her. The captain of the *Hind* described it:

> Monday, September 9th, the frigate was near cast away . . . yet at that time recovered; and, giving forth signs of joy, the general, sitting abaft with a book in his hand, cried out unto us in the Hind, 'We are as near to Heaven by sea as by land'. . . . The same Monday night, about twelve, the frigate being ahead of us in the Golden Hind, suddenly her lights were out . . . In that moment the frigate was devoured and swallowed up of the sea.

The next year Walter Ralegh took over his half-brother's charter and sent out a reconnaissance expedition to act as the basis for a later colonizing venture. To the area round Roanoke

Island, which they found delightful, Ralegh gave the name Virginia: it was located a little farther south than the later American state. To this Virginia, therefore, in 1585 Ralegh's first colonizing venture set out, the ships being under the command of his cousin Richard Grenville who, nevertheless, did not himself take part in the settlement. But it was not yet seen that colonies needed farmers rather than soldiers and women as well as men, and the settlement was never organized for agriculture, relying instead on the Indians for food. In 1586 Drake looked in on the colony and, finding the settlers distressed, took them back to England. Ralegh then leased his rights to a London company who, in 1587, sent out the first true colonizing venture – with women and children among the settlers. They, too, were landed on Roanoke Island and, for a moment, stand revealed with their Governor John White and the first English child born on American soil – 'Virginia' Dare. Then the picture fades. The settlement was left to fend for itself during the Armada crisis, and by 1591 the settlers had disappeared. There was after all to be no Tudor empire.

Naval Conflict with Spain

The Tudor impulse towards wider trade, however, was not exhausted and was to lead to conflict with Spain. Such a conflict was perhaps inevitable, given the determination of Catholic Spain to exclude foreigners from her empire and the envy which its wealth naturally aroused. It is also claimed that Protestants took to trade because their attitude to life (and not only to religion) was independent and because many of them felt that to succeed in the world was a sign of divine favour. At all events earnest Protestantism was a mark of many of the English seafarers, and it was strengthened by the experiences some of them went through at the hands of the Inquisition searching out heresy in Spanish ports.

The birth of English distrust of Catholic Spain can be dated. It occurred in 1568 at San Juan de Ulloa on the Gulf of Mexico, where John Hawkins's third slave-trading expedition arrived after a voyage that had not gone smoothly. The Portuguese had been alerted to the purchase of slaves on the Guinea Coast, so that

Hawkins had had to fight to get them; the Spaniards on the Main no longer traded willingly and in some cases had to be forced to trade at all. A storm drove Hawkins and his six ships into San Juan. This port was a busy one – the centre of the Spanish silver traffic with Mexico. While Hawkins was there a Spanish fleet of thirteen ships appeared, which was only admitted to the harbour after a pledge of peace. The pledge was broken by the Spaniards and Hawkins was only able to get two of his ships away. Some of his men had to be left ashore, where they were slaughtered or sentenced to service in Spanish galleys. Between the English seamen and Spain there was in future only hostility.

Exploits of Drake

One of the ships that escaped from the Spaniards on that disastrous day at San Juan was commanded by a young kinsman of Hawkins named Francis Drake, who was determined to have his revenge. The son of a Protestant farmer in Devon, he had served his apprenticeship in a coastal collier. Religious zeal, the thirst for gain, a strong combative instinct, and a grand talent for seamanship combined to make Drake the greatest of privateers. He waged a private, unofficial war against the Spaniards, to whom he was known as 'El Draque', the devil or serpent; but they also said admiringly 'that if he was not a Lutheran there would not be the like of him in the world'. As for his own men, they gave him the respect due to a king, remaining bareheaded in his presence and living only for his approval.

In 1572 Drake set off for Nombre de Dios on the north side of the Panama isthmus, to launch a commando-style attack with 75 men on the very centre of Spanish colonial power. "I have brought you to the mouth of the Treasure of the World," he told them. But there was no treasure there then, so instead he had to waylay the silver train as it jogged across the isthmus from the far side, to which it was shipped direct from the mines in Peru. With the help of some French Huguenots this was done, and Drake sailed home the richer by £20,000.

Five years later, he received the Queen's commission to execute a more ambitious enterprise, directed against the Spanish empire of the Pacific. With three ships, of which the *Pelican* (renamed *Golden Hind*) of 120 tons was the largest, he made a sixteen-day passage of the Magellan Straits and was then driven far south by tremendous storms, which separated him permanently from the two smaller ships but also resulted in a major geographical discovery. For he established that the Tierra del Fuego, south of the Straits, was an archipelago and not the beginning of the southern continent – which was supposed (in Drake's day and much later) to provide a necessary counterpoise in the antarctic to the known extension of the northern continents into the arctic.

Passing north into the Pacific, Drake made several easy hauls of unprotected Spanish treasure; in one place he found the precious metal stacked in bars on a quayside which was deserted in the afternoon heat. Then he pursued and boarded near the equator a ship loaded with sufficient bullion and jewels to repay all the perils of his voyage. But the alarm was now raised to the south, so Drake continued northwards as far as 38° N., where he looked for the North-West Passage and landed to claim the coastline north of Mexico for his queen – a claim which was used against the Spaniards after the lapse of two centuries. Finally, he headed west for the Spice Islands and the Portuguese half of the world. Three tons of cloves and a trade treaty were obtained from a sultan in the Moluccas, but the cloves had to be jettisoned in a last adventure, when the *Hind* was nearly lost on a rock off Celebes. And so home round the Cape of Good Hope.

In the autumn of 1580 the little ship tied up in Plymouth harbour and yielded up her crew, bursting with seamen's tales, to the curiosity of the crowd. They were the new legendary men, latter-day Argonauts, who had circled the earth to bring back the golden fleece. Even a Spanish noble expressed his reluctant admiration of Drake's achievement:

> It is a thing that terrifies me, the voyage and the boldness of this low man, the son of vile parents . . . Yet it is a positive and accomplished fact that he undertook that navigation.

It is also a positive fact that the enterprise yielded a colossal profit to the Queen, to Drake, and to all the backers of the expedition. The total lay somewhere between £400,000 and a maximum of £1,500,000 which was talked of at the time.

After such an exploit, war with Spain must follow. Indeed, the second English circumnavigator of the world, Thomas Cavendish, crossed the path of the Armada as he returned home with further plunder. But this was eight years later. In the meantime Drake had struck at Vigo on the coast of Spain itself and then swept like a hurricane into the Caribbean against San Domingo and Cartagena. In 1587, when vast Armada preparations were under way in the harbours of Spain, it was the turn of Cadiz, where his devastating success taught his opponents the superiority of sailing-ships to their Mediterranean oared galleys, even in harbour waters. Since Philip of Spain had successfully asserted a claim to the throne of Portugal (1580), Portuguese harbours had also to be dealt with: for two months Drake preyed on supply ships heading for Lisbon, the chief Armada base, and finally he waylaid a Portuguese carrack in the Azores, whose cargo covered the entire cost of his expedition twice over.

The Armada – Spanish and English Ships

But the decisive contest came at last. Out from the Tagus the Armada sailed, spreading its canvas before a southerly wind that confined the English ships to the Channel. Just over one-half of the Spanish vessels which entered English waters were 'great ships' (*naves*) and 40 of these 64 were provided from their mercantile marine, then second only to the Dutch. They had nearly 20,000 soldiers on board, but their main object was to break through the Channel and gain control of the narrow seas between England and the coast of the Low Countries about Dunkirk, where the Duke of Parma awaited them with three times as many soldiers and a host of invasion barges. No general action was to be fought by the fleet until the whole convoy was mustered for the final crossing. This it was the concern of the English fleet to prevent at all costs. They had 172 gun-carrying vessels as against the Spanish total of 124 large and small, mostly merchantmen collected for the occasion but including a hard core of 34 vessels belonging to the Queen's Navy.

What were these ships like? The normal type of warship was now the galleon, the English form of which was developed chiefly by John Hawkins. As Treasurer of the Navy from 1578 to 1587, his energy and nautical skill resulted in the building of a number of excellently designed vessels, of which the 450-ton *Revenge* was one of the first and most typical. With a length of 92 ft, a beam of 32 ft, and an armament of nearly 50 guns, she was worked and fought by a crew of only 250 – a reduction of manpower in relation to tonnage which made it possible for Hawkins to improve the pay and to a modest extent the victualling of the Queen's ships. The largest vessels of this period, which were 600-tonners, had four masts and eight sails: square lower and top sails on the fore and main masts, triangular lateen lower and top sails on the two mizzen masts. Top-gallant sails were sometimes introduced on the fore and main masts, Hawkins having made their use less hazardous by constructing top-masts which could be struck in foul weather.

With a proportion of length to beam of three to one, the newer type of ship could sail closer to the wind; it could also mount more guns. Henry VIII had begun the practice of equipping his ships with heavy cannon and piercing their sides with gun-ports in order to carry them near to the water-level, where their recoil would shake the vessel least. But in early Tudor ships the existence of high fore- and after-castles separated by a deep waist severely restricted the gun-space on the upper decks. These were therefore lowered by Hawkins, who decked over the waist so as to provide something like a flush top-deck, except indeed for the raised quarter-deck at the stern. As for the guns, the English speciality was the culverin and demi-culverin, firing shots of seventeen and nine pounds respectively. They were of brass construction, moulded in one piece and of course muzzle-loaded, with an accurate range of about a thousand yards. In the Armada campaign that range was all-important, for the Spanish guns, though much fewer, could deliver an overwhelming weight of shot over a shorter distance.[1]

The average size of the merchant ships which served with the

[1] The English fleet mounted 1,972 guns (over 4-pounders), the Spanish 1,124, but the respective weight of shot was 14,677 lb. and 19,369 lb. (M. Lewis, *The Spanish Armada*, p. 78).

Royal Navy against the Armada was only 200 tons, but the bigger vessels mounted both whole- and demi-culverins, which they always needed for their long voyages into dangerous waters. Many of them were carracks, whose armament was restricted by the combination of high fore- and after-castles with a deep hold for cargo. Lastly, among the many types of smaller vessel which played a part we may distinguish the pinnaces, equipped with oars and a single sail: each large ship had its own pinnace, towed or even carried on deck, which it employed for easy communication with other ships and the shore.

Since the Spaniards had orders to postpone battle and the English dared not risk the heavier weight of enemy gunfire at short range, there was no dramatic general action during the nine days when the Armada, in well-kept crescent formation, was sailing at only three knots up the Channel. Limited engagements took place off Portland Bill and the Isle of Wight, but the rest of the fighting was scrappy and spasmodic. Nevertheless, both sides became gradually exhausted, and the Spaniards gladly sought a respite by anchoring in Calais Roads: they needed to provision their ships and make sure that Parma was ready for the combined operation from the Netherlands.

The Spanish Defeat and Its Effects

The English fleet under Lord Howard of Effingham, with Drake as second-in-command, had now reached its maximum size through the arrival on the scene of a division which had been watching Parma. That night they sent eight fireships down the wind and tide against the Spaniards, who, suspecting that they were charged with explosives, cut their cables in a panic, and headed for the open sea. Next day, with order already lost, they were forced into a decisive battle off Gravelines, during which they had to fire at long range and soon ran out of heavy shot. The English could then for the first time bring their guns to bear effectively at point-blank range, with the result that at least three of the most powerful Spanish vessels were lost to the enemy and many more half-wrecked. Their whole fleet would have been driven on shore, had not the wind changed from north-west to south-west, so that the scattered ships could stand out to sea. Their commander, Medina Sidonia, decided to break off action by fleeing north. Drake had prophesied before the battle, "The duke of Sidonia shall wish himself at St Mary Port among his orange trees," but his way home lay round the rock-bound coast of northern Britain and the Atlantic shore of Ireland. Inadequately supplied with ammunition, Howard broke off the chase at the Firth of Forth; but high winds and reduced morale did the rest.

Flavit Deus et dissipati sunt ('God blew and they were scattered') was the pious inscription on the commemorative Armada medal. The Spaniards lost from all causes 33 out of 64 *naves* and a slightly smaller proportion of their lighter vessels. Allowing for the brutal executions of ship-wrecked Spaniards which were ordered by the English authorities in Ireland, their loss of life may be estimated at two-thirds of the entire Armada force. The English lost not more than 100 lives in action, but up to one hundred times as many from typhus, food-poisoning and other diseases on board ship.[1]

This sanguinary victory, renowned throughout Europe, firmly established an English tradition of maritime skill and prowess, which gives an aura of magic to the whole Elizabethan age. Before that time the English had not regarded themselves as a seafaring nation before all others. Now they did, and many generations looked back upon the reign of Elizabeth I and its great mariners. Such men as Drake, Hawkins, Frobisher and Grenville had humbled Spain and kept the Catholic world at bay. The voyages of discovery, colonization and trade were all felt to be bound up with the national struggle against Spain and the Pope, in which even wavering English Catholics felt a reluctant pride. Moreover, these deeds found a chronicler of genius in Richard Hakluyt, author of *The Principal Navigations, Voyages and Discoveries of the English Nation*. First published as a single, close-packed quarto in 1589, by 1600 it had swollen to three volumes, with prefaces proclaiming that England's future lay on the sea, the pathway to commerce and colonization. Hakluyt served her sea tradition in the same way as Foxe her Protestantism.

[1] M. Lewis, *The Spanish Armada*, pp. 50, 208–9, and 181.

The Post-Armada Years

The power of Spain, however, though humbled was by no means crushed. A second Armada set sail eight years after the first, though the combined effects of a heavy gale and poor morale prevented it from reaching England or Ireland. Meanwhile Elizabeth continued the war mainly by land, spending at least four times as much on expeditions to keep the Protestant cause alive in the Netherlands and France as she did on the efforts of her seamen. Unsuccessful projects for intercepting Spanish treasure included that in which Grenville and the *Revenge* were lost after fighting fifteen men-of-war for fifteen hours.

> What became of his body [wrote Ralegh], whether it were buried in the sea or on the land we know not: the comfort that remaineth to his friends is, that he hath ended his life honourably in respect of the reputation won to his nation and country, and of the same to his posterity, and that being dead he hath not outlived his own honour.

A much bigger failure followed in 1595–6, when Drake and Hawkins were unwisely given joint command of an expedition to the Caribbean, where both of them died with their mission unaccomplished.

Though a good deal of booty was won by the individual efforts of privateers, the future lay with pioneering efforts to tap the trade of the east, where the Portuguese possessions had now passed under Spanish sovereignty. On two such voyages every ship was lost, though a handful of survivors made their way back to tell the tale; on the third, in which John Davis was blown back through the Magellan Strait, the result was hardly more encouraging.

> To be short, all our men died except sixteen, of whom there were but five able to move. The captain was in good health, the master but indifferent, Captain Cotton and myself swollen and short-winded . . . and one boy in health: upon us five only the labour of the ship did stand. The captain and master, as

> occasion served, would take in and heave out the topsails . . . and all of us at the capstan.

Undeterred, Davis entered the Dutch service in order to study the route round the Cape of Good Hope, returning to act as chief pilot to the first expedition of the newly formed East India Company. The four ships sent out in 1601 did not reach home again until after the Queen's death, but their success was the final Elizabethan triumph, for it inaugurated the era of England's oceanic trading fleets.

5

THE RURAL SCENE

APART from London and perhaps half a dozen of the leading provincial towns, the life of Tudor England was all directly linked with the countryside, on which the people of market and even county towns were almost as dependent as the villagers themselves. The new maritime interests described in the last chapter therefore stirred the nation as a whole less profoundly (so far as we can now judge) than a change which was taking place in men's attitude to the land. To a much greater extent than ever before it was looked upon as a business proposition, from which whoever held rights over the land was entitled to extract the maximum of profit for himself without regard to the interests of dependants or neighbours. Its vigorous and often ruthless exploitation brought wealth to some people, deep poverty to others, and a general turmoil and unsettlement which every Tudor government in turn attempted to remedy.

The Crisis on the Land

The circumstances which unsettled rural life in this way lay largely outside the possibility of government control. The rise in population, which enormously increased the demand for land by which to live, was happening all over Europe, as was noticed in Chapter 1. So was the rise in prices, which enabled the possessor of land to make bigger profits on corn, meat, and dairy produce. And it was the ready market for English cloth on the Continent[1] which made the first half of the sixteenth century a period when sheep farming paid particularly well. In two respects, however, government action in pursuit of other objects made the crisis on the land more acute.

[1] See p. 94.

The dissolution of the monasteries by Henry VIII has already been described as one of the first steps towards the English Reformation. But it also had big social effects: not only did the monks cease to be the source of some almsgiving and other direct help to the poor, but – what was very much more important in the long run – the huge and on the whole conservatively administered estates of the monasteries passed into new hands. The process was continued through the sale of the chantry lands after 1547 and of some of the lands belonging to bishoprics at the beginning of the reign of Elizabeth, who was also forced to sell much Crown land to pay for the wars she could not avoid. Thus by the end of the century a large proportion of the soil of England had come under the control of new owners – courtiers, merchants, sea adventurers, and especially the younger sons of landed families, who had no share in the original family estate. On the whole, they were the sort of people who would be most determined to make the land pay, even if its original inhabitants suffered in the process.

Debasement of the Coinage

The English government also bore some responsibility for the rise in prices. At the beginning of Henry VIII's reign, the speed at which the young king spent his father's accumulated treasure on a magnificent court and preparations for an unnecessary war did something to produce inflation; and in 1526 Wolsey found it expedient to reduce the weight of the silver coinage so as to increase the amount of money in circulation, though his reduction left English silver coins on a par with those of the Continent. At the end of the reign, by which time the rise in European prices had made war much more expensive, so that neither taxation nor the plunder of the monasteries could meet Henry's military needs, he went in for debasement on an altogether larger scale. What Henry began, the duke of Somerset continued, with the result that in seven years (1544–51) the quantity of precious metal in the silver penny fell to one-sixth of what it had been in the time of Henry VII. The Crown made a profit of about £500,000 by minting six times as many coins from the same amount of bullion.

This drastic operation had a double effect on prices. They rose because there was a greatly increased quantity of coin in circulation; they also rose because every trader added to his charges, to cover himself against the chance of being paid in the most debased of the various qualities of more-or-less silver coin (the bad coin circulated most rapidly because everybody tried to get rid of it). A proper recoinage was not achieved until 1561, when the bad money was called in for melting down and a new silver currency issued very quickly and profitably with the help of a loan raised by Elizabeth's financial expert, Sir Thomas Gresham, in Antwerp. Thus England for a time suffered a particularly rapid inflation, which made real estate more precious than ever. Hence in part the ruthlessness with which the landowners on Edward VI's Council suppressed the popular rising in 1549: it was a direct threat to their class interests at a time of economic crisis.

To sum up, the two movements of the rise of population and of prices gave a greatly enhanced value to land. More people had to be fed and therefore more corn grown and more animals pastured, at a time, too, when the demands of England's staple industry made the wool on the sheep's back much more valuable than the mutton. Estates therefore changed hands very rapidly, as we have seen. At the same time even small scraps of land acquired a new importance, if they could be brought into more intensive use by the much discussed process of enclosure.

Enclosure

In Wales and Scotland, on the moors of northern England, and to a smaller extent in almost every English county it was still possible to make enclosures or 'intakes' of unused land, and there is no doubt that this kind of enclosing went on all the time, but especially when high prices gave an extra incentive to the hard work of clearance. As nobody suffered by it, it roused little discussion. But in the central and east midlands, and in some smaller areas elsewhere, open-field agriculture was practised: the strips in the big arable fields had all to be cultivated according to the same pattern, and the surrounding common or 'waste' was all required for the existing village livestock. Here enclosures created trouble out of all proportion to their geographical extent, because they disturbed an established routine.

Such enclosures were made in several different ways. The lord of the manor often sought to regain control of demesne land, especially if it had been let on short lease. Such parts of it as lay directly round the manor house could then be converted into a single compact farm. The lord's demesne strips lying scattered in the open fields were more difficult to consolidate: long negotiations would be needed in order to acquire possession of intervening strips either by exchange or purchase. The lord might also wish to turn some or all of what had once been villein land into large enclosed areas, which could be let at high rents to big farmers or even farmed under his own direction. This would involve still more opposition from small copyholders[1] and others clinging desperately to the strips in their possession.

While the lord through his bailiff was the principal encloser of the arable, it must be noticed that freeholders and other substantial yeomen farmers were also out to get full control of their lands in the open fields by consolidation and enclosure. Some yeomen were better off than some lords of manors, and could afford to buy up any land which fell vacant for addition to their own farms. Moreover, both lords and substantial farmers were interested in arranging for common pasture land to be enclosed. This was especially advantageous for the grazing of large flocks and herds, but might ruin the small farmer who, if deprived of the common, could no longer keep the sheep which provided essential manure for his arable strips.

It is clear that a good deal of enclosure was going on at this time, though its extent can easily be exaggerated. Even in the midland region on which it centred, most of the land was still unhedged in the early eighteenth century: Leicestershire, for example, during the Tudor period had between 30 and 40 per cent of its arable land enclosed, which represented 3–4 per cent of its total area. What are less clear are the specific reasons for enclosing, other than the general rise in prices.

[1] See p. 85.

Sheep-Farming

The contemporary impression was that most of it was for sheep-runs, made with a view to cashing in on the high price of wool. This was certainly the aspect of the enclosures on which critics concentrated their attention, for it was true that sheep needed far less labour than corn, so that laying down land for sheep-grazing might mean the turning away of men or, in extreme cases, the depopulation of a whole village. Thus More, in a famous and whimsical passage in the first book of *Utopia*, remarks as a phenomenon of the England of his day that

> sheep . . . these placid creatures, which used to require so little food, have now apparently developed a raging appetite, and turned into man-eaters.

At mid-century a Protestant preacher, Thomas Becon, likewise complains that

> whole towns are become desolate, and like unto a wilderness, no man dwelling there, except it be the shepherd and his dog.

And at about the same date an anonymous writer 'showed the decay of England' by an argument which maintained that, every time a plough was put out of use by the increase of sheep, 6 persons lost their employment and 7½ persons their potential supply of bread. "And now they have nothing," he concludes, "but go about in England from door to door, and ask their alms for God's sake."

It is probably right to conclude that in the first half of the sixteenth century most enclosures were for sheep (or cattle) and that some part of the very numerous deserted medieval villages which have been rediscovered in recent years owed their enforced abandonment to the fact that they lay inside an area – possibly of very poor soil – which was now turned over to pasture. But sheep-farming did not necessarily involve enclosure, nor enclosure sheep-farming.

As to the former proposition, some landlords made their

fortunes by pasturing excessive flocks on common lands to the disadvantage of smaller men whose rights they infringed there. It is noteworthy that, when Ket assembled his 16,000 followers outside Norwich in 1549 to protest against the encroachments of the gentry upon the rights of the poor, he was much less explicit about enclosures than in his demand 'That no lord of no manor shall common upon the commons.'

Other Uses of Enclosures

Enclosure did not necessarily involve sheep-farming, although the price rise stimulated every land-holder to try to get the most from his land: John Norden, who practised as a surveyor at the end of the century, thought that enclosure usually added one-half to its value. The demand for wool had then eased off to some extent, but popular farming handbooks suggested many possibilities – especially for farmers who were within reach of the huge and varied food market offered by the capital. The first English-language handbook was Master Fitzherbert's *Book of Husbandry*, which ran through eight editions between 1523 and the death of Elizabeth. A famous successor was composed by the verse-writer Thomas Tusser, whose original *Hundred Good Points of Husbandry* grew rapidly into five hundred. He was an advocate of enclosure for all purposes:

More plenty of mutton and beef,
Corn, butter, and cheese of the best,
Where find ye (go search any coast)
Than there where enclosure is most?

There were many other new books on tree-planting, bee-keeping, and livestock and arable farming in all their branches, so that any enterprising landholder might be encouraged to enclose simply to have freedom to experiment. Enclosed ground was needed, too, for a number of special crops: flax, for linseed oil as well as linen-weaving; woad, madder, and saffron for dyeing; and the hops, which had been introduced from Flanders early in the century to improve the quality of the Englishman's beer.

Gainers and Losers

Many men therefore had good cause to welcome the rising prices, which were advantageous to everyone who controlled what other people wanted – and land was wanted above all. Thus landowners were obviously gainers, provided they were free to put up their rents. This was the case wherever farmland was let for a short, fixed period or simply at the will of the lord. On the former demesne lands in particular, lords had made a point of keeping the leases short, so as to be able to rack-rent the tenant by a series of increases. Even where the letting could not be terminated by the lord, it was often possible to exact a big payment each time an heir took over. In other ways, too, a grasping landlord with the help of a cunning bailiff or lawyer could often extract payments to which he was not legally entitled from tenants who were too ignorant or too frightened to resist. There was ample reason for the prayer used in Edward VI's time: "O Lord, we pray thee that the landlords may not rack or stretch out the rents."

But the big landowners, on whom public attention was chiefly focused, were not the only gainers. Small freeholders and the holders of long leases were also getting more money from their crops without having to increase their basic expenses. A large proportion of the former villein families, too, now held land 'by copy of the court roll of the manor', and these copyholds might be secure for one life, three lives, or for as long as the heir paid the rent and other dues originally prescribed. So the rural community comprised in one way or another a growing class of yeomen, who were able to keep their expenses down and their profits up and could often improve their position still further by taking over additional pieces of land from a less efficient or less lucky neighbour.

This was the class that, before the end of Elizabeth's reign, was either building or, more often, rebuilding or adding to its farmhouses all over England – whether the stone houses of the Cotswolds or the black-and-white timbered buildings of the west midlands. Stone or brick chimneys and fireplaces, glazed windows, new plastered ceilings, and panelled walls were all evidence of growing wealth. William Harrison conjures up their comfortable situation in his *Description of England* (1577):

> Yet will the farmer think his gains very small towards the end of his term if he have not six or seven years' rent lying by him . . . besides a fair garnish of pewter in his cupboard, with so much more in odd vessels going about the house, three or four feather beds, so many coverlets and carpets of tapestry, a silver salt, a bowl for wine (if not a whole nest), and a dozen of spoons to furnish up the suit.

At the same time, there were many people for whom this world of rising prices involved difficulties and even disaster. A good many lords of manors derived their rentals chiefly from agreements which they were powerless to alter. One such is made to declare despondently, in an anonymous dialogue composed about 1549:

> In all my life time I look not that the third part of my land shall come to my disposition, that I may enhance the rent of the same.

Although he might have some capital to fall back on, his income in terms of purchasing-power would be falling all the while. Still worse was the plight of short-term leaseholders and mere husbandmen who held their farms on a year-to-year basis, for they would have no accumulated reserves to help them pay an exorbitant rent. They might try to eke out a living by working for other farmers – in midland villages about one man in five was at least partly dependent on wages – but that was a hopeless prospect in the event of a substantial turnover from ploughland to pasture.

Gentry and Peasantry in Wales

To what extent the ranks of the dispossessed in general were swollen from copyholders and other tenants who were cheated of their rights is one of the many uncertainties in the complicated story of the agrarian changes. But in Wales it seems clear that the introduction of English land law at this period, enabling land to be bought and sold freely, often with the help of mortgages, created a legal chaos of which the rising Welsh gentry took full advantage.

Along the coastal strip of South Wales, with a lime soil and easy access to the sea, hillside pasture was enclosed to grow corn, which was sold as far away as London. In the north, the scattered farms of former tribal territory were consolidated into big estates, which the new practice of primogeniture preserved intact for many generations. Here the profit lay in the grazing of black cattle for the English market and in growing wool, both for direct sale to England and to supply the native cloth industry centred on Oswestry and Shrewsbury. In either case the gentry class built up its fortunes on land ownership, while the bulk of the Welsh population became merged in a single landless peasantry.

Tudor Governments and the Social Problem

'Depopulating enclosure' was exposed, condemned, and combated by a long series of proclamations, royal commissions, interventions by the Council, and statute laws. But peers, MPs, and even Councillors either would not, or dared not, take effective steps to restrict the liberties of the dominant landowning class. One of the very few exceptions was the duke of Somerset during his brief period of power in Edward's reign; he proposed to take action "in spite of the devil, private profit, self-love, money and suchlike the devil's instruments". But all that even he achieved was a modest tax on sheep. The enclosure movement died down to some extent in Elizabeth's reign, more on account of lower wool prices than through effective legislation. But four years after her death her successor proclaimed, "The king is not unmindful of the abuse of enclosures and of the loss he suffers by depopulation."

But the persistence of unsettled conditions on the land accentuated a wider problem of poverty, with which the government was driven to grapple. Poverty was of course an old problem: but rising population, soaring prices, and (to a very minor extent) the loss of monastic charity combined with the fact that people were now more readily on the move to create a menacing situation, not only in villages up and down the country but in more concentrated form in London and the principal towns. For wage-earners who had no other source of income – a class which must have included a high proportion of all those who left the land at this time, hoping to better themselves in the towns – the evidence all goes to show that it was more difficult to live than at almost any other period in our history.

Unlicensed beggars and vagabonds were a direct threat to society, against which government, parliament, and the local justices of the peace were all ready to co-operate. There were believed to be about 10,000 of them at large in early Elizabethan times,

Plate 6. *The 'Ark Royal'*. An anonymous woodcut of c. 1588. Built in 1587 by Sir Walter as the *Ark Ralegh*, the ship was sold to the Queen and so became Howard of Effingham's flagship against the Armada. She was of 800 tons and carried 55 guns – an unusually large ship for the time. She would have been brightly painted over the whole upper hull, either in the Tudor colours of white and green or in the reds, yellows and purples popular at the time. (Cf. text p. 74.)

Plate 7. *The Armada in the Channel.* From *Expeditionis Hispanorum in Angliam vera Descriptio* (1588). The book contains a series of beautifully hand-coloured plans, based on Howard's own narrative, showing the progress of the Armada and the movements of the English ships along the whole of the course from off Cornwall to the North Sea. This print shows the position on July 30th 1588, when, against a fresh south-west wind, Howard led out his ships from the shelter of Plymouth Sound along the line shown stretching to the bottom of the picture. A further squadron of English ships is also portrayed tacking its way westward along the coast in order to gain the advantage of the wind to the rear of the Spanish crescent. The picture (covering time as well as space) shows the English fleet in final possession of the weather gauge, with all their ships gathering to the rear of the Spanish fleet. (Cf. text p. 75.)

Plate 8. *The Old Scotch Plough.* A very rare surviving specimen, last used in the 1880s and now in the Stranraer County Museum. Its overall length is 10¼ feet and it is in its original state, except that a third rung should join the two handles (or 'stilts'), that the right-hand stilt itself is reconstructed, and that the coulter (which once descended through the hole in the iron plate on the beam) is missing. The share now on the plough was used for hard and stony soil, but this type of plough was regularly provided with another which could be fitted for easier conditions. Except in some parts of the Highlands and Islands, these ploughs were very widely employed in Scotland down to the close of the eighteenth century and even later. (Cf. text p. 92.)

Plate 9. *The Manor of Feckenham, Worcestershire.* From a map drawn in 1591 by John Blagrave and copied by John Doherty in 1746.

Feckenham was in a royal forest area, but from the 14th century some enclosures had been allowed. In 1591 Elizabeth granted the manor to Sir Francis Knollys who had this map-survey drawn up, on which the holdings of the tenants are shown by letters of the alphabet and other signs. 'A+', for instance, denotes the lord's land and 'H' lands belonging to the parish as a whole. An asterisk (*) indicates the common fields and meadows, and it can be seen how these open fields were being encroached upon. For instance, in Chester Field John Bunde, William Clarke and Ralf Bowes (AA, BB and DD respectively) were private landholders and, in the common pasture of Perry Hill Field, Edward Robinson (NN) possessed a barn and two pieces of land. The court house and mill, naturally, belonged to the lord.

For a full account of this manorial map, see the essay 'The Character of England in maps' in E. Lynam's *The Mapmaker's Art* (1953). (Cf. text pp. 81–2.)

NORTH
PARTE OF CORNEWALLE
PARTE OF DEVONSHIRE
PLIMMOVTHE
NORTH
WEST
EAST
SOVTH
SOVTH

Plate 6 and 7

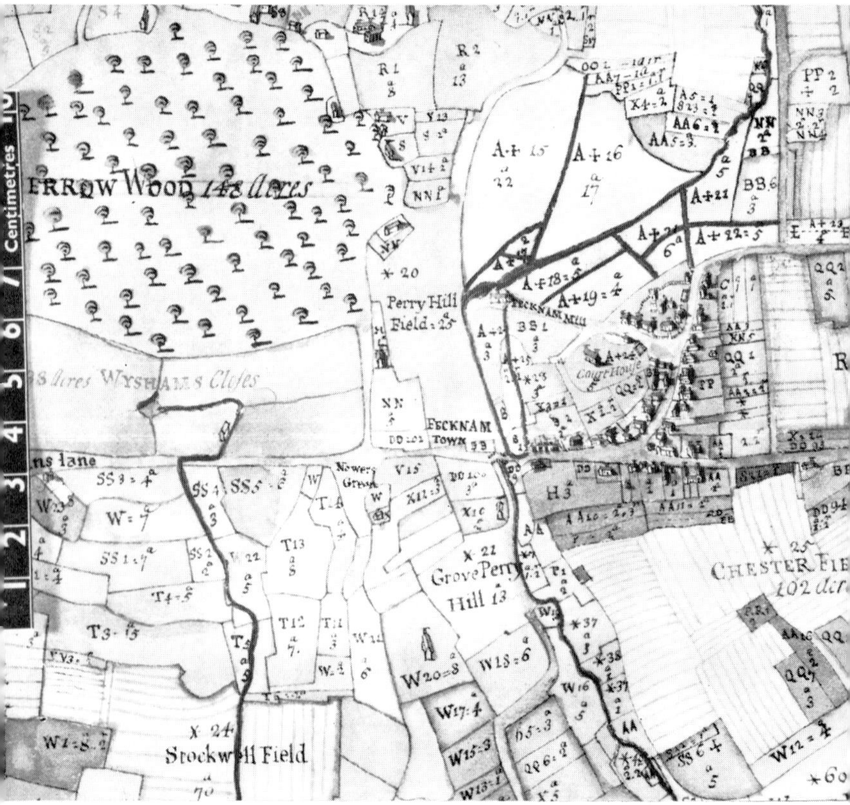
Centimetres
ERROW WOOD 148 Acres
88 Acres WYSHAMS Closes
Perry Hill Field 25
FECKNAM TOWN
Court House
Nowers Grove
Grove Perry Hill 13
CHESTER FIE
102 Acr
Stockwell Field
ns lane

Plate 8 and 9

and they often travelled in groups strong enough to overawe the people of the villages and market towns through which they passed. Thomas Harman specifies 23 different forms of roguery practised by them, in his lively but scarcely objective account of "the abominable and detestable behaviour of all these rowsy ragged rabblement of rakehells". Apart from the crimes they committed, their life of idleness was itself an offence against God in the Protestant view, which regarded hard work as every man's duty.

Although the Tudor governments soon came to admit that the aged, the crippled, the chronically sick, and widows and orphans might have other reasons for begging besides an innate distaste for work, they were slow to accept the fact of unavoidable unemployment as a sufficient cause: the able-bodied beggar deserved only punishment. By an Act of 1495 he was to be put into the stocks; in 1531 he was sentenced to be 'tied to the end of a cart naked and be beaten with whips till his body be bloody', after which he must be sent back to his place of birth or regular residence. For a time in Edward VI's reign, the persistent vagrant was liable to be enslaved or even hanged. However, London, in response to an eloquent plea from its first Protestant bishop, Nicholas Ridley, was allowed to add a fifth institution to the four hospitals already endowed out of confiscated Church lands, namely, St Bartholomew's and St Thomas's for the sick, Bedlam for the insane, and Christ's Hospital for destitute children. This was the old royal house of Bridewell near Blackfriars, which became, not just the lodging for vagrants that the bishop desired, but a formidable 'House of Correction'. In the time of Elizabeth such Houses were built in many places at local expense, so that, after a 'sturdy beggar' had been whipped, he could be sent to the house of correction nearest his birthplace and compelled to work.

It is more agreeable to notice the proliferation of another, older institution for the poor, in the clusters of Elizabethan almshouses still to be seen in many villages and old towns. In Yorkshire, for instance, they provided a refuge for two and a half times as many aged poor at the end of the Tudor period as at its beginning. Moreover, about 1550 the whole volume of charitable bequests, of which the bulk was directed either to poor relief or education, began to grow, until after seventy years the continuous rise in prices did not prevent it from reaching in real values as high a level as was ever attained in pre-Reformation days.

Elizabethan Social Legislation

But in the time of Elizabeth individual generosity was joined by State action, based in part on municipal experiments such as had been made in London. Thought out in the calm of the Privy Council, the Poor Law Act of 1598 (slightly modified in 1601) relied on the justices of the peace as the proper instrument to alleviate distress, which the bad harvest of that decade had abundantly shown to be a national problem. In each parish they were to appoint annually from two to four householders, who were to act together with the churchwardens as Overseers of the Poor. They were to levy a compulsory poor rate within the parish, so that a stock of raw materials – 'flax, hemp, wool, thread, iron, and other necessary stuff' – could be provided to employ whoever was fit to work. Pauper children were to be apprenticed till the age of 24 (girls till 21 or previous marriage) and the old and sick relieved out of the rate, if necessary within 'fit and convenient places of habitation', which the overseers were entitled (but failed) to erect. A rich parish with few poor was to be required to help other parishes in the same county (this also was asking too much of human nature), and work-shy persons who refused to carry out the tasks appointed were to be sent as vagabonds to the house of correction.

Responsibility for its poor was thus assigned to each parish. The system had many drawbacks, as will be seen later, but it kept the pauper alive on however meagre a basis and continued to function for nearly two and a half centuries as one of the mainstays of English society. It remained for a long time without parallel on the Continent, where the local community was not usually placed under any compelling legal obligation to save the poor from starving outright.

Much poverty was directly caused by the unemployment prevalent in a period of change in agriculture and intermittent depressions in the woollen industry. To relieve poverty was only one part of the task before the government: it had also to try to find jobs for people. One method was to encourage the introduction of new industries by foreigners, of which some examples will be given in the next chapter. But the most striking venture was what we might call Cecil's 'National Plan', the Statute of Artificers of 1563 – a document of 8,000 words on nine parchments stitched together to make a 14½-foot roll.

In the main this was a perhaps wrong-headed and certainly ineffectual attempt to bring back the stability of the past. Special advantages were given to employers of labour in agriculture. Anyone not otherwise lawfully employed could be compelled to enter their service at any time, while in the harvest season

> the justices of the peace may cause all such artificers and persons as be meet to labour . . . to serve by the day for the mowing, reaping, shearing, getting or inning of corn, grain and hay.

Conversely, financial barriers of various heights were set up to restrict entry to the more attractive industrial and professional occupations. Above all, there was to be good order everywhere: industry was to be entered through a compulsory seven-year apprenticeship; all employment was to be for a year at a time; and everyone's wages were to be fixed by the justices of the peace.

The effects of the apprenticeship clauses on the towns will be considered later. In country districts the law may have done a little to check the turn-over to keeping sheep as a way of saving labour, but this had already passed its peak. But the provisions for the fixing of wage-rates, though marred by the fact that the only penalties were those prescribed for exceeding the rate, represent an effort to grapple with a thorny set of problems. The justices were not to fix them arbitrarily but as a regular annual duty to be discharged at the Easter quarter sessions of the county,

> calling unto them such discreet and grave persons as they shall think meet, and conferring together respecting the plenty or scarcity of the time and other circumstances necessary to be considered.

Since the Council, to which the justices were mainly responsible for their actions, was often in sympathy with ill-used workers, it is reasonable to suppose that the assessments, which seem to have been made fairly regularly for about a century, were not generally unfair. Thus the Statute of Artificers may take its place alongside the other social measures of Elizabeth's government as a serious effort to grapple with the needs of a rapidly changing situation.

Scottish Rural Life

The picture in Scotland is less one of change than of the continuation of old methods. Because of the very different political situation Scottish landowners were not, like the Welsh, forced to adopt new practices, and the dominance of mutually suspicious clans in the Highlands, together with the harsh climate and soil, meant that old ways persisted.

As far as agriculture was concerned, the old in- and out-field system was still followed. The in-field near the village settlement was kept in permanent cultivation under oats and barley and was constantly manured. From time to time pieces of the out-field were ploughed up and sown with the same crops as the in-field until the soil was exhausted. Then it was rested for about five years, while another part of the out-field was farmed. Both fields were divided into strips or 'rigs' and worked communally. The plough was heavy and wheelless, making no more than a triangular cut in the soil as it was hauled along by sometimes as many as twelve oxen. The Highlanders used ponies for ploughing, but obtained most of their grain from outside and sold some fish and timber in return, floating the logs downstream to markets such as Perth. One of the troubles was the short three-year leases (or 'tacks') on which land was held, for these discouraged any improvement by the tenant, as John Major remarked in 1521 in his *History of Greater Britain:*

> If the landlords would let their lands in perpetuity, they might have double and treble the profit that now comes to them – and for this reason: the country folk would then cultivate their land better beyond all comparison, would grow richer and build fair dwellings.

On the Crown lands, however, the 'feu-ferme' tenure (perpetual inheritance in return for a fixed annual money rent) provided a more encouraging situation from the tenants' point of view.

Pasture was important for meat and dairy produce and the export of skins and hides, though arable farming, driven from the valleys by badly drained land, competed for use of the hill-sides. Cattle were often sent from the Highlands and islands to be marketed in the Lowlands. In the south of the country, some English cattle even shared the hill pastures in the summer, a matter for complaint to the Scottish Privy Council: "The English sheep and horse and others are suffered to go and pasture within the bounds of Scotland."

So static a society had no social problems comparable with those of England, where it was the very pressure of change that produced strains within the social fabric. The use of land of some sort was easy to obtain and, even if farming were for little more than personal subsistence, it yielded enough food to cushion the farmers against the blows of the increase of price or lessening of demand. This was one reason for the wide divergence of Scottish from English practice regarding the relief of the poor.

Between 1574 and 1597 the Scots parliament passed a series of four laws, providing for a compulsory poor relief assessment and its administration by the 'kirk sessions' of minister and elders in every parish. But the able-bodied poor were not intended to receive any relief, and what was intended for the rest was not in fact given, for by 1700 the compulsory assessment was being levied in only three Scottish parishes. But a good deal of private charity went into the building of almshouses, and for the rest the poor depended mainly upon voluntary collections at the church door.

6

INDUSTRIAL GROWTH

We have already seen that the first national trade of England was the wool trade. In Tudor times wool was still the chief foundation of English wealth, though most of it was now turned into cloth on English looms instead of being exported as raw material to the Continent. The Staplers' Company which sold wool abroad was already declining fast when it suffered a further blow through the cession of Calais, where the staple trade had long been centred, after its capture by the French in 1558. Meanwhile, in Henry VII's reign the cloth trade with the Netherlands had been put on a firm basis by the commercial treaty known as the *Magnus Intercursus*, the cloth being normally sent to Antwerp 'white' – to be finished and dyed by the more advanced techniques known to the Netherlanders. Although their country passed under the sovereignty of Spain, the first half of the sixteenth century marked the Golden Age of Antwerp, and the Merchant Adventurers' Company, based on London, derived big profits from its monopoly rights in the sale of English cloth there.

The Woollen Industry

By 1550 the sale of London shortcloths had reached the record total of 132,000, which was about three times the figure for 1500. But the English merchants had been helped by the fact that English prices were rising more slowly than those of the Continent, thus enabling them to buy cheap and sell dear. This advantage was lost when English price levels rose as the result of the efforts made by Northumberland in 1551, and more effectively by Cecil and Gresham on Elizabeth's behalf in 1561, to rescue the English coinage from the debasement which had stimulated exports.

Political and religious difficulties interrupted the Antwerp trade even before the city fell a prey to the 'Spanish Fury' in 1576 (when 8,000 citizens were massacred), and the Merchant Adventurers eventually found a Protestant port of entry to Europe for their goods at Middelburg on the island of Walcheren. In sum, although the decade from 1575 to 1585 was a boom period, the reign of Elizabeth began and ended with a serious slump in the woollen industry, as the merchants pushed their losses back along the line to the homes of the weavers and the wool-growers.

We too may go back along the line to remind ourselves of the basically unchanged methods of production. John Hooker of Exeter, uncle of the famous divine, describes the making of the local cloth called 'Devon dozens':

> Wheresoever any man doth travel, ye shall find at the hall door . . . the wife, their children, and their servants at the turn spinning or at their cards carding, by which commodities the common people do live . . . The weaver buyeth the yarn of the spinster, the clothier sendeth his cloths to the tucker or fuller, and then the merchant or clothier doth dye them in colours, or send them to London or elsewhere to his best advantage.

Alongside these traditional activities, however, there had emerged some mechanical improvements in the textile industries as a whole, together with the manufacture of several new types of cloth. The gigmill for raising the nap on the cloth preparatory to shearing dates back to the later Middle Ages, but it became more prominent in Tudor times and continued to spread, although its use was forbidden by law in 1551, when the start of the long depression made it desirable to maximize employment. The first English textile invention of any note was the stocking-frame in 1589, but the hostility of the hand-knitters delayed any widespread use until well into the following century. The same attitude was adopted by the workers even more effectively in the case of the 'Dutch loom', by which a number of ribbons or tapes could be woven simultaneously: it was in use on the Continent at about the same date as the invention of the stocking-frame, but is not known to have reached England until the reign of James I, when there were loud outcries against 'that devilish invention brought in by strangers'.

The new types of cloth introduced to England in the sixteenth century were known collectively as the 'new draperies'. They included bays (or baize) and says, arras, grogram, and mockado – light fabrics of a worsted description, which were brought into East Anglia by Protestant refugees from the Spanish Netherlands. They received official encouragement in the way of religious freedom, tax relief, and exemption from trade restrictions; by 1572 four thousand such weavers were bringing fresh prosperity to Norwich, and there was a second important nucleus of foreign craftsmen in Colchester.

However, the cloth industry was more rural than urban. Three contributory factors were the fulling-mills and other water-powered machines, which had to be located by fast-running water; the desire to escape the apprenticeship and other trade regulations which the gilds enforced in the towns; and the cheap labour supply to be tapped in the countryside, where spinning and – to a smaller extent – weaving could be a part-time occupation. The carding of wool and distaff-spinning were easily combined with looking after animals, and much rough cloth was woven in cottage homes. From such small beginnings a flourishing industry was built up by clothiers or other 'putters-out', who bought wool in quantity and gave out the material to the various classes of workers who processed it, until the completed cloth was in their hands. This rural industry produced a quality which fitted in well with the export trade to Antwerp, in which the finishing and dyeing were usually done abroad, though the clothiers also sold country-made cloth in the towns, where they themselves had their homes and warehouses. In a few cases, indeed, the dissolution of the monasteries encouraged them temporarily to mass their weavers there for supervision under one roof: thus William Stumpe, the clothier who got possession of the abbey buildings at Malmesbury, was put on record as able to supply 100 men for the French war in 1545.

Metal-Working

But while cloth-making in its various forms was the main Tudor industry, others were growing rapidly in importance. It was an age when men everywhere were fascinated by the search for metals. Henry VIII sought for gold in Wales, and the right to exploit precious metals was among the privileges of the Mines Royal Company which Elizabeth incorporated in 1568. This company prospected for copper and lead in the north and west, operated mines in Cumberland through a Bavarian firm with Tyrolese miners, worked copper in Cornwall, and for a time smelted it at Neath in South Wales. Another monopoly, which was established in the same year, was the Mineral and Battery Works. This made wire in twelve thicknesses at Tintern for the spikes of carding-boards, improved fish-hooks, and countless domestic purposes; the product was exported as far as Turkey and North Africa. Some of the wire was made of brass, which was in great demand for cannon, and the company was able to prepare this alloy of copper and zinc, thanks to the discovery of calamine in the Mendip Hills.

The pewter ware which began to replace wooden trenchers and rough pottery on the tables of the middle class was based on Cornish tin and Welsh and Mendip lead supplies; both lead and tin were also exported separately. Although there was a marked decline in large orders for lead to roof new churches and a considerable supply was in any case available from the plundering of the monasteries, it was in demand for the windows and drainpipes of Elizabethan mansions. Leaden bullets were also exported from Bristol to the troubled Continent.

The needs of war gave a great impulse at this time to the ancient iron industry. As early as 1496 the blast furnace was introduced into England, which made it possible to supply increased quantities of malleable iron for the use of the smith and also to produce fire-backs and other simple domestic equipment very readily from castings. But from the reign of Henry VIII onwards the great new achievement was the casting of cannon, which were supplied complete with superior cast-iron shot. These were mostly of sizes below the demi-culverin of the larger warships, but in the smaller pieces Elizabethan England supplied all her own needs and drove an extensive export trade with the Dutch and other Continental powers. Between 1570 and 1600 the annual output of cannon rose from 500–600 tons to a maximum of 1,000 tons, most of which were cast in the Sussex Weald.[1]

Kent and Surrey – where such names as Abinger Hammer recall the water-driven forge equipment of a long-dead past – were also important iron-working counties. Some of the Kentish iron no doubt went to feed the first English slitting-mill, which is believed to have been set up at Dartford in 1590; this cut bar-iron into narrow rods ready for the nailer. Some southern iron may even have found its way as far as Sheffield, which was already a centre for steel cutlery. But the nearer the industry advanced to the south coast, the more it competed with shipbuilding in eating up the woodlands: four tons of wood had to be burnt into two tons of charcoal in order to smelt one ton of iron. One consequence was some dispersion of the iron industry into other regions, such as Glamorgan and Monmouthshire, where the iron ore deposits were a Tudor discovery. In 1565 a London goldsmith set up an ironworks at Pontypool, which supplied much of the material needed at Tintern: the result was the consumption of 6,000 beech trees in three years. Another consequence, of more importance in the long run, was the increased demand for coal.

Coal-Mining

Coal had been used to some extent in Roman Britain, but it was difficult to mine and carry and was therefore not in much regular demand so long as wood was plentiful. But the requirements of the iron and shipbuilding industries plus the fuel demands of a rising population now created a scarcity, which was most marked in London, where in the period 1540–1640 the cost of firewood rose nearly three times as fast as the general level of prices. This gave a great stimulus to mining in the Newcastle area, from which the coal could be readily conveyed by sea to the Thames-side wharves.

[1] H. R. Schubert, *History of the British Iron and Steel Industry*, pp. 250–1, where an example is given of a cast-iron Elizabethan full-culverin from Pevensey Castle: its weight is 40 cwt, length 10ft 11in.

In 1580 the quantity brought in was already 15,000 tons, and in the next 25 years the amount was increased almost fivefold. At the same time Newcastle coal was being distributed to other towns which felt the pinch, wherever the seaports and navigable rivers of eastern and southern England gave convenient access. In the same way coal from Glamorgan reached south-west England, helping to make the Bristol Channel area into almost a single economic unit: one part of the Bristol anchorage became known as the 'Welsh Road'. Coal was also sent across the sea to Ireland and in much larger amounts to the Continent from Newcastle, which exported 36,000 tons in 850 shiploads in 1594.

Since any method but surface-digging of coal was difficult and hazardous, the increased demand resulted in various technical improvements. Boring-rods were introduced for testing underground seams; machines operated by horse-whims or waterwheels came into use for drainage; and the first wooden rails were laid for moving the heavy trucks along cramped passage-ways. The toil and risk nevertheless got worse as the pits deepened. But meanwhile the spread of the use of coal to one industrial process after another, to saltpans, limekilns, glass-blowing establishments, soap-boilers, brickworks, and breweries, helped to make this an era of almost revolutionary economic development.

Sources of Capital

The very existence of new industries and new processes on such a scale implies the availability of capital. Some of it was provided by big landowners, especially for the opening-up of mines on their own estates. Another, in all senses irregular, source was the plunder which Drake and the privateers wrested from the Spaniards. But the largest Elizabethan fortunes were commercial in origin. Some members of the Merchant Adventurers' and Levant Companies, for example, were probably richer than even the leading metalworkers, whose enterprises were still of modest proportions. Merchants could make financial deals more easily after 1567, when Sir Thomas Gresham built the Royal Exchange in London; this provided much greater facilities for merchants than the earlier customary meetings twice a day in Lombard Street. Here credit terms could be haggled over and loans obtained. But by far the best source of loans was Antwerp, which had cornered the trade of all Europe and with it the organization of European finance. In the Middle Ages the Church had condemned the demanding of interest on loans–taking literally the words of Christ, 'Lend, hoping for nothing again'. Even as late as Shakespeare there was enough popular suspicion of moneylenders for *The Merchant of Venice* to find a ready audience. But Antwerp moneylenders were active long before this and charged in Edward VI's reign, for instance, interest as high as 14 per cent. For, as Sir Thomas Wilson asked in his *Discourse on Usury* (1572):

> What man is so mad to deliver his money out of his own possession for naught? or who is he that will not make of his own the best he can?

Not only merchants and industrialists but also the Crown itself applied for loans in Antwerp, where Sir Thomas Gresham was the royal financial agent.

Smaller Industries

Such comparatively large-scale ventures as have been considered, requiring capital for their birth and growth, were not typical of the general run of English industry. This was mainly small-scale in towns as well as villages. Coventry, for instance, in the 1520s had ninety separate trades, and Northampton and Leicester about sixty each. Many of them (35–40 per cent) were connected with such day-to-day things as clothing (e.g. cappers, tailors and shoemakers), food (e.g. butchers, millers and bakers) and building (e.g. masons and stone-slaters) and were concerned far more with providing the country round through their shops and markets than with exports. Later in the century, in a typical midland county town such as Leicester, the producers of household goods were still important – chandlers, cutlers and haberdashers, for instance.

Yet there were many other industries somewhere in between the great capitalistic ventures and these more typical domestic ones: ventures that might require large capital but which could equally well be run simply as a family concern. Fishing was important among these, partly because, as the government was quick to see, it encouraged a supply of seamen for the defence of the state. After the Reformation, when many Catholic customs fell into disuse, that of Friday fish-eating was continued and was even enforced by law in 1548, with the addition of Saturday. In 1563 Wednesday also was added to these Protestant fish days, so that, counting in Ember days and Lent, there were more fish days than others. William Cecil, Elizabeth's chief minister, proclaimed his purpose:

> Let the old course of fishing be maintained by the strictest observation of fish days for policy's sake; so the sea coasts should be strong with men and habitations, and the fleet flourish more than ever.

In the earlier part of the century intensive fishing was largely confined to the east coast, to which the herring had recently moved from the other side of the North Sea. English fishermen concentrated on drying the fish, since native salt was not suitable for preserving it. Yet in this form it could be exported as far as the Mediterranean, feeding the ships' crews on the way. Apart from the east coast, there was fishing off Iceland, and towards the end of Elizabeth's reign English ships had become more important than all their rivals in the cod fisheries off Newfoundland.

Fishing grounds as far away as Iceland and Newfoundland attracted ships from all the chief ports – Plymouth, for instance, contributing fifty vessels to the one-hundred-strong Newfoundland fleet in 1594. But as far as coastal waters were concerned, only the eastern ports were of much importance, though in the west pilchards were caught on a growing scale and exported to Spain and Italy.

There were many others of these middling-sized industries. Connected with fishing and with the preservation of meat, there was salt manufacture. This had long been concentrated in Cheshire and Staffordshire, where it was made from natural inland brine. In Tudor times it was extended to the Tyne and Wear, where sea water was used. From this salt was obtained by evaporation, coal being employed to speed the process. There was also glass made in Sussex by Huguenot immigrants; a paper-mill at Dartford, started by an immigrant German; and gunpowder manufactured on the

Evelyn estates near Chilworth in Surrey. A soap-boiling industry was concentrated in London, where sugar refining was also established after the devastation of Antwerp in 1576. London increased its silk-weaving, too, and Flemish tapestry-makers established themselves in Norwich.

Position of the Gilds

Ever since the Middle Ages industry in the towns had been carried on through the craft gilds, and each craft – bakers, chandlers and carpenters, for instance – had its own gild. The normal way of entry to the craft was by apprenticeship to a master-craftsman, usually for seven years. But the apprentice could look forward to a secure future with sick and religious benefits thrown in, including prayers for his soul after death. Customers also benefited, for the gild kept a watch on the quality of the goods produced. Yet by Tudor times the system was breaking down. It was becoming difficult for the apprentice to become a master, since the qualifications required were more and more those of wealth and birth. He could become a 'journeyman' (one who worked for wages by the day – '*journée*' in French) in which case he could not take part in the government of the gild, which only the masters managed, or in that of the town, which was run by the top men of the different gilds. The Chantries Act of 1547 deprived the gilds of such parts of their lands and property as were devoted to religious purposes – 'the maintenance of any anniversary or obit[1] or of any light or lamp in any church or chapel' – while the tendency for towns to spread beyond their legal boundaries meant that the areas where gild authority held good became insufficient. At the same time the continued movement of the cloth industry into rural districts (as already noticed) put the most important English industry largely beyond gild control.

The compulsory apprenticeship clauses of the Statute of Artificers of 1563 were intended to restore something of the power of the gilds. But although they remained nominally in force until 1814, their effect was limited. For the simpler handicrafts, the seven-year period prescribed in the law was much too long, and

[1] A memorial service for the soul of a dead benefactor.

its exaction merely supplied the master with free labour. In many cases the judges got round the law, both by saying that apprenticeship served in one craft gave the right to practise any other, and by interpreting a phrase in the law referring to crafts 'now used or occupied within this Realm' as implying exemption for any craft invented or introduced after 1563. And in so far as the gilds nevertheless succeeded for a time in insisting on 'lawful apprenticeship' for workers in the old chartered towns where they were strong, the result was to increase the tendency for industry to move to other areas, where justices of the peace were unlikely to be strict about enforcing apprenticeship – except in the special case of pauper apprentices, whose indentures took a charge off the rates.

The sons of freemen of chartered boroughs usually had the right to trade there by inheritance, whatever their training, a fact which underlines the undemocratic attitude of the gilds and their increasing remoteness from the mass of working craftsmen. Amalgamations of gilds often widened the gap: in 1598, for instance, the goldsmiths of Hull absorbed the gilds of plumbers, musicians and basket-makers of the town. By such developments the specialist concern of the gilds in the details of manufacture was weakened and masters might well be less skilled than the ordinary workmen. In 1529 some poor working goldsmiths complained that the leading members of their gild 'were but merchant goldsmiths and had but little knowledge in the science' and for this impertinence were thrown into prison. Their harsh treatment shows that the very character of the gilds was changing. In London they developed into the Livery Companies (each known by its distinctive dress or livery) and John Stow in his *Survey of London* (1598) listed sixty of them as represented at the Lord Mayor's banquet in 1532. Among these sixty, twelve (the mercers, fishmongers and goldsmiths, for instance) became the 'great companies' whose leaders were the most important men of the City and largely controlled its government. Like the unknowledgeable goldsmiths of 1529, they were not craftsmen but merchants. Wealth in Tudor England was merchant wealth, and the great men of the London craft companies knew this as well as any merchant of the Merchant Adventurers or other companies which traded over distant seas.

Monopolies

These great commercial companies were monopolies: that is to say, they had the sole right to trade their goods to certain defined areas of the world – as the Merchant Adventurers had the monopoly of exporting English cloth anywhere between the mouth of the Somme and the Skaw. These monopolies were obtained by royal charter in return for, usually, both initial and annual payments to the Crown. The main reason for this form of organization was royal poverty – increased, as it was, by rising prices – though in trading to distant parts of the world some firm organization was essential. The same royal needs ensured that industry, too, should be run by chartered companies on monopolistic lines. The Evelyns manufactured gunpowder under a monopoly which even entitled their agents to dig for saltpetre in the grounds of private houses, and Christopher Schutz of the Mineral and Battery Works had the sole right of making brass. And there was some industrial advantage about monopolies, too, in cases where new crafts or crafts newly introduced from abroad needed a respite from competition while they established themselves.

In any case there was nothing new about the practice of monopoly, which the medieval craft gilds had always tried to enforce on a local basis for the benefit of their own members. In most places the gilds no longer had such an effective control of manufacturing standards, prices, and wage-rates, which were now supervised to an increasing extent by the national government through laws and orders administered by the justices of the peace. Royal monopolies could therefore be regarded as a natural accompaniment of the growth of national power in the sixteenth century, especially as it was still widely accepted that careful control did much more than unbridled competition to encourage the growth of trade.

But since privileged producers of goods in big demand could charge as much as they liked, the result was felt everywhere in exorbitant prices. The scandal was increased by Elizabeth's use of monopolies as a cheap and handy means of rewarding her servants and courtiers: Ralegh, for example, had exclusive rights over tavern licences and the sale of playing cards. During the depressed decade of the 1590s, accordingly, the system came to be felt as a serious grievance. The law courts could not help, since the grants were made by royal prerogative, and in 1597 parliament appealed unsuccessfully to the Queen herself. When parliament assembled again four years later there were angry demonstrations and proposals for legislation, which the Queen met by professing to have been ignorant of the hardships created: ten monopolies would be cancelled at once, and leave was given to bring others before the judges. The faithful Commons were duly pacified, and Elizabeth took leave of them (for the last time, as it turned out) in the moving speech already quoted.[1] Nevertheless, the whole question was to boil up again in the reign of her successor, who came from a country whose economic problems were of much smaller dimensions.

Industry in Scotland

In Scotland industry was in its infancy. This was partly because the demand was small and local and partly because industry was to some extent monopolized by the royal burghs. These were towns which grew up on royal lands and had received their charters from the king himself – as against the more numerous other towns whose charters came from Scottish lords. In early days the royal burghs controlled the trade of whole counties, and they alone still had the right to trade abroad. In these boroughs, therefore, the emphasis was more on trade than industry and craftsmen were subordinate to merchants. Craftsmen could only become freemen of such boroughs if they abandoned their crafts and concentrated upon trade – a ruling that set all small craftsmen against merchants. The wish to protect their privileges led the royal burghs to look suspiciously on newer towns and to oppose their growth – as, for instance, Aberdeen tried to stifle Fraserburgh and Stirling Falkirk. Here they failed, and between 1517 and 1571 only seven new royal burghs were established as against twenty-five others. Still, the privileges of the royal burghs were maintained: only their merchants traded salt and skins to the Low Countries through the Scottish staple port of Veere, or took cloth into Bordeaux and

[1] See p. 22.

the Baltic (mainly to Danzig) and salt and coarse linen to England. Some of these merchants, such as Heriot of Edinburgh, became rich and, having the monopoly of foreign trade, they controlled most of the shipping of Scotland, which was increasing fast. In 1596, for instance, the fleet which traded with Bordeaux for wine contained eighty ships, nearly all of them Scottish-owned.

Yet there was industry too, some branches of which – such as cloth-finishing – were controlled by the royal burghs. Cloth-making never flourished after the English manner, in spite of attempts to attract foreign workmen to establish it. Undyed rough cloth was, however, woven freely in all towns, and in the country districts too, by humble 'websters'. Salt was produced round, and exported from, the Firth of Forth, though like the English salt it was unsuitable for preserving fish. Some lead was mined: but more important than this was coal-mining – in some ways more advanced than in England and Wales because of the shortage of timber in Scotland. As in the rest of Britain, the mines most eagerly exploited were those near the coast – Fifeshire coal supplied all east Scotland. Before 1600 some Scottish coal was finding its way to London, and more would come when James VI became James I of England. There was some English collaboration in the mining of Scottish coal. In 1566, for instance, Bevis Bulmer, a mining engineer from the north of England, was working in Scotland, and in 1598 the Englishman Gavin Smith was associated with James Aitchison (goldsmith to James VI) in inventing a pump for draining mines. But all these were small beginnings, and there is very little that stands out in the picture of Scottish industry in the sixteenth century. Its great age still lay far in the future.

7

SHAKESPEARE'S ENGLAND

A PICTURE of the England of Shakespeare can be built up in many different ways – from other dramatists and poets, from chroniclers and antiquaries – as well as from Shakespeare himself. It was an age anxious to record and celebrate time past and to describe time present, both for the benefit of the unborn and as an expression of its own restless curiosity. The English language had reached a height of beauty and gave birth to a many-sided literature. In their brown leather bindings and heavily inked print the works of the Elizabethans crowd the shelves and cry out to be used as evidence. But we have space to cite only three or four volumes at all extensively, namely, Stow's *Survey of London*, Harrison's *Description of England*, Camden's *Britannia*, and more occasionally the *Poly-Olbion* of Michael Drayton.

Descriptive Writings

John Stow (1525?–1605) worked as a tailor in London for thirty years, and in 1598 produced his *Survey*, which is a mixture of history and painstaking observation – a sort of handbook to London and its customs. His likeness can still be seen in the alabaster effigy erected by his wife in the church of St Andrew Undershaft, Cornhill.

William Harrison (1534–1593) was rector of Radwinter in Essex and a canon of Windsor. His *Description of England* was first published in 1578 as an introduction to Holinshed's *Chronicles*.

William Camden (1551–1623) was an usher and, later, headmaster of Westminster School, who spent his holidays on the antiquarian tours which provide the basis for his *Britannia*. This famous work, which covers the whole of the British Isles, appeared in six Latin editions (1586–1607) before the first of several translations into English was made in 1610.

Michael Drayton (1563–1631) was a Warwickshire poet, whose *Poly-Olbion* ('having many blessings') is replete with patriotic sentiments:

Of Albion's glorious isle the wonders whilst I write,
The sundry varying soils, the pleasures infinite . . .

It was written over a period of nine years (1613–22), providing almost a canto to a county, but there is no certainty that the author derived his inspiration from much personal visiting.

The Vanities of Life

The English of Shakespeare's day lived as full-bloodedly as they did, partly perhaps because of their close familiarity with death. Disease struck swiftly and frequently in the crowded capital; Elizabethan adventurers left their bones to bleach on many distant shores; and not a few noble lives ended on the scaffold. The Jesuit, Robert Southwell, who spent three years in prison awaiting execution, had good cause to trace the skull beneath the flesh:

I often look upon a face
Most ugly, grisly, bare and thin;
I often view the hollow place
Where eyes and nose had sometimes been;
I see the bones across that lie,
Yet little think that I must die.

And there is Ralegh, whom James I was to send to his death on Tower Hill, haunted by the cruel power of Time,

Who in the dark and silent grave,
When we have wandered all our ways,
Shuts up the story of our days.

But while the story lasted, they made the very most of it in every respect – even in the way men wore their clothes. In the England of Shakespeare, the richer of them dressed more finely than in any age since and, with their ruffs, pleated doublets and hose, outshone their women. The 'new draperies' were put to good use and sometimes to ones that excited female sneers. 'I scarce knew him,' exclaims a woman in Thomas Dekker's *Shoemaker's Holiday* of a nobleman's son, fresh to the army, seen strutting before his men:

> Here he wore a scarf, and here a scarf, here a bunch of feathers and here precious stones and jewels and a pair of garters; O monstrous! like one of our yellow silk curtains at home . . .

And, if some men imagined that it added to their bravado and swagger to be seen smoking like the Indians of North America, there were others like the shoemaker's wife in the play above who detested the habit: "these filthy tobacco pipes . . . God bless us, men look not like men that use them".

Homes of Rich and Poor

From the man to the house he lived in. Here there were as great differences between rich and poor as in dress, and there were regional differences too: the east was richer than the west, in spite of such pockets of prosperity as Exeter and Bristol. Here is Richard Carew's description of peasant houses in his *Survey of Cornwall:*

> Walls of earth, low thatched roofs, few partitions, no glass windows, and scarcely any chimneys, other than a hole in the wall to let out the smoke.

Yet, as we have seen, wherever men could take advantage of the rise in prices they could do well: it was the wage-earners who sank. Over most of the country it was probably true, for instance, that, as Harrison said, window glass "is come to be plentiful and . . . cheap", and that old men commented on "the multitude of chimneys lately erected, whereas in their young days there were not above two or three, if so many, in most uplandish towns of the realm". Harrison also remarked on the springing up of new buildings in his time:

> Every man almost is a builder and he that hath bought any small parcel of ground, be it never so little, will not be quiet till he hath pulled down the old house . . . and set up a new.

This was true whether of half-timbered or stone cottages, or of great houses such as the sumptuous Burghley House or the more restrained Longleat, which Camden described as 'a very fair, neat and elegant house in a foul soil'. In the halls of such houses the Elizabethan plays were performed, and their occupants beguiled the wet winter afternoons promenading in long galleries adorned with wall-paintings and tapestries.

Houses, however, are homes more than buildings and many of the pleasures of life are enjoyed in them. Among these food is always important. Harrison reckoned that the coolness of the climate ensured much eating among the English:

> The situation of our region lying near unto the north doth cause the heat of our stomachs to be of somewhat greater force: therefore our bodies do crave a little more ample nourishment than the inhabitants of the hotter regions are accustomed withal . . . It is no marvel therefore that our tables are oftentimes more plentifully garnished than those of other nations . . .

Certainly one that was 'plentifully garnished' was that of the poet Ben Jonson, who set himself to tempt a friend to supper:

> *Yet you shall have, to rectify your palate,*
> *An olive, capers, or some better salad*
> *Ushering the mutton; with a short-legged hen*
> *If we can get her, full of eggs, and then*
> *Lemons, and wine for sauce; to these, a coney*
> *Is not to be despaired of, for our money;*
> *And though fowl now be scarce, yet there are clerks,*
> *The sky not falling, think we may have larks.*
> *I'll tell you more, and lie, so you will come:*
> *Of partridge, pheasant, woodcock, of which some*
> *May yet be there.*

Jonson speaks only of 'wine for sauce' but, if Harrison is right, there were very many wines drunk at the table. He speaks of 56 sorts of light wines and strong ones 'according to the number of regions from whence they come'. And there was a variety of cheese. Writing of Cheshire, Camden remarked that "cheeses be made here in great number of a most pleasing and delicate taste, such as all England. . . . affordeth not the like". On more prosperous tables they would go with wheaten bread, but Harrison notes that the poor

> are forced to content themselves with rye or barley, yea, and in time of dearth . . . with bread made either of beans, peason or oats . . . and some acorns among.

Nevertheless a poor man's food was not always so wretched, for Harrison also writes of craftsmen and farm labourers whose diet

> consisteth principally in beef and such meat as the butcher selleth, that is to say, mutton, veal, lamb, pork etc., whereof he findeth great store in the markets.

From the house into the rectangular walled garden, divided into four regular sections by paths and with its splashing fountain in the middle. The Elizabethans delighted in wild and garden flowers and in herbs and vegetables too, and there are frequent references to them in literature. In his delicate poem *Prothalamion* Edmund Spenser speaks of 'nymphs' gathering flowers in a meadow beside the Thames:

> *Of every sort which in that meadow grew,*
> *They gathered some; the violet pallid blue,*
> *The little daisy that at evening closes,*
> *The virgin lily, and the primrose true,*
> *With store of vermeil*[1] *roses. . . .*

And in his *Poly-Olbion* Drayton rolls the names of garden vegetables round his mouth as though their very sound delighted him:

> *The colewort, cauliflower, and cabbage in their season,*
> *The rouncefall, great beans and early ripening peason;*
> *The onion, scallion, leek, which housewives highly rate;*
> *The kinsman garlic then, the poor man's Mithridate;*

[1] Vermilion (*O.E.D.*)

The savoury parsnip next, and carrot, pleasing food. . . .
The turnip, tasting well to clowns in winter weather.
Thus in our verse we put roots, herbs and fruits together.

The Face of the Land

Beyond the garden stretched the countryside, where the ceaseless activity of man overlaid old scars with new. Drayton notices this, alive to what now perhaps would be called 'agricultural archaeology':

The ridge and furrow shows that once the crooked plough
Turned up the grassy turf, where oaks are rooted now:
And at this hour we see the share and coulter tear
The corn-bearing glebe, where sometimes forests were.

Some of the most recent marks were made by enclosures – hedges and ditches cutting across the pattern of the open fields and commons. Of these Harrison writes, remarking also the social changes that accompanied them. He is aware of

> encroaching and joining of . . . land to land, whereby the inhabitants are devoured and eaten up and their houses either pulled down or suffered to decay.

And he goes on to describe how a few prosperous men were coming to dominate the village community:

> The ground of the parish is gotten up into a few men's hands, yea sometimes into the tenure of two or three, whereby the rest are compelled either to be hired servants unto the other or else to beg.

Yet such enclosures, however painful, could lead the way to improved farming techniques, always an object of Elizabethan curiosity. Camden notices how in Denbighshire, although not enclosing country, the farmers managed to enrich their poor soil with ash fertilizer:

> After they have with a broad kind of spade pared away the upper coat . . . into certain turfs, they pile them up on heaps, put

> fire to them and burn them to ashes, which being thrown upon the ground . . . causeth the hungry barrenness thereof to fructify.

But perhaps the most significant changes in the countryside went on below its surface, as the exploitation of minerals spread into new areas. In visiting Glamorgan, where coal and iron were beginning to be worked, Camden noticed only that the region to the south of the mountains was 'the richest part of the county and thick set with towns'. But he detected the growth of what was later to be called the Black Country in south Staffordshire, "which has pit coal and iron mines, whether to its advantage or disadvantage can best be determined by the inhabitants". He also saw Birmingham under its modern aspect, "swarming with inhabitants and echoing with the noise of anvils, for here are great numbers of smiths".

This new world of industry was already to some extent at war with the countryside, swallowing up the woods in a way that made many Elizabethans anxious. "Within these forty years we shall have little great timber growing," lamented Harrison. Camden described Sussex as

> full of mines everywhere, for the casting of which there are furnaces up and down the country and abundance of wood is yearly spent.

But he was more explicit in his comment on the situation in the Forest of Dean:

> Since that rich mines of iron were here found out, those thick woods began to wax thin by little and little.

Glass-making, too, devoured the forests. How rapidly is suggested by an incidental reference to the wood-consumption in Stow's account of the accidental destruction of a London glass factory in 1575:

> A glass house, wherein was made glass of diverse sorts to drink in burst out into a terrible fire . . . The same house in a small time before had consumed a great quantity of wood by making of glasses; now itself having within it about forty thousand billets of wood was all consumed to the stone walls.

The Elizabethans were just beginning to appreciate the extent of their coal resources and to see that they might have to be very widely used. Harrison remarked of the coal-mines:

> We have such plenty in the north and western parts of our island as may suffice for all the realm of England: and so must they do hereafter indeed, if wood be not better cherished than it is at this present.

Of the coal-mines themselves Drayton speaks, describing in poetic and rather over-drawn terms some shafts near Darlington:

> *Three black and horrid pits, which for their boiling heat,*
> *(That from their loathsome brims do breathe a sulphurous sweat)*
> *'Hell Kettles' rightly called.*

And he goes on to write of the port of Newcastle already famous for its export of sea-coal, giving the River Tyne speech for the occasion:

> *As of those mighty ships which in my mouth I bear,*
> *Fraught with my country coal of this Newcastle named,*
> *For which both far and near that place is no less famed*
> *Than India for her mines.*

And, in more down-to-earth fashion, Camden makes the same point, speaking of

> The abundance of sea coal vented hence [i.e. from Newcastle] unto which a great part of England and the Low Countries of Germany are beholden for their good fires.

Coal was also beginning to replace wood for salt-boiling. Camden, speaking of the town of Nantwich in Cheshire, gives a good account of how salt was produced there:

> It hath only one salt-pit . . . fourteen feet from the river, out of which they convey salt water by troughs of wood into houses adjoining, wherein there stand little barrels pitched fast in the ground, which they fill with that water and at the ringing of a bell they begin to make fire under the leads[1] whereof they have

[1] Cauldrons, perhaps of lead.

> six in every house, and therein seethe the said water: then certain women, they call them 'wallers', with little wooden rakes fetch up the salt from the bottom and put it in baskets, they call them 'salt-barrows', out of which the liquor runneth and the pure salt remaineth.

Camden also reminds his readers that the ancient Derbyshire lead mines were still in operation – yet another competitor for vanishing wood supplies. Of the Peak district he says:

> In these mountains, fertile lead stones are daily digged up in great abundance; which upon the hilltops lying open to the west wind they melt with mighty great fires of wood in troughs or trenches, which they dig of purpose for it to run into and so make it up into sows.

The Elizabethan Town

Enfolded by the green countryside lay the towns of Shakespeare's England - many of them still surrounded by their walls and ditches, though some had overflowed these boundaries and invaded the fields and orchards beyond. Exeter, with an estimated population of 7,000 or more, was then the fifth or sixth largest provincial city, yet its Chamberlain gives a clear picture of its narrow limits in a paper written in 1559:

> It is not altogether foursquare but declineth somewhat towards a roundness, and containeth in circuit or compass 1600 whole paces after 5 foot to the pace, which after 1000 paces to a mile containeth a mile and a half and somewhat more. It is pendant towards the south and west, in such sort that the streets, be they never so foul or filthy, yet with one shower of rain they are cleansed.

Here or at Chester or Shrewsbury the showers still fall on streets of timber-framed, black-and-white houses, along which prosperous Elizabethan burgesses once bustled. The shop or office faced the street on the ground floor, with kitchens and storerooms behind. The first floor held the main living-room, with its leaded windows and carved front jutting out over the passers-by. There were one or two floors of low-ceiled bedrooms above, and finally attics – though employees and servants were often accommodated in the extensive cellars.

London and Its Expansion

London, which altogether dwarfed the towns of the provinces, was spreading all the time, as Stow frequently points out. Between Aldgate and the Tower, for instance, houses had been built on "the ditch without the walls of the city, which of old time was used to be open", and a whole suburb had newly grown up beyond Bishopsgate:

> This Hog Lane stretcheth north towards St Mary's Hospital without Bishopsgate, and within these forty years had on both sides fair hedgerows of elm trees, with bridges and easy stiles to pass over into the pleasant fields . . . which is now within a few years made a continual building throughout, of garden-houses and small cottages; and the fields on either side be turned into garden-plots, tenter houses, bowling alleys and such like.

Land in the City itself had a correspondingly great value. Stow relates from the experience of his own father the high-handed action by which Thomas Cromwell, the much-feared minister of Henry VIII, enlarged the garden of his new house in Throgmorton Street.

> The house being finished, and having some reasonable plot of land left for a garden, he caused the pales of the gardens adjoining to the north part thereof on a sudden to be taken down; twenty-two feet to be measured forth, right into the north of every man's ground; a line to be drawn there, a trench to be cast, and a high brick wall to be built. My father had a garden there and a house standing close to his [Cromwell's] south pale. This house they loosed from the ground and bare upon rollers into my father's garden, twenty-two feet, ere my father heard thereof . . . No man durst go to argue the matter.

Perhaps to modern senses the most unpleasant feature of town life in Tudor times would be the smells and dirt: the street was the obvious place to get rid of house refuse, and the gradients were seldom so convenient as at Exeter. In Dekker's *Shoemaker's Holiday*, the master summons his apprentices to clean the street outside his shop: "Come out and sweep me these kennels,[1] that the noisome stench offend not the nose of my neighbours." In London, however, most of the stinking streams that ran down to the Thames from the northern slopes were already being closed in. Stow, for instance, refers to the Walbrook, which once entered the Thames as a broad tidal creek in the vicinity of Cannon Street:

> This watercourse, having divers bridges, was afterwards vaulted over with brick and paved level with the streets and lanes wherethrough it passed; and since that, also houses have been built thereon, so that the course of Walbrook is now hidden underground and hardly known.

Such paving over of the streams that ran through the metropolis was also one way of meeting its ever-growing need for fresh water. This had been a problem ever since the Middle Ages, and many Elizabethan citizens spent their money on solving it for their own immediate neighbourhood. Thus Stow describes how in 1577 a cloth worker named William Lamb rebuilt a conduit in Holborn:

> The water he caused to be conveyed in lead from divers springs to one head, and from thence to the said conduit . . . more than two thousand yards . . . at his own charges, amounting to fifteen hundred pounds.

In most cases the supply, whether of spring or river water, had to be carried home from the street. But Stow also mentions "Thames water conveyed into men's houses by pipes of lead from a most artificial forcier, near unto London Bridge": the first water-wheel pump had been set up there in 1581.

Almshouses and Schools

Private charity was likewise active, in many towns and in some villages, with the building of almshouses and schools. At Stoke Poges, for example, the recusant Lord Hastings in 1573 endowed

[1] The surface-drain or channel of a street (*O.E.D.*)

'the rude forefathers of the hamlet' with a hospital for four poor men and two women, each of whom was to have a chimney in his room, four loads of firewood and £3 6*s*. 8*d*. a year, and every second year 'a blue gown of broadcloth of four yards'. Stow names many similar foundations in London, such as the one in Golden Lane, north of the ancient watch-tower of the Barbican, where "Richard Gallard of Islington, esquire, citizen and painter-stainer of London, founded thirteen almshouses for so many poor people placed in them rent-free". The same writer refers to the 'notable grammar school' of the London Merchant Taylors, but it is perhaps more interesting to observe the example of London spreading to the provinces. Thus Camden records, on his visit to Berkhamsted in Hertfordshire:

> In the very town itself nothing is worth sight, save only the school which John Incent, Dean of Paul's in London, a native of the place, founded.

This dated from 1544, but farther north he noticed such Elizabethan developments as the two new Rutlandshire schools at Uppingham and Oakham, which led him to remark that such schools were now to be found even in the smaller market towns.

Amenities of London Life

On the Southwark bank of the Thames, opposite the crowded city crowned with the spires of more than a hundred churches, Stow describes the riverside as built over 'more than a large mile in length'. Here the citizens enjoyed themselves at tennis and football:

> The ball is used by noblemen and gentlemen in tennis courts, and by people of meaner sort in the open fields and streets.

They also crowded to cock-fights and to see the baiting of bulls and bears, particularly 'in bear gardens on the Bank's side, wherein be prepared scaffolds for beholders to stand upon'. But Stow also knew of nobler exhibitions there:

> Of late time hath been used comedies, tragedies, interludes and

histories, both true and feigned; for the acting whereof certain public places hath been erected.

In fact London, then as now, was a metropolis which provided entertainment both for its permanent residents and numerous visitors.

For the latter group at least, staring at the sights was as important as the more organized enjoyments. Among famous buildings Gresham's colonnaded Royal Exchange, which the Queen opened in 1571, was the newest, but St Paul's and London Bridge were supreme. The great bulk of St Paul's dominated the sprawling, narrow streets on both banks of the river and was plainly visible for miles around. It was one of the largest cathedrals in England – longer than the present structure and, when Elizabeth came to the throne, much higher. The spire rose 489 feet into the air, to which Stow with pardonable pride added a further 31 feet; but he wrote from memory, for in June 1561 it was struck by lightning and burnt down to the level of the great central tower on which it stood. London Bridge was as wonderful as St Paul's and seems so to our eyes too, looking at it in the contemporary panoramic views of the city. It carried a double row of houses divided by a central street and, while from the street itself there may have been little view, from the houses upon the bridge the scenes of movement must have been magnificent. Stow says of it:

> It is a work very rare, having with the drawbridge twenty arches made of squared stone. . . . It seemeth rather a continual street than a bridge, for all the bridge is replenished on both the sides with large, fair, and beautiful buildings, inhabitants for the most part rich merchants and other wealthy citizens, mercers and haberdashers.

A Maritime Nation

Downstream from the bridge clustered the masts of ships, their hulls slapped by the tidal water. Few Londoners could have been unaware of the sea beyond their river and the England of Shakespeare never forgot it, for it provided her trading wealth and her defence from foreign enemies. 'Who is ignorant', asks Stow,

> that we have no mines of silver or gold . . . so that the increase of our coin and bullion cometh from elsewhere; and yet nevertheless we be both fed, clad and otherwise served with foreign commodities and delights . . . which thing cometh to pass by the means of merchandise only.

For such reasons Elizabethan England encouraged trade, and also because it trained seamen to serve in war. This was why the State kept up the old Church practice of compulsory 'fish days', upon which Harrison remarks:

> It is lawful for every man to feed upon whatsoever he is able to

Plate 10. *The Stocking Frame.* This was invented in 1589 by the Rev. William Lee of Woodbridge, Suffolk and was a device to knit stockings flat, so that they could then be seamed by hand. The machine formed rows of loops and passed them on to rows of needles or barbed hooks – like the process of simple hand-knitting. The 'frame' was called so because the knitting part of it, where the loops and needles were (i.e. between the worker's hands in this picture), was mounted on a frame. The invention was slow in spreading, so that even as late as 1641 there were fewer than a hundred frames in England and Wales. Yet the basic principles were so sound that the machine was not superseded for over two centuries. (Cf. text p. 95.)

Plate 11. *A Fulling Mill (1607).* Fulling was the process by which woollen cloth was beaten while wet so that it matted and shrank and was thickened. As early as the 13th century it was found that this could be done mechanically, and the fulling mill was one of the earliest examples of the use of powered machines in industry. Water-power was used, turning a water-wheel (I) and so rotating a shaft (G) to which a series of projecting cams (H) was attached so that, as the shaft turned, the wooden hammers were raised on the projections to thud onto the cloth in the tub (kept wet by a water-inlet at D). Mixed with the water in the tub was fuller's earth which acted as a detergent, removing the grease and dirt from the cloth. Such machines continued in use until well into the 19th century, and as late as 1963 one was still working at Sunnybank Mills, Rossendale, Lancs (for which see W. H. Chaloner and A. E. Musson's *Industry and Technology* – note on illustration no. 183). (Cf. text p. 96.)

Plate 12. *Bird's-Eye View of Shrewsbury from the East.* A water-colour drawing by an anonymous draughtsman of the late 16th century.

This shows very well the appearance of a prosperous market town of the time – still surrounded by its walls, though beginning to expand beyond them, and with its churches, castle and market cross. The drawing formed part of a collection of maps and charts which once belonged to William Cecil, Lord Burghley, who wrote the note 'ye Welsh gate' by the bridge at the top of the picture. (Cf. text p. 115.)

Plate 13. *Old Edinburgh.* From a 1670 engraving by Wenceslaus Hollar. The city is shown spreading south from the spine of the 'Royal Mile' between the Castle on the left and Holyrood Palace on the right. St. Giles's Church, with the Parliament House beside it, is on this street, between the castle and the centre line of the picture. The city is still walled, though beginning to burst its boundaries on the south side, where field strips (or 'rigs') can be seen. The New Town was not founded till 1767, and open country lies between the north side of the city and the port of Leith at the top right of the picture. (Cf. text pp. 125. 269.)

Plate 10

Plate 11

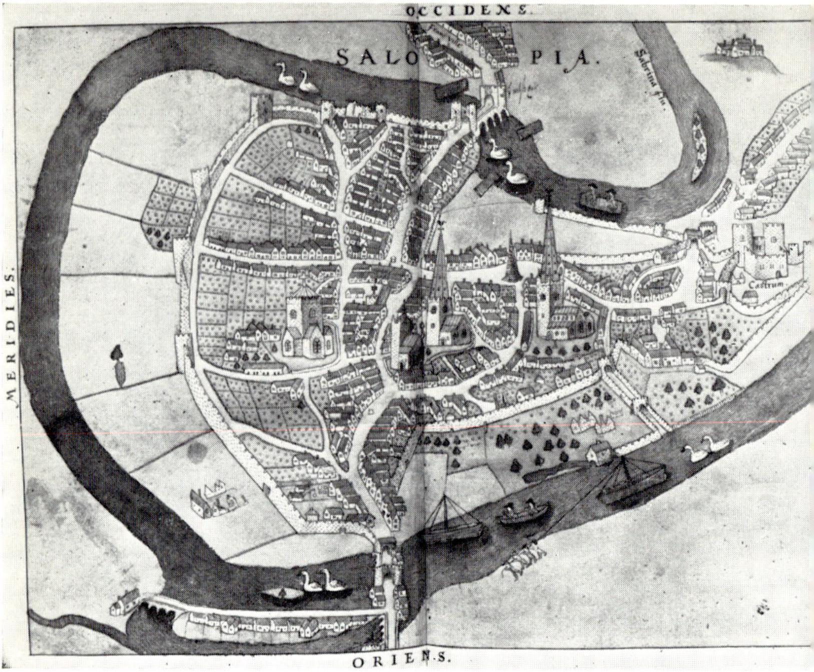

Plate 12

Plate 13

purchase, except it be upon those days whereon eating of flesh is especially forbidden by the laws of our realm . . . There is great consideration had in making of this law, for the preservation of the navy and maintenance of convenient numbers of sea-faring men.

This Elizabethan concern with seamen and the perils as well as the profits of seafaring is revealed in the writing of the time. Clarence in Shakespeare's *Richard III* shows it in the terror of his nightmare:

Lord, Lord! methought what pain it was to drown:
What dreadful noise of water in mine ears!
What sights of ugly death within my eyes!
Methought I saw a thousand fearful wracks:
A thousand men that fishes gnawed upon;
Wedges of gold, great anchors, heaps of pearl,
Inestimable stones, unvalued jewels,
All scattered in the bottom of the sea.

John Donne in his poem *The Storm* illustrates it:

Then note they the ship's sicknesses, the mast
Shaked with this ague, and the hold and waist
With a salt dropsy clogged, and all our tacklings
Snapping like too-high-stretched treble strings.
And from our tattered sails, rags drop down so,
As from one hanged in chains a year ago.

But two lands, still in some degree strange, were known to Englishmen through other means than perilous sea voyages.

The English View of the Welsh

Wales had begun a steady development – especially among the gentry class whose sons were going to Oxford, where in 1571 Jesus College was founded mainly for Welshmen. Or they went to London to share in the opportunities of the time. Englishmen, too, were feeling a new interest in the Principality – and not only for the mineral wealth that it was supposed to contain. Shakespeare introduced into *Henry V* the forthright Fluellen, of whom the king exclaimed, "There is much care and valour in this Welshman," and with whom he claimed kinship of race:

> *King Henry*: For I am Welsh, you know, good countryman.
>
> *Fluellen*: All the water in Wye cannot wash your Majesty's Welsh blood out of your body, I can tell you that: God bless it and preserve it . . .
>
> *King Henry*: Thanks, good my countryman.
>
> *Fluellen*: By Jesu I am your Majesty's countryman, I care not who know it; I will confess it to all the world.

And Dekker introduced the two Welsh knights, Sir Owen ap Meredith and Sir Rees ap Vaughan, into his two plays, *Patient Grissil* and *Satiromastix* respectively. The same pride of country that Fluellen showed is revealed by Sir Owen too in this snippet of dialogue between a Welsh widow named Gwenthyan, Sir Owen and a certain Farneze:

> *Gwenthyan*: Sir Owen gramarcye whee: Gwenthyan Manda gen y, ac welloch en Thlawen en ryn mogh.
>
> *Farneze*: . . . Oh my good widow gabble that we may understand you.
>
> *Sir Owen*: . . . Is talk in her British tongue, for 'tis fine delicates tongue, I can tell her, Welsh tongue is finer as Greek tongue.
>
> *Farneze*: A baked neat's tongue is finer than both.

The Welsh language certainly was strange to English ears, and Harrison is on more familiar ground when he speaks of the qualities of the Welsh soil:

> It hath been commonly reported that the ground of Wales is neither so fruitful as that of England, neither the soil of Scotland so bountiful as that of Wales: which is true for corn and for the most part.

A Scot on Scotland

For Scotland we must take down another book from the shelves. This is the translation of the significantly named *History of Greater*

Britain, both England and Scotland by John Major, originally published in Latin in 1521. Major was born near North Berwick and was one of the most learned Scotsmen of his day, studying at Cambridge and Paris and lecturing at Glasgow and Saint Andrews.

The great division in Scotland was between the Highlanders and Lowlanders. Major speaks of this as the difference between the 'wild Scots' and the 'householding' ones who controlled the government of the State. He writes:

> Just as among the Scots we find two distinct tongues, so we likewise find two different ways of life and conduct.

And he adds that:

> Our householding Scots . . . these men [i.e. the Highlanders] hate, on account of their differing speech, as much as they do the English.

He goes on to describe the Highland dress:

> From the mid-leg to the foot they go uncovered; their dress is, for an over-garment, a loose plaid and a shirt saffron-dyed. They are armed with bows and arrows, a broadsword and a small halbert. They always carry in their belt a stout dagger single-edged . . . In time of war they cover the whole body with a coat of mail made of iron rings.

Camden helps to fill in the picture when he speaks of these "Highlandmen" as "divided into companies called Clans", and adds that "they commit dreadful outrages by plundering and murdering". He was also aware of the turbulence of the whole region of the Scottish border: even on Hadrian's Wall, this classical enthusiast found that there were parts which "we durst not go and view, for fear of the moss-troopers." Some of the marauders were English, but cattle-stealing was a special temptation to the impoverished Scots. Camden quotes a vivid description of their activities from the pen of a Scottish bishop, John Lesley, who published a Latin history of his native land at Rome in 1578.

> They go forth in the night through by-ways. All the day time

> they refresh their horses and recreate their own strength in lurking-places appointed beforehand, until they be come . . . at length in the dark night where they would be. When they have laid hold of a booty . . . they return home, likewise by night, through blind ways only . . . And so crafty and wily these are that seldom or never they forgo their booty . . . unless it happen that they be caught by their adversaries . . . tracing them directly by their footing . . . But say they be taken, so fair spoken are they and eloquent . . . that they are able to move the Judges . . . if not to mercy, yet to admiration.

The bravery of such men was not in question, nor indeed of all the Scots – to whom Harrison pays tribute from a strongly English point of view:

> In martial prowess there is little or no difference between Englishmen and Scots: for albeit that the Scots have been often and very grievously overcome by the force of our nation, it hath not been for want of manhood on their parts but through the mercy of God showed on us, and His justice on them, since they have always begun the quarrels.

Harrison reckoned that, on the principle that the farther north men live the more they eat, the Scots filled themselves even more lustily than the English, though with deplorable results:

> In Scotland likewise they have given themselves . . . unto very ample and large diet . . . They far exceed us in overmuch and distemperate gormandize and so ingrosse their bodies that divers of them do oft become unapt to any other purpose than to spend their times in large tabling and belly cheer.

Turning from the people to the land, Harrison recognized, as an Englishman conscious of such things, that the Scots possessed

> not only plenty of quarries (. . . of sundry kinds of marble, hard stone and fine alabaster) but also rich mines of metal.

Such stone was ideal for building and, though John Major remarks that short leases discouraged men from building good houses 'though stone abound', yet it was much used in the main towns. It is, however, surprising that Major calls Perth 'the only walled town in Scotland' (which Camden contradicts). He wishes it were not so:

> If towns in general had even low walls I should approve of it as a means of restraining the robbers and thieves of the realm.

Camden is predictable about Edinburgh, and his description has no surprises:

> This city in regard of the high situation, of the wholesome air and plentiful soil, and many noblemen's towered houses built round about it . . . reaching from east to west a mile . . . is worthily counted the chief city of the whole kingdom; strongly walled . . . well peopled and frequented.

But his picture of Glasgow comes as something of a shock:

> The most famous town of merchandise in . . . Clydesdale: for pleasant site and apple trees and other like fruit trees much commended, having also a very fair bridge supported with eight arches.

It was also, as Major records,

> the seat of an archbishop and of a university poorly endowed and not rich in scholars.

And surprisingly, in view of his own university experience, and the national love of learning, which led to the foundation of a fourth university as the 'town's college' of Edinburgh in 1582, Major comments sourly:

> I look with no favour on this multitude of universities; for, just as iron sharpeneth iron, so a large number of students together will sharpen one another's wits.

This reads like the remark of a man suspicious of change. Yet in 1521, ahead of many men of his time on both sides of the Border, he looked towards an eventual union between Scotland and

England. His words may serve as an introduction to the new world of Stuart Britain:

> To God . . . I pray that He may grant such a peace to the Britons that one of its kings in a union of marriage may by just title gain both kingdoms – for any other way of reaching an assured peace I hardly see.

THE STUART CENTURY

8

KING AND PARLIAMENT, 1603-1640

THE period of 118 years during which the Welsh Tudors ruled in England showed big advances towards the making of a British people. A strong monarchy worked through an efficient Privy Council, controlled a loyal parliament, and commanded the support of the local gentry in their capacity as justices of the peace. Parliament had gained in importance by frequent royal use, giving its sanction to the main political changes of an eventful age. The Church had been brought under the direct control of the Crown, so that the final authority was the same as in the State. Through its simple and dignified liturgy and in its capacity as a national institution, that Church was destined in spite of many strains to command the affection of many Englishmen and the assent at least of most.

England had also developed her economic strength, applying capital to natural resources in a way that dimly foreshadowed the more opulent future. The greater part of this capital came from the merchant community, for with the help of chartered companies English commerce ranged more widely than ever before. The keel of a naval tradition was laid, too, in the enterprises of adventurers and privateers as well as in the national victory over the Armada. All these achievements were mirrored in a golden age of literature. Finally, there was the completion of the union of Wales with England and the improvement of Anglo-Scottish relations, pointing to the possibility of a fully united Britain.

James VI and I

The unification of the island was brought a clear stage nearer when James VI of Scotland, as the great-grandson of Henry VII's daughter Margaret by James IV, succeeded the last of the Tudors as England's James I. The two countries, while remaining separate in all else, now acknowledged a single king, and the crosses of their patron saints, St George and St Andrew, were merged in a new flag, the 'Union Jack', flown originally as a national emblem at the jack-staff of a ship. To England the accession of James came as a relief, for not till the very close of her reign did Elizabeth name him as her successor and it was feared that the next heir (James's cousin, Arabella Stuart) might be subject to Catholic influences.

James styled himself 'King of Great Britain': he only once revisited Scotland, so the flow of official business between London and Edinburgh helped to bind the two countries together. A legal bond was also established, when the English judges ruled, in an action about land ownership (Calvin's Case), that Scots and English born after 1603 shared a common nationality. Yet the king's high-sounding title hid a very real distinction between the two states under one crown.

His Power in Scotland

For Scotland James was a masterful king, ruling with a greater ruthlessness from the safety of London than he would have dared to do from Holyrood. "Here I sit," he said, "and govern it with my pen; I write and it is done." Through his Scottish ministers he controlled his Privy Council absolutely, and with its help and the rigging of elections he managed the committee called the 'Lords of the Articles', to whom the Scottish parliament in practice handed over its powers. This parliament met only once every few years to pass large quantities of Acts in a single day: it was no more than the rubber stamp of the King. The judges, too, were under his control and even local government, inasmuch as he influenced the election of burgh officials and set up justices of the peace.

With such a machinery of government, James attempted to make his commands respected in the wild and lawless mountains and islands of the north and north-west. Here some examples had to be made, though the means were harsh. The chief of the MacGregors, who terrorized the area of Loch Lomond, was taken, even though under a safe-conduct, and hanged and the very name of the clan abolished. The chiefs of the southern Hebrides were lured aboard a ship and imprisoned; they were not released until they promised to be answerable for the peace of their clansmen and to send their sons to Lowland schools. The lands of the earl in distant Orkney were taken over by the Crown and the earl and his son executed in Edinburgh. Yet the Outer Hebrides resisted James. In spite of attempts to wipe out the Gaelic language, it continued to be spoken there and widely through the north-west, while with their language many clans clung to their religion, the old Catholicism unshaken by the Reformation. Whatever theory might say, James more truly reigned over one and a half kingdoms than two and had no more than a claim on the rest of his inheritance.

James made himself master over the Church. Against the Calvinist idea that it should be governed by an elected General Assembly, James put forward rule by bishops chosen by himself. From stamping out freedom of debate in this Assembly, the King went on to restrict its meetings; on one occasion he banned a sitting and outlawed members bold enough to attend. The Assembly grew weaker while the powers of the bishops increased: they were seated in parliament, given authority over dioceses as in England, allowed to preside over church courts and reinstated in confiscated church lands. More and more James was drawn as by a magnet to the practices of the English Church. Most Scotsmen, however, were not attracted, and James divided them deeply from the Crown when he wrung the 'Five Articles of Perth' (1621) from a reluctant Parliament and General Assembly. Among these Articles that which insisted on kneeling at Holy Communion angered many Calvinists, who saw in it a clear step back to Roman practices. The Presbyterian Church under James, although cowed, was forced to await better times, when the rule of the 'Saints' was to lay the bishops low.

The Plantation of Ulster

Though a quieter Ireland would mean less trouble for him in the Hebrides, it was more as King of England than Scotland that James exercised his powers across the Irish Sea. To the original hostility between Anglo-Normans and Irish, the English Reformation added religious bitterness[1] – dangerous if Spain should want an Irish stepping-stone to English shores. In Elizabeth's reign adventurers, such as Drake, tried to secure against this threat by a colonization of Ulster. This led only to an Irish rebellion, which occupied the last years of Elizabeth and which in 1601 was made worse by the landing of 3,000 Spaniards at Kinsale. When James came to the throne, therefore, the need to quieten Ireland was real: hence a far more determined colonization of the whole north-east than the Elizabethans had attempted. Irish gave way to English and Scottish landowners and Ulster, from being the most Celtic part of Ireland, was made the most British. In the course of twenty years it became the home of about 20,000 Scottish Presbyterian farmers and English speculators – such as those citizens of London who gave their name to Londonderry. Other Scotsmen, bludgeoned into the beginnings of a new peace at home, found energies to spare for ventures farther afield than Ulster. Scottish settlers carried their name across the Atlantic to Nova Scotia under a charter given to Sir William Alexander in 1621. The colony was, however, abandoned to the French in 1632, partly because the settlers were few and the climate harsh, but also because its abandonment might help Charles I to obtain the balance of his French wife's dowry. The time when Scotsmen would help to people a British empire was not yet.

Divine Right of Kings

In Scotland James by a mixture of law, persuasion and force had given body to the name of king. In England, however, the monarchy he inherited from the Tudors was already a very solid institution. Elizabeth had inspired both respect and love, so that

[1] See p. 11.

the enthusiasm which greeted James's accession promised a support for his throne no less than had been given to her. Yet to manage his new subjects, and especially the English parliament, James would need tact. The rights of the Crown – the 'prerogative' powers – were supported by custom and law, but they were beginning to be challenged by strong forces in the state. If James attempted to underline his powers, to spell them out in order to assert them, he might merely weaken his rule.

James, however, was not only a king but a philosopher whose interest was statecraft and whose pleasure the defining of his own powers within the State. In 1598 he had produced his own textbook of kingly rule – *The True Law of Free Monarchies* – and later he lectured the English judges on the same theme:

> That which concerns the mystery of the King's power is not lawful to be disputed; for that is to wade into the weakness of Princes and to take away the mystical reverence that belongs unto them. . . . It is atheism and blasphemy to dispute what God can do. . . . It is presumption and high contempt in a subject to dispute what a King can do, or say that a King cannot do this or that; but rest with that which is the King's revealed will in his law.

James believed that a king's powers were given him by God and that he ruled by 'Divine Right'. At the outset such a claim seemed unnecessary, for custom already allowed the King great authority: in the control of the Church, for instance, in deciding foreign policy, in choosing ministers, and in shaping and administering the law. Moreover, when the later years of his reign brought successive challenges to his powers, the readiness with which James leant upon this theory of divine right could be seen as a confession of weakness – the borrowing of an extra prop for the throne.

James's son, Charles I, in the eventful years of his reign (1625–49), leant even more upon this prop, for whereas James was a man of argument, Charles was a man of conviction. Though he seldom spoke of divine right, he consistently based his conduct upon the deduction that it meant "A subject and a sovereign are clear different things". Dignified, devout, artistic, and athletic – in many ways all that a king should be – Charles (as we shall see in due course) was to bring ruin upon himself, and to a great extent also upon his country, by failing to keep his promises. This was because in his view a subject had no status for bargaining with his sovereign. But we must return to the situation as it was in 1603, when Charles as a child of three first entered the palace of Whitehall from which he was eventually to be led to the scaffold.

Puritan and Arminian

From very ancient times the Crown had played a large part in the government of the Church – in helping to choose the bishops, for instance, who were great officers of state. At the Reformation, when the King had displaced the Pope as head of the English Church, his power there became almost autocratic, though it was to some extent challenged in Elizabeth's reign (as we have already seen) both by Catholic recusants and by the various types of Puritans. When James came to the throne, Puritanism was more outspoken in its demands, which opposed not so much the royal supremacy but the use that was made of it. It was the duty of the Crown, in the opinion of the more extreme Puritans at least, to complete the overthrow of the papal system in England by abolishing the orders of bishop and priest and recognizing only 'presbyters', of whom some were lay elders and others called by their congregations to become ministers. What proportion of the population shared this view of church organization or the characteristic Puritan doctrine of predestination[1] it is impossible to say; but the bishops as a class were not well liked and there may have been wide support for the minimum Puritan demand for the removal of such relics of the Catholic past as the wearing of priestly vestments, the use of the sign of the cross in baptism, bowing at the name of Jesus, and kneeling to receive the Sacrament.

In the reign of James I this Puritan temper in the nation was challenged by an opposite opinion, called Arminianism after a Dutch theologian, Jacob Harmensen; he tried unsuccessfully to turn the Calvinists on the Continent back from predestination to the more liberal doctrine, held by Catholics and Lutherans, that

[1]See p. 3.

salvation is open to all men. In England the leader was Lancelot Andrewes, bishop of Winchester, master of fifteen languages, a great preacher, and highly regarded by Elizabeth as well as James. While firmly rejecting papal authority, Andrewes supported the Catholic structure of church government by bishops and priests, the use of vestments and ceremonial as part of a decent order of worship, and the retention of a Prayer Book drawn from Catholic as much as Protestant sources and teaching. James, who prided himself on his knowledge of theology, did not accept the Arminian view of salvation but welcomed the exaltation by English Arminians of the authority of the bishop. For his Scottish experience led him to regard the strict control of the lower clergy by bishops, who could be relied upon to elevate the dignity and authority of the Crown, as essential in order to suppress the democratic tendencies which he had learnt to associate with Puritan presbyterian ministers.

The Authorized Version of the Bible

Before he reached London the new king was presented with a petition from several hundred clergy, asking for fewer ceremonies and more preaching: at that time less than one half of those who had been ordained held the bishop's licence as being qualified to preach. As a result he summoned a conference at Hampton Court between his bishops and four leading Puritans from the universities, memorable for the decision to produce an improved translation of the Bible – one of the few tasks in which both parties in the Church could collaborate. The 47 translators who made the Authorized Version of 1611 built of course upon the labours of other men – nine-tenths of their New Testament is said to be recognizably founded on Tyndale – but they wrought and polished a masterpiece of poetic prose, which for more than two and a half centuries held an unchallenged pre-eminence in church and home. Its influence on all religious teaching and discussion was profound. But as the first English 'classic', read by everyone who could read at all and by most people with reverential awe, the Authorized Version also influenced secular literature, both prose and verse, and even the common form of speech. Thus a modern American scholar writes: "One testimony to the way in which the

Bible – and the Book of Common Prayer – have interpenetrated English life is the magical language and rhythm of rustic speech in Hardy's novels."[1]

Otherwise, the Conference achieved only some minor reforms over such matters as the provision of more preachers, for an unfortunate allusion to 'presbyteries' reminded James of his sufferings in Scotland and of what he took to be their lesson: 'No bishop, no king.' The sequel was the strengthening of the powers of the bishops, a proclamation which required that all clergymen should accept in full the rules for church services, and the expulsion from their livings of the three hundred who refused to obey. Having thus created by his actions the first important body of Nonconformists outside the Church, James continued to regard the Puritans primarily as a political danger. Another indirect consequence, which seemed wholly insignificant at the time, was that a hundred persecuted Independents, after an unsuccessful migration from the eastern counties to Holland, sailed from Plymouth in November 1620 and made their landfall at Cape Cod; only one half of these Pilgrim Fathers survived the first winter to establish the Puritan faith in the New World.

Charles I, in contrast to his father, was an Arminian from personal religious conviction. He believed in a church which preserved the beauty and dignity of ancient traditions and he hated the idea of predestination, with its implication that low-born men might be fore-ordained to be saints and called of God to lay down the law to their betters. In return, his clergy laid increasing stress upon divine right and what followed from it – that resistance to the king was a sin. In the words of a sermon by a royal chaplain:

> No subject may, without hazard of his own damnation in rebelling against God, question or disobey the will and pleasure of his sovereign.

Accordingly, when the see of Canterbury fell vacant in 1633, Charles chose an out-and-out Arminian, William Laud, as archbishop, with a programme of establishing authority in the Church of England and eradicating its Puritan tendencies. Since every important body of religious opinion still believed in a single

[1] D. Bush, *English Literature in the Earlier Seventeenth Century*, p. 72.

national church, the only question at issue was who was to control it.

Conflict Over Foreign Policy

Opposition to the king's prerogative in church matters was accompanied by attacks on his powers in foreign policy. Elizabeth had been revered to a great extent because of her leadership of her people in a resistance to Spain which united the causes of Protestantism and national defence. James, who was pacific by disposition and saw no profit in continuing the war, made peace with Spain in 1604 and in general followed a pro-Spanish line of policy. This was all the more remarkable as his reign began with the unearthing of successive plots to kidnap, depose, and annihilate him, each of which had a Catholic background. The third of these, in which Guy Fawkes was found tending his 36 barrels of gunpowder in the vaults on the eve of the state opening of parliament overhead, was commemorated by a special service in the Prayer Book and the institution of a public holiday which lasted until Victorian times. Its effect on the English people as a whole was to strengthen and perpetuate their fear and dislike both of the Catholic minority at home and of the great Catholic powers of the Continent. But James enforced only intermittently and with reluctance the new anti-Catholic laws now passed by parliament.

Instead, the King was largely dominated by the Spanish ambassador Gondomar, who even secured the execution of the last of the great Elizabethan adventurers, Sir Walter Ralegh, nominally for the plot to depose James, but actually because he had involved himself against royal orders in fighting Spaniards in South America. But the royal policy became increasingly complicated after the outbreak of the Thirty Years War in 1618. James was a pacifist, but he did not wish to see the Protestant cause in Germany completely overthrown; he was the friend of Spain, but Spain's allies deprived Frederick the Elector Palatine, the husband of James's daughter Elizabeth, of his throne and country. The sequel was a double failure. First, James sent his son Charles with the favourite Buckingham to carry out a long-planned scheme for a royal marriage in Madrid, in connection with which the Spaniards were to be induced to do something for Frederick. After hanging about for five months in Madrid, Charles and Buckingham returned empty-handed, to be greeted with bonfires of rejoicing by the anti-Catholic populace. This was in 1623, and next year James tried the alternative of an expedition to rescue the Palatinate, but parliament grudged the expense, even in a Protestant cause: the result was a military fiasco. To make matters worse, the alliance which it involved with the Dutch had necessitated the tame acceptance of a cold-blooded massacre by them of English merchants on Amboina, resulting in the forced abandonment of the Spice Islands trade by the East India Company.

Charles I did no better. Immediately after his accession, he carried through arrangements already made for his marriage to a Catholic French princess, Henrietta Maria, in hopes of an alliance with France against Spain. A sea and land attack on Cadiz, however, failed miserably. Four years later, when his quarrel with parliament made continued warfare financially inexpedient, he was in the unpromising position of having both France and Spain as enemies and had failed to save his small ally, the French Huguenots besieged in La Rochelle. Peace was restored, and England became a mere onlooker at the later stages of the great Thirty Years War on the Continent. In 1639, when the Dutch and Spanish navies fought a pitched battle in English territorial waters off Dungeness, the only reaction on which the Government ventured was to authorize Spanish troops to march over English soil from Plymouth to Dover so as to circumvent the Dutch control of the English Channel.

The prestige of Drake's homeland had sunk very low. In 1621 parliament had aroused James's intense indignation by resolving that

> the urgent affairs concerning the King, state and defence of the realm . . . are proper subjects and matter of . . . debate in parliament.

The King with his own hand tore this Protestation out of the still existing volume of the Commons' Journals; but neither he nor his son could conjure away the growing resentment at the use made of the royal prerogative in the conduct of foreign relations.

Parliament and the King's Servants

It was, of course, also a part of the royal prerogative that the king was entitled to choose and dismiss his own ministers. These were members of the Privy Council, which was still the primary instrument of royal government, initiating Bills in Parliament, controlling the prerogative law courts, and sending out orders to the justices of peace in the countryside. The great officers of state had their seat in it of right – men such as Robert Cecil, the son of Elizabeth's great minister, who was secretary of state to James, or the ambitious and industrious London merchant, Lionel Cranfield, who rose to the treasurership. Into this body of experienced men James introduced a different sort of servant – the royal favourite, whose main qualification was charm of person. The first was Robert Carr, who accompanied James from Scotland as his page: after rising to an earldom and the office of lord chamberlain, he was implicated in a murder scandal which reflected deep discredit upon the whole life of James's Court. George Villiers, the younger son of a Leicestershire knight, rose in the same way but to greater heights. In 1614 he was the King's cupbearer, in 1619 lord high admiral, in 1623 duke of Buckingham – the first new dukedom since Northumberland's in Edward's reign. As Clarendon[1] says in his *History of the Rebellion*:

> His ascent was so quick that it seemed rather a flight than a growth; and he was such a darling of fortune that he was at the top before he was seen at the bottom.

Buckingham's meteoric rise inspired jealousy among the professional councillors and mistrust in the nation at large. For he sailed close to the Catholic wind, leaning towards Rome himself and marrying a wife who, though a conforming Anglican, was a Catholic at heart. His absolute dominion over the minds of James and Charles, coupled with his inefficiency as a commander, extravagance, and reckless amassing of privileges for his family and friends, fanned the hatred of the Commons to fever-pitch. "The duke of Buckingham," said Chief Justice Coke, "is the cause

[1] See pp. 165, 171.

of all our miseries . . . the grievance of grievances." So keen was the resentment that the House of Commons repeatedly demanded the duke's dismissal, only to meet with the blank refusal of Charles I: "I will not allow any of my servants to be questioned amongst you, much less such as are of eminent place and near unto me."

In August 1628 the rule of the favourite ended with his murder at the hands of a discontented army officer. Thirteen more years were to pass before parliament was in a position to assert, through the execution of Strafford, a power of punishing ministers who ruled against its will.

The King Above the Law?

The king's position as a law-giver goes back to the very earliest times: as late as the Tudor period it was still in some respects being strengthened. The ultimate supremacy of the Pope over the Church courts had then passed to the king and new prerogative courts had been set up, where there were no juries and law was administered in the royal interests. It is not surprising, then, that in the intensely legalistic seventeenth century James I should claim that all law, whether it took the form of statutes or of judgements in the common law courts, flowed from him as the fountain head. In addition he claimed the right – which the Tudors had exercised without challenge – to declare or set aside law by proclamation. Such law-making by prerogative had been opposed by Chief Justice Sir Edward Coke, who argued that even the Crown was subject to the law, which stood above all persons and causes. One of the most learned of all judges, he searched far into the past for precedents to establish his case, and found one in Magna Carta, by which he claimed that King John had been bound to observe the law. "Magna Carta," he declared in 1628, "is such a fellow that he will have no sovereign." Thus was seventeenth-century antiquarianism put to practical use, for Magna Carta had hitherto been regarded with general veneration but not as applicable to current needs. Coke's view won wide acceptance, and the great charter was henceforth seen as a bastion of English liberty even by the moderates in parliament, such as Sir Edward Dering, who declared:

I shall be very glad to see that good old decrepit law of Magna Carta, which hath been kept so long and lain bedridden, as it were – I shall be glad to see it walk abroad again with new vigour and lustre.

Coke's opposition to the Crown had long since cost him his judgeship, but he was listened to with great respect in parliament, which to an increasing extent considered that its whole existence was threatened, not only by the vague claims of divine right but by the whole development of the royal prerogative. All the lines pointed the same way. If the king's religious policy succeeded, Puritanism would be brought to an end; if his foreign policy went unopposed, then Catholicism would triumph in Europe and might well recross the Channel; if the king could maintain in office such ministers as Buckingham, then parliament was reduced to a cipher in administration; and finally, if the king could claim to be above the law, then their functions as a legislative body might be deemed superfluous.

The above is a rough sketch of the position as viewed through the eyes of the parliamentary politicians. There was of course another side to the argument. Historically, the demands they were making were so wildly in excess of parliament's earlier share in the government of England that they could fairly be called revolutionary. Practically, too, they ran counter to the general trend away from representative assemblies and towards autocracy in most parts of the Continent. But two factors gave special force to their demands. One was the steady growth during a period of rather more than two centuries of a new class of society, with an economic strength which gave it self-confidence and a social cohesion which had enabled it to turn the House of Commons into 'the organ of the gentry'.[1] The other factor was the pervasive emotional influence of Puritanism. Its belief in individualism appealed to the rising gentry who applied themselves seriously to the improvement and extension of their estates, to prudent merchants impatient of royal charters and other restrictions upon economic enterprise, and to lawyers for whom unbridled competition among individuals meant profitable arguments in the courts of common law. Puritan respectability, on the other hand,

[1] The expression used by R. H. Tawney.

pointed an accusing finger at the laxity and extravagance of the Court.

Parliament and Finance: Monopolies

We may now turn to the subject of finance, since this provided the field for the direct trial of strength between the two forces now striving for mastery of the machine of state. The charge of extravagance was not mere prejudice. James I in the first seven years that he was on the throne gave away £88,000 to Scotsmen alone, and in 1611 and 1612 another £63,600 was bestowed on peers, mostly those of Scottish extraction. Buckingham had £50,000 from Charles I in 1625 and £40,000 more in 1627 on a kind of expenses account; and by 1630 about £125,000 a year was being spent on pensions, partly for services rendered but much of it as 'an extravagant system of outdoor relief to a minority of highly favoured noblemen.'[1] But it is also clear that legitimate government expenditure was rising rapidly. Under the influence of an increase in population, estimated at 30 per cent during 1600–42, the inflation of prices continued. From 1624 onwards the normal cost of administration was heavily swollen by warfare on the Continent which James had tried hard to avoid.

As for revenue, at the end of James's reign the yield of the customs (thanks partly to the change in price levels) was two and a half times what it had been at the beginning. But this was now the king's biggest source of regular income, for the rents of Crown lands did not keep pace with the inflation and in any case the early Stuarts followed Elizabeth's policy of disposing of Crown lands as a way of rewarding courtiers and officials. The sale of honours and titles, such as the new rank of baronet, roused hostility among influential members of the older peerage and was suspended by Charles in 1628. And as its difficulties increased, the Crown found it harder to meet them by borrowing from its subjects, who doubted its capacity to repay them. This applied even to the tax-farmers, a body of gentry and merchants who from 1604 onwards paid a lump sum in return for the right to collect the customs duties;

[1] L. Stone, *The Crisis of the Aristocracy 1558–1641*, p. 421.

they had often been induced to lend the king additional sums on the security of the customs.

Considerable importance therefore attached to the employment of monopolies as a form of indirect taxation, however clumsy and costly. In spite of Elizabeth's acknowledgment that the royal prerogative in this respect had been badly if unintentionally abused, by 1621 there were said to be 700 monopolies again in existence. Monopolists paid a premium and in some cases a percentage of profits for their concession, which brought in revenue to the Crown without the expense and trouble of collecting it. But for the subject their activities meant that he had to pay a higher price for what was often an inferior commodity, produced without the stimulus of competition. In some cases the scandal lay chiefly in the big profit pocketed by the holder of the monopoly from licensing other people to trade: in 1612 the earls of Salisbury, Suffolk, and Northampton were making respectively £7,000, £5,000 and £4,500 a year through rights of control over the sale of silk, currants, and starch. In other cases a trade was ruined by mismanagement, as when a future lord mayor of London, William Cockayne, secured a monopoly of cloth-finishing, in connection with which the export of unfinished cloth was prohibited. The Dutch refused to buy the home-finished article, and by the time the trade was handed back to the Merchant Adventurers to be run in the old way, part of the market was irrecoverable.

Monopolies were particularly obnoxious to the class of rising but not yet very wealthy merchants, who could not afford to buy a share in one for themselves and were adversely affected by the operations of others. They were well represented in parliament, with the result that in 1624, when James needed parliamentary support for his foreign policy, he found it prudent to allow his prerogative in this matter to be restricted by the Statute of Monopolies. This conceded a 14-year monopoly for any genuine invention – the beginning of modern patent protection – but forbade the grant of any other type of monopoly to any individual. Since parliament had no general wish to interfere with the privileges of overseas trading companies or the surviving gilds, charters granted to 'corporations, companies, and fellowships' were exempted from the statute. Monopolies accordingly continued during the first fifteen years of Charles I's reign, though the holders had now to be organized as a group, which was often contrived under the patronage of some courtier. In 1639 the Treasury was receiving nearly £100,000 a year from such organizations as the 'London Society of Soap Boilers', who paid £10,000 down for their charter and promised £8 more for every ton of soap they sold. As they had the right to ban all rival soaps after testing for suitability, their own sales should not have been difficult to arrange, for the washing public was at their mercy.

The strength of parliament lay above all in its control of taxation. Throughout the reign of James I it struggled to restrict the king's power – which had the support of the law courts – of levying extra customs duties or 'impositions'. On Charles's accession it carried the matter further by offering only an annual grant of the older customs duties of 'tonnage and poundage', hitherto granted to each sovereign for life. Charles therefore resorted to such measures as the exaction of forced loans. But by 1628 he needed money for his military expenditure so badly that he gave his assent to a new limitation of the royal powers in return for a grant of direct taxes. The Petition of Right (1628) sought to close the door to the levying of taxation without consent of parliament, both by an explicit statement of its illegality and by prohibiting imprisonment without trial, martial law, and forced billeting of troops – the three instruments employed in raising the forced loans. Next year, however, the quarrel flared up again, when parliament claimed disingenuously that the Petition of Right also debarred the king from collecting indirect taxes without their consent, such as the much disputed tonnage and poundage. Before its proceedings were interrupted by royal order, the House of Commons passed three resolutions, in which whoever enforced the payment of, or voluntarily paid, the tonnage and poundage to which parliament had not agreed was bracketed with the introducer of popery or Arminianism as 'a capital enemy to this kingdom and commonwealth'.

Prerogative Government, 1629–40

"Parliaments," said Charles I, "are of the nature of cats, they ever grow cursed with age." However, there was little risk of his parliaments being allowed to fall into this fatal degeneracy. Between 1625 and 1629 he had summoned three, but their four sessions lasted only a little longer than twelve months; and he now dissolved the houses, which were not summoned again for eleven years. The mere fact that parliament could be set aside for so long looked ominous, especially to those who were aware of the situation in France, where parliament had not met since 1614. The grievances which had been voiced at Westminster continued to heap themselves up, while the financial ones in particular assumed a new importance, since it was by financial exactions of all kinds that the Crown was asserting – or from another standpoint, reasserting – its ability to rule unfettered by parliament and its grants.

The royal government was not universally regarded as a form of tyranny: it commended itself to High Churchmen, as we shall see, and there were many benefits for the poorer classes. The Privy Council and the prerogative courts were very active during this period in enforcing the enclosure laws, the poor law, and the Statute of Artificers, and in their anxiety to avoid unrest took measures to stop employers from turning workers adrift at times of trade depression. In the matter, too, of aristocratic violence it appears that "The Privy Council and Star Chamber now felt able to deal more severely with such cases as came before them."[1] But the overriding interest of the Crown was financial, as can be clearly seen in its handling of the big schemes for draining the fens, in which James I had secured the services of the Dutch engineer, Vermuyden. In 1638 Charles himself became the 'undertaker' of the project, on the basis that he would eventually receive 57,000 acres out of a total reclaimed area of 400,000 acres; meanwhile, he was taking a full third of the part actually drained. The rights of fishermen and fowlers were extinguished by levying a drainage tax which they were too poor to pay; when the Civil War came, much of the reclaimed land was seized back by the fenmen.

Tonnage and poundage continued to be collected without any parliamentary sanction, in spite of the protests of merchants. The Crown lawyers burrowed into ancient records for obsolete laws which could be made to serve again. Thus men whose income ex-

[1] L. Stone, *The Crisis of the Aristocracy 1558–1641*, p. 238.

ceeded £40 a year were fined for having failed to apply for knighthood; others who had turned ancient forest into farmland were fined as though the royal privileges in the forests still had meaning. The tax-farmers were outraged by an increase in the 'rent' for their farms, and a much wider section of the community felt themselves aggrieved by the spread of monopoly grants to companies. But the financial grievances of all the moneyed classes came to a head in the matter of 'ship money' – a contribution to the cost of the Navy which had long been levied in lieu of actual ships from the seaports and coastal counties: this was now extended to towns and counties inland. In 1635 John Hampden challenged the legality of the payment demanded from his Buckinghamshire estate, but in spite of the Petition of Right seven out of the twelve judges supported the king's claim 'on such grounds and reasons as every stander-by was able to swear was not law'. Swear they might, but by this time the royal budget balanced as it had not done for more than a generation, which meant that Charles and his advisers might be able to dispense permanently with parliaments.

The place of the dead Buckingham in the councils of the king was taken by Thomas Wentworth (later earl of Strafford) and bishop Laud. The latter had been an intimate of Buckingham, but Wentworth was a member of the parliamentary opposition until 1628, when he came to believe that it was in danger of creating a revolutionary body. "The authority of a king," he said, "is the keystone which closeth up the arch of order and government." As a believer in good government, he then placed his immense energies at the king's disposal. The head of a great Yorkshire family, he became a dominant figure as president of the Council of the North, retaining this post even after he was made (in 1633) lord deputy of Ireland. There his name was a byword for ruthless and efficient administration.

In the same year Laud, on his promotion to the archbishopric of Canterbury, addressed to him the famous words, "In the state indeed I am for *Thorough.*" Though Laud himself was chiefly concerned with 'putting things through', as we might term it, in church affairs, he was instrumental in securing the appointment of Juxon, the bishop of London, as the first ecclesiastic to hold the office of lord treasurer since the reign of Henry VII. Like Charles,

Laud was a convinced Arminian, and (unlike Lancelot Andrewes) he believed in making the Church conform to a single pattern. The Puritans were therefore to be forced to observe the ceremonies of the Prayer Book, to submit their writings for the censorship of Church authorities, to abandon their 'lecturers' (private preachers financed by wealthy Puritans), and to accept discipline imposed by the archbishop and the prerogative Court of High Commission. The persecution under Laud took no man's life – a fact which did not stop the House of Commons from insisting on his execution in the last year of the Civil War – but in a deeply religious age it outraged many consciences. In a country which had long lost the habit of rebellion, there was no immediate open resistance; but a widespread feeling of discontent (to which trade depression also contributed) caused many thousands of Englishmen to emigrate to Massachusetts, so that a Puritan New England arose as a kind of would-be counterbalance to old England.[1]

The Scottish National Covenant

But the application of the same religious policy in the northern kingdom produced an explosion. Brought up in England from the age of three, Charles had even less natural sympathy than his father with the Scottish Kirk. On his first visit to Scotland in 1633 he created a new bishopric of Edinburgh, and in the same year church finances were overhauled, with the result that the clergy obtained a legal minimum stipend about three centuries ahead of their Anglican brethren. But the nobles began to fear the loss of the church lands of which they had possessed themselves at the Reformation, while the people at large took alarm at the issue in 1635 of a Book of Canons, without the approval of either the General Assembly or the parliament. This gave the king the title of Head of thc Church, and announced that a new service book would be introduced and made compulsory. In Scottish eyes this new liturgy proved to be more 'Papistical' than the English Book of Common Prayer, which Laud would have preferred to impose. On 23 July 1637 the attempt to use it in St Giles's church, the cathedral of the new bishop and the Scottish equivalent of Westminster

[1] See p. 215.

Abbey, provoked a riot touched off by the throwing of a stool at the minister's head – an approving tablet still marks the spot where the thrower sat.

The sequel was the signing with due solemnity of a National Covenant for 'the defence and preservation of the true religion, liberties, and laws of the kingdom', first by the four orders of nobility, gentry (lairds), ministers, and burgesses in Edinburgh, and then by the people at large. The Scottish bishops fled to England for succour. But they left behind them a very formidable body of opponents among men of all classes, whose patriotic feelings and warlike instincts were bound up with a religious obligation that rested upon the conscience of the individual. As the marquis of Argyll, the most powerful Scottish nobleman of the day, was to say two decades later, when his adhesion to the Covenant had brought him on to the scaffold:

> God hath laid engagements upon Scotland. We are tied by Covenants to religion and reformation . . . and it passeth the power of all the magistrates under heaven to absolve from the oath of God.

Thus the English parliamentary revolution began in Scotland, where religion more than politics was the driving-force.

9

THE CLASH OF ARMS

In 1639–40 the interaction of events in Scotland and England was decisive for the fate of both kingdoms. Having failed in negotiations with the Scottish Covenanters, Charles with difficulty raised an army in the northern counties. But when his cavalry had crossed the border, it beat a precipitate retreat into Berwick before the infantry of the Covenanters under the command of Alexander Leslie, a veteran of the Thirty Years War on the Continent. For nearly twelve months an uneasy truce prevailed, during which Charles summoned the English Parliament, only to dissolve it after a three weeks' session (April–May, 1640) when money for war was refused and it seemed likely that the Commons might openly proclaim their support for their fellow-Puritans in Scotland. The latter meanwhile, not content with strengthening their army on the border, also reconstituted their parliament after the King had prorogued it, and replaced the Lords of the Articles by a more representative committee working in close agreement with the General Assembly of the Church.

The Scots at Durham

Wentworth, now earl of Strafford and the King's chief lay adviser, offered the help of an army from Ireland to reduce the Scots to obedience, and pending its arrival went himself to take charge in the north. But he had got no farther than York when Leslie's army, after a skirmish at Newburn, crossed the Tyne and drove the royal garrison out of Newcastle. By the end of August the Scots were in control of all Northumberland and Durham and of the northern coal trade. On the advice of a Council of Peers, which he summoned to York, Charles suspended the so-called Bishops' Wars at the cost of a payment of £850 a day to the Scottish army, too large a sum to be raised by any extra-parliamentary method. In November the 'Short Parliament', already mentioned, was followed by the first of the many sessions of what is known to history as the 'Long Parliament'. The eleven years of personal rule were over; parliamentary institutions in Britain had survived their most dangerous crisis.

The opposition to the King was led by John Pym, a Somerset gentleman who had first entered the Commons in 1614 and was a persuasive as well as an experienced debater; he was a Presbyterian and had close relations with the City merchants. Pym also had close relations with the Scots army in the north, for he was as aware as they were of the value of that army to the parliamentary cause. "No fear of raising the parliament as long as the lads about Newcastle sit still," said one of the Scots. In fact, they did not go home until the following summer, when they were paid in full and were followed to Edinburgh by the King himself. He then gave Leslie an earldom and made numerous concessions to the Scottish parliament, in the vain hope of detaching it from the side of the parliament at Westminster, which was just completing its triumphant first session.

First Session of the Long Parliament

All the classes which had been injured by Charles's personal government gained some redress: the gentry in the ending of proceedings to enforce knighthood, in the reduction of the areas of the royal forests and the abolition of ship money; the merchants in an Act abolishing tonnage and poundage and a ban upon impositions; and the lawyers through the abolition of the prerogative courts. And the security of parliament itself was assured by the Triennial Act, which provided machinery for holding an election automatically if three years should pass without a session of parliament, and by a special Act to forbid the dissolution without its own consent of the parliament then sitting. These were revolutionary measures, biting deeply into the royal prerogative. But few members were content with these gains alone: they wished to pull down those royal ministers who had been the servants of divine right. Before 1640 was out, Strafford and Laud were impeached for high treason and sent to the Tower. Impeachment, however, failed, since it was not treasonable for ministers to carry out royal commands and there was no proof of the accusation that could bear investigation. While Laud was left in prison, Strafford was condemned by an Act of Attainder which, without attempting to prove it, declared that he was a traitor and should die. This was no law without the King's consent but, with the London mob outside his Whitehall palace threatening the Queen's life, Charles gave Strafford over to the scaffold.

All this brought civil war near – except for the fact that Charles was incapable of war because he had no party. For nine months parliament was united, but in the late summer of 1641 a split opened which by autumn was a chasm. This rift, reflected in the nation, gave the King followers who would fight.

Events Leading to War

There were two main issues: the government of the Church and the control of the army. The Church question concerned the place of the Prayer Book and bishops. The extreme Calvinists wished to abolish the episcopal system 'root and branch', but these were a minority in the House and in the country generally. Most of the Commons were prepared to continue with an amended Prayer Book and less powerful bishops: early in the following year the latter were deprived of their seats in the House of Lords. Prayer Book and bishops at least helped to preserve a traditional framework for the Church and to defend it against a flood of radical changes.

The question of the control of the army was brought to the forefront by the Irish revolt. When Strafford fell before the triumphant English Parliament, the Catholic Irish rose to avenge the wrongs of many years. Some thousands of English and Scottish settlers were massacred, still larger numbers died of privation, and refugees poured across the Irish Sea with tales of Irish ferocity, which were rushed into print under such titles as *The Rebels' Turkish Tyranny*.

An army would have to be raised, but who was to control it? His bitter opponents dared not risk putting a force at the disposal of the King, while others saw reason to dread the power that its control by parliament might put into the hands of Puritan extremists. In these circumstances the conviction grew among more moderate men that, if it came to a choice between the tyrannical tendencies of the Crown and a Puritan tyranny, then the former was preferable. Reform had gone far enough: to go farther would be revolution. Both in Church and State they began to look for the old paths.

Pym was aware that the initiative was slipping away from him, so he tried to seize it again with a Grand Remonstrance which recounted point by point the grievances that the Commons had accumulated against the King from the start of the reign. Once passed it was to be published, so that the people could judge the issue and see the nature of the threat to liberty. It was in fact a revolutionary appeal by the Commons to the people, causing one of the moderate members of parliament, Sir Edward Dering, to exclaim indignantly:

> When I first heard of a Remonstrance..... I did not dream that we should remonstrate downwards and tell stories to the people.

Many moderates swung to the Royalists in the House and, when the Remonstrance was passed by a mere eleven votes, it was plain for all England to see that the King had a following in the House which, on some issues at any rate, was little smaller than Pym's. The isolation of the Crown was ended and a civil war a possibility. Emboldened by his success, the King attempted to arrest Pym and four other leading members in the House of Commons; but they had fled to the City, which called out its train-bands to protect the parliament-men. This was on both sides the language of war; attention was now turned from the debating chamber to the battlefield.

The Two Sides

The war that broke out in August 1642 was not, however, a clear-cut conflict between King and Parliament. The King took the field with about one-third of the Commons members on his side and a big majority of the peers. It has also to be noticed that the situation was more fluid than we might expect: some MPs changed over during the war – Dering, for instance, resigned the king's commission in 1643 – and some noble houses were so inconsistent in their views that two earls charging in the King's Guard at the battle of Edgehill faced their heirs in the parliamentary ranks. Very broadly speaking, it was a war between the more and the less developed parts of the nation. The parliamentarians or Roundheads had their chief strength in the prosperous south-east, in London and almost all the ports, and in the inland trading towns. The royalists or Cavaliers were strongest in the feudal and partly Catholic north, in Wales, and in the rural counties of western England. Although there was a minority of opponents waiting for its chance in every district, the fact that Parliament controlled London and other sources of economic power (such as the customs levied at the ports) gave it the better chance in a prolonged conflict.

Except for individuals prompted by strong religious and moral feelings, such as the Bedfordshire tinker's son, John Bunyan, the poorest classes were not much concerned with the war. When the armies were assembling on Marston Moor in the third year of the conflict, a labourer is reported to have expressed surprise on learning that King and Parliament had 'fallen out'; and in the final campaign in the south-west the peasantry mustered as 'Clubmen' to defend their cattle impartially against the depredations of either side. London was probably an exception, as the feelings of the mob had been worked up during the excitements of the Long Parliament: at all events, we are told that all classes co-operated in throwing up the earthworks against the royal advance upon the city in the autumn of 1642. Methods of conscription were tried by both sides, but the fighting was done mainly by the classes which had a stake in the country, landowners leading out their tenants and merchants sending their apprentices to muster in the train-bands.

Arms and Tactics

In both camps, if men of position fought in the ranks, they did so in the cavalry, usually with their own horses: their pay, three times the infantryman's, reflected their superior status. Their armour consisted of a light helmet or 'pot', a 'back and breast' of iron, and a leather coat underneath; their weapons, a sword and a pair of flintlock pistols; and the tactics they were taught were to charge home, so as to bring the weight of the horse into the attack. There was a further social division in the infantry, where the pikeman was thought superior to the musketeer. Certainly he needed a superior physique to wield a sixteen-foot pike while wearing armour and sometimes encumbered with a sword as well. Yet musketeers proved increasingly useful as the war went on, even though their matchlocks took long to load and could not be fired without the use of loops of 'match', which had to be kept alight continuously, and two sorts of powder; flying sparks provided an extra hazard on windy days, while the glowing match was liable to betray the musketeer's exact position at night.

The pattern of the war was one of innumerable skirmishes and fairly frequent sieges, but big battles were few. This was partly at least because the rival forces did not advance against each other

Plate 14. *The House of Commons in 1624.* This is probably the earliest picture of the House and indicates its separate importance in the 17th century. The Chamber is St. Stephen's Chapel, where the Commons sat from 1549 to 1834, and the aisle dividing the members is a reminder of the arrangement of the chapel choir stalls. Obviously the room is too small: there were 467 members in 1603 and there was never space for all of them. The Speaker is in the chair and, in front of him, the Clerk of the House records the day's business in the Journals. On the Speaker's right, in the front row, the few Privy Councillors sit – the royal spokesmen in the House. At the bottom of the picture, an offender against the privileges of the House kneels bareheaded at the bar in the custody of the Serjeant-at-Arms. (Cf. text p. 249.)

Plate 15. *Westminster in 1647.* This is another Hollar engraving. On the left is St. Stephen's Chapel, where the House of Commons met (see plate 14) and from which the Five Members came down to the river steps and escaped from Charles I to the City. In the centre is Westminster Hall, where Strafford and Charles I were tried and on the right is the Abbey – as yet without its western towers, which were not added till the early 18th century.

Plate 16. *"The Royal Oak of Britain".* A bitter Royalist cartoon against Cromwell and his rule. Cromwell stands directing the cutting down of the oak tree which represents the ancient English State: Crown, Church, law and popular liberties are all doomed. But Cromwell's henchmen will themselves be judged: those who haul on the tree ('the fickle mob rushing downhill') will fall into the abyss when at last the oak gives, and the pigs who feed on dropped acorns are only fattening themselves for slaughter. Even those who lop off and carry away the branches are fools, dismissed with the comment: 'when the tree falls anyone can gather wood'. The only solid part of the scene is the house which sums up Cromwell's rule – 'the maw of money, the Charybdis of taxes'. But Cromwell himself stands on 'a slippery place' over the mouth of hell, and the heavens thunder their judgement – 'slowly but surely'.

Plate 14

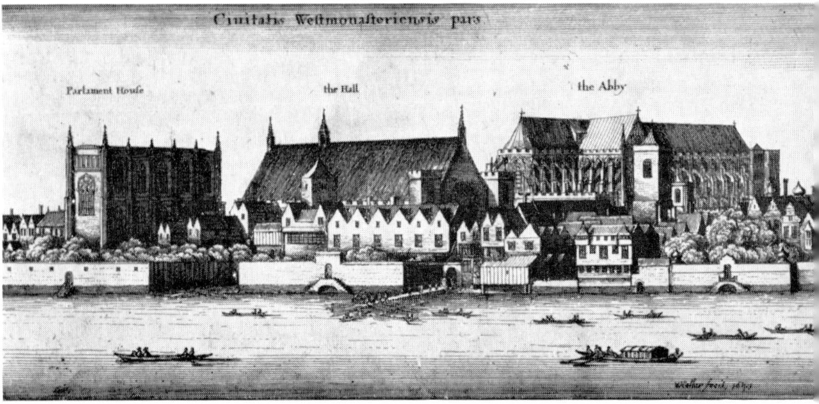

Plate 15

Plate 16

from firmly and completely held rear areas. On the contrary, not only cities, such as Gloucester, Hull, and Plymouth, but defensible mansions, such as Basing House, the home of the Catholic marquis of Winchester, and even, in the case of Lichfield, a fortified cathedral, stood out like islands in hostile seas. It is significant that the only big strategic design of the war, namely the King's plan for a triple advance against London in 1643, came to nothing because his troops refused to leave unconquered enemy strongholds in their rear. Some of the sieges were therefore key events, such as that of Bristol, which capitulated very quickly to the king's nephew, Prince Rupert, and the defence of Gloucester later in the same year (1643), which acted like a tonic to the flagging parliamentary cause.

The royalists had brought their heavy guns to Gloucester, and they employed miners from the Forest of Dean to help to breach the walls, and also to divert the stream which drove the corn mills and to try to cut off the supply of drinking water. But the townspeople countermined the royalist diggings and reinforced their walls with earth embankments. They pumped in water from the Severn and set up treadmills to grind their corn. They replied to airborne propaganda – papers attached to arrows, reading "Essex is beaten like a dog" – by setting lights in towers, so that the London train-bands under his command, as they came over the crest of the Cotswolds on the last stage of their long march, should know at once that they were still holding out. And in the end the siege was raised, the royal troops abandoning their water-logged mines and trenches as the banners of the earl of Essex fluttered into sight.

The Battles: Marston Moor

In the First Civil War of 1642–6 three battles may, however, be singled out as crucial events. Edgehill, in October 1642, was the first general engagement. Indecisive in itself, it revealed a brilliant cavalry leader in the King's nephew, Prince Rupert, who had seen action on the Continent at sixteen; it also marked a stage in the meteoric rise of Captain Oliver Cromwell. A Huntingdonshire squire (remotely connected with Thomas Cromwell), he had

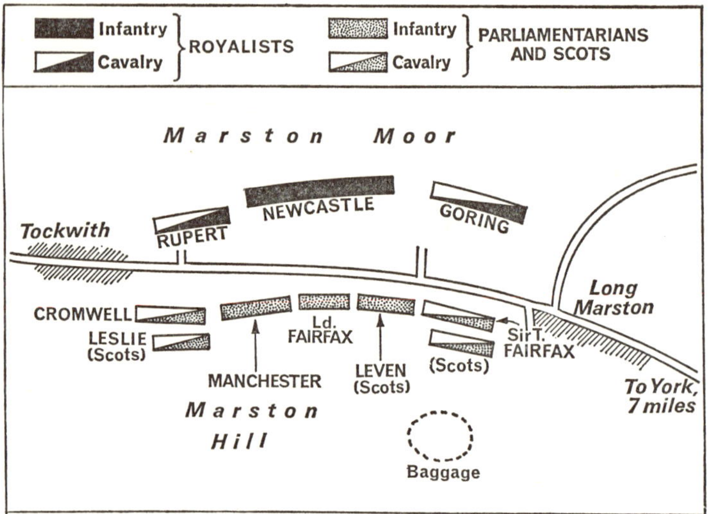

BATTLE OF MARSTON MOOR 1644

had nothing to do with military matters until past the age of forty, but had become an MP in 1628 and figured prominently in the early debates of the Long Parliament as a Puritan of deeply held convictions. When war began, he raised and took command of a troop of sixty horse from the eastern counties; from Edgehill onwards, his resolute and disciplined leadership of cavalry carried him steadily upwards. Both the prince from the Palatinate and the fenland squire figured prominently in the battles of Marston Moor in 1644 and Naseby in 1645. The latter was decisive in the sense that it disposed of the King's last full field army; but Marston Moor deserves special attention, not only because larger armies took part than at Naseby but because Marston Moor settled the fate of the north; having lost the north, the most the King could have achieved by a victory at Naseby was a stalemate.

Apart from its size, Marston Moor stands out as the one big battle in which the King's forces were pitted against the armies raised by the parliaments of both kingdoms. Shortly before the death of Pym in December 1643, they had joined together in the Solemn League and Covenant, involving the adoption by England of a new settlement of religion, to be made 'according to the word of God and the example of the best reformed Churches'. Though the Scottish presbyterian system was not expressly named in this formula, it was understood that England was to go presbyterian, both by the Scots and by the English House of Commons, which was now mainly presbyterian in outlook. In January 1644, accordingly, Alexander Leslie (earl of Leven) and his nephew David Leslie, who was likewise a veteran of the Thirty Years War, had begun to move south with 18,000 foot and 3,000 horse.

In April the Scots linked up with an army of Yorkshiremen under the two Fairfaxes (father and son) and forced the royalist marquis of Newcastle to shut himself inside York. Beyond the four-mile circuit of the walls, the allies were joined by the earl of Manchester and his Eastern Association army (a single force made up of what had been separate county units in the east of England). To the King the prospect of the fall of York, the capital of the north, was alarming. "If York be lost," he wrote to Rupert, "I shall esteem my crown little less," so he directed his nephew to cross the Pennines from Lancashire to relieve it. Having done this and forced the parliamentary armies away from York to Marston Moor, seven or eight miles off, Rupert followed them there, to catch them off their guard, half on and half off the moor. It was the opportunity for a crushing victory, but Rupert was forced to throw it away while he waited for the marquis of Newcastle to bring his army out of York. The parliamentary forces had time to regroup themselves and face battle.

In so far as the local conditions permitted, the layout of a battle at this period followed a fairly regular pattern. The cavalry were drawn up on the flanks and infantry in the centre, where each company would have a central core of pikemen protecting the more numerous musketeers, who stood six deep. The best-drilled regiments were, indeed, capable by this time of forming a line three deep, in which the front two ranks knelt and stooped for the firing of the more effective simultaneous 'salvo'. But the usual practice was still to fire in rotation, each man moving to the back of his file of six in order to reload, a process which filled the three minutes that brought him again to the front. Meanwhile, it was the business of the pikemen to hinder the intervention of the enemy cavalry, until the signal was given to attack, when the 'push of pike' might be formidable.

About a hundred yards in front of the main body of infantry it was usual to station a 'forlorn hope' – a small body of musketeers whose task was to break the first shock of the enemy's onset before retiring to their own lines. Light artillery was generally placed in the gaps between the infantry companies – sakers, minions and drakes, firing a shot of five pounds or less; they were charged from powder barrels, liable to be exploded by accident.

Behind the cavalry and infantry were reserves of each, and behind them the heavy artillery – demi-culverins, for instance, firing a nine-pound shot. But such guns could only be moved with six or eight horses or oxen, and were mainly used for sieges. At the very rear was the baggage train, where the wagons containing food, clothes, and reserve ammunition were guarded by a ring of men armed with firelock muskets, which dropped no ash or sparks to set the powder alight.

Though only Prince Rupert's Order of Battle survives to guide the historian, it was in this general fashion that the armies were drawn up on Marston Moor by about four o'clock in the afternoon of that eventful July 2nd, 1644. For three hours after their deployment the sun shone fitfully on the flags of infantry and horse and Rupert's great black and gold, blue and silver standard. Some massed uniforms also showed up, for the men of the Eastern Association were partly fitted out in red and on the royalist side there were Rupert's 'Bluecoats' and the 'Whitecoats' under Newcastle; the troops also bore a special distinguishing mark, which in the case of the parliamentarians on this occasion consisted of pieces of white cloth or paper. Then in the evening, when smoke showed that the royalists were cooking supper, a single cannon shot gave the signal for the parliamentarians to launch their attack.

By far the greater part of both armies were infantrymen, who provided the slogging heart of the action. Yet the direction of the battle was dictated by the horse – as so often in the Civil War. An opening cavalry charge, made by Cromwell and the younger

Leslie, from the Parliamentary left, scattered Rupert's horse and exposed the whole right flank of the Royalist infantry, who were engaged on their front by the infantrymen under Fairfax and Manchester. But on the Parliamentary right the opposite happened. The cavalry of George Goring routed the greater part of the younger Fairfax's horse and turned on the unprotected right flank of the Parliamentary and Scottish foot, beginning to roll them up – except for a superb stand made by two Scottish regiments. Only when Cromwell and Leslie brought their victorious cavalry behind the battle to this wing, did the tide turn. They defeated Goring and joined with the Scottish and Parliamentary infantry in a final push against Newcastle's foot, who died almost to a man. Thus, to a greater extent than any other major battle of the Civil War, this action illustrated the decisive role of cavalry in the warfare of that era.

Marston Moor was the last battle of the Civil War in which the parliamentary forces served as separate units. Next year they were merged by parliament into a single 'New Model' army, nationally recruited and paid, in which strict military discipline was combined with freedom of worship for all forms of Puritanism. Under the younger Fairfax and Cromwell this army overwhelmed the King's forces at Naseby in June. Then in September Charles's last hopes faded when David Leslie, at Philiphaugh in south-east Scotland, reversed the series of brilliant victories in which the marquis of Montrose with Irishmen and men from the Hebrides had routed the Covenanters throughout the Highlands. In 1646 the King became the prisoner of his enemies, but another five years were to pass before the decision reached on these battlefields was accepted as final.

The Establishment of the Republic

In England the two forces which had won the war – the Parliament, now largely Presbyterian, and the Army, in which the Independents or Congregationalists and other smaller Puritan sects flourished under Cromwell's protection – were soon at loggerheads regarding the future of the country. So were Scots and English, regarding the religious settlement in both kingdoms. Charles, from his place of confinement in the Isle of Wight, signed an Engagement with the Scottish Covenanters: they were to invade England on his behalf, and he undertook (with many mental reservations) to establish Presbyterianism in England for a minimum period of three years. The ensuing Second Civil War, however, lasted only a couple of months. Fairfax crushed the royalists of south-eastern England (where there had been least action in the first war) at Maidstone and Colchester, while Cromwell subdued those of South Wales and quickly disposed of the Scottish invaders by attacking them from the rear at Preston. Supreme in England, the Army reduced the House of Commons to an obedient 'Rump' of less than one hundred members and carried out its vow 'to call Charles Stuart, that man of blood, to an account for the blood he had shed'.

After a pretended trial in Westminster Hall, King Charles died with great dignity on the scaffold, a martyr in his own view for the cause of the Church of England. The House of Lords was then abolished, and England became a Commonwealth in what the new Great Seal of the Realm hailed as 'the first year of freedom by God's blessing restored'.

Six days after his father's execution, however, Charles II was formally proclaimed King of Great Britain in Edinburgh. His hopes lay at first in the virtually independent Catholic Ireland which had developed from the rebellion of 1641. But in August 1649 Cromwell set about its reconquest, which was marked by two terrible massacres: at both Drogheda and Wexford the defeated Catholic garrisons were murdered in cold blood or (as Cromwell preferred to express it) 'made with their blood to answer the cruelties which they had exercised upon the lives of divers poor protestants'. The exiled king then pinned his hopes upon his father's friend, Montrose, until his defeat and death at the hands of the Covenanters showed where the power in Scotland still lay. At last he was driven to sign both Covenants, was received by his Scottish subjects as a king pledged to the Presbyterian faith for both his kingdoms, and was eventually crowned at Scone.

Thus the position of the army, which now had the effective power in England, was directly challenged by its fellow-Puritans across the border. On the refusal of Fairfax to move against Scotland, Cromwell replaced him as commander-in-chief and headed the invasion. In September 1650 he was hemmed in by Leslie at Dunbar, but the latter made a rash move down from the hills; this gave Cromwell his chance. Many Scots as well as most of the English saw the finger of God in a victory in which 3,000 casualties were inflicted and 10,000 prisoners taken at the cost of less than 30 English lives. Exactly a year later, when Cromwell left the way open for Charles to march down into England, the result was all that the great general could have desired – the crushing defeat of the Scots at Worcester, far from home; Charles's flight into exile; Scotland laid at the feet of her conqueror; and peace insured for his lifetime at least, in three kingdoms united by his sword.

As Caesar, he ere long, to Gaul,
To Italy an Hannibal,
And to all states not free
Shall climacteric be.

So wrote the young Puritan poet Andrew Marvell of Cromwell in 1650. The prophecy of continued military triumphs proved right. In 1652–4, indeed, a naval war against the Dutch for trade[1] involved big defeats alongside big victories – as did two later struggles against the same skilful rivals in 1664–7 and 1672–4. But the fleets of the English republic also sailed the Mediterranean, from which they had expelled the last royalists under prince Rupert, and made their influence felt in Italy and North Africa; and both Jamaica and Dunkirk were wrested from Spanish hands. One problem, however, Cromwell could not bring to a satisfactory solution – that of establishing a 'free state' at home.

Why the Republic Did Not Last

The Commonwealth had come into existence in a time of change and ferment. In every parish Puritan churches were being established, in which Presbyterian, Independent, and Baptist ministers replaced the Anglican incumbent; a strict code of morals was being enforced on a reluctant public, which hated to see the theatres closed and Christmas celebrations denounced as papist; and wiser reforms were drafted at least in many fields, including legal

[1] See p. 212.

procedure, the parliamentary franchise, and education. An advance towards political democracy and even a primitive form of communism based on the Bible had for a time some backing in the army. Colonel Rainborough, on the eve of the Second Civil War (in which he was killed), had argued with his fellow-officers in memorable words:

> The poorest he that is in England hath a life to live as the greatest he. And therefore I think it's clear that every man that is to live under a government ought first by his own consent to put himself under that government.

In 1649 an extremist group among these so-called Levellers acquired the name of 'Diggers', through an abortive attempt to cultivate some unused ground on a Surrey hillside as a protest against landlordism. In the same year their leader, Gerrard Winstanley, stated in his *New Law of Righteousness*:

> All the men and women in England are all children of this land: and the earth is the Lord's, not particular men's who claim an interest in it above all others.

Cromwell was hostile to Levellers of all kinds, assuring the Council of State, "If you do not break them, they will break you." The most popular and influential figure among them, John Lilburne, who had suffered as a Puritan propagandist at the hands of the Star Chamber, was imprisoned more than once under the Republic and ended his days as a convert to Quakerism. Winstanley also became a very active member of this new sect, to which its founder George Fox had given a strongly radical tone, denouncing 'steeple houses' and declaring that true religion was to be based on the guidance of the individual conscience or Inner Light. But the propertied classes remained firmly entrenched in power, and when James Harrington dedicated his *Oceana* to Cromwell in 1656, the Utopia he described was a community in which a wide suffrage and vote by ballot still left the main legislative power with the men of property. His book led, however, to the establishment of what seems to have been the first public debating society in England, the Rota Club of 1659.

It is a sad fact that, whether because or in spite of all this ferment of opinion, the central problem of finding a suitable legal basis for the reconstruction of the State was not solved. The Rump of the Long Parliament, which from 1649 onwards shared the executive power with the Army in the Council of State, clung to its legal right of continuance under the Act of 1641. On April 20th, 1653, Cromwell finally lost patience and closed down the House in person with men of his own regiment, using words which characteristically identified his own impatience with Divine Providence: "In the name of God – go!"

The first attempted replacement was an unworkable Assembly of Saints, nominated through the Puritan churches and contemptuously nicknamed the Barebones Parliament from one of the City representatives, a Baptist minister called Praise-God Barbon; this body was induced to dissolve itself after only five months. The Army officers then endowed the country with a written constitution, the Instrument of Government. This placed the supreme executive power in the hands of Cromwell as Lord Protector, eventually with the right of nominating his own successor; the legislative and taxing power was assigned to a new parliament of one, and later of two, chambers. But all in vain: there were old-style quarrels about their respective rights, especially regarding taxation, and none of Charles I's uses of the prerogative appears to have been more widely resented than the rule of the major-generals, whom Cromwell placed for a time at the head of a kind of regional administration.

While Oliver Cromwell lived, people dared not do more than sigh for a return to traditional monarchy. But he died in his sixtieth year (September 3rd, 1658) bequeathing the Protectorship to his son Richard, a ruler of a very different temperament: "I will not have one drop of blood spilt for the preservation of my greatness," he is reported to have said. In January 1660 control over a very confused situation was seized by George Monk, commander of the army of occupation in Scotland, who marched on London. Quarrelsome military leaders had replaced the Protector, and the Rump of the Long Parliament had reassembled: but Monk held free elections to a convention parliament, which recalled the King.

The Restoration of Charles II

So Charles II came into his own. Six days before he was proclaimed in the capital, Samuel Pepys wrote rather cautiously in his diary:

> Great joy yesterday at London, and at night more bonfires than ever, and ringing of bells, and drinking of the King's health upon their knees in the streets, which methinks is a little too much.

Perhaps it was too much, for the new king's character had not been improved by nine years of wandering in exile on the Continent. Time was to show that his notorious profligacy – he became the father of nine illegitimate children – was combined with a cool cynicism which enabled him to outwit his subjects. Yet the joy which greeted the Restoration was justified, inasmuch as it marked a new beginning.

Charles II, riding in state to London along the Dover Road, was entering a very different world from that which his grandfather had approached from Edinburgh in 1603. He had shown some awareness of this in his Declaration of Breda, published from exile by arrangement with Monk, which was more generous in tone than the detailed settlement which he left to the hands of the Convention Parliament. But in considering what was restored or not restored, three background facts must be kept in mind. Although twelve regicides (and one other leading republican) were made to expiate their crime on the scaffold, the Divine Right of Kings could never look the same after a king had been defeated and executed by rebellious subjects. The modified doctrine of Passive Obedience, or the duty of non-resistance to the Lord's Anointed, was no more than an unconvincing substitute. Nevertheless, an accommodation was feasible because these rebellious subjects had also been taught a lesson; they had found it impossible to establish any satisfactory form of government without the weight of tradition and appeal to loyalty of the ancient monarchy. And there was a third fact, which the Stuarts ignored to their cost. Although Puritanism as a moral force was largely discredited by what men now jeered at as the 'Rule of the Saints', the hatred and fear of

Catholicism on which it was partly based had lost none of its vigour.

As regards the direct conflict of interest between Crown and Parliament, only the gains made by the Long Parliament before the outbreak of the Civil War retained the authority they had received originally by royal assent. This covered two main classes of legislation – the measures against the prerogative courts and those forbidding the various forms of non-parliamentary taxation. In the other measures of that period two changes were, however, introduced. The law excluding the bishops from the House of Lords was repealed and, what was far more important, the Triennial Act was replaced in 1664 by a new law of the same name. This repeated the requirement that parliament should meet at least once in three years, but abolished the arrangement for holding elections if necessary without the participation of the sovereign.

Thus it might seem at first sight as though the opposition gained nothing additional by the later stages of the struggle which brought Charles I to the scaffold. But the position of parliament was in several ways stronger than it had been before the Civil War. The new king was granted a peacetime revenue of £1,200,000 a year, which was only half of what Cromwell had spent though more than any king had had before. In practice, however, he received much less than this, partly at least because neither the customs nor the new excise duties on beer, etc., which had been started by Pym, yielded as much as was expected in the early years of the reign, when they were entrusted to tax farmers. Moreover, the spending of the money was jealously watched by the Commons, who set up committees to examine the royal accounts. The intrusion of such committees into what had been the exclusive concern of the Crown arose first during the Civil War, when parliamentary committees controlled such things as trade, military and naval expenditure, and the sale of confiscated lands. Charles II could not claim, as his predecessors had done, that the mysteries of government were beyond the understanding of subjects: though functioning as offshoots of the Privy Council rather than of the House of Commons, committees of this kind became a regular feature of the system of government, from which the Cabinet was ultimately to be derived.

Religion: The Clarendon Code

The second great conflict of interest on the eve of the Civil War had been that between the supporters of the bishops and the Prayer Book and their Puritan opponents. Here angry passions obstructed any fair settlement, for Cavalier squires and parsons saw a good chance to avenge in the name of principle the humiliations and loss of land or living which they had suffered under the Rule of the Saints. A settlement was complicated by division among the Puritans. During the war the army had been the home of the Congregationalist, Baptist, and many smaller sects whose main belief was in the sanctity of the individual conscience and whose main support came from Cromwell himself. Their standard of doctrine was their own, often peculiar, interpretation of the Bible, with which no one was entitled to interfere. In the words of one soldier: "If I should worship the sun or moon like the Persians, or that pewter mug on the table, no one has anything to do with it." But this was not at all the view of the Presbyterians, who believed in a strict discipline of creed and behaviour enforced by a highly organized Church. Besides its entrenched position in Scotland, Presbyterianism had had many supporters in the Long Parliament and was influential in the City of London.

As the Presbyterian leaders included noblemen of the type of the two parliamentary military commanders, the earls of Manchester and Essex, while their followers tended to be much less radical in political and social outlook than the Independents, they had become the natural allies of the moderate royalists in the moves which brought back the king. The Church of England therefore had good cause to abandon revenge for compromise, at least with this section of its opponents. For this object a conference was summoned at the bishop of London's lodgings in the Savoy; but in spite of royal support it failed completely to agree upon some modifications to the Prayer Book which might have brought many Puritans back into the fold of a comprehensive national church.

Instead, the Cavalier Parliament, which had been elected in 1661, devoted much of its energies in its first few years – it was not dissolved until January 1679 – to a series of laws for the repression of Nonconformists or (as they now began to be called) Protestant Dissenters. The result was that, down to the twentieth century, both England and Wales suffered from a pronounced social and political cleavage which had its origins in a much shorter-lived religious persecution. These laws were known collectively as the Clarendon Code from the name of Charles's chief minister, who had been made lord chancellor while he and his master were still in exile. But there is no reason to think that Clarendon initiated legislation which his royal master certainly deplored.

In 1661 the Corporation Act debarred from the membership of any town council persons failing to receive the Sacrament 'according to the rites of the Church of England'. Next year the Act of Uniformity made the restored Prayer Book (which included a new prayer of thanksgiving with reference to 'the seditious tumults which have been lately raised up amongst us') the only legal form of worship. All clergy had to use it; those who had not been ordained by a bishop must obtain such ordination; and all teachers, whether ordained or not, must make a declaration of conformity with 'the liturgy now by law established'. On St Bartholomew's Day (August 24th) two thousand clergy who refused to conform were duly expelled from their livings. In 1664 and 1670 two Conventicle Acts provided increasingly severe penalties for the holding of unauthorized religious services. And in 1665, when the Plague had caused nonconforming ministers to return to their stricken congregations, the Five Mile Act forbade them to come within that distance of any city or borough or of any parish where they had served. So Parliament preserved the religious monopoly of the established church, at the cost of losing many clergy of sensitive conscience and encouraging a perfunctory adherence by seekers of valuable office in church or state. The two greatest embodiments of the Puritan genius in literature, Milton's *Paradise Lost* and Bunyan's *Pilgrim's Progress*, both date from this era of persecution.

The Social Aspect of the Restoration

The settlement of 1660 also had a social aspect, which worked out to the benefit of the enterprising class – landed gentry, rising merchants, and lawyers – who had been in the forefront of the struggle against the Crown. The years of civil war, in which they had triumphed over their royalist opponents, had exposed them for a time to new rivals from below. For the ferment of religious controversy, together with the unsettlement of individual lives and fortunes by the fighting, brought the political and social discontent of the underdog suddenly to the surface. Tenants lost their bonds of respect for landlords, servants for masters, the uneducated for the educated. But although its connection with the Army had given some temporary importance to the Levellers, as we have seen, the effective control of the country had rested in the hands of the property-owning classes. This position was confirmed by the settlement of 1660, which made the predominance of the landowners securer, if possible, than ever. During the preceding fifteen years confiscations and forced sales of Crown, Church, and Cavalier estates had resulted in the setting up of many new families of landed gentry from among those who had sided with parliament. The Crown and the Church recovered their lands at the Restoration, as did the other victims of outright confiscation – but not the much larger number of royalists who had sold land under the pressure of fines inflicted by parliament. In this way the number of estate-owners was increased, and a body of enterprising new men made their entry into the landowning class.

Becoming conformist in their religious observances, they were made justices of the peace and helped to rule the countryside. A few even climbed into the ranks of the aristocracy: Monk, the younger son of a Devonshire knight, became duke of Albemarle. Yet in many ways these men, like their allies among the prosperous merchants and lawyers, had earned their advancement. They had placed the royal powers within limits which it would be perilous for any future king to transgress, and they had written into the English political tradition the notion that government in some sense exists for the governed. To expect more of Cromwell and his contemporaries would be to judge them as gods rather than men.

Events in Scotland: The First Union

What of the settlement in Scotland? In one sense, the Restoration was more complete than in England. The Scottish parliament had passed a Triennial Act to secure its future position in 1640 – a year ahead of the English – and the king had been forced to agree that the chief officers of state, privy councillors, and judges should be appointed by him with the advice of parliament. But in 1661 the Act Rescissory cancelled at one stroke the legislation 'of all pretendit parliaments since the year 1633'. In another sense, however, the events of those crowded years had left deeper marks upon the life of the smaller country. Argyll and two other Scottish leaders, who were executed after the Restoration for high treason, set the example of firm adhesion to the National Covenant, which was to be the dominant factor in the politics of the following generation. There was also the remembered experience of eight years of parliamentary union.

In the period 1652–60 the Cromwellian conquest had resulted in the conversion of the two kingdoms into a single Commonwealth. Five Scots sat among the 140 representatives of the churches in Cromwell's first experimental assembly, 21 and 30 respectively among the 460 members summoned to the first and second parliaments of the Protectorate. So small a proportion at first sight justifies the mordant comment of a Scottish Presbyterian divine, one of those who had been foremost in wishing to impose Presbyterianism in England when power seemed to be on the side of the Scots:

> As for the embodying of Scotland with England, it will be as when the poor bird is embodied in the hawk that hath eaten it up.

Yet Scotland had been in many ways a gainer by the union. Even the English garrison, with its five large forts and more than twenty smaller outposts, had hurt the pride of the Scots more than their pockets, for law and order were maintained as never before, and the economy also profited directly from the military expenditure, much of which was financed from England. A by-product was thc establishment of one of the smaller military posts at Lerwick in the Shetlands, from which the Dutch were extruded to the profit of the native fisheries. The fuller development of the use of justices of the peace was one of several improvements in the judicial system. A higher level of taxation was to some extent compensated by the introduction of some new industries, such as glass-making and framework knitting; and the free trade which opened the way to severe competition from across the border also gave the Scots an all-important access to English colonial markets overseas. The historian bishop Burnet, looking back on his boyhood in Edinburgh and Aberdeen, wrote: "We always reckoned those eight years of usurpation a time of great peace and prosperity."

For the moment, however, it was the end of the usurpation which Scotland celebrated. When England at last restored the King for whom the Scots had fought and lost two great battles, his loyal subjects in Edinburgh marked the occasion by a firework setpiece, in which a flaming Cromwell was chased by the Devil into a final explosion. The Union too was exploded, though the common Crown remained. There were no more Scottish members at Westminster, and the trade barriers were renewed. But it is significant that within ten years both a commercial treaty and a union of parliaments had again been proposed, and that "when these projects fell through, disappointment was real".[1]

The Resettlement of Ireland

Ireland, too, had been brought into a parliamentary union with England, but the Catholic Irish majority had neither vote nor seat. In this case the real legacy of the Commonwealth and Protectorate was a shifting of the balance between Catholic and Protestant to the very long advantage of the latter. "This ascendancy," writes its latest historian, "was to control the life of Ireland down to the nineteenth century."[2] At the end of a decade of civil strife, in which about one-third of the population fell by the sword or famine or disease, Cromwell's army imposed the last and biggest of the plantations. Ten counties were systematically made over to time-expired soldiers and adventurers from England; the original inhabitants could either remain as labourers on the land of aliens or remove themselves to inferior soil in Connaught. This savage programme, which in intention was almost an act of genocide, lost much of its effect because many of the soldiers intermarried with the Irish and were lost to the 'ascendancy'. But it is

[1] G. S. Pryde, *A New History of Scotland,* II, 17.
[2] J. C. Beckett, *The Making of Modern Ireland 1603–1923*, p. 109.

to be borne in mind that throughout the Civil War period the English had had cause to fear the landing on their shores of hordes of wild Irish. This fear was not dissipated by the fact that the small force of 2,500 men which Charles I succeeded in bringing over in the winter of 1643–4 was quickly defeated and to a large extent enlisted on the other side.

Yet the Ulster Presbyterians, who followed the Scottish example in rallying to the support of Charles II after his father's execution, were taken into favour by Henry Cromwell, the Protector's younger surviving son, who was one of four commissioners for the administration of Ireland. They were able to bring over additional ministers from Scotland, and most of the parish churches in the north-eastern province passed into their hands. For in both islands the deepest cleavage was that between Protestant and Catholic. This was clearly and cruelly shown in Cromwell's Irish warfare; it was to be shown again, though in less cruel terms, in the politics of the English Revolution of 1688–9.

IO

THE SETTLEMENT

ON the morning of February 23rd, 1689, the Banqueting House in Whitehall Palace was arranged for a solemn spectacle. At one end crowded the members of the Lords and Commons, the Speaker holding the mace, while Yeomen of the Guard stood motionless round the walls. At the other end was a dais, empty save for a canopy of state beneath which two formal chairs were placed. Outside the hall, the wide space bounded by the Holbein Gate and the wall of the tilt-yard was filled with a great crowd, which spread all the way to Charing Cross. The occasion was the offering of the English Crown to William and Mary and the mood was festive, for since William's landing at Torbay on November 5th the capital had lived under the threat of a return to civil war. At last the doors at the dais end opened and William and Mary, the Prince and Princess of Orange, appeared and took their places beneath the canopy. The Speakers of the Lords and Commons advanced, the new Declaration of Rights was read out loudly in the hushed hall, and the marquis of Halifax in the name of both Houses formally offered the Crown to the Prince and Princess. "We thankfully accept," replied William, "what you have offered us"; although his reply was not in doubt, a great shout went up in the hall, below the glorious ceiling of Rubens, one of whose panels by way of contrast shows Government treading down Rebellion. This shout, heard from the hall, was taken up by the crowds outside, who were soon rewarded by the sight of a slow procession of members of both Houses making its way to the Holbein Gate where, amid the brilliant colours of heralds and pursuivants and the sound of drums and trumpets, William and Mary were proclaimed King and Queen of England.

From Restoration to Revolution, 1660–89

What had gone wrong that, less than twenty-nine years after the welcomed restoration of Charles II, the King should once again be repudiated by the English people and his crown offered to the head of a foreign state? The main trouble was that neither Charles nor James II accepted the Restoration settlement – though Charles was the more cautious of the two in flouting it. Both men were attracted to the Catholic faith held by their mother, which Englishmen of all classes saw in the light of Foxe's book and the Gunpowder Plot. Both were dazzled by the brilliance of the France of Louis XIV, the triumphs of its armies, the polish and wit of its arts, and the unchallenged supremacy of a Crown whose rule was not hampered by any national parliamentary assembly.

The Attempt to Reduce the Power of Parliament

Yet the English Parliament existed – an important barrier on the road to a home-made copy of the French state. To use compulsion against it was too dangerous, but its members might be bribed by grants of pension and place or influenced by pressure on voters at elections. Clarendon, after his fall from power in 1667, wrote in exile about both these devices. First, of bribery and influence:

> The chief men of the court . . . instead of pressing what was desirable upon the strength of reason or policy . . . desired rather to buy . . . votes and concurrence by promises of reward and preferment.

Secondly, of pressure in elections (by-elections caused by the death of members):

> In the places of those who died, great pains were taken to have some of the King's menial servants chosen: so that there was a very great number of men in all stations of the court . . . who were members of the House of Commons.

It was the Earl of Danby, lord treasurer from 1674 to 1678, who carried these forms of influence to their highest point – and a pamphlet of 1679 asserted that 214 MPs were taking government money in various forms.

Towards the end of Charles II's reign, and much more in that of James II, the Crown employed the device of remodelling corporation charters so as to influence borough elections. Traditionally, such charters came from the king and they could be manipulated to ensure compliant electorates – and juries, too. In 1683, for instance, a new charter was drawn up for London, by which no lord mayor, recorder or sheriff could be appointed without royal approval; since these officials could influence the conduct of elections and the nomination of juries, they could ensure that these went as the Crown wished. James II remodelled some corporations three or four times in a year, and that of Maldon in Essex six times!

The Crown also tried to obtain some sort of financial independence of Parliament. Charles II was always short of money, even when in the middle years of his reign mounting prosperity gave a big lift to the receipts from customs and excise. One reason lay in the notorious profligacy of his Court and a general lack of system in the conduct of the royal finances. The hereditary revenues of the Crown, consisting mainly of rents from Crown lands, dried up as a result of successive sales: already in 1663 the rents had fallen to half of what they had been in 1660, and they fell further through the sale of land to the value of £1,300,000 in the 1670s. In 1672, when the expense of the Second Dutch War was followed by that of preparations for the Third,[1] Charles adopted the short-sighted expedient of the Stop of the Exchequer, a (temporary) suspension of interest payments on the royal debts which made it harder for him to borrow in later emergencies.

One constructive measure was that between 1671 and 1684 the practice of farming the taxes was brought to an end. This produced a direct economic advantage to the Crown because the collection cost much less than before; also an indirect advantage, through the institution of the customs and excise services, whose members might have a useful vote to cast in the Crown interest at elections or even, in the case of the top posts, provide support for the Crown in

[1] See p. 173.

Parliament. But in a period when expensive military preparations were unavoidable, Charles could only achieve financial independence by accepting money from outside – from Louis XIV, whose foreign policy required a friendly, or at least a neutral, England. In 1670–8 he received an average of £123,664 a year from French sources, and the renewal of these subsidies in 1681 made him independent of parliament for the rest of his reign. Suspicion of the existence of this financial dependence upon France obviously strengthened the appeal to patriots of those who opposed the Court.

Charles II and Catholicism

Each move which brought England to an increasing extent within the orbit of the great French monarchy appeared as a move not only towards despotism but towards Catholicism. Louis XIV was known above all as a persecutor of Protestants, through the flight of many thousand Huguenots to England which both preceded and accompanied his revocation of the Edict of Nantes in October 1685. Though Charles did not identify himself as a Catholic until he received absolution on his death-bed, the conversion of his younger brother James in 1669 marks the period from which he at least entertained the idea of a reconversion of the nation to be accomplished with French help. In the following year an alliance was made with France by the treaty of Dover, whose most secret clauses contained an offer of French money and troops for this purpose, while the less secret provided for a surprise attack on Holland. The Third Dutch War duly followed in 1672–4, but the rest did not go according to the royal programme. Making a use of the prerogative which he had tentatively proposed ten years earlier, Charles issued a Declaration of Indulgence to suspend the operation of the penal laws against both Protestant and Catholic Dissenters. When Parliament met to vote supplies for the war, it half-suspected what had happened and by financial pressure forced Charles both to revoke the Declaration and to accept an addition to the Clarendon Code, aimed especially against the Catholics.

By the Test Act of 1673 the holders of any civil or military office were required, not only to receive Communion as members of the Church of England, but also to sign a specific declaration of disbelief in the doctrine of transubstantiation, about which no Catholic could possibly equivocate. James resigned the office of Lord High Admiral and bided his time. Charles, a more skilful politician by far than his younger brother, would never pursue an autocratic policy which risked his throne. He therefore dropped the Indulgence policy and reigned within the law until the close of his reign, when the money supplied by Louis XIV (as already mentioned) enabled him to rule without summoning Parliament, in quiet defiance of the Triennial Act to which he had given his assent in 1664.

The Rise of Political Parties

Nevertheless, it was out of the opposition to Charles that English political parties were born. The earl of Shaftesbury, who had served the King as chancellor of the exchequer and then lord chancellor, bitterly resented the trickery over the treaties of Dover, made known only to two Catholics (and two future Catholics) among the members of the so-called Cabal ministry to which he had then belonged. He became the implacable enemy of the King and his new minister, lord Danby, and set himself to organize the opposition now growing up in the Cavalier Parliament – much changed by the by-elections of many years. In 1675 Shaftesbury founded in London the Green Ribbon club, which flourished in an atmosphere of general suspicion regarding the activities of the Court, as expounded for instance in *An Account of the Growth of popery and arbitrary government in England*, anonymously published by Andrew Marvell, at this time MP for Hull. Thus the Court party ruled under the angry eyes of a Country party.

Then in the late summer of 1678 the whole nation was shocked and alarmed by the disclosure of the 'Popish Plot'. Seven persons were supposed to have been paid to shoot, stab, and poison the King; this many-sided event was to be followed by a massacre of Protestants and a French invasion of Ireland; James was to mount the throne and rule under the direction of the Jesuits. So absurd a story was believed because people wanted to believe it and because its author, the utterly contemptible adventurer Titus Oates, was as clever as he was wicked.[1] Shaftesbury deliberately aggravated the panic, in which a number of innocent Catholics were sentenced to death for treason and the Second Test Act was passed to exclude them permanently from both houses of Parliament; he also made the most of the disclosure (arranged by Louis XIV for his own ends) that Danby as the king's chief minister had been employed in obtaining money for his master from France. Danby was impeached. To save his head, Charles dissolved the parliament which had begun in ecstasies of loyalty eighteen years before.

In the next two years three parliaments sat for short periods. In each of them Shaftesbury and his friends had a clear majority in the Commons, which they used to try to force upon Charles an Exclusion Bill to exclude James from the succession; they hoped to replace him by the Duke of Monmouth, one of Charles's illegitimate sons, who would have reigned as Shaftesbury's puppet. He was the Absalom of the brilliant satire *Absalom and Achitophel* with which John Dryden, the first poet laureate, envenomed the controversy. So violent was the struggle that England seemed to be on the verge of a new civil war provoked by rival parties. Charles played for time until popular feeling at last turned against the Plot, by which he himself had never been taken in. He then summoned the third of these 'Exclusion Parliaments' to meet in Oxford, where he had plenty of supporters; prorogued it suddenly, before Shaftesbury and his friends had time to concert plans for resistance; and (as we have already seen) ruled as he pleased for the last four years of his reign.

Shaftesbury died in exile; two of his leading supporters went to the scaffold for supposed complicity in the Rye House Plot against the life of the King. What remained was a division between two political parties. The 'Whigs', who were for the time being discredited, had at their head a group of the proudest nobles, who believed in a monarchy under their strict control and for the most part cared little for religion of any kind; their main support,

[1] D. Ogg, in his authoritative *England in the Reign of Charles II*, II, 562, 575, describes him as 'a profound psychologist', noticing for example his use of the dress of a Doctor of Divinity – he had taken the degree at Salamanca – 'to create what in some circles is called "presence" '.

however, came from the merchant class and the Protestant dissenters in all classes. The 'Tories', on the other hand, were the party of Church and King, predominant among the squires and their rural dependants and held together by the distribution of offices and pensions to its members as the party of the Court.

The names were originally given by opponents. 'Whig' meant a Scottish covenanter rebel, 'Tory' a Catholic Irish bandit – not altogether inept in either case, for the Whigs included some Presbyterians and many Cromwellian rebels and the Tories the supporters of a crypto-Catholic monarchy. An early mention is to be found in the diary of a Yorkshire Nonconformist minister:

> I being at Wallinwells, October 24 1681, they were discoursing about a new name lately come into fashion for Ranters, calling themselves by the name of Tories. Mistress H. of Chesterfield told me a gentleman was at their house and had a red ribband in his hat. She asked him what it meant: he said it signified that he was a Tory. "What's that?" said she. He answered, "An Irish rebel." Oh, dreadful, that any in England dare espouse that interest. I hear since that this is the distinction that they make instead of Cavalier and Roundhead – now they are called Tories and Whigs.

The Reign of James II

The autocratic powers which Charles had striven to attain by devious ways and with great political finesse, his less intelligent and more obstinate younger brother sought to complete by blunter methods. Ascending the throne as an acknowledged Catholic, he was well received by a parliament elected under the remodelled charters.[1] It contained no more than forty opposition members, and voted the new king an income of £1,500,000 for life. And on July 6th, 1685, exactly five months after his accession, his army crushed a Whig rebellion in south-west England, led by the Duke of Monmouth, who paid for it with his head. The battle of Sedgemoor was indeed a pitiful affair, in which a force of about 4,500 men, mainly unemployed woollen workers and Puritan small

1. See p. 172.

farmers, was pitted against three times as many Regulars. But the Bloody Assizes, where intimidated juries enabled Judge Jeffreys to hang 300 yokels and transport another 800 to the West Indies, gave the country a terrible further demonstration of the long arm of the royal power.

In November Parliament reassembled, under the shadow of the appointment of Catholic advisers by the new king and such minor indications of the wind of change as a government order forbidding the customary bonfires on the Fifth. Loyal as they were, both Houses rejected the royal demand that they should repeal the anti-Catholic laws; and when they asked for reassurances about religion, they were at once adjourned, not to be summoned again while James was king. But the judges, with Jeffreys promoted to the lord chancellorship, gave the help that Parliament refused. In June 1686 they ruled by eleven to one in favour of Sir Edward Hales, a Catholic who was prosecuted under the Test Act on becoming governor of Dover Castle. When he was allowed to plead successfully a royal dispensation from the obligations of the Act, the way lay open for the King to admit his co-religionists to the Privy Council, to key posts in the universities, and – most ominously – to commissions in the royal army. For each summer James assembled about 16,000 men to receive their training on Hounslow Heath, in the immediate neighbourhood of the capital.

From dispensing with the anti-Catholic laws in individual cases, James proceeded to their complete suspension by his two Declarations of Indulgence, which proclaimed toleration for both Catholic and Protestant dissenters. These lost some of their intended effect when the Protestant beneficiaries, suspecting that religious liberty would soon be swallowed up again in the rule of Rome, failed to rally to the support of the throne. But the King persisted, and seven bishops who ventured upon a written protest, which was handed to him in private by the Archbishop of Canterbury upon his knees, were prosecuted – but acquitted by a London jury – on a charge of 'uttering a seditious libel'. At this juncture, too, the birth of a son to James's Italian Catholic queen meant that it was no use supposing that the death of an elderly sovereign would automatically bring better days.

The Revolution of 1688 in England and Scotland

In this way three years of James's rule united bishops and Nonconformists, Tory and Whig leaders, and (so far as we can judge) the all-important rank and file of the nation in a common dread of the permanent establishment of a persecuting Catholic autocracy, French servitude transferred to English soil. A petition bearing Whig, Tory, and episcopal signatures was therefore smuggled over to Holland, requesting the intervention of the Stadtholder, William Prince of Orange, a resolute and prudent ruler, who had been called to power by the Dutch before he was 22 in the crisis of a French invasion which followed the treaty of Dover.[1] His mother was James's sister, and he had married his cousin Mary, James's elder daughter by his first marriage, (to a daughter of Lord Clarendon). Thus Mary was the next heir to the throne after the infant James Edward. But what mattered most in William's eyes was the chance of securing Britain as a firm ally of his native land in its long struggle against the overwhelming power of Louis XIV.

William landed at Torbay on November 5th, 1688, and moved his Dutch army with politic slowness upon London, gathering the support which made a battle unnecessary and giving James every chance to escape to France. In the New Year a Convention Parliament was elected, which prepared the Declaration of Rights. This document declared that James's use of the dispensing and suspending powers and other high-handed actions (enumerated under 13 heads) were 'utterly and directly contrary to the known laws and statutes and freedom of this realm'; pretended that James had abdicated; and offered the throne to William and Mary as joint sovereigns in the manner narrated at the beginning of this chapter.

The thinly disguised English Revolution of February 23rd, 1689, might or might not be accepted by the foreign powers, to whom James was busily applying for help; it certainly had no legal validity for his northern kingdom. However, their experiences since 1660 made the Scots more ready to follow the English line than they had been at the revolution of forty years earlier. In 1661

[1] See p. 173.

the Edinburgh parliament which passed the Act Rescissory had passed another 392 Acts in six months, the effect of which was to make the king almost absolute. The Lords of the Articles resumed their earlier powers, and episcopacy was restored to the Church. The two Covenants, embodying the deepest aspirations of a large part of the Scottish people, were declared treasonable; attendance at the episcopal church services was enforced by fines; and attendance at other forms of service – the conventicles which began to meet on the hills and moors – was eventually made a capital offence.

Ministers had to be presented to their livings by the lay patrons (a system abolished in 1649) and approved by the bishop; about 270 refused to accept this and were ejected. Although about half of these were subsequently won back by Letters of Indulgence, the south-west became the centre of a determined opposition, which erupted into the Pentland Rising of 1666; simmered during the descent of the 'Highland Host' in 1678 (when the government sent a force composed mainly of Highlanders to keep order in the area); and boiled over again next year, when the Covenanters won a skirmish at Drumclog and were defeated by the Duke of Monmouth at Bothwell Brig. Charles's reign ended with the vividly remembered horrors of the 'Killing Time', directed especially against the Cameronians, a sect of Covenanters who preached 'nae king but Christ', and partly inspired by James as his brother's commissioner for Scotland.

Nevertheless, the great majority of the Scottish people had passively accepted the royal policy, which had not reimposed the Prayer Book and had left presbyteries and kirk sessions to function as before at the local level. James began his reign with a Scottish parliament as loyal as the English; a rebellion in the south-west under the younger Argyll failed even more rapidly and completely than Monmouth's, with which it was meant to synchronize. Catholics were placed in office in Scotland, and although parliament refused (as in England) to repeal the laws against Catholics, James's Declarations of Indulgence were accepted with relief by extruded Presbyterian ministers who were at last able to return to their parishes. Thus there was no general movement of resistance in Scotland; the invitation to William and Mary was a purely English affair. But a Convention Parliament in Edinburgh agreed, on the day of their coronation at Westminster, to substitute them as sovereigns in place of James, who was declared to have forfeited the throne by his tyrannous acts, particular reference being made to the 'great and insupportable grievance and trouble of prelacy'.

The Revolution Settlement, 1689–1701

In principle the battle against an absolute Crown had been won at the Restoration: prerogative had been cut down, and it seemed to be clear that in the last resort the Crown was dependent on Parliament rather than the other way about. But it was all 'in principle' and 'in the last resort': there was no constant watch upon the practice of royal rule, no insistence on details and precise limits: it was as if Parliament had shut the door on absolutism and not locked it. The Revolution settlement did lock the door: it emphasized what had already been done and extended it, and dealt in the practical details of the limitations on royalty. It consisted of a variety of Acts passed during the whole reign of William III – all of them in one way or another putting bounds about the monarchy. The most important were: in 1689, the Mutiny and Toleration Acts and an enlarged version of the Declaration of Rights which was enacted as the 'Bill of Rights'; in 1694, a new form of Triennial Act; in 1697, the Civil List Act; and in 1701 the Act of Settlement, the provisions of which, however, did not take effect until after the death of William's successor, namely Mary's sister Anne. It will be convenient to consider these measures as a single whole, as having important lasting effects upon the monarchy, upon Parliament, and upon the national religion.

The Crown was settled upon William and Mary as joint sovereigns, the regal power being entrusted specifically to William alone; after them, upon the children of Mary, upon Anne and her children, and finally upon the children of William in the event of his remarriage after Mary's death. Mary died childless in 1694; William did not marry again; and the death of the last of Anne's children in 1700 provided the occasion for the above-named Act of Settlement. It having already been laid down in the Bill of Rights that no person who was a Catholic or married to a Catholic could inherit the throne, recourse was had to the surviving Protestant daughter of Elizabeth, daughter of James I, and the crown was assigned where it still remains, namely 'to the Princess Sophia and the heirs of her body being Protestants'. In order to underline their grudge against William III, a member of the Dutch Calvinist Church, the Tories also inserted in the Act of Settlement the requirement that the sovereign must be an Anglican communicant; but the important aspect of the Act was of course the fact that it made the title to the throne purely parliamentary, since there were 57 Catholic heirs who had a better blood claim to it than Sophia.

The revenue of the Crown was divided into two parts, of which one was to be public and under parliamentary control, leaving only a 'civil list' of £700,000 a year as the part to be placed freely at the disposal of the sovereign. Apart from some complicated arrangements which were almost immediately repealed as being unworkable, he was still left free in theory to choose and direct his ministers at his own discretion. But in future a royal pardon was not to be allowed to protect against impeachment, and (until 1870) no naturalized alien could be admitted to the Privy Council. A very much more significant restriction of the royal powers was a change made in the terms of appointment of the judges, which protected them from dismissal except at the request of both houses of parliament.

The law-making and tax-levying powers of parliament were expressly safeguarded by the Bill of Rights, which deprived the Crown of any claim to suspend laws and of the lesser dispensing power 'as it hath been assumed and exercised of late', and which stated clearly

> that levying money for or to the use of the Crown by pretence of prerogative without consent of parliament for longer time or in other manner than the same is or shall be granted is illegal.

The regularity of its meetings, which was another source of power, was at the same time assured through the Mutiny Act. This authorized the Crown to maintain a standing army, which was otherwise illegal in peacetime under the Bill of Rights, but only for a single year: thus an annual session of parliament was (and still is) necessary in order that a disciplined military force may be kept in existence.

But a parliament which met regularly might still be exposed to undue influence on the part of the Crown. This danger was mitigated by the new Triennial Act, which prescribed the holding of a general election at least once in three years. This strengthened the position of MPs as representatives of the electorate, made political controversy more vigorous, and weakened the position of the Crown because it so often had new men to manage. The Act of Settlement proposed to prevent such management by excluding all office-holders under the Crown from membership of the House of Commons; but this project, which would have aggrandized the House of Lords and rendered impossible the co-operation between the ministers and the lower house out of which the Cabinet system was slowly emerging, was very quickly abandoned. Meanwhile the long-continued French wars gave the Commons an automatic increase of authority, since the ability of the Crown to go on fighting depended on the voting of taxes, especially the land tax. Based on a valuation of estates made in 1692, this became for a century the chief form of direct taxation: in war years it commonly rose from one or two shillings in the pound of assessed value to a height of four shillings, causing the Tory MPs who represented the landed interest to make unbridled, though for a long time unsuccessful, attacks on the royal foreign policy.

In Church matters, the Tories had things more their own way. The refusal of the Protestant dissenters to support James against their Anglican persecutors obviously entitled them to relief as part of the new settlement of the nation's affairs. What they received by the Toleration Act was a rather grudging concession of freedom of worship for persons meeting openly in places registered for the purpose, subject to the acceptance by their ministers of all except three (and part of a fourth) of the Anglican Thirty Nine Articles. They were still formally barred from civil and military office – though not from serving their country in the ranks of the armed forces – and excluded from the universities with their many social and cultural advantages. In one respect, however, the High Church lost face, for about 400 of its most conscientious clergy, including the Archbishop of Canterbury and six bishops, while accepting the expulsion of James as a regrettable necessity, could not bring themselves to take the oath of allegiance to William as their lawful king. The withdrawal of these Non-Jurors from the Church underlined the willingness of others, once equally loud in their championship of Passive Obedience to the Lord's Anointed, to swallow their old convictions.

The settlement of English institutions which has now been outlined was, of course, a mere paper settlement unless it could be effectively defended against the Jacobites, as James's supporters came to be called. His flight to France, misrepresented as an abdication, was for the purpose of securing help from Louis XIV. Britain accordingly joined Holland and other powers in an eight-year struggle against France. A naval victory off Beachy Head gave the French command of the Channel for two of those years, and although the Anglo-Dutch fleet restored the situation in a battle at La Hogue in May 1692, so that the threatened French invasion of England never took place, British arms gained little success on the Continent. The treaty of Ryswick (1697) accordingly marked a mere breathing-space before a greater struggle, the War of the Spanish Succession (1702–13), in which a similar alliance fought to prevent France from securing possession of Spain with its empire and trade. In both contests the French war aims included the restoration of James II or, after his death in September 1701, of his son James Edward to the British throne.

The Revolution in Ireland

In this precarious situation great importance attached to the course of events in Scotland and Ireland: in both countries Stuart hopes were destined to be defeated, but in very different ways and with very different long-term results. Ireland may be treated briefly first. In 1689 the Catholic Irish rose spontaneously on behalf of their Catholic King, and the Protestants lost possession of the whole island except for the two Ulster towns of Enniskillen and Londonderry. The latter was saved at the last moment by the forcing of a boom across the river-mouth after enduring a siege of fifteen weeks, in which thousands died of fever and outright starvation: "I saw 2s. a quarter given for a little dog, horse blood at 4d. a pint," writes one of the survivors. Ulster alone was then held for William until the following summer, when he crossed over with an army drawn from most of the Protestant nations of Europe. James, who now had Dublin as his capital, covered it with a smaller army than William's but from a stronger position, on the far bank of the river Boyne. However, on a day which is still a public holiday in Northern Ireland, the Blue Dutch Guards resolutely forced a passage, the undisciplined Irish infantry fled, and only the presence of a French contingent prevented James's retreat from becoming a rout.

Though he retired to France, the war in Ireland went on for another year, to end with a second big defeat of Irish and French forces at Aughrim, the surrender of Limerick, and the treaty made there. Forfeitures reduced to one-seventh the portion of the soil of Ireland left in Catholic ownership, and new penal laws were imposed which were a breach of the spirit, if not of the actual wording, of the treaty. Catholic worship was never actually forbidden, but no Catholic bishop and no member of a religious Order was entitled to live in Ireland and there was, in theory at least, a ban on Catholic schools and on the sending of children to receive a Catholic education abroad. Catholics were forbidden to bear arms and, with a view to depressing the status of the surviving

Plate 17. *The Treaty of Union.* This treaty was drawn up in 1706 after nine weeks of negotiations between English and Scottish commissioners; and the following year was passed as the Act of Union by the parliaments in London and Edinburgh. The picture shows the 25th and final article of the treaty and the beginning of the signatures – the Archbishop of Canterbury and the Scottish Chancellor Seafield heading them, and the other commissioners signing after: English on the left and Scottish on the right. (Cf. text pp. 188–9.)

Plate 18. *The Quayside, Bristol, c. 1720.* This picture shows Bristol as a flourishing port – in 1700 it was second only to London with a population of 25,000 to 30,000. It was the centre of the wine trade with Spain and Portugal (note the barrels on the quayside) and, in the early 18th century, till superseded by Liverpool and Glasgow, both of the slave trade with the West Indies and of the imports gained through this trade – sugar, tobacco and cotton. It was, too, the centre for the export of the woollens of the midlands and south-west (occasioning the two laden horses in the centre of the picture?) and was engaged in the export of Birmingham metal-work (of which there is, perhaps, evidence in the nearest shop). Many of the houses appear to be of stucco or lath and plaster: brick was not used in Bristol before 1700 (see p. 362 of N. Pevsner's *North Somerset and Bristol* – Penguin 'Buildings of England' series.)

Plate 19. *Key House, Falkland.* Falkland is rich in 18th century houses and this (date 1713) represents a type which appeared in Scotland just before 1700 – the sort of house that merchants, farmers or the clergy might live in. The interior is as symmetrically arranged as the outside: with two rooms on each floor and fireplaces at the gable ends.

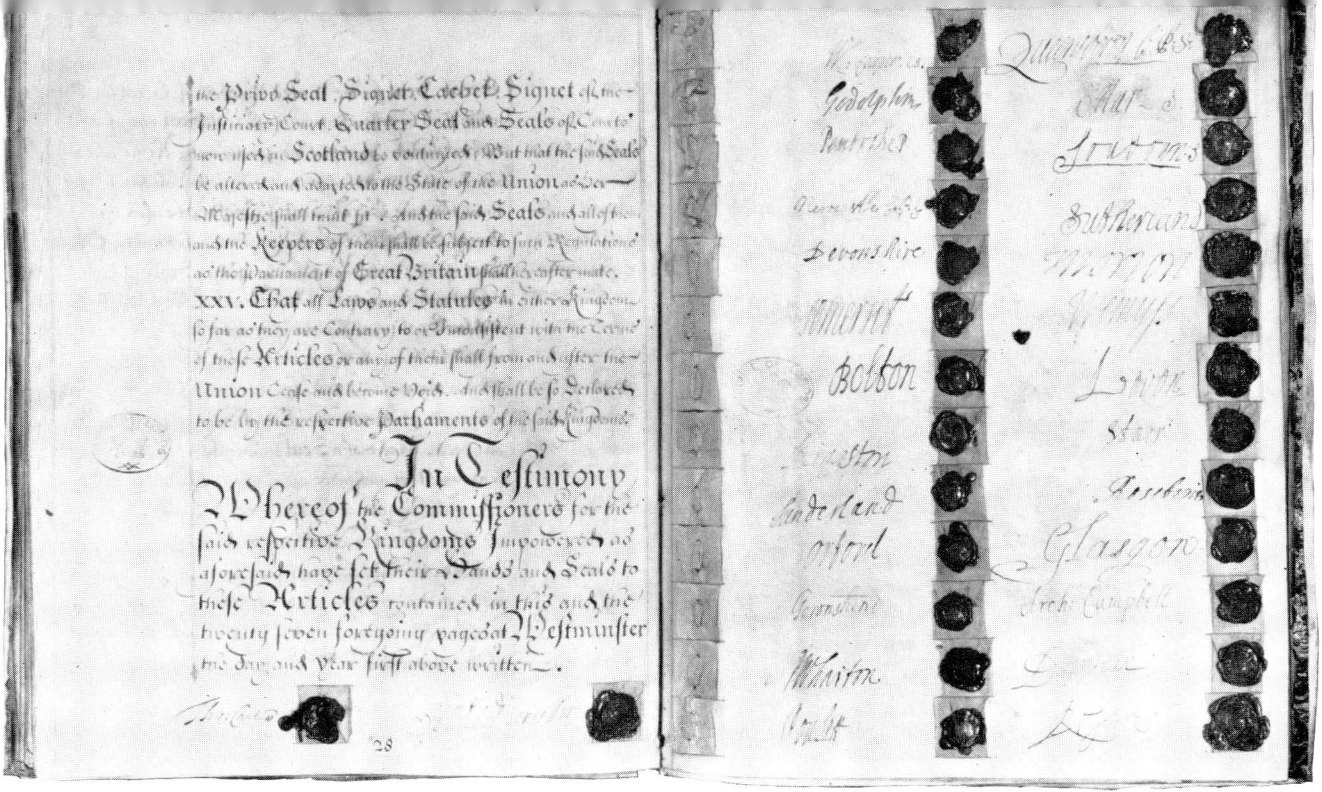
the Privy Seal, Signet, Cachet, Signet of the Justiciary Court, Quarter Seal and Seals of Courts now used in Scotland be continued; But that the said Seals be altered and adapted to the State of the Union as Her Majesty shall think fit; And the said Seals and all of them and the Keepers of them shall be subject to such Regulations as the Parliament of Great Britain shall hereafter make.

XXV. That all Laws and Statutes in either Kingdom so far as they are Contrary to or Inconsistent with the Terms of these Articles or any of them shall from and after the Union cease and become Void, And shall be so Declared to be by the respective Parliaments of the said Kingdoms.

In Testimony Whereof the Commissioners for the said respective Kingdoms Impowered as aforesaid have set their Hands and Seals to these Articles contained in this and the twenty seven foregoing pages at Westminster the day and Year first above written.

28

Plate 17

Plate 18

Plate 19

Catholic gentry, the lands of Catholics had to be divided equally among all male heirs. Finally, in 1699 the English parliament, jealous of an Irish woollen industry based on cheaper labour than their own, prohibited all exports of woollen goods except to England, where high duties already ensured their exclusion.

If the above measures could be excused to some extent by the fear that the Catholic Irish might again rally to the support of James, nothing excuses the meanness of the treatment meted out to the Presbyterians, who had been the backbone of the resistance to James in Ulster. No equivalent of the English Toleration Act of 1689 was passed for their benefit. Instead, in 1704 the Irish parliament expressly reimposed the test of Anglican Church membership upon all office-holders, so as to drive the Presbyterians out of the corporations of Belfast and Londonderry. Six years later, even the small state subsidy for their ministers was taken away.

Events in Scotland, 1689–1706

The ill-treatment of the Presbyterians in Ulster was to some extent due to the resentment of the High Church against the triumph of their brethren in Scotland. There the overthrow of the bishops, the abolition of the royal supremacy, and the return to the full Presbyterian system were the main features of the Revolution settlement. The General Assembly, meeting for the first time since 1653, was a democratically elected body which represented national feeling more fully than the parliament did and was well aware of its own importance. Indeed, the Presbyterian divines claimed an 'intrinsic power' of holding the Assembly at their own discretion, which William with some difficulty modified into an arrangement for its summons annually by a royal commissioner. Meanwhile the episcopal church fell into the background as a non-conformist body, treated at first with considerable harshness.

The Scots parliament, which itself negotiated the Revolution Settlement, also acquired a new standing. It now became entirely a lay organization, in which the clerical 'estate' was not included; the Lords of the Articles were abolished; and special committees could now be appointed in which no officer of state could vote. The number of shire representatives was considerably increased and the franchise extended to all burgesses in the royal burghs, so that it became more nearly the equivalent of the parliament in England.

But the settlement only underlined the difference between the two separate societies of the Highlands and the Lowlands. Well-adapted as it was to Lowland needs, among the Highlanders it aroused the strong hostility of a Catholic element and of a still larger body of opinion which clung to its traditional loyalty to a Stuart king. The lead was taken by John Graham of Claverhouse, a hunter-down of Covenanters whom James II had rewarded with the title of Viscount Dundee – the 'bonny Dundee' of the song and the 'bloody Clavers' of Covenanting imprecations. This formidable character defeated a government force with a wild Highland charge in the Pass of Killiecrankie, where he fell dying from his horse. His followers were then worsted at Dunkeld by a newly embodied regiment of the Cameronians, who had many wrongs to avenge. Next spring (1690) they were finally defeated at Cromdale, and the stronghold of Fort William was erected under the shadow of Ben Nevis as a sign of government determination. At Glencoe, however, this determination acquired a sinister reputation. Oaths of allegiance were demanded from the Highland clans by the start of 1692, as a way of bringing things to a head and identifying enemies still unreconciled. Yet in fact the chiefs came in to take the oaths: all except Macdonald of Glencoe, who by accident was late. On the advice of the Scottish under-secretary in London, Sir John Dalrymple, a terrible revenge was taken. Soldiers from Fort William – mainly Campbells, traditional enemies of the Macdonalds – were sent into Glencoe and for some time were treated as guests by the clan. Then they suddenly turned on their hosts and slaughtered them, killing the chief himself and thirty-seven others including two women and two children. There was as much muddle in this as policy, but the deed was so treacherous and savage that it left a stain on the King and the Revolution Settlement which time did not eradicate from the Highland memory.

This act did much to embitter relations with England, for it was in London that it had been prepared. But another matter worked in the same way, namely the Darien scheme. This was a plan to colonize the isthmus of Darien, about 150 miles south of the modern Panama Canal – obviously not a suitable place for a colony that encroached upon Spanish territory, since it was close to the nerve-centre of their colonial empire. However, it was decided upon under the auspices of the newly founded Company of Scotland Trading to Africa and the Indies (1695). At the outset this company had much English backing, for it offered a way by which English moneyed men could get round the trading monopolies at home. But they were not keen to be involved in a dubious colonial venture, particularly when Spain was an ally. So the English shareholders withdrew their capital and the Scots went on alone, employing a capital of £400,000, which was half of all the available national resources. Three separate expeditions were made, but all failed. This was blamed on England: and it is true that William III had instructed English colonial governors to refuse help (1699). Yet it was not a straight case of commercial jealousy, other considerations being involved, such as the delicate negotiations over the succession to the Spanish throne, which was a prime interest for England and made it necessary to keep on good terms with Spain.

Such differences as these only underlined the fact that Scottish and English paths were beginning to diverge. This was shown plainly in foreign policy, which for England had become a dominant concern ever since the accession of William III had swept her into the leadership of the European struggle against France. In 1701 the outbreak of the War of the Spanish Succession sent British armies under Marlborough back to the Continent, where Scottish regiments such as the Greys played a notably gallant part. But the conflict did not seem vital to the interests of Scotland, which tried again, as in the Darien venture, to dissociate herself from her century-long involvement in a foreign policy dictated from London. In the Wine Act of 1703 the Scots parliament made trade arrangements with France in spite of Queen Anne's declaration of war, and in the same year in its Act anent Peace and War asserted the right to participate in any future declaration of war or any treaty-making by Anne's successors on the Scottish throne. Finally, the Act of Security, which the Queen vetoed in 1703 but was forced to accept in 1704 in order to get supplies, indicated that the throne might again become separate. Unless specific measures were taken to protect Scottish institutions from foreign interference, Scotland would not adopt the Hanoverian succession, even though she could find no Protestant claimant closer than the duke of Hamilton, who was descended from James II, the grandfather of James IV of Scotland.

England was alarmed, since all her hopes were centred upon the Hanoverian succession and the successful conclusion of the European struggle, both of which were imperilled by the Scottish decision. She embarked on a policy of threat and conciliation. The Alien Act of 1705 was the threat, by which the Scots would be treated as foreigners and all trade between the two countries prohibited, if the Hanoverian succession were not accepted in Scotland by the end of the year. Yet conciliation lay in the invitation to renew negotiations for a parliamentary union, which had been discussed in 1702 without success. The shock of these events now produced a willingness for compromise, which issued in a Treaty of Union (1706). This was turned into the Act of Union, passed by both parliaments the next year.

The Anglo–Scottish Union

The Act of Union in the main gave each country what it wanted – England an agreed succession and a single parliament and Scotland security for her Church and a far wider scope for her trade. The succession was to be that laid down by the English Act of Settlement. The two parliaments were to be merged in a single 'Parliament of Great Britain', where the Scots were to have 45 members in the Commons and 16 in the Lords. This did little justice to the Scots, whose population was nearer one-fifth of the English and Welsh than the one-eleventh that this suggested. Nevertheless it was a compromise between the 38 that the English proposed and the 50 claimed by the Scots. Separate Acts provided for the security of the widely different established church in each country, and the two legal systems likewise remained distinct, no appeals lying from Scotland to the English courts in Westminster Hall. England and the colonies were opened to Scottish traders as freely as to English, and the customs and excise rates were to be on the same English basis. The two currencies were merged, so that the wide difference[1] between the values of the Scottish and English pound disappeared. Taxation presented a problem, since Scotland could hardly be taxed in the same way as her more wealthy neighbour; it was eventually agreed that she should contribute only about one-fortieth of what England then paid in the land tax. Furthermore it was not just that Scotland, with her low national debt, should help towards paying off the high English one, as she would do through the customs and excise. It was decided, therefore, that England should pay to the Scots nearly £400,000 as an 'Equivalent' – a form of compensation.

These were the main features of the treaty, whose enactment created the state of Great Britain and freed the energies of her people to develop the interests of the combined nations at home and abroad. In detail the settlement was not wholly equitable. The basing of Scotland's parliamentary representation upon taxable capacity rather than estimated population was ungenerous; the taking of appeals from the Scottish courts to the House of Lords was dubiously excused by the wording of the treaty, which only exempted the Scots from the appellate jurisdiction of 'courts sitting in Westminster Hall'; and the guaranteed independence of the Scottish Church was infringed as early as 1712 by an act to restore lay patronage of livings. In its broad concept, however, the Act of Union was a sensible blend of the ideal and the practical, in which good sense on both sides of the Border prevailed over the counsels of pride and prejudice. While twentieth-century Scotland has its revisionists, to most British people the treaty seems a part of the natural order. In the words of an eminent historian of the period, "The union was no more good or bad than the law of gravitation."[2]

By 1707 the great institutional problems of the preceding century had all been worked out: the succession question; the relationship between Crown and Parliament, between the Crown and the law, and between the Church and the Protestant Dissenters; and the increasingly inconvenient separation between the two halves of a small island. Having decided these high matters, Britain seemed set for stability at last – especially in view of the mounting

[1] See p. 206.
[2] Sir George Clark, *The Later Stuarts 1660–1714*, p. 281.

tide of success abroad. In 1704–8 the duke of Marlborough had won resounding victories over the armies of Louis XIV at Blenheim, their first defeat for two generations, Ramillies, which carried him across the French border, and Oudenarde, which led to the capture of Lille. Only at Malplaquet in 1709 did a further victory involve him in heavier losses than the enemy without achieving any strategic result.

The attempt to set an Austrian in lieu of a French prince upon the throne of Spain, which was the original war aim of Britain and her allies, was doomed indeed to failure: but even here the struggle had brought the possession of the Rock of Gibraltar (1704), to which the island of Minorca was to be added four years later as the first British strongpoint in Mediterranean waters.

The Conflict of Parties

Yet the second half of the Queen's reign proved to be as stormy as the first, with party strife rising to a bitter climax. William III had been reluctantly accepted by the Tories as a necessary evil, in order to preserve the Church of England; after the death of his popular Stuart queen, Mary, in 1694 they viewed him with positive dislike, as a foreign ruler who had involved their country in an expensive French war. The Whigs, on the other hand, had welcomed the fact that William's title to the throne was purely parliamentary, and regarded the war as necessary for the defence of liberty against autocracy. Moreover, Whig merchants benefited from contracts for military supplies and from raising the loans to government which became the nucleus of the National Debt, whereas Tory squires (as we have seen) felt the cost of the war in land tax at four shillings. Queen Anne's keen personal devotion to the Church of England made her the natural ally of the Tories; but in the first part of her reign she found the support of Whig ministers essential for the war. The Whig party was always strong in the House of Lords, and it was a Whig majority in the House of Commons which passed the Act of Union with Scotland.

A run of success proved to be their undoing. Confirmed in power by an election in 1708, the Whigs began to lose their popularity in the country because they made it their policy to continue the war until total victory, which might mean an indefinitely long-drawn-out and wasteful conflict. After two years the Queen seized her chance to replace Whig ministers by Tories, and then got the result confirmed in an election which gave the Tories a majority of more than two to one. Supported by the royal favour, they repeated their win at the next triennial election in 1713, which was held a few months after they had made peace at Utrecht. The way for this had been prepared by a brilliantly persuasive pamphlet *On the Conduct of the Allies* from the pen of their chief party propagandist, the future Dean Swift; by Britain's desertion of her allies; and by the opening of secret negotiations with France while the war nominally continued. The Queen created twelve new peers to provide a Tory majority in the House of Lords, and the dismissal of Marlborough likewise cleared the path for the peace-making. While the rest of Europe did not quickly forget Albion's perfidy, Britain rejoiced in her territorial and commercial gains: acknowledgement of her claim to Newfoundland (except for limited French fishing rights), the Hudson Bay region, and Acadia; the cession of Gibraltar and Minorca; the Spanish Asiento[1] and other advantages for her trade.

In home affairs too, the atmosphere of conflict was made more acute by the rapid development of political journalism. The Whig cause had the support of Steele and Addison, the essayists, in the *Tatler* and *Spectator*, whose short lives ran in succession between 1709 and 1714. The extreme Tories were championed by Swift in the forty numbers of the *Examiner*, the more moderate by Defoe, formerly an ardent Whig. Defoe's periodical, *The Review*, followed the politics of his paymaster, the lord treasurer, Robert Harley earl of Oxford, who had himself been born and bred a Whig. Amid much angry discussion the new ministry proceeded to gratify its friends in cathedral close and country vicarage by passing two measures against the Protestant dissenters, which would have had a big cumulative effect if they had not been repealed early in the next reign. The Occasional Conformity Act of 1711 forbade the device – used throughout the following century – by which ambitious dissenters qualified for civic office by a single formal attendance at the Anglican Sacrament while retaining their nonconformist

[1] See pp. 297–8.

church membership. The Schism Act, which came into force on the day of Anne's death, would have had even more far-reaching consequences, for it aimed at the closing-down of all nonconformist schools teaching anything more than the three Rs. The main issue of the day, however, was that of the succession to the ailing Queen. The Tories had passed the Act of Settlement in favour of the princess Sophia in the same spirit in which they had accepted William – as a necessary evil: but was it really necessary?

Although the treaty of Utrecht had bound France to respect the decision made in 1701, the power of Louis XIV might nevertheless be brought to bear on behalf of James Edward as the legitimate heir. This thought was made all the more attractive to many Tories because they saw that their action in ending the war had ruined their credit with the house of Hanover, which had wanted it to continue: this was an important issue with the Elector George, who had fought in person, when his mother's claim passed to him on her death in April 1714. A section of the party – how large a section can never be known – might therefore have fallen in with any scheme for bringing James Edward over to seize possession of his father's throne, whatever the risks in Church and State. And at the end of July 1714 the ambitious leader of the extreme wing of the Tories, the secretary of state, Henry St John viscount Bolingbroke, was left in control of the government. The Queen dismissed his rival Harley, whom she disliked both for his moderate religious opinions and for his immoderate drunkenness.

Death of Queen Anne

James Edward, however, had refused even to simulate a return to the Protestant faith. This shook the opinion of all but the most headstrong Tories in a country where ballad-mongers could present it as an issue above parties:

Whoe'er is in place I care not a fig,
Nor will I dispute between High Church and Low,
'Tis now no dispute between Tory and Whig,
But whether a Popish successor or no.

After three days Queen Anne, now lying on her death-bed, handed the white staff of the lord treasurership to another moderate, the duke of Shrewsbury. By so doing she underlined the failure of Bolingbroke, who had found it too late to take any effective action, and pronounced the doom of the Tory party, which she had striven to support. Two days later, the last Stuart sovereign was at rest, and the elaborate arrangements made nine years earlier for the protection of the realm pending the arrival of her successor from Hanover came smoothly into force.

II

THE GROWTH OF PERSONAL LIBERTY

THE great struggle between King and Parliament in the seventeenth century, which among much else was a contest between the spirit of autocracy and that of liberty, extended the boundaries of freedom for ordinary men. This remains true, although (as this chapter will show) at first only the upper classes had the full enjoyment of this freedom. Many of these gains were enjoyed through the nation's representatives in parliament: its complete liberty of speech, its full control of taxation, the regularity of its meetings, the discontinuance of attempted alternative methods of legislation by proclamation, and the like. But the triumph of the common law courts over the Star Chamber and other instruments of the royal will, while advantageous above all to lawyers, preserved an important liberty for the people at large, namely the right to trial by jury. Two other examples may be given of liberties won at this time, of which the value extended far beyond the field of politics.

Habeas Corpus and Freedom of the Press

In 1679, when the exclusion struggle[1] was at its height, the Habeas Corpus Amendment Act greatly improved the working of the ancient writ, under which the friends of an imprisoned person could have him produced before a judge to show whether or not he had been deprived of his liberty by lawful sentence of a court. In Charles II's reign its use was still being thwarted by judges not making themselves available to issue it, or by the writ being dodged through transfers of prisoners from place to place, or through their removal to the Channel Islands and other parts of the king's dominions where the writ of the common law courts did not run. All these points were satisfactorily covered, so that an English

[1] See p. 175.

subject henceforth received full protection against the danger that he might be left to languish indefinitely in prison, while his trial on a criminal charge was deliberately postponed to suit the convenience of the government. Scots law, like that of Continental countries, has no Habeas Corpus writ, but a law against 'wrongous imprisonment' was made in 1701.

A second reform was the discontinuance in 1695 of the requirement that all printed matter should be submitted for censorship before it could lawfully be published. The control formerly exercised by the Star Chamber had been put on a statutory basis by the Licensing Act of 1662, when different classes of books were assigned to different authorities:

> All books of history . . . or other books concerning any affairs of state shall be licensed by the principal secretaries of state . . . books of divinity, physic, philosophy or whatsoever other science or art . . . by the lord archbishop of Canterbury and lord bishop of London or by either one of the chancellors or vice-chancellors of either of the universities.

This law also aimed at the eventual limitation of the number of master-printers to twenty for the entire country, not counting the King's Printer, two university printers, and one press to be allowed at York. When William of Orange landed at Torbay in 1688, so large and important a town as Exeter could not produce a printer for his proclamations

It was fortunate that this stringent measure required periodic renewal: it was in abeyance from 1679 to 1685, and ten years later it was allowed to lapse finally on rather slender grounds, not of principle, such as Milton had expounded forty years before in *Areopagitica* – "A good book is the precious life-blood of a master spirit" – but apparently because of objection taken to the monopoly of the Stationers' Company, with whom all books had to be registered. The new liberty was in fact important as the beginning of a movement towards the free expression of opinion which was to make eighteenth-century Britain widely envied. The first daily newspaper, the *Courant*, was published in 1702; by 1714 the number of such papers had grown to seven. Yet the law of seditious libel still weighed heavily upon both authors and publishers: in

Anne's reign one judge declared that any criticism of government was sedition. The critics, such as Swift and Defoe, were certainly not silenced, however, though the latter was fined, pilloried, and imprisoned for one of his political pamphlets, and a further curb was applied to all political writers by the introduction of a stamp duty on newspapers and pamphlets.

Religious Liberty

This rather half-hearted abandonment of a political censorship came about chiefly because a religious censorship could no longer be applied by the Established Church against Protestant dissenters. In return for the support they had given to the Church of England in the struggle against James II, the Protestant nonconformists could now worship in their own churches, of which about a thousand are said to have been opened in William's reign; apart from the abortive law of 1714, they could also run their own schools. But it was a severely restricted liberty: the Anglican Sacrament was exacted as a condition for holding office under the Crown and even for membership of the corporations governing the towns. As most MPs were elected either directly by, or under the influence of, such corporations, the dissenters were in practice almost shut out of Parliament. Oxford and Cambridge were barred to them, but they were welcomed at the Scottish universities, to which some Welshmen also went from their own dissenting academies. While these disabilities affected only the well-to-do, more widespread resentment was caused by the fact that legal marriages could only be performed by the Anglican clergy. In spite of the Toleration Act, dissenters ranked as second-class citizens.

Still less liberty was granted to the Roman Catholic minority, of whose size we have no certain knowledge except that in 1692 they were served by more than one hundred priests. As citizens they were hardly even second-class. Not only were they excluded from any public office and from membership of either House of Parliament by the two Test Acts, but as a precaution against Jacobite plots they were forbidden to possess arms or a horse worth more than £5 and were debarred from residence in the cities of London and Westminster. The celebration of Mass involved in theory the penalty of life imprisonment, so priests often practised their profession under some kind of disguise. However, except when there was some scare or the mob was aroused, the Catholic community lived in freedom but also in separation from their fellow-citizens – a situation which was made tolerable by the existence of a number of old gentry families, which could organize Catholic services in an unobtrusive way. In London, from which Catholics were not in practice excluded, their worship centred upon the Portuguese and Sardinian embassies.

The Privileged Position of the Gentry

The classes whose liberty expanded most rapidly in this period were the gentry and the merchants. Through their hold on the House of Commons they seized control of the state, asserting broad principles of freedom as they did so, though by the end of the century MPs had narrowed their concept of freedom to mean chiefly the assertion of their own privileges as members of parliament. In 1701, for instance, the House of Commons imprisoned seven Kentish gentlemen who presented an unwelcome petition in favour of war, and declared their action to be 'scandalous, insolent and seditious'. But the general trend of their management of state affairs was towards the freedom of their class from inconvenient state controls such as the laws against enclosure, commercial and industrial monopolies, and the old pattern of social regulations. They laid the world open to individual enterprise.

In the countryside the landed gentry were supreme. As unpaid justices of the peace they dealt with all but the gravest crimes and also administered the affairs of their county. At their discretion they licensed ale-houses, fixed the price of bread, regulated wages, enforced the poor law, and repaired the roads and bridges. Tasks which up to the Civil Wars had been performed under the eye of the Privy Council, which frequently added new ones, were now performed or left unperformed by the light of self-interest, except when proceedings were taken before the assize judges.

Having spent lavishly at election time to secure their return to Parliament, the members of this class used their powers as legislators to their own benefit. In 1671 the first game law forbade the smaller freeholders whose land was worth less than £100 a year to shoot game on their own property, and one of the very few laws of King William's reign to receive full Tory approval was one to facilitate the preserving of pheasants. In 1673 a bounty on corn exports was combined with the duty on imports to guarantee for estate owners the steady profits needed to support an increasingly opulent way of life.

Secure in these matters, the gentry class set about building its houses in the new French and Dutch fashions, with hipped roofs and sash windows, and laying out its gardens with tree-lined avenues and gravel paths. In his *Memoirs* Sir John Reresby, a prominent Yorkshire Cavalier, describes the process. In 1668 he writes:

> It was this year that I began to build that side of the house towards the church . . . with stone, which was before only laths and rough cast, and to lay the garden walls in lime and sand . . . I made this summer . . . the fountain in the middle of the parterre and the grotto in the summerhouse and brought the water in lead pipes. I then built the north side of the house also with stone, which was roughcast before.

Two years later he took the interior of the house in hand:

> This year I was confined to Thriberge to make new ceiling or limework to most of the rooms throughout the whole house . . . and to new-wainscot several of the rooms and to paint the whole house. I was the first in these parts that began to rebuild or repair my house according to the mode of that time, which others have since followed.

In 1671 he was again improving the house and outbuildings:

> This year I took in that part of the park with a wall that lies beyond the ponds to the south. It was this summer also that I paved the courts and built the long stable to the house at Thriberge. I built the barn and ox-house of stone which stands northwest of the house instead of one of laths and lime which stood in the very front of it.

And in 1674 he was occupied with the gardens:

This spring I set that walk with ashes and sycamores that leads down to the ponds and so to the park wall . . . And though I might have planted trees of better kinds, yet I found that these agreed best with the soil and were of the speediest growth. I then made also the two lowest fish ponds in the park and stored them with tench and carp.

Such great houses formed the centre of their neighbourhood, linked with other such centres but not entirely separate from the humbler life circling round them. At such times as Christmas and New Year the landlord was one with his tenants – if we may judge by Sir John Reresby's account from Christmas 1684:

The four first days all my tenants of Thriberge, Brinsford, Deneby, Mexbrough, Hoton Roberts and Rotherham dined with me. The rest of the time some four score gentlemen and yeomen with their wives were invited, besides some that came from York, so that all the beds in the house and most in the town were taken up. There were seldom less than four score . . . that dined in the house every day and some days many more. On New Year's Day chiefly there dined above three hundred, so that whole sheep were roasted and served so up to feed them. For music I had five violins, besides bagpipes, drums and trumpet.

Yet the tenants may not always have felt cause to join in the festivities of the gentry, for often enough the common land on which they relied for fuel and rough grazing was being taken from them with or without the law. Sir John Reresby protected the common where his own interests were involved, as this entry of 1671 shows:

I commenced suit against the Countess Dowager of Strafford . . . for planting a warren and opening a quarry upon the common, which I opposed as a freeholder . . . but it went no further, my lord of Strafford and her ladyship both consenting that the warren should be destroyed and the quarry filled up.

Nevertheless, only a year earlier he had done much the same thing himself:

> I added some field land to it [the old deer park], which I exchanged with the tenants for other land, with a brow or cliff of wood belonging to the common . . . and encompassed it with a stone wall.

Commercial and Industrial Freedom

Sharing with the gentry as heirs of the revolution of the seventeenth century, there were the merchants and industrialists, many of whom put their money into land and so qualified as gentry in their own right. Sometimes, however, the movement went the other way – when landowners exploited mineral wealth on their estates, for instance, as did the Pryse family of Gogerddan in Cardiganshire. Wealth could be both made and used in many directions, and while land ownership continued to carry prestige, greater profit was often to be found in trade, industrial production and finance. As someone put it in 1674:

> I choose rather to keep my estate in money than in land, for I can make twice as much of it that way, considering what taxes are upon land and what advantages there are of making money upon the public funds.

This wealth found its way into parliament and local affairs and was exerted to produce a state offering the widest opportunities to men of ambition.

In overseas commerce they were concerned to liberate themselves from the control of the Dutch and establish their own privileged position in the colonial markets: this was the programme of the Navigation Acts[1]. At home the general trend may be seen in the encouragement of the wholesale corn merchant, through the relaxation in 1663 of the old laws against regrating and engrossing, and the gradual abandonment of regulations which standardized – and discouraged free enterprise in – the nation-wide woollen industry. "As the worthy makers of those good laws are now asleep," lamented a lover of standardization in 1691, "so are their laws too." In particular, free enterprise benefited from the decline of the gilds, which had no place in the life of new industrial areas, such

[1] See pp. 212–13.

as the teeming suburbs outside the precincts of the City of London, and were out of fashion even in the older towns. The ambitious entrepreneur no longer risked the interference of jealous fellow-gildsmen with his prices and processes; the justices of the peace might step into the gap, but there was no central authority requiring them to do so and for the most part they would have neither the knowledge nor the desire to interfere with industry.

The demand for freedom to develop new enterprises went hand in hand with the demand for a free market in labour. "In a free nation," wrote Bernard Mandeville, a Dutch immigrant physician who published the satirical *Fable of the Bees* (1714), "where slaves are not allowed of, the surest wealth consists in a multitude of laborious poor." One impediment to the freedom of the employing class was the institution of apprenticeship, which protected the skilled worker but held up the supply of the unskilled. In Mandeville's words: "Men who are to remain and end their days in a laborious, tiresome and painful station of life, the sooner they are put upon it, the more patiently they'll submit to it ever after." Not only were the unapprenticed 'put upon' their occupation younger, but these 'illegal men' – as those who had served a statutory apprenticeship called them – would tend to be more docile. The obligation to serve the seven-year period had first been suspended under Cromwell to help ex-soldiers to find employment; it had been waived in London in order to attract workers during the rebuilding after the Great Fire[1]; and by 1700, when the House of Commons expressed its hostility in general to such 'restraint of trade', only the most strongly organized and conservative crafts seem to have been able to enforce the system at all fully.

The mobility of labour was, however, to some extent impeded by the law of Settlement, a tightening-up of earlier practice made in 1662, when some parishes were experiencing a heavy demand for poor relief from one-time soldiers wandering in search of support. This Act gave every parish the formal right to send away within forty days any new arrival who seemed likely some day to become a burden upon the rates. Justified as it was in the eyes of ratepayers, who found the poor who were born within the parish a sufficient burden to cope with, the measure obviously hampered

[1] See p. 249.

employers in expanding industries. The lawyer and historian, Roger North, wrote of the poor as being 'imprisoned' in their villages: "Men want the work and the work men and are by laws kept from accommodating each other." In 1697, accordingly, the rule was relaxed in favour of immigrants whose parish of birth would issue a certificate, undertaking to receive them back if they should at some later time require relief.

The Unrestricted Flow of Capital

In matters of trade and industry and the supply of labour, the endeavours of the moneyed classes were all on the side of liberty. It was the same too with financial affairs – in the making available of the capital which lubricated the whole trading machine. Here the main instrument was the bankers, whom Clarendon described as 'a tribe that had risen and grown up in Cromwell's times and never were heard of before the late troubles'. Clarendon was about right: the regular London bankers appeared between 1640 and 1675. They came first from among the goldsmiths who, when Charles I had frightened moneyed men by seizing – temporarily – the bullion deposited in the Tower, began themselves to accept deposits. Other features of modern banking soon followed, such as the issuing of notes and discounting of bills of exchange and accepting of cheques. Bank notes originally were receipts for money deposited, bearing a promise to repay a particular sum to the depositor. About 1670 the promise of payment was extended to any 'bearer' of the receipt; thus the bank-note was born, to be recognized as legally negotiable in 1704. The 'discount' business was a natural way for the bank to employ its spare cash, while the idea of the modern cheque may be traced back to the depositors with the goldsmiths, who wrote orders for the payment of money from their account to named persons.

But the most important part of a bank's activities is the lending for interest. Early bankers soon found out that they could make use of their deposits in this way, since it was unlikely that everyone would want to withdraw their whole balance at the same time. In any case, loans could be made in notes without taking coin from the bank at all. Only a proportion of a bank's deposits had to be kept to meet current demand – the rest could be lent out or invested in trade and industry.

Alternatively it might be lent to the government, though banks were nervous after the royal seizure of Tower bullion (mentioned above) and the 'Stop of the Exchequer' in 1672, which caused half the banks to collapse. Interest rates rose high in the face of such risks: shortly after the Stop, Charles II was paying 10 per cent. It was to meet the increasing government need for funds in the great French wars that the Bank of England was founded in 1694, with a subscribed capital of £1,200,000 to be lent to the government at 8 per cent. As confidence in the Bank grew its interest rates dropped, till by 1714 they were only 5 per cent – a fall which affected general interest rates as well. So credit was available to finance the growth of industry and commerce, while every kind of business transaction was facilitated by the use of bank-notes and bills of exchange. Yet another help was the recoinage of 1696, when fraudulently clipped coins were replaced by a more reliable currency under the supervision of Sir Isaac Newton as Master of the Mint.

Bank loans were only one way of financing such expansion. The issue of stocks and shares was another; before 1700 news about the stock market was appearing, for example, in John Houghton's weekly journal called *A Collection of Letters*[1]. The dealers, he said, were to be found 'chiefly upon the Exchange[2] and at Jonathan's Coffee House, sometimes at Garroway's and at some other coffee houses'. Such were the unpretentious origins of the London Stock Exchange, and in many cases of insurance companies too. Marine business, for instance, was attracted to Lloyd's Coffee House in the 1680s, and marriage risks to Pilkin's Coffee House from about 1710. Fire insurance began in the later 1660s, but reliable life insurance still awaited the development of statistics. The needs of the trading world demanded such institutions, and providing them became itself an important part of business.

[1] See p. 240.

[2] i.e. Gresham's Royal Exchange, as rebuilt after the Great Fire; the Stock Exchange had no building of its own until 1773.

Development of Communications

Communications were also of obvious importance to the free activity of the trader, and in the late seventeenth century the first halting steps were taken towards their improvement. The roads were supposed to be kept in repair by the farmers of each parish, who were to provide six days labour a year under the control of an amateur surveyor: but they were not usually interested in the passage of anything but their own farm carts. In 1663, therefore, the first Turnpike Act was passed to enable toll roads to be established in Hertfordshire and two neighbouring counties, but the tolls which were to pay for better upkeep were easily evaded; the Act had no successor until 1690. A lady who made extensive journeys in that decade found the roads very variable – from Knaresborough to York, for example, was 'the worst riding in Yorkshire' and the Derbyshire hills made 'travelling tedious and the miles long'. Her most significant reflection, however, was when she observed that in 1698 she had covered 1,045 miles "of which I did not go above a hundred in the coach."

Stage-coaches first appeared about 1640 and developed fairly rapidly after the Restoration. But John Ogilby's *Britannia*, a road book published in 1675, indicates road conditions which would dispose people in general to prefer to ride a horse rather than be shaken about in a springless vehicle. The value of these early coach services to the business community was also reduced by their high cost and low speed: the fifty-odd miles between London and Oxford could be performed in one day in summer only, and the charge was a shilling for five miles. A more solid gain was the growth of postal services. In 1635 it was possible to send a letter at least 120 miles in a day, or from London to Edinburgh and back in six days. The Commonwealth made the post office into a well organized government monopoly, partly for purposes of espionage. Under Charles II the state remained in charge, with a fixed tariff varying by distance for destinations at home and abroad, and the enterprise of a merchant provided a London penny post for letters and packages up to a weight of one pound. Post boys, using relays of horses, now travelled along all the main roads out of the capital, but the crossposts between provincial towns were not well provided for until the following century.

Heavy goods were normally transported by water, as in many instances were lighter goods, including people. It is therefore a very important fact that between 1628 and 1683 the amount of shipping in coastal employment was trebled, and by the end of the century the capacity of the colliers, which were now in great demand, may even have quadrupled. Rivers, too, in which England is so rich, were more and more crowded with boats and barges, although their navigation was in many cases seriously impeded by fords, fishing-weirs, damming for corn mills, and shallows caused by silting. However, individuals sometimes took them in hand, as did Sir Richard Weston of Sutton Place in Surrey, who between 1635 and 1653 made much of the River Wey navigable by locks and cuts. Also Andrew Yarranton, an iron-master, who deepened the Stour, examined the courses of several other rivers, and in a far-sighted book in two parts, called *England's Improvement by Sea and Land* (1677, 1681), recommended 'making rivers navigable in all places where art could possibly effect it'.

Liberation of Trade in Scotland

In Scotland the pace of change was far slower than in England, yet there too men were beginning to demand wider scope for their desire to enrich themselves. But the Highlands were still apart, only interested in the outside world as the source for grain, malt and cloth, which they exchanged for their timber, sent down the Ness and Tay, and for their cattle, marketed in the country round the Firths of Tay and Forth.

There were no great changes in agriculture, where the short leases discouraged improvement. However, if minerals such as coal were discovered, such leases made it possible for the landlord to evict his tenants and abandon farming for mining.

The privileges of the royal burghs with their sole right to engage in trade and manufacture lay like a blanket over Scottish economic life, smothering change. Those who wished to strip away these privileges were the nobles and lairds, many of whom sought the right to set up 'burghs of barony': about a hundred new ones were authorized between 1660 and 1707, though less than half became 'real burghs'.[1] Strongly represented in parliament, the nobles and lairds concerned aimed at extending the powers of their burghs until they rivalled the royal burghs. Privileges of foreign trade were strongly contested,[2] but by 1672 burghs of barony had finally established the right to sell retail whatever was produced in Scotland. In the period 1660–1707 about 250 grants were also made to landlords for the establishment of weekly markets or annual fairs in country areas, outside any burghal control.

Scotland was still too poor for full industrial freedom to be practicable. Instead, Acts were passed in 1661 and 1681 to offer exclusive privileges to any foreign capitalists who would set up industries. Native capitalists, too, were encouraged by import bans to set up privileged joint stock companies: between 1681 and the Union about fifty of these came into existence to make textiles, pottery, paper, soap, gunpowder, and other commodities. As in England, banking developed to meet the new industrial needs as well as those of government. The Bank of Scotland was founded in 1695, with exclusive rights and a capital of £1,200,000 Scots (£100,000 sterling). In 1704–5 the general depression which overtook industry caused a four months suspension of cash payments; but the credit of the Bank easily survived this crisis, of which one lasting result was the withdrawal of English shareholders from participation in this Scottish national institution.

The Liberties of the Poor

The benefits in the shape of increased liberty of individual action, which resulted from the long struggle against the Crown, went chiefly to those classes of people, whether Englishmen or Scotsmen, which had taken the lead in that struggle. But were the poor better or worse off than before? Eventually of course, they inherited all the great political and legal advances that had been made, though for the time being these meant little to them. In some

[1] G. S. Pryde, *New History of Scotland*, II, 32 (footnote 4).
[2] See p. 105.

ways the triumph of Parliament was directly disadvantageous to them – the Settlement law, the ending of Crown supervision over the activities of the JPs, the falling into disuse of the laws against enclosures, and the levying of excise duties mainly on beer, the staple drink of the humbler classes, are some examples. But it is easy to exaggerate this aspect of a complex situation: the latest full-scale economic study of the period concludes that "the picture of a ruthlessly materialistic ruling class exploiting wage-earners and the poor is not borne out by the facts."[1] The most important of these is the steady rise in wages during the second half of the century.

This was not due primarily to a scarcity of labour, for the same period saw the decline and disappearance of the plague, whose ravages for centuries had affected the death-rate among the poor in the slum quarters of the towns more than the rich, who could (and often did) escape into the country. Its visitations in 1603, 1625, and 1636 were almost as severe as that of 1665, to which Pepys's Diary and Defoe's fictitious *Journal of the Plague Year* have given celebrity. But the 70,000 deaths in London on that occasion were followed by an astonishingly rapid abatement of the disease in all parts of Europe, attributed to the elimination of the plague-flea-carrying black rat by the brown. By 1700 the poor had an increased 'freedom to live'.

In spite of rising wages, the availability of poor relief remained an important factor in the life of a country where, according to a statistical estimate of 1696, cottagers and paupers formed a quarter of the population. In each parish it was administered by unpaid overseers of the poor, often farmers or shopkeepers serving in rotation. The justices by this time seldom interfered with the choice of the parish in this matter, though they were supposed to approve the amount of the rate levied and the expenditure recorded in the accounts. Here are some items from the accounts of a Gloucestershire parish in the 1680s:

> To Joane Web for tending of Goody Hoskings four months at 10s. a month £2–00–00
> For milk for Goody Hoskings £1–05–06, for candles and soap

[1] C. Wilson, *England's Apprenticeship 1603–1763*, p. 136.

for her £0–06–00, coal and wood £0–04–00, a bed pan and other necessaries, £0–04–06
For burying of her..............................£0–10–06
Given Goody Evans, her husband being in prison and she and her children being in Great Want, at several times in money and coal £0–14–00

Since 'Goody' was 'a term of civility applied to (married) women in humble life',[1] these examples clearly relate to the 'deserving poor'. Some parishes had their own poor-houses in which the old and feeble or orphaned children could be maintained. But this was expensive, and no doubt many overseers made use of such helpers as Joane Web.

A harsher attitude was adopted towards the able-bodied poor, who were believed to enjoy the liberty of deliberate idleness at the expense of all industrious persons and to the detriment of the national economy. Obdurate vagrants might be committed to Houses of Correction, by this time hardly distinguishable from county gaols. As rates went up, efforts were made to find a wider solution. In 1696 Bristol experimented with a single workhouse to serve all its parishes, and was able to claim that "All do something though perhaps some of their labours comes to little, yet it keeps them from idleness". This project was imitated in many other towns, such as Norwich, whose building accommodated a thousand poor, and the City of London. There the workhouse established in Bishopsgate in 1699 received children from all the parishes, who worked at spinning or knitting and elementary education as well, and beggars or vagrants for hemp-beating and other tasks; the result was a rate of discharge of 500 persons a year. To keep these institutions effective, however, either for industry of any kind or as deterrents for the work-shy, required conscientious and expert administration; in most places the guardians found it much easier to slip back into doling out outdoor relief on the traditional lines.

The status of the individual Englishman was clearly improved by the existence of the right to poor relief, even if it was open to abuse; it was not necessary to look farther afield than Scotland to

[1] *O.E.D.*

see what suffering the absence of any real equivalent caused in times of widespread famine, such as the 'seven ill years' at the turn of the century. In addition, he gained at this time through an increase in private charity, some of it taking the traditional form of the provision of almshouses or funds to supply needy families with food and clothing, but a growing proportion assigned to organizing instruction for their children. It is noteworthy that in London, Norwich, and Bristol alike, one-third of all surviving charitable trusts date from the period 1660–1714. The most promising new development of this kind was the Charity School movement under the auspices of the newly formed Society for the Promotion of Christian Knowledge: although the schools were designed to inculcate Anglicanism, qualifications for humble industrial or domestic employment, and a very elementary education – in that order, for some at least of their pupils they opened the doors to independence, self-respect, and liberty of the spirit.

We cannot tell whether the events of the seventeenth century had extended the liberty of the individual to enjoy life. The failure of the Puritans to consolidate their power in politics ensured the survival of many traditional pleasures, which they had wished to suppress. And yet the Restoration comedies of such writers as William Wycherley, with their witty denigration of all the bourgeois virtues, do not necessarily mean that the upper class had succeeded in capturing enjoyment. Perhaps it is more easily measured in the freedom of the countryside – the Maypole, the morris dancers, the hunting of the hare, the musket competition at the butts, the click of bowls on the green, the arguments on the alehouse bench. Even there, one liberty of self-expression seemed to be on the decline, as a more or less standard English came increasingly into fashion. In 1678 the last sermon that we know of was preached in Cornish; lowland Scots, while it encroached upon Gaelic in the mountains, was coming increasingly to resemble the other English of the south; and it was even noticed that the native tongue 'wears out more and more in south Wales, especially since the Civil Wars'.

'John Bull'

In 1712 John Arbuthnot, a fashionable physician and Tory propagandist of Scottish extraction, wrote five pamphlets on the war, in which John Bull is agreeably contrasted with Lewis Baboon. Unlike the scoundrelly Frenchman who sells liveries, John is "an honest plain-dealing fellow, choleric, bold, and of a very inconstant temper . . . a boon companion, loving his bottle and his diversion; for, to say truth, no man kept a better house than John, nor spent his money more generously". John Bull was quickly accepted as the very personification of British liberty, to be depicted by cartoonists as the broad-paunched proprietor of a small estate. Rightly so, for the events of the preceding century had secured the liberties of just such as he.

12

THE BRITISH OVERSEAS

So far we have considered the British as they developed in their island base. In the course of the Stuart century, however, they had burst their bounds to settle in the West Indies, along the east coast of North America from the Carolinas to Maine, and to a small extent in Newfoundland and Nova Scotia. They also acquired scattered trading stations on both sides of the Indian peninsula and in West Africa, and strategic outposts in the Mediterranean at Gibraltar and Minorca. To what was this astonishing expansion due? Religious and social discontent; the enthusiasms of the explorer, the adventurer, and the missionary; and international political rivalries – all these played a part. But above all there was the desire to capture trade.

Rivalry in Foreign Trade

The people of this age had what may seem to us an exaggerated idea of the value of a favourable trade balance, measured conveniently in terms of bullion, as an indication superior to all others of the growth of national power and prosperity. This was pithily stated in *England's Treasure by Foreign Trade*, a book first published in 1664 which ran through six editions in a century:

> The ordinary means to increase our wealth and treasure is by foreign trade, wherein we must ever observe this rule: to sell more to strangers yearly than we consume of theirs in value . . . because that part of our trade which is not returned to us in wares must necessarily be brought home in treasure . . . The balance of the Kingdom's account ought to be drawn up yearly, or so often as it shall please the State to discover how much we gain or lose by trade with foreign nations.

Although a permanent board of trade was not established until 1696, Charles II had for a time a 'committee of trade and plantations', with the philosopher John Locke as secretary and the future Whig leader, lord Shaftesbury, as president. "It is trade and commerce alone," declared the latter, "that draweth store of wealth along with it."

Seventeenth-century people also believed that there was a fixed amount of wealth in the world: one country could only be enriched at the expense of another. This sharpened national antagonisms everywhere so that, as religious differences became less bitter, economic jealousies took their place. The Dutch, for instance, who had been the Protestant allies of England in the sixteenth century, in the seventeenth became her deadly rivals – the national enemy in three wars. Such rivalries became all the more dangerous as the state took over from the trading companies the direction of economic policy, making it the servant of national interests. Trading therefore became bound up with the national power which could win the wars caused by economic jealousies; it followed that naval strength and the training of seamen became important to the state. In all this there was nothing to encourage co-operation between trading nations, and it became the main object of each to stifle foreign competition. In England the instrument for this was the group of Navigation laws, especially those of 1651 and 1660.

The Navigation Acts

These had two main intentions: firstly to strengthen English shipping by excluding foreign vessels from our carrying trade, and secondly to monopolize the most valuable colonial products. Therefore only English and colonial ships were henceforth allowed to trade between the colonies and England, and certain 'enumerated commodities' (by 1714 sugar, tobacco, cotton, ginger, indigo, dye-woods, naval stores and rice) were to be exported from the colonies to England alone. These enumerated articles were either thought to be profitable for resale on the Continent or important to English manufacturers or essential to the power of the state. Sugar, tobacco, ginger and rice came in the first category; cotton, indigo and dye-woods in the second; and naval stores for shipbuilding in the last. While such measures ensured a sale for these colonial products, they prevented the colonies searching out the highest bidders and forced them to accept the prices offered in the English market. On the other hand, English consumers were also bound to the colonial supply in some at least of these articles. Tobacco planting, for instance, was forbidden in England, though the low prices ensured by the constant flow of supplies would in any case have made it unprofitable. The idea of empire that the Navigation Acts enshrined was that of a closed system, in which the colonies supplied the mother country with vital raw materials and goods for re-exportation, and took from her all the manufactures they needed. For about a century the colonies accepted this situation, but obviously it could not last for ever.

The Navigation Acts legislated so strictly for colonial trade because in the seventeenth century it became more and more difficult to organize distant trades except on a colonial basis – or at least on that of permanent trading stations which eventually became colonial. Europe was an exception, of course, and so (it turned out) was the Ottoman Empire, because these were stable and developed territories where access to ports and harbours was all that was necessary. They already produced goods which had only to be collected and needed imports which required no more than safe delivery. In most of the areas, however, where trade went hand in hand with the establishment of colonies, the materials England needed were not yet being produced; their production awaited the labour and capital to be supplied by colonists. Furthermore, the fierce economic competition of the later seventeenth century and the exclusive trading policies followed by the European Powers meant that access to the sources of raw materials had to be seized from – or at least defended against – rivals. From these considerations sprang the growth of colonies.

The West Indies

Of all the colonies the most important to England in the seventeenth century – and for some way into the next – were those round the Caribbean. This can be seen from the list of colonial articles 'enumerated' in the 1660 Navigation Act. With the exception of naval stores, which (if colonial) came from North America, and of Asiatic indigo all came from near those favoured waters. William Penn, who gave his name to the colony he founded, pointed out the importance of this area in his *Account of the Province of Pennsylvania* (1681):

> What is an improved acre in Jamaica or Barbados worth to an improved acre in England? We know 'tis three times the value, and the product of it comes for England and is usually paid for in English growth and manufacture.

And he went on to state the importance of colonial settlement in more general terms – in its stimulus to shipping and the crafts dependent on it:

> The plantations employ many hundreds of shipping and many thousands of seamen; which must be in divers respects an advantage to England, being an island and by nature fitted for navigation above every country in Europe. This is followed by the depending trades, as shipwrights, carpenters, sawyers, hewers, trunnel-makers,[1] joiners, slop-sellers, dry-salters, iron workers, the Eastland merchants, timber sellers and victuallers with many more trades which hang upon navigation.

Colonists moved early into the West Indies, where before mid-century they were established in the Bermudas and Barbados, as well as in Honduras on the mainland. Jamaica was seized from Spain in 1655 and next year a landing was made in the uninhabited Bahamas; the treaty of Utrecht added St Kitts, which had been first occupied by English settlers in 1623. Once acquired, however, their value depended on three factors: ease of access, which made it more practicable to exploit small islands than vast hinterlands; suitability for saleable crops, of which sugar became the most important; and the procurement of a large supply of suitable labour. Apart from the initial outlay, slaves cost no more than their keep and, unlike indentured white labourers, could be made to work long hours in a tropical climate.

Thus the slaves from West Africa, whose first introduction we

[1] truck-makers (*Webster's Dictionary*).

have noticed in the sixteenth century, were now imported on a much larger scale: between 1640 and 1651, for instance, the number in Barbados rose from 1,000 to 20,000. West Africa in this way became part of the Caribbean economic area, in which by 1714 the British had replaced the Dutch as the principal purveyors of slaves. This invidious and highly profitable distinction Britain retained until the slave trade was belatedly abolished by Act of Parliament in 1807. Its organization was entrusted to the Royal African Company of 1672, which quadrupled its nominal capital in the first sixteen years of its long life and was still conducting about one-sixth of the trade as late as the 1730s. By that time, however, its main function was the upkeep of the forts, such as Fort James on the River Gambia, which was ceded to England (by other Europeans) in 1664, and other protected trading posts along the Gold and Slave Coasts farther south.

Slaves, sugar, tobacco, and later, cotton – these were the subjects of trade which for England bound the Atlantic region into a single whole. There was also increasingly a trade in less basic commodities, especially rum, which the New England colonies produced from West Indian molasses for export to England, where it helped to pay for their supplies of manufactured goods. At the centre of this economic system the western English ports benefited particularly. At Bristol customs receipts went up 1,000 per cent between 1614 and 1687; after the Restoration there was also rapid growth at Liverpool, which built the first wet dock in 1709.

The Twelve American Colonies

Twelve more colonies, predominantly of a different character, were strung out along the North Atlantic coastline between the Appalachians and the sea. Virginia had struggled into existence in 1607, as the property of a company in London which never paid a dividend and was wound up in 1623; by that time their colony had about a thousand white settlers. New England was inaugurated by the Pilgrim Fathers in 1620, but its effective development began a decade later, when the Massachusetts Company was formed of intending emigrants, with the result that the population rose in the next ten years from 1,000 to 14,000. Other, smaller ventures sprang from this, three of which – Maryland, Rhode Island, and Pennsylvania, which was the last of the twelve – had the merit and attraction of religious toleration. The first and third of these had individual proprietors in control. Lord Baltimore made Maryland originally a refuge for his fellow-Catholics, the Quaker William Penn the younger in 1681 brought in, not only his co-religionists but also Welsh Baptists (numerous enough to require books in their own language) and many refugees from the Continent.

But although geography made them part of the Atlantic economic system, these colonies did not fit snugly into it. Apart from the big tobacco-growing estates of Virginia and some unsuccessful efforts to produce silk, oils, and fruits of the Mediterranean type in the Carolinas as a special venture early in the reign of Charles II, they did not offer those semi-tropical materials which made the Atlantic area so important to England. Even rum required molasses from elsewhere – and in any case these were predominantly colonies of settlement rather than trade.

They had been settled chiefly by small men of the skilled artisan or farmer class, whose main concern was not trade with Britain so much as the carving out a living for themselves in a new world. This appears from American colonial prospectuses, which put the stress on small farming. Such, for instance, as this of 1622:

> With what content shall the particular person employ himself there when he shall find that for £12. 10*s*. adventure he shall be made lord of 200 acres, to him and his heirs forever. And for the charge of transportation of himself, his family and tenants he shall be allotted for every person he carries 100 acres more. And what labourer soever transport himself thither at his own charge, to have the like proportion of land upon the aforesaid conditions and be sure of employment to his good content for present maintenance.

Some of the earlier emigrants were Puritans who went – to New England especially – to escape the Anglican church discipline. Typical of these was the minister Thomas Higginson, who in these words made his goodbyes to the vanishing English coast:

> We will not say as the separatists were wont to say at their leaving of England, Farewell Babylon! Farewell Rome! But we will say farewell dear England! Farewell the Church of God in England and all the Christian friends there! We do not go to New England as separatists from the Church of England; though we cannot but separate from the corruptions in it. But we go to practise the positive part of the church reformation and propagate the gospel in America.

From the reign of Charles II onwards the colonial population included transported criminals and a considerable class of indentured labourers, poor emigrants who raised the money for their passage by binding themselves for a term of years to employers in the colonies. But in most parts life was a constant battle with harsh natural conditions, even for a free man. John Winthrop, the first governor of Massachusetts, describes for instance in his *Journal* an episode just after Christmas 1630, when a party in an open boat were driven ashore at Cape Cod on their way to Plymouth, the first capital of the colony. Having no hatchet to cut firewood, four of them perished from exhaustion; friendly Indians disposed of the bodies under piles of timber, as the soil was frozen too deep for grave-digging and the wolves must somehow be kept off. There is nothing of the travel brochure about this picture. Settlers had also to endure isolation from their fellows in the American wilderness and from all contacts with home. John Winthrop tells how the first news of the Civil War was brought to Massachusetts by two fishing boats on February 12th, 1643 – six months after its start.

Not every colony was acquired peacefully. New York, formerly named New Amsterdam, was seized from the Dutch in 1664, closing a geographical gap in the line of English colonies and an economic gap as well, which had enabled the Dutch to trade within the colonial system. Charles II wrote of it to his sister in obvious satisfaction:

> You will have heard of our taking of New Amsterdam, which lies just by New England. 'Tis a place of great importance to trade. It did belong to England heretofore, but the Dutch by

degrees drove our people out and built a very good town, but we have got the better of it and 'tis now called New York.

Yet, whether they were acquired peacefully or not, these American colonies were primarily colonies of settlement whose population by 1714 was about 340,000. Such colonies did not fit into the trading pattern – they produced goods not so different from England herself and so were often in financial difficulties, needing English manufactures, especially textiles and hardware (such as spades and hatchets, as we have seen above), but lacking the money with which to buy them. They were permanently on the depressed end of the balance of trade. Virginian tobacco was in great demand both for home consumption and re-exportation; it helped for instance to balance England's own shaky balance of trade with the Baltic area. Naval stores were important, too – increasingly so after 1650 – but most of them came from Scandinavia and the Baltic: the very imports that caused that imbalance of trade just mentioned. American were larger than Baltic masts but, where medium ones were needed, those from the Baltic were thought to be better. American cotton as yet hardly existed, and that enumerated under the Navigation Acts came almost entirely from the West Indies.

Other Ventures in North America

Away to the north of New England was Nova Scotia, which under French rule was named Acadia. This cannot be properly considered as a colony till 1713, when possession ceased to be disputed by the French. Farther north again was Newfoundland, which John Cabot had first claimed for England and which the Elizabethan Humphrey Gilbert had failed to colonize. In spite of the grant of part of it to Sir George Calvert for settlement in 1621, its main importance lay in the fertile cod-fishing grounds, to which not only English but also French and Portuguese fishing fleets went each summer. The fish were salted and dried on shore and the catch brought back to Europe in the autumn, so that at mid-century the 2,000 or so settlers were less important than the much greater number of seasonal visitors: in 1626 there had been

150 boats from Devon alone. The English fishing interests feared the competition of a permanent settlement and persuaded the government to ban it – so far at least as the coasts were concerned (and nowhere else mattered). The government continued to pay great attention to the fishing interests, even after annexation was confirmed in 1713, because they believed this trade to be vital for training seamen – a constant reservoir of men for the naval and merchant power of the country. On this power the preservation of the system of the Navigation Acts depended.

Nine hundred miles to the west were the vast expanses of Hudson Bay, round whose southern shores Indians and bears had things much to themselves. A company was formed under Prince Rupert in 1670, partly with the now antiquated idea of searching for a north-west passage, but also with the more practical intention of trading English guns and hatchets for Indian furs. From the start it was a rich man's company, with £300 as the price for a full share, and it is not surprising that as late as 1721 there were only fifty shareholders. Yet in its first eighteen years its nominal capital trebled – partly, no doubt, because for the first fourteen it paid no dividend! But it was also put to the expense of defending its trading posts against the French, who were engaged in the same trade along the line of the St Lawrence. Until that quarrel was settled much later, its activities were limited; the Hudson's Bay Company stood rather in the wings while the seventeenth-century scenes in the drama of trade and empire were enacted.

Trade with the East

At the other side of the world the East India Company, founded at the start of the seventeenth century, had become by its end the greatest of the trading companies. All round the Indian coasts its stations were scattered – from Surat and Bombay in the north-west to Madras and elsewhere on the Coromandel coast, on to Masulipatam in the east and to Calcutta in the north-east of the sub-continent. It says something both for its own activities and its skill in siting that Calcutta, Bombay and Madras are three of the four largest cities of modern India. Yet, except for Bombay (which was ceded to Charles II by the Portuguese on his marriage to

Catherine of Braganza and by him given to the East India Company), the organization had no territorial sovereignty, leasing its 'factories' from Indian rulers. What impelled the Company to defend its stations and introduce land and sea forces into the area was the growing weakness of the Mogul Empire, which left the factories open to attack. With the death of Aurungzebe in 1707 the Mogul Empire broke up and some defence became the more urgent as India sank into anarchy. There was also rivalry with the Dutch and, between 1698 and 1708, with a second English company (the 'General Society') which was established with parliamentary backing by merchants opposed to the monopoly of the older company.

The East India Company brought into England luxury products of Asia in great demand – raw and woven silk, cotton materials, porcelain and carpets (but very little tea at this stage, mainly because it was a Chinese rather than an Indian product). But there was little that it could sell in return for these things, for India had no mass market for English goods. The difference could only be made up by a large export of silver, and this was looked on with horror by an England conditioned to believe that the precious metals were the only true wealth – though it was plain that the value of the goods imported was far greater than that of the silver which paid for them.

Half-way to India – at the eastern end of the Mediterranean – was the Levant, where trade was carried on by the Levant Company. All this area was part of the wide and still spreading Ottoman Empire, which in this century was pushing its way into the heart of Europe itself. The Levant Company carried on trade at three centres – Constantinople, Smyrna and Aleppo – where it had permanent representatives. At Aleppo there were fifty Englishmen and a Company chaplain together with an English consul. The trade was very similar to the East India Company's but much better balanced, since the Turks were in a position to import as well as export goods. The Turkish product most in demand was raw cotton, followed by wine, oils and alum. Lewis Roberts, a Beaumaris merchant who had two sons in the Levant Company, recorded cotton together with many other goods:

> Galls for dyers, aniseeds, cordovants,[1] wax, grogram,[2] yarns, chamlets,[2] carpets, gems from India, spices from Arabia, Mohairs and raw silks brought overland from Persia and goat's hair.

In at any rate partial return for these things the Company exported predominantly English cloth – it is thought that the Turkish Empire took up to a quarter of the total cloth exports – and also lead and tin, together with re-exports of Indian spices and indigo.

Decline of the Chartered Companies

Although they had been for so long in the vanguard of English trading activities overseas, in the later seventeenth century the Companies were beginning to decline. One reason for this lay in the fact that the protection of merchants abroad was more and more the concern of the Royal Navy. Its ships had first entered Mediterranean waters under the Commonwealth flag; by 1713 they sailed them regularly. Fleets were also sent from time to time into the Baltic. Thus the East India and Hudson's Bay Companies were the only ones which continued to protect their members as in earlier periods – and these two long retained their strength.

But what chiefly affected the fortunes of the Companies in general was the transference of control over the nation's economic policy from the king's hands to those of parliament. Its members did not think of the Companies first and foremost as a convenient source of revenue, but as a commercial device which benefited the largest merchants rather than the man of medium resources, and London, where the Companies had their headquarters, rather than the outports in the provinces. Many MPs were themselves men of medium resources from those outports. Thus at various dates between 1671 and 1712 the admission fees to the Russia, Eastland, and Merchant Adventurers' Companies, all of them conducting European trades, were either lowered by degrees or disappeared outright. The trade of the Levant and Royal African Companies was opened by rather slower stages, but by 1700

[1] High-grade leather.
[2] Fabrics made of mohair, etc.

parliament had adopted for commerce the principle which it announced for the regulation of industry: "Trade ought to be free and not restrained."

More and more the state was taking control of external trading relations. The Methuen Treaty of 1703, for instance, wrenched the whole course of the traditional wine trade with France towards trade with Portugal. A duty of £7 per tun on Portuguese wines as against £55 on French was an economic pistol pointed at the national enemy. Because of it port and madeira appeared on British tables – to the financial rather than the bodily benefit of the consumer, as gout became the characteristic malady of the upper classes.

In customs duties generally the state – pushed by manufacturers and merchants – moved away from the idea that customs merely raised revenue to the conception that they should control the whole volume of production and trade. Most export duties, therefore, disappeared about the turn of the century; in the case of corn they were actually succeeded by an export bounty, so that (to the predictable pleasure of landowning MPs) grain could be sold abroad at under cost price. Thus landlords, merchants and manufacturers had taken over from the Crown the direction of economic affairs: one of the most important results of the revolution of 1688.

Growth of Scottish Commerce

Scotland was influenced by the same economic ideas as the south: the same fear of a flow of silver overseas and the same insistence on a favourable balance of trade. 'In future', said Sir Thomas Craig in his *De Unione Regnorum Britanniae* (1605),

> our people must pay very particular attention to the manufacture of cloth, for thence will proceed our ability to import wines, merchandise, and those things on which men set store. Otherwise we shall find it hard to raise the money to pay for our imports.

But in fact Scotland was so little developed that she needed to import a great deal: timber, flax and hemp from Scandinavia and the Baltic area; wines and silks from France; from the Netherlands spices and fine textiles; and from England various manufactures, which again included textiles – to take only a few examples. To pay for these Scotland employed her traditional exports of fish, salt, hides, cattle, coal, and linen. But all except the last of these had the character of raw materials, which commanded low prices as compared with luxury imports.

One way in which the state tried to redress the balance was by widening the privilege of engaging in foreign trade, which up to the Restoration was legally monopolized by the royal burghs. Other burghs were included by a law of 1672, which was modified to their disadvantage in 1690; but three years later foreign trade was thrown open to any place, whether burgh or not, which was willing to contribute to the land tax paid by the royal burghs. Secondly, the English Navigation laws had their counterpart in a Scottish Navigation Act of 1661, which was, however, directed primarily against the English rather than the Dutch. Since England after the end of the Cromwellian regime treated the Scots as foreigners in matters of commerce, her ships and trade were as far as possible to be excluded. This in turn produced a third course of action. It was forbidden to export raw materials, such as hides, linen yarn, and wool, which could be used for home manufactures, or to import them in manufactured form from abroad.

In 1693 one of the many Acts for setting up companies to conduct such manufactures refers explicitly to

> the great advantages that arise to other nations, and particularly to our neighbour nation of England, by the erecting and carrying on of manufactories, especially those of cloth.

But the Scots were handicapped by scarcity of capital, skilled craftsmanship, and commercial experience, while the English wars against Holland and France cut off important lines of trade, so that many east coast ports began to decline. The sequel was the disastrous Darien scheme, which has already been described because its failure led indirectly to the Act of Union. Nevertheless, it would be wrong to conclude that the Scots in the two generations before the union of parliaments achieved nothing overseas.

In New Jersey and South Carolina, the proprietors allowed

organized settlements of Scotsmen to be made in the reign of Charles II. More important, the English colonies as a whole being short of manpower welcomed individual Scottish settlers, and a Scottish Privy Council document of 1666 shows that, in some cases at least, it was the approved policy to send them:

> Supplication by James Dumbar, merchant bound for Barbados, as follows: out of zeal for his country and promoting of trade and the credit of Scotsmen in the foreign plantations, he has by warrant of the justices of the peace seized several vagabonds and idle persons to carry to the said plantations. . . .
>
> The Lords hereby authorize justices of peace to apprehend vagabonds and to deliver them to the petitioner for transport to the Barbados; and ordain the magistrates to deliver to him such prisoners as are willing to go to Barbados.

We do not know how widespread and effectual this 'zeal for the credit of Scotsmen in the foreign plantations' may have been, but it was at least a promising beginning.

Finally, it may be noticed that Glasgow during this period began the rise which was to make it, after the Union, one of the principal British trade links with the overseas world. A Glasgow professor declared during the Cromwellian union that it "thrives above all the land . . . our people has much more trade in comparison than any other". Some of this trade was done with Ireland and the Scottish Highlands, but the most lucrative part was the trade in colonial products. Athough this became illicit at the Restoration, it seems clear that tobacco and sugar from the English colonies continued to flow along the established routes to the quaysides on the Clyde. On a close estimate[1] the rise in population, which raised Glasgow from fifth to second place among the cities of Scotland, was from 7,644 in 1610 to 12,766 in the year after the Union, when an enumeration was carried out by the magistrates.

[1] G. S. Pryde, *A New History of Scotland,* II 78; H. Hamilton, *Economic History of Scotland in the Eighteenth Century,* p. 18.

13

SCIENTIFIC AND TECHNICAL ADVANCES

In the early years of the seventeenth century John Donne cast a bewildered eye on the progress of the new Science:

> *The new philosophy calls all in doubt,*
> *The element of fire is quite put out;*
> *The sun is lost and the earth, and no man's wit*
> *Can well direct him where to look for it.*

This 'new philosophy' was that preached by Francis Bacon, for a time lord chancellor to James I. Though he was not a scientist himself, in such books as the *Novum Organum, or Indications concerning the Interpretation of Nature* (1620) Bacon proclaimed the view that science in co-operation with nature could transform the life of man. "Nature to be commanded must be obeyed," he wrote, for nothing could be done against the very conditions of existence. It was necessary first to observe nature and then, from a multitude of particular instances, to build up a pattern of natural law. As one of the chief officers of state, he knew what he was talking about when he said that "Nature like a witness reveals her secrets when put to torture." This process of torture was patient experiment – a long third-degree examination by question and answer. As a result of this, since seventeenth-century science was always close to practical things, inventive genius would be stimulated and life made easier. "The real and legitimate goal of the sciences," he claimed, "is the endowment of human life with new inventions and riches."

Scientific Pioneers

These ideas were not influential till later in the century, and Bacon himself was satisfied to speak to the future. "I shall content myself," he wrote, "to awake better spirits, like a bell-ringer which is first up to call others to church." However, he knew that he was not alone in his bell-tower, for the *Novum Organum* mentions with respect the *De Magnete* of William Gilbert,[1] who died just after James's accession. Here Gilbert was already using the methods that Bacon approved and, like him, was interested not in vague theories but in 'the commerce of the mind with things'. Like Bacon, too, Gilbert believed in a close relationship between science and industry, he himself learning how to forge iron and getting to know miners, iron-workers and seamen. It was from Robert Norman, a seaman and compass-maker who in 1581 had published *The New Attractive*, that Gilbert discovered that a suspended needle dips from the horizontal in a way which could be given a value for different parts of the world. From this, and from various magnetic experiments, Gilbert concluded that the earth itself was a magnet, which explained both the dip of the needle and its pointing to the north. From his absorption with the earth he turned to the universe, becoming the first scientist in England to support the Copernican idea that the sun was its centre. Looking farther into space, he concluded that the fixed stars were at widely differing distances from the earth and so at a stroke revealed the staggering immensity of the setting in which the earth hangs. "How immeasurable then," he exclaimed,

> must be the space which stretches to those remotest of fixed stars! . . . How far removed from the earth must the most widely separated stars be and at a distance transcending all sight, all skill and thought!

It was in the reign of James VI and I that the first great British mathematician made his appearance in the person of John Napier, laird of Merchiston Castle, Edinburgh. In 1614 he invented logarithms, the fruit of twenty years' study, though their final form was settled with the help of Henry Briggs, a professor at Gresham's College in London. Napier also gave to arithmetic the idea of the decimal point and devised a machine ('Napier's Rods') for multiplication and division. Another professor at Gresham's College in James's later years was Edmund Gunter, who further developed

[1] See p. 38.

trigonometry; he invented a simple form of slide rule as well as the surveyor's chain with which his name is still associated.

From 1616 onwards William Harvey, a physician at St Bartholomew's Hospital, London, was delivering his annual lectures to the College of Physicians in which he expounded his great discovery of the circulation of the blood. He showed that the heart is a pump, working by muscular action to drive the blood from one side of the heart round the body to the other. He had dissected no fewer than 80 species of animals, but as he had no microscope it was impossible for him to detect the part played by the capillaries in taking the blood from the arteries to the veins. The greatest discovery in the history of physiology was made known to the world in a Latin treatise *De Motu Cordis et Sanguinis*, which Harvey published at Frankfort in 1628. As physician to Charles I – he was later to figure in the royal entourage at the battle of Edgehill – he dedicated his book to the king, making a neat analogy between the place of the heart in the body and that of the Crown in the state: "The animal's heart is the basis of its life . . . equally is the King the basis of his kingdom."

The Royal Society

It is significant that the first English version of Harvey's book appeared in 1653, for it was in the ferment of ideas at the time of the Civil War that English science first became an organized movement. By 1645 the new experimental philosophy was being discussed at weekly meetings of a so-called 'Invisible College', chiefly centred at first on Gresham's College, London, but later also upon the university of Oxford. There the moving spirit was John Wilkins, the author of a book arguing the possibility of human life on the moon, who was Warden of Wadham College and Cromwell's brother-in-law. Six months after the Restoration he became the first chairman of a permanent organization, designed to hold weekly meetings for a membership to be restricted to 55 peers and professed scientists. As Charles II frequently attended the meetings, the lack of any financial basis beyond the members' subscriptions – ten shillings entrance fee and a shilling a week – was no bar to the attainment of a charter of incorporation as 'The Royal Society of London for Improving Natural Knowledge' (1662); in March 1665 the Society published the first number of its still continuing *Philosophical Transactions*.

The draft preamble to the statutes of the society, which is believed to have been written by Robert Hooke, set out clearly the Baconian direction of its studies – applied rather than pure science:

> The business of the Royal Society is to improve the knowledge of natural things and all useful arts, manufactures, mechanic practices, engines and inventions by experiment . . .

And Hooke made the same point in the formal dedication of his book *Micrographia* to the king, where he contrasts the comparative unimportance of his own academic studies with the more practical pursuits of others:

> There are, Sir, several other of your subjects now busy about nobler matters: the improvement of manufactures and agriculture, the increase of commerce, the advantage of navigation . . .

Everything was to be practical, even the very language in which science was expressed – as Thomas Sprat proclaimed as early as 1667 in his *History of the Royal Society*. "The Royal Society," he wrote,

> have exacted from all their members, a close, naked, natural way of speaking; positive expressions, clear senses; a native easiness: bringing all things as near the mathematical plainness as they can: and preferring the language of artisans, countrymen and merchants, before that of wits or scholars.

These early members of the Royal Society performed their experiments before the whole body and discussed them afterwards. Some of their names are familiar to all who have even the slightest knowledge of seventeenth-century science: Robert Boyle the so-called 'father of chemistry', the physiologist William Harvey, Robert Hooke the mathematician and astronomer, the botanist Nehemiah Grew, the astronomer Edmund Halley, Isaac Newton the mathematician, and the architect Christopher Wren.

Growth of Scientific Ideas

Robert Boyle, the son of the first earl of Cork, was to affect deeply the whole technology of the coming industrial revolution. Although he considered himself first as a chemist, he is known also for the improved air pump which Robert Hooke and he constructed from a German original. In this 'new pneumatical engine' the two men created vacuums though, as Boyle wrote: "We never were able totally to exhaust the receiver or keep it when it was almost empty . . . from leaking more or less." Boyle found that in a vacuum sound would not carry and that fire and breathing were impossible. He discovered, too, that air and other gases at a constant temperature have a volume that varies according to the pressure: the more pressure the less volume. "There is a spring or elastical power in the air," Boyle wrote, and compared it to the resilience in wool. To contemporaries the vacuum pump was a toy which could be made to produce the strangest effects. "We tried several experiments in Mr Boyle's vacuum . . . ," wrote the diarist John Evelyn: "a man thrusting in his arm upon the exhaustion of the air had his flesh immediately swelled, so as the blood was near breaking the veins: he drawing it out we found it all speckled." But it had important scientific and technological results: widening the knowledge about the behaviour of gases, bringing nearer an understanding of the part oxygen plays in combustion and the blood, and helping to provide a mechanical concept of the working of the heart. Its most important technological development was the steam pump invented by Savery and Newcomen.[1]

Robert Hooke, the son of a poor parson in the Isle of Wight, was the curator of experiments to the Royal Society and one of the greatest experimental physicists in history. We have already noticed his work with Boyle, for whom he made much apparatus. His mind ranged over a vast field, coming near to the discovery of the wave theory of light and hitting on the idea (even before Newton) of a mechanically moved universe. He claimed, indeed – perhaps truly, except that his quarrelsome vanity leads us to doubt

[1] See p. 235.

him – to have anticipated Newton in the 'inverse square law'[1] in astronomy and the theory of gravity itself. One law he was certainly responsible for – the axiom on which the study of elasticity is founded: extension is proportional to force (*ut tensio, sic vis*). Elasticity led him to the springs of watches, whose future accuracy he ensured by inventing the balance wheel. From the boundlessness of space he turned to the smallest things, inventing a micrometer for fractional measurements and discovering the existence of organic cells when experimenting with the microscope. His book *Micrographia* (1665) describes this miniature world – perhaps giving birth to Swift's fictional expression of it in *Gulliver's Travels* (1726). The language of *Micrographia* is simple enough to meet the most exacting requirements of the Royal Society. Of the point of a needle seen through a microscope he observes that it 'appears a broad, blunt and very irregular end', and of a razor's edge that it seemed no thinner 'than the back of a pretty thick knife'. He throws off comments on the way – amusing to us but at that time quite matter-of-fact: for instance, on what was then indeed the common louse:

> This is a creature so officious that 'twill be known to everyone at one time or another, so busy and so impudent, and so proud and aspiring withal that it fears not to trample on the best.

And, with that seventeenth-century bias towards the practical, he remarks, on easily reading a twopenny piece with the Lord's Prayer, Apostles' Creed, the Ten Commandments and six verses of the Bible inscribed on it, that

> if this manner of small writing were made easy and practicable . . . it might be of very good use to convey secret intelligence without any danger of discovery or mistrusting.

The microscope transformed the possibilities of discovery through observation. It was used by Nehemiah Grew to revolutionize the study of botany. In his book *The Anatomy of Plants* (1682), Grew revealed the basic fact of plant sexuality. 'The same plant is both male and female', he asserted, and showed that flowers are the sexual organs and how reproduction takes place

[1] See p. 231.

through transference of pollen. 'All flowers have their powders . . . they are that body which bees gather and carry upon their thighs'.

From the dust of pollen to the scattered stars: such was the sweep covered by the science of the time. Yet the interest was mainly upon the stars, among which man's thought could wander more rationally after the work of Hooke, Halley and Newton. Hooke has already been noticed and Newton must yet be – his thought dominating the time. Between them Edmund Halley demands some mention, if only because of the comet which bears his name and whose orbit he calculated in 1682. Before him comets were so mysterious and apparently uncaused that they were thought to be supernatural – warnings from the gods of doom or blessings to come. So Halley's comet, blazing above the newly crowned and perjured Harold in 1066, warned of his fate at Hastings. Now this explanation was found threadbare – as Halley himself wrote in his *Ode to Newton*:

Now we know
The sharply veering ways of comets, once
A source of dread, nor longer do we quail
Beneath appearances of bearded stars.

Sir Isaac Newton

By the calculation of the orbit of his comet Halley had brought comets under the rule of law. His friend Isaac Newton was to do the same with the universe itself. He revealed the force of gravitation, binding our system to the sun as its centre and the moon to the earth, and estimated the strength of the attraction by the inverse square law[1]. In place of a universe subject to irrational forces, Newton established a mechanical system in which, after the initial act of creation (which Newton accepted), the universe moved strictly according to its own laws. Everywhere Newton tested this theory it met the facts: the tides were explained, for instance, and the uneven orbit of the moon, together with the very slight

[1] Bodies attract each other with a force inversely proportional to the square of their distance apart.

variation in the angle of the earth's tilt known as the 'precession of the equinoxes'.

Newton also drew up his 'laws of motion' – the basis of modern dynamics. Many of these are so familiar today that their statement seems obvious: that, for instance, the movement of a body from rest necessitates an applied force or that 'to every action there is always opposed an equal reaction'. The latter is Newton's third law of motion – explained with the greatest simplicity in his own words:

> Whatever draws or presses another is as much drawn or pressed by that other. If you press a stone with your finger, the finger is also pressed by the stone. If a horse draws a stone tied to a rope, the horse . . . will be equally drawn back towards the stone.

The dates of these discoveries are difficult to fix because Newton was slow to publish his conclusions, and this led to bitter quarrels between him and his rivals (with Hooke, for example, over the discovery of the inverse square law). It was not till 1687 that Halley was able, by paying for the work himself, to persuade Newton to publish the great *Mathematical Principles of Natural Philosophy* (originally in Latin). What we have so far considered of Newton's work appeared in this great book.

Yet Newton went further when, in 1704, he wrote *Optics, or a Treatise on the Reflexions, Refractions, Inflexion and Colours of Light*, which showed that these phenomena too were held fast in the grip of physical law. Here again, much of the work described by Newton he had done long before: such, for instance, as his important discovery that light is a compound of seven colours – the colours of the spectrum, which can be separated out by a prism. To some extent an ordinary convex lens will separate out the spectral colours, as Newton found in the telescopes he used. But as this blurred the image by edging it with colour, he wrongly concluded that a telescope depending on such lenses could never be satisfactory. However, the Scottish astronomer James Gregory had suggested as early as 1663 a reflecting telescope with a convex mirror in place of an object lense. This Newton built, presenting a nine-inch-long improved version of it to the Royal Society, who still possess it.

Isaac Newton was essentially a mathematician, bringing mathematical principles to the solution of physical problems. But those he dealt with mostly concerned movement, in which the various parts of the problems were constantly changing in relation to each other: the moon, for instance, revolving about the turning earth and both circling the sun. Mathematics in Newton's time had no theoretical tools to deal with such cases, and it was left to Newton to provide them. The device he hit upon was the differential calculus, in which he may have been anticipated by the German mathematician Leibnitz – one of the principal tools of modern science and engineering. "If I had stayed for other people to make my tools and things for me," said Newton in quite a different connection, "I had never made anything of it." Whether it was polishing lenses or providing such mathematical computers as the calculus, Newton did everything for himself.

Rationalism

In bringing so much of the physical world under the control of law, Newton and the other scientists of the seventeenth century, though very few in number, led the way to a gradual adoption of a more rational view of life: in proportion as the boundaries of the natural world widened, those of the supernatural shrank. The process can be illustrated by the growth of a more sceptical attitude towards witches. Sir Francis North, a leading judge in the reign of Charles II and later lord chancellor, who himself had scientific interests, is said by his brother to have feared the clash with popular prejudice, so much that he 'dreaded trying a witch'. His brother was present, however, when he had to try an old man for wizardry at Taunton Dene. He was supposed to have bewitched a girl of 13, so that she had fits in which she spat out pins, and his defence of malice and imposture carried no weight with the rustic jury. The judge nevertheless contrived to save him by putting a local JP in the witness box, who gave his own impression that the girl bent her head to simulate convulsions, and then picked up the 'magic' pins between her teeth from the front of her dress.

> As the judge went down stairs out of the court, a hideous old woman cried, "God bless your lordship." "What's the matter, good woman?" said the judge. "My lord," said she, "forty years ago they would have hanged me for a witch, and they could not; and now they would have hanged my poor son."

The last executions for witchcraft took place, in England and Scotland respectively, in 1712 and 1722.

Increasingly, religion also came under critical examination. This was not at all the intention of Newton, who believed that his work had proved rather than excluded the existence of God. As he put it: "This most beautiful system of the sun and planets and comets could only proceed from the council and dominion of an intelligent and powerful Being." Several of the early members of the Royal Society were clerics and others, like Boyle, men of deep faith. Yet the drift of their scientific outlook was bound to extend to religion and to undermine popular belief in many miracles. Samuel Pepys, who was elected President of the Royal Society in 1684, gave in that year a chill look at the story of Noah:

> Noah's ark must needs be made of some extraordinary timber and plank, that could remain good after having been a hundred years in building, whereas our thirty new ships are rotten within less than five. Moreover Mr. Sheres computes from its dimensions that six months would have sufficed to have built what Moses assigns an hundred years for.

Technology: The Early Steam-engine

This new scientific attitude was bound to influence religion in the end, but its starting-point was often practical – the improvement of navigation, for instance. The more accurately the movement of the stars and planets could be predicted, the easier would be that of ships. Better telescopes would follow naturally, and better microscopes too.

Boyle and Hooke had invented the vacuum pump; and while, as we have seen, men like Evelyn treated it as a toy, there were others (not only in Britain) who saw that it might be put to practical use. As early as 1698 a military engineer and prolific inventor, named Thomas Savery, patented a machine for raising water by steam pressure. Four years later, he described it in *The Miner's Friend or an Engine to raise water by Fire*, the paper being addressed significantly to the Royal Society:

> At the request of some of your members at the weekly meeting at Gresham College, June 14th 1699, I had the honour to work a small model of my engine before you and you were pleased to approve of it . . . Your honourable Society are the most proper judges of what it may be to mankind.

Unfortunately, Savery's engine easily blew up, and it seems to have been chiefly the need to secure the benefit of his patent rights that caused him to be made a partner in the enterprise which produced the first commercially successful steam-engine, installed at Dudley Castle coal mine in Warwickshire in 1712. Its designer was Thomas Newcomen of Dartmouth, 'a dealer in iron tools with which he used to furnish many of the tin mines'; besides his practical knowledge of Cornish mining problems, he was so far in contact with scientific thought that he corresponded with Hooke.

Newcomen's 'fire-engine' produced steam at safe atmospheric pressure, which was admitted to the bottom of a cylinder so as to drive a piston to the top; a jet of cold water then condensed the steam, so as to create a vacuum which allowed the pressure of the atmosphere to drive the piston down again. The piston was attached to one end of a rocking beam; at the other end a pump rod was suspended over the mine shaft or other aperture through which water was to be sucked up. When the inventor died in 1729, his pump had largely solved the problem of flooding, which had brought work to a standstill in many of the deeper coalpits of northern England.

Increasing Use of Coal

In many parts of Britain coal-mining was a rapidly expanding industry: the growth of population increased the demand for domestic purposes, while the shortage of wood was also causing more trades to adapt their manufacturing processes to the use of coal as fuel. The most important English mines were those in Northumberland

and Durham, in the valleys of the Tyne and Wear. Nearness to rivers and the coast was important because most of the coal travelled by water: the port of Newcastle was crowded with ships to take it abroad and down the east coast to London and the mouths of all the navigable rivers. Already the areas closest to the Tyne were being worked out (no very deep mines then being possible) and wagons were bringing the coal down to the river from as much as ten miles away. Increasingly, railed wagon-ways were being built to reduce the physical difficulties and the expense of land transport. Yet so great was the demand for coal that, even in the Midlands, mining was expanding and the wagons were supplying the growing towns. In Staffordshire many of the seams were as thick as ten to twelve yards.

In Scotland the story is the same. On the south side of the Firth of Forth coal was mined extensively between Edinburgh and Haddington, and on the north for seventy miles along the Fifeshire coast. Some coal from the valley of the Clyde was also shipped from Dumbarton. But the most remarkable evidence of expanding enterprise was the construction of mine galleries under the sea, such as a visitor found at Culross, near the head of the Forth, in 1618:

> The mine hath two ways into it, the one by sea and the other by land . . . At low water, the sea being ebbed away and a great part of the sand bare, upon this same sand did the master of this great work build a circular frame of stone, very thick . . . so high withal that the sea at the highest flood can neither dissolve the stones so well compacted in the building or yet overflow the height of it. Within this round frame they did dig forty foot down, right through a rock.
>
> At last they found that which they expected, which was sea-coal . . . In the space of eight and twenty years they have digged more than an English mile under the sea, so that when men are at work below, an hundred of the greatest ships in Britain may sail over their heads.

Of the industries dependent on coal, salt-making was important in both England and Scotland. The evaporation of salt from sea-water heated in iron pans, which required six tons of coal per ton of salt, flourished, as we might expect, along the coal-bearing east coast districts of Scotland and in England at the mouth of the Tyne. "Here is such a cloud of smoke as amongst these works you cannot see to walk," wrote a touring baronet from Shields in 1636. The output of the Scottish pans, which were more scattered, may have been still larger. But England also had salt made from brine pumped out of pits at Northwich, Nantwich, and Droitwich. In 1670 it was found that these pits contained 'a hard rocky salt that looks clear like sugar candy'; since this yielded ten times as much salt from a solution as the natural brine yielded, the eventual eclipse of both the older methods of salt-making was now foreshadowed.

Other industries which now used much coal included glass-making (with an output of about 10,000 tons a year by the close of the century), the firing of pottery, soap-boiling, brewing, and building: the last because of the gradual displacement of scarce English timber by brick, which had to be baked. The metal industries, too (bronze, brass and lead especially), increasingly depended on coal. Iron, however, used charcoal for smelting and was pressing upon the shrinking forests – unable to make use of the growing coal supplies because of the sulphur and other impurities in the coal, which spoiled the iron. The drain on the forests was a matter of great concern and its results were important: the migration of the iron industry from the over-worked woodlands of the Weald to the West Midlands; a growing reliance on imported Swedish iron; and the stimulus to technical change in the search to find some way to smelt iron by coal.

The Iron Industry: Coke-Smelting

With the development of the iron industry, the West Midlands boomed. "Within ten miles of Dudley Castle," wrote Dud Dudley, an illegitimate son of the 9th Baron Dudley, in his *Metallum Martis* in 1665, "there be near 20,000 smiths of all sorts and many iron works." These iron works smelted the iron ore into pig iron, to be refined in turn to wrought iron by the smiths, working at home with no more complex aids than an anvil, tongs and hammers and a fire. However, some processes were more advanced than this and already demanded factory organization: the rolling and slitting mills, for instance, where iron was first rolled into thin plates and then slit into thin rods, some of them as small as $\frac{1}{4}$in × $\frac{1}{8}$ in, required for the making of nails. Birmingham became the great centre for the manufacturing side of the industry, though to some extent every village smith was a manufacturer of iron wares. Besides nails, swords and knives, Birmingham craftsmen produced the day-to-day equipment of the seventeenth-century household: locks and keys, hinges, firebacks and grates, pins, horses' bits, and so on.

But much of this iron, worked up in Birmingham and elsewhere, came from Sweden, where there was no shortage of timber and the cost of the smelted metal was low. This unpalatable economic fact was recognized as early as 1661, by those petitioners from Lewes, who complained that

> the vast quantities of woods and iron mines which the Swedes have . . . together with the cheapness of the workmen, enables their making of iron at much lower rates than can possibly be done in any parts of this nation.

Yet for about sixty years after the Restoration a static English iron production was only able to support an expanding manufacture with the help of Swedish imports.

This was a situation which cut across all the economic self-sufficiency of the time and, with coal production rising, there were naturally attempts made to harness coal to iron production. Dud Dudley in his book wrote of his own efforts in this direction:

> I have held it my duty to endeavour . . . the making of iron . . . with pit coal, sea coal, peat and turf, for the preservation of wood and timber so much exhausted by iron works of late.

But he described his methods so vaguely that it is not at all clear what he discovered. We move into clearer light, however, with Abraham Darby – the first of a dynasty of iron-makers – who in 1709 successfully smelted iron with coke. In a letter written many years later, his daughter-in-law described the modest start of this technological break-through, when he

> about the year 1709 came into Shropshire to Coalbrookdale and with other partners took a lease of the works, which only consisted of an old blast furnace and some forges. He here cast iron goods in sand out of the blast furnace that blowed with wood charcoal; for it was not yet thought of to blow with pit coal. Sometime after he suggested the thought that it might be practicable to smelt the iron from the ore in the blast furnace with pit coal: upon this he first tried with raw coal as it came out of the mines, but it did not answer. He, not discouraged, had the coal coked into cinder as is done for drying malt, and it then succeeded to his satisfaction.

But, as we shall see later,[1] the invention was very slow in spreading.

Science in Agriculture

In industry, science and technology met to the enrichment of both. It was the same in agriculture: new ideas fostered by the Royal Society were tried out in gardens and farms which, for scientists who were interested, took on the aspect of laboratories. Landowners who adopted these ideas were the rich, who could afford to experiment and had some leisure to think about their farming. This was especially true in Scotland, where the nobility were the main improvers: the 9th earl of Argyll, the 6th earl of Haddington, and the 2nd earl of Stair respectively planted new trees, clover and root crops. And Lady Henrietta Mordaunt, marrying into the Gordon family, added to her dowry such unexpected benefits as the English plough, foreign grasses, and southern methods of hay-making.

Special interest was shown at this time in gardens, with their tree-lined walks and orchards. John Worlidge, for instance, who in 1669 wrote his *Systema Agriculturae* (for a long time a standard work), gave 106 pages to such things as trees, silkworms, orchards and bees, and only three to stock-breeding. John Reid, in his *Scots Gardener* (1683) made the same emphasis, himself describing the subject-matter of the two parts of his book:

> The first is contriving and planting gardens, orchards, avenues,

[1] See p. 308.

> groves; with new and profitable ways of levelling; and how to measure and divide land. The second, of the propagation and improvement of forest and fruit trees, kitchen herbs, roots and flowers, with some physical herbs, shrubs and flowers.

With the new interest, gardens all over Britain flourished. The Oxford Botanic Garden was founded in 1621, the Edinburgh Physic Garden (later the Royal Botanic Garden) in 1670; John Evelyn, too, spent many years laying out the gardens of Wotton in Surrey, where he planted trees and terraced an artificial hill. His two books – *Sylva* (1664) on trees and *Terra* (1676) on horticulture – brought to these matters the experimental methods of the Royal Society to which he belonged.

Some attention was also being paid to more general farming. In 1681–3 and 1692–1703 there appeared John Houghton's weekly *Collection of Letters for the Improvement of Husbandry and Trade*, which attempted in a serious and scientific way to popularize new ideas: the cultivation of potatoes, for instance, which 'begin to spread all the kingdom over' and 'are a pleasant food boiled or roasted and eaten with butter and sugar'. In fact this idea was a non-starter, for potatoes did not do well in England at this time. Nevertheless, Houghton considered 'our inhuman civil wars' as a turning-point, after which 'our gentry, who before scarcely knew what it was to think . . . fell to such an industry and caused such an improvement as England never knew before.' There is some truth in this for, in agriculture as in trade and industry, the civil wars freed the gentry to follow their own advantage and even set the state on their side.

Many of the great changes of the eighteenth century were anticipated on a small scale at this time. In Norfolk, especially, men such as Colonel Walpole (father of Sir Robert) were introducing Dutch ideas of crop rotation with the help of turnips, clover and artificial grasses, and were marling their sandy soils so that they would retain moisture. All over England – and in Scotland too – lime was in use as a fertilizer: it was baked in farm kilns fed from the increasing coal supplies. Crop rotation not only enriched the soil, and by abolishing fallow brought more into cultivation so that corn could be exported – Scotland sent much to Norway –

but also enabled more cattle to be kept alive in the winter. For this purpose roots and clover were important, as was silage which some farmers began to make. Scotland raised cattle for the English market – sending, it is said, 20,000 beasts through Carlisle in 1662, and developing a regular export, which twenty-five years later is thought to have ranked second only to linen. And even before the Restoration, ideas for agricultural machines were being put forward – a double-furrow plough, for example, and a corn driller. The air was filled with hope: "Any land," said Walter Blith in his *English Improver Improved* (1652), "may be made rich and as rich as land can be."

All this activity, whether in farming or industry, was a fruit of the new experimental attitude to nature which science expressed. Nevertheless, at the level of day-to-day life, science was still applied as crudely as ever. Men suffered as they had always done – as Sir John Reresby reminds us in this account of a riding accident in 1677:

> My horse was forced to go upon a slippery stone, so that he fell flat upon my right leg and put my knee out of joint . . . At the last they found four that pretended to be versed in that art [of bonesetting] but so little understood it that they put me to a great deal of pain to no purpose, for they set my knee wrong.

14

LONDON IN THE REIGN OF QUEEN ANNE

In Queen Anne's reign London was already very large: it had spread far beyond its Roman and medieval walls, absorbing on the west, round the great loop in the river, the neighbouring city of Westminster, while on the south it was joined by its single bridge to the suburb of Southwark. Along the north bank, from opposite Rotherhithe to Vauxhall beyond Westminster, it stretched for four miles, though it was generally less than a mile wide. Conrad von Uffenbach[1], a German traveller who, in 1710, spent five months in England and wrote of them in his *Travels*, climbed to the top of the new St Paul's and was astonished at the city he saw:

> From the top one can see almost the whole city, especially in the direction of Westminster. The prodigious size and length of it is amazing, though it is not so very wide.

Another visitor – the Frenchman François Misson[1] – in 1698 had already made the same point (in his *Memoirs and Observations*), though more summarily: "I believe I may venture safely to affirm that London, including Westminster, is the biggest city in Europe." It was not only the largest in area but in population too, for about 600,000 people lived in its seething streets. Perhaps, too, it was the dirtiest European city, its huge population providing the main market for northern coal. As early as 1661 the diarist John Evelyn (in his *Fumifugium: or the Smoke of London Dissipated*) had written of "this horrid smoke which obscures our churches and makes our palaces look old, which fouls our clothes and corrupts the waters." And von Uffenbach on the visit to St Paul's already mentioned, remarked how the cathedral, which was only just

[1] See Appendix I, 11 and 12, for the experiences of these two foreign visitors outside London.

completed, "is already so black with coal and smoke that it has lost half its elegance." Buildings lost 'elegance' but the people their health: even William III found his asthma so aggravated by the London air that he deserted Whitehall and St James's for Hampton Court and Kensington.

The River

This straggling and smoky capital depended for much of its character upon the Thames, which bound it together and linked it to the world beyond. Von Uffenbach thought it "prodigiously convenient that, because London is for the most part built along the river, one can go almost anywhere by water". Along the north bank the continuous line of buildings at the water's edge was broken into by stair-openings where swaying ferry boats waited for passengers: 32 of them between London Bridge and Horseferry, Westminster, and 16 of them on the south bank. Some of these stairs, above the bridge, were named after the noblemen whose houses had once stood by the river – for instance, the Essex, Arundel and Surrey stairs. But, below the bridge, where the masts of the shipping clustered and the gulls cried, the names were saltier: Ship Brew House, Dick's Shore, Pickle Herring and Three Mariners' Stairs.

While some ferry boats were large enough to take a coach and horses, the ordinary ones were simple but sturdy rowing boats. "You sit at your ease upon cushions," says Misson, "and have a board to lean against; but generally they have no covering, unless a cloth which the watermen set up immediately, in case of need, over a few hoops." Von Uffenbach was more impressed by the discomforts of such travel:

> There is always a fairly stiff breeze on the river even in the height of summer; thus it is especially difficult to boat on the Thames, because men's wigs look so frightful and, if there is a shower, get quite wet.

Wind and rain, however, were not the only daunting features of ferry-boat travel, if 'Ned' Ward is to be believed. Edward Ward was the owner of the King's Head Tavern near Gray's Inn and the writer of much hearty prose and verse. Between 1698 and 1709 he produced in monthly instalments *The London Spy*, a series of narrative sketches of London life. In one of these he describes how he and a companion, wanting to cross the river, came down to the waterside, where

> a jolly grizzle-pated Charon handed us into his wherry, whipped off his short-skirted doublet, whereon was a badge to show whose fool he was, then fixed his stretcher, bid us trim the boat and away he rowed. But we had not swum a yard or two before a scoundrel crew of Lambeth gardeners attacked us with such a volley of fancy nonsense that it made my eyes stare . . . "You couple of treacherous sons of Bridewell: how dare you show your ugly faces upon the river of Thames to fright the Queen's swans!"

Yet the great were removed from these vulgar contacts and sheltered from the rudeness of the weather. They owned their own barges, with a covered cabin in the stern and rowers in the forepart: splendid with gilded lanterns on the cabin roof and great billowing flags at bow and stern. Misson describes them as

> a sort of pleasure boat, at one end of which there is a little room handsomely painted and covered, with a table in the middle and benches round it; and, at the other end, seats for 8, 10, 12, 20, 30 or 40 rowers. There are few persons of great quality but what have their barges, though they do not frequently make use of them. Their watermen wear a jacket of the same colour they give for their livery, with a pretty little silver badge upon their arm, with the nobleman's coat-of-arms embossed in it.

London Bridge

The most eye-catching feature of the Thames at London was still the great bridge, covered almost continuously with shops and dwellings, which had been admired by Stow. The scene below the arches was also a striking one, especially as the ebb-tide forced its way through the narrow openings. "We turned down to Thames side," says Ned Ward, "when the frightful roaring of the bridge waterfalls so astonished my eyes and terrified my ears that . . . I could hear no voice softer than a speaking trumpet." Only the brave were prepared to shoot these falls; most passengers went ashore at the last stairs before the bridge and walked round it, leaving the waterman to bring the boat through. It is thought that in the mid-eighteenth century about fifty people a year were drowned in these waters.

However, some good came from the menacing sweep of the current, for it was used to work water-wheels to pump water into the City. As early as 1580, such a wheel was set up at the north end of the bridge and others were added later. When John Macky wrote his *Journey through England* in 1714, he remarked on this device:

> There is a curious engine at this bridge which, by the flux and reflux of the tide, raises the water to such a height as to furnish most parts of the city, and especially the breweries, with Thames water.

This partial blocking of the river by the piers of the bridge had the further effect of damming the flow of the stream above the bridge, so that in very severe winters the river froze. This was considered a great wonder at the time and Misson set it down:

> We every now and then read in the Annals of the Thames being frozen two or three months together and carts being driven where ships used to sail; but the greatest of all these winters was in 1684. The Thames had a universal bridge over it, on which there was a fair held for two months together. There were whole streets of shops . . . rope-dancers and puppet shows . . . There was bull-baiting and bear-baiting and a whole ox was roasted upon it.

But Misson need not have gone so far back as 1684, for in the very year in which he wrote (1698) the Thames was frozen so solid that a coach-and-six was driven upon it.

Nevertheless, with all its disadvantages, the bridge was a fine sight – though never again so splendid as with its turreted Tudor superstructure, much of which vanished in the Fire, and the rest of which was pulled down afterwards. Then more sober and uniform buildings were laid upon it – still impressive but no longer dreamlike. In any case the bridge could only be appreciated from outside it, as von Uffenbach saw:

> We had gone twenty yards over it without being aware that we were on the bridge . . . One does not take it for a bridge because it has on both sides large and handsome houses, the lower storeys of which are all shops. Well over halfway across the bridge . . . is a single place about eight feet long where there is not a house and the Thames can be seen through the iron palings.

The Built-up Area

Away to the west and north of the river, the builders hammered their way into the fields and pastures surrounding the capital – though more slowly to the west, since St James's Park and Hyde Park blocked the way. By 1700, however, to the north of St James's Park, the limits of the built-up area pressed beyond Piccadilly to the line of Bolton and Bruton Streets, continuing north-east to Golden and Soho Squares (the latter just off the Tyburn Road – modern Oxford Street). Thence it inched farther north-east to Bloomsbury and ran north of Red Lion Square, Gray's Inn and the Charterhouse to the neighbourhood of Shoreditch, when it turned south to cut the Whitechapel Road and reach the Thames at Stepney. On the south bank it is not possible to draw even so rough a limit as this, the built-up area being very small. Except for a thicker wedge of buildings at Southwark, the houses merely lined the Thames from Rotherhithe to Lambeth, here becoming even sparser in the southward bend of the river past Lambeth marsh.

Yet, although London had expanded so greatly, it is still possible to consider it in Anne's reign as focused upon the two centres of Westminster and the City. Round the former was the world of government and fashion, while that of trade and finance surrounded the latter. And, just as the fashionable world expanded round Piccadilly, so the business world spread west from the City along the line of the Strand and the area of Covent Garden.

Westminster

The world of Westminster might be expected to revolve around the Court, but in the reigns of William III and Anne it did not spin that way. William III avoided London so far as he could and Anne was ill and retiring. In any case, in 1698 Whitehall Palace was burned so completely that sixteen years later John Macky could only record that "there remains now little worth mentioning besides the banqueting house . . . one of the prettiest pieces of architecture in Europe." Queen Anne, therefore, was forced to live in the Tudor St. James's Palace, to which Wren made additions.

Perhaps St James's Park, rather than the Palace, was the centre of fashionable London. It was the great place for walking, for no coaches were allowed there, except those of the Queen, the duke of Marlborough and the duke of Buckingham, whose new mansion lay at the western end, where Buckingham Palace is today. "Pray, sister," asked Mrs Pinchwife in William Wycherley's *Country Wife* (1675), "where are the best fields and woods to walk in, in London?" – receiving the unequivocal answer: "Mulberry Garden and St James's Park and, for close walks, the New Exchange." Von Uffenbach speaks of the cows and red deer which grazed among the strollers in St James's, while Misson reports in more detail:

> It has very fine walks of elms and lindens, a fine Mall, a large canal, and several other . . . basins of water. The time for good company is at noon in the fine days of winter, and very late at night in hot days in summer. On holidays and Sundays, the common people take their walks thither in whole shoals.

There, on weekdays at least, the fashionable world displayed itself, the 'beau' strutting in his coloured silk waistcoat and heavy wig, which contained a pound of hair and cost from thirty to forty guineas. Ned Ward had no patience with vanity of this sort: such a person, says he, "is a Narcissus that is fallen in love with

Plate 20. *Napier's Rods.* This calculating device was described in Napier's book *Rabdologiae* (1617). Though primarily used for multiplication, it could also be used to divide. In this picture only the two left-hand of the three blocks of rods constitute the calculator. It will be seen that this is made up of a set of eleven vertical wooden rods, each divided into nine squares. In the left-hand rod, and in the top squares of the others, there are single digits written, which represent the numbers to be multiplied together. In the lower squares of all save the left-hand rod are the multiples of the side and top digits, arranged so that the tens and units are separated by a diagonal (in this picture, however, the engraver has made several mistakes). While the left-hand rod stayed fixed, the others could be moved about so as to make all sorts of variations in the figures to be multiplied.

The right-hand block of rods is arranged to show a calculation: the multiplication of the figure 5978. To multiply this by 3, for example, the end figure of the product is read as 4 (in the right-hand rod) and the others obtained in succession by adding the diagonals from rod to rod going left (e. g. 2+1=3, 2+7=9 etc.). The final figure is 1, which is left over. This gives the correct product 17934.

When the multiplier was a figure of more than one digit, the process had to be gone through for all of them – setting the partial products down and adding them up, allowing for the correct placing of the figures in the sum. (Cf. text p. 226.)

Plate 21. *Charcoal-Burning.* This print, dated 1763, shows well the devastation of woodland caused by charcoal-burning, mainly in the production of iron – for which oak and beech were best. It shows, too, the stages in the process. After felling, the wood was cut into 3ft. lengths and stacked (beneath the trees). A central pole was then set up, round which the wood was piled in a small cone. Horizontal layers of wood were subsequently laid in a circle around the central cone, till the base was twenty to thirty feet across; and other lengths of wood were added (as in the centre figure of the middle row) till the cone was complete (bottom left). This was then covered with turf or clay (bottom right) and vent-holes made in the stack. Finally, the central pole was removed and the cone lit by introducing burning charcoal through the hole at the top (figure on extreme right). After 2½ to 3 days the charcoal was raked out of the collapsed cone and taken to the forges. (Cf. text pp. 98, 113, 237, 308.)

Plate 22. *Bartholomew Fair.* From a 1733 engraving by William Hogarth. This fair, originating in the 12th century, lasted till 1855 and was the most popular of the London fairs: it was described at its height by Ben Jonson in his *Bartholomew Fair* (1614). It became notorious for swindlers and pickpockets, whose profits nevertheless sank as first the fashionable world and then the respectable middle class deserted it. Hogarth illustrates well the seedy rowdiness to which its booths and alleys had sunk by this time. (Cf. text pp. 253–4.)

Plate 23. *Gin Lane.* From an engraving after a drawing by William Hogarth, 1751. This picture did much to arouse the conscience of the nation against the evils of cheap gin during the years 1720–50. In London alone during 1733 there were about 6,500 dram-shops of the sort shown at the bottom left of the picture – where the legend on the arch proclaims, 'Drunk for a penny, dead drunk for twopence, clean straw for nothing'. But gin was sold also by the distillers (see upper right) and by small shops of every variety; and wages were often paid in it. In consequence, especially in London, the death rate soared. Hogarth indicates this and harshly points out other evils in the wake of the gin habit: rioting, suicide, and the neglect of children and property – a ruinous world in which only the pawnbroker does well. This was the situation that the Gin Act of 1751 gradually transformed – mainly by stringent limitations on the sale of the liquor. (Cf. text pp, 266 292.)

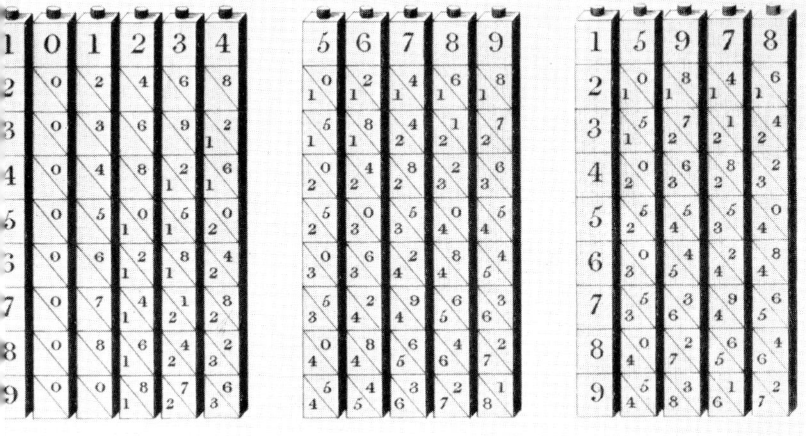

Plate 20

Plate 21

Plate 22

Plate 23

himself and his own shadow . . . His head is a fool's egg which is hid in a nest of hair."

Near by was the meeting-place of parliament, with St Stephen's Chapel, where the Commons sat, conspicuous amid the huddle of buildings between the river and Westminster Hall. The smallness of this Commons chamber was even then notorious, and von Uffenbach was justified in his comment on this:

> The room is small, and it is amazing that so many members and human beings can assemble together here. We were assured that, when Parliament is sitting, it is so crammed full that scarce another person could get in without risking suffocation.

It is all the stranger, then, that the native-born Edward Hatton gives no hint of this legislative crush, describing the chamber in estate-agent's language as a "commodious building accommodated with several ranks of seats covered with green, and matted underfoot, for 513 gentlemen".

The City

About a mile and a half down-river from Westminster was the City – the work-a-day world where fortunes were made, whose inheritors later perhaps would loll on the green benches in the Commons or stroll under the St James's linden trees. The heart of it still lay within the circuit of its old walls, though the buildings had long since spread beyond. Panoramic views of the time suggest a fine city, dominated by the whole upper part and superb dome of St Paul's, and made interesting by the cluster of church spires. Yet, less than forty years before the accession of Anne, it had been four-fifths burned in the Great Fire – with 13,200 houses and 89 churches lost and 100,000 people rendered homeless. Misson gives the outline of the tragedy without emotion, as known to him a generation afterwards:

> On Sunday the 2nd of September, about two in the morning, the fire began at a baker's, in that part of the town where all the streets were narrow and all the houses built of deal. In a very short time the fire spread all about, and made so speedy and

> furious a progress that by the next evening the greater part of the city was nothing but a heap of rubbish. It continued three whole days, till Wednesday morning. There were 13,200 houses burned down, which stood upon the space of 436 acres . . . fourscore and nine churches, taking in St Paul's cathedral, and a great many handsome public edifices.

The City in Queen Anne's time, therefore, was a new place – bridge, cathedral, churches and houses all new. Most of the houses had been rebuilt as early as 1672, after the holders of private property rights had defeated all ideas of a planned city, so that the buildings had been allowed to go up again on what were roughly the old medieval street sites. King Street and Queen Street – opening up the Guildhall to the river – were the only two important new thoroughfares laid out on the waste. Rebuilding Acts stated that the new houses must be of brick or stone and regulated their height according to the importance of the street: four storeys in the 'high and principal streets', three in the 'streets and lanes of note' and two in 'by-lanes'. So these uniform houses were put up decently enough, though without much architectural design, by the masons and bricklayers, carpenters and glaziers, who flooded into the city after the Fire. Misson gives these houses a qualified approval and contrasts them with what they replaced:

> For these fifteen or twenty years, nay ever since the Great Fire, the people of London have built in a manner polite enough. Before that time, their houses were the scurviest things in the world, as appears very plainly from whole streets still remaining, nothing but wood and plaster, and nasty little windows with but one casement to open. The storeys were low and widened one over another all awry and in appearance ready to fall. Now the houses are built with brick, with even fronts, without magnificium indeed . . . but with symmetry and neatness enough. All very lightsome, the windows large and sashed, the roofs all ceiled, and the ground and first floors universally wainscotted . . . Balconies are very much in use . . . They cover with tile and build generally high enough.

The Work of Wren

Of the churches burned in the Fire, some were not rebuilt, but as many as 51 were redesigned by Wren. The intimacy of their interiors was partly necessitated by the cramped sites; yet Wren believed in any case that the services held in them should be audible to the whole congregation. He experimented ceaselessly with various forms of centralized church plan: carved wooden galleries, running round the whole church save for the east end, were important elements in the idea. The churches were built in brick and Portland stone, and their spires and towers (rising above a city no more than forty feet high) punctuated the skyline in a variety of harmonious shapes. But most important of all, of course, was Wren's rebuilding of St Paul's.

When John Macky wrote of the cathedral in 1714, it was just four years since Christopher Wren's son had climbed to the lantern on top of the dome and placed the last stone in position. Macky had observed the building from all over London and beyond: "This noble pile," he wrote, "with its noble cupola, is seen from all the adjacent counties and gives an august and venerable aspect to the approaching travellers." He described it as 'the first outside of any church in the world', and it certainly was a most triumphant blending of the Gothic urge for length in a cathedral with the centralized, domed buildings associated with Renaissance architecture on the Continent. Yet in some ways its appearance of complete symmetry was an ingenious contrivance – achieved by increasing the height of the nave walls to hide the flying buttresses which supported the roof, and by providing the dome with an outer casing (concealing two inner domes of a different shape) which had little to do but look beautiful.

New St Paul's and Other Sights of the City

The cathedral was 35 years in building – not surprising in view of its great size and the lack of modern machines – and, according to Edward Hatton, had at some periods employed 500 workmen at a time. However, Ned Ward had seen some of those workmen and was not impressed:

> We observed ten men in a corner, very busy about two men's work . . . The wonderful piece of difficulty the whole number had to perform, was to drag along a stone of about three hundredweight in a carriage, in order to be hoisted upon the mouldings of the cupola; but they were longer in hauling it half the length of the church than a couple of lusty porters would have been carrying it all the way to Paddington without resting.

He went on to say – anticipating the guide-books:

> You must remember . . . this is work carried on at a national charge, and ought not to be hastened on in a hurry, for the greatest reputation it will gain when it is finished will be that it was so many years in building.

Yet finished it was – and immediately the trippers took over, scratching their names on the stonework and discovering the delights of the whispering gallery. Von Uffenbach was one of them:

> Right at the top of the tower we found countless names written in chalk or scratched on the stone, so we had ours done also by our men.
>
> The vaulting comes down into this gallery in such a way that . . . when two persons stand with their backs turned exactly opposite to each other, and one of them speaks quite quietly looking towards the wall, the other will hear distinctly everything he says over on the other side.

No doubt many of these early name-carvers at St Paul's had practised their art in the Tower of London – already well-established as one of the main sights of the capital. It was still sometimes used as a prison, it contained great stores of weapons and gunpowder, and it housed the Royal Mint; but for ordinary trippers it was a zoo and museum, where wild animals paced and snarled and where armour was on show. And it contained the crown jewels. Misson remarked that "anybody may see them for a shilling", while von Uffenbach was surprised that "they are not kept in an elegant and vaulted chamber, as they well deserve to be, but in a gloomy and cramped den".

Four of the hot and heavy days of August were enlivened by the Bartholomew Fair, covering a wide area round the Smithfield meat-market. Its commercial significance had much declined, but it was still an important occasion of enjoyment. There were swings where the children climbed and dived – described rather ponderously by Ned Ward:

> We turned round the outside of the Fair, at the back of the booths, where we found . . . children in flying coaches, who insensibly climbed upwards, knowing not whither they were going but, being once elevated to a certain height, they came down again according to the circular motion of the sphere they moved in.

There were all sorts of side-shows, such as the wax-works, where Ward was "astonished at the liveliness of the figures who sat in such easy postures" and was amused to see some slow country youth quite taken in:

> When he had looked round him and pretty well feasted his eyes he turns about to the girl that shows 'em: says he – "They are woundy silent. I pray you, vorsooth, can they speak?" At which the young damsel fell a-laughing, saying: "You must speak to 'em first and then, perhaps, they'll answer you." With that, the foolish ignoramus did as he was bid, crying to one of the figures: "How d'ye, forsooth? – you in the black hood."

And, of course, there were pedlars, selling all manner of trifles. Their thin voices come down to us across the unheeding jostle of Ned Ward's London: "Will you buy a mouse-trap, or a rat-trap? Will you buy a cloth brush, a hat brush or a comb-brush?" There must have been many of them on the streets of the metropolis. Lady Wishfort's maid, a character in William Congreve's *The Way of the World* (1700) had been rescued from this dead-end job with a generosity that she was not allowed to forget:

> Thou bosom traitress that I raised up from nothing . . . go set up for yourself again . . . with your threepenny-worth of small ware, flaunting upon a packthread, under a brandy-seller's bulk, or against a dead wall by a ballad-monger. Go, hang out

an old frisoneer-gorget[1] with a yard of yellow colberteen[2] again . . . an old gnawed mask, two rows of pins and a child's fiddle; a glass necklace with the beads broken, and a quilted nightcap with one ear . . . These were your commodities . . . this was the merchandise you dealt in.

The Life of the Streets

Emerging from the City through the old walls at Ludgate, Fleet Street ran westward into the Strand and so linked up with Westminster. Here the mercantile and financial centre met the social and political one. It was a bustling middle-class district, where uniform brick houses looked through their sash windows across basement areas into the street. In these streets the hackney coaches jostled and pressed, to the oaths and cracking whips of the coachmen, but at least they ran according to a known scale of charges which could not be exceeded. Macky found them

> very necessary conveniences not to be met with anywhere abroad . . . Here you have coaches at the corner of every street, which for a shilling will carry you within a reasonable distance. . . . There are 700 of them licensed by Act of Parliament, and carry their numbers on their coaches.

But although, like a large sedan chair, they were covered in, they had no glass in the windows and their strap under-slinging gave a rough ride. "May those that like it enjoy it," said Ward, nursing his bruises after a coach ride, "for it has loosened my joints in so short a passage, that I shall scarce recover my former strength this fortnight."

At night, some at least of the streets had lights – "dazzling", according to Ned Ward. Misson describes them:

> Instead of lanterns, they set up in the streets of London lamps which, by means of a very thick convex glass, throw out great rays of light which illuminate the path for people that go on foot tolerably well.

[1] A woollen collar or wimple (*O.E.D.*)
[2] Lace resembling network (*O.E.D.*)

He claims that the lamps were alight till midnight, but Ward noticed that, by eleven, "the glittering lamps . . . were now dwindling to a glimmering snuff". It was wise to be home before the taverns emptied, especially on a Sunday, the only day free for working men. "How are the streets inhabited, sirrah?" asks Lord Rake of a waiter in Vanbrugh's *The Provoked Wife* (1697), only to be reminded: "It's Sunday night, they are full of drunken citizens."

Along these bustling streets, then, whether by day or night, the people of Queen Anne's London moved on their affairs. Some to the coffee house or the theatre, others to the rougher pleasures of cockfighting or bull-baiting and some, no doubt, to the darker world of crime.

Coffee-houses

There were 500 coffee houses in Queen Anne's time, with such names as The Bell, Dick's, and Sarah's (all in Fleet Street), offering their customers coffee, tobacco, the newspapers and good talk. And business could be combined with relaxation, as at Jonathan's in Change Alley, where dealers in stocks congregated, and Lloyd's in Tower Street, the origin of the great society of underwriters of marine insurance. The literary world could be found at Will's in Covent Garden and Church affairs were discussed at Truby's, while the Grecian was the haunt of scholars and the St James's of Whig politicians. There were chocolate houses, too, such as the Cocoa Tree where Tories met and White's in St James's Street, where the exclusive world of fashion took its first pinches of captured Spanish snuff. Misson spoke of the coffee houses as "extremely convenient":

> You have all manner of news there: you have a good fire, which you may sit by as long as you please; you have a dish of coffee, you meet your friends for the transaction of business, and all for a penny if you don't care to spend more.

Theatres and Other Diversions

The Theatre Royal in Drury Lane and the Queen's Theatre in Haymarket (the latter for opera) were the two main theatres in London, drawing their audiences largely from the surroundings of St James's, though Queen Anne never went to either. Seats cost roughly five shillings in a box, three shillings in the pit, and two shillings in the gallery, for performances which started at about 6.30 p.m. Anne's reign was no period for great drama, nor for great actors, and it seems that the audience paid only casual attention to the stage. Misson, at any rate, gives this impression:

> The pit is an amphitheatre, filled with benches without back-boards and covered with green cloth. Men of quality . . . some ladies of reputation . . . and abundance of damsels that hunt for prey, sit altogether in this place, higgledy-piggledy, chatter, toy, play, hear, hear not.

The gallery was usually occupied by the footmen of the fashionable playgoers, who copied the behaviour of their masters, as an advertisement in the *Female Tatler* (December 9th, 1709) indicates:

> Drop't near the playhouse in the Haymarket a bundle of horse-whips, designed to belabour the footmen in the upper gallery, who almost every night this winter, have made such an intolerable disturbance, that the players could not be heard, and their masters were obliged to hiss them into silence. Whoever has taken up the said whips is desired to leave them with my Lord Rake's porter, several noblemen resolving to exercise 'em on their backs, the next frosty morning.

A stentorian voice must have been the main necessity for an actor of that time, to penetrate the massive indifference of his audience.

There was no such indifference among spectators at cockfights, however, who gambled furiously upon their outcome. To von Uffenbach, cockfighting was "a sport peculiar to the English". He describes the cockpit near Gray's Inn: it was

> round like a tower and all round it there are benches in tiers on which the spectators sit. In the middle is a round table which is covered with mats, on which the cocks have to fight . . . The people, gentle and simple (they sit with no distinction of place), act like madmen and go on raising the odds to twenty guineas and more . . . If a man has made a bet and is unable to pay he is made to sit in a basket fastened to the ceiling and is drawn up in it amidst peals of laughter.

In many parts of London, too, there were enclosures for the baiting of bulls and bears – a form of brutal entertainment rather than an occasion for gambling. Here also, von Uffenbach was a cool observer, sitting on the raised benches which bounded on two sides the open space of the bear garden, and recording what he saw:

> First a young ox or bull was fastened by a long rope to an iron ring in the middle of the yard; then about 30 dogs, two or three at a time, were let loose on him, but he made short work of them, goring them and tossing them high in the air above the height of the first story . . . Several had such a grip of the bull's throat or ear that their mouths had to be forced open with poles . . . They brought out a small bear and tied him up after the same fashion. As soon as the dogs had at him, he stood up on his hind legs and gave them some terrific buffets; but, if one of them got at his skin, he rolled about in such a fashion that the dogs thought themselves lucky if they came out safe from beneath him.

There were, of course, many other diversions to occupy the Londoner – some so little organized that observers were unlikely to notice them. Misson, however, remarks a form of football, which flourished without the help of rules.

> In winter footballs is a useful and charming exercise: it is a leather ball about as big as one's head, filled with wind: this is kicked about from one t'other in the streets, by him that can get at it, and that is all the art of it.

Without rules or referee, this game must often have become a brawl – all the more so since, as Misson remarks, "anything that looks like fighting is delicious to an Englishman". He noticed how, if two little boys quarrel in the street, the passengers stop, make a ring round them in a moment and set them against one another . . . During the fight, the ring of bystanders encourage the combatants with great delight . . . and never part them while they fight according to the rules. And these bystanders are not only other boys, porters and rabble, but all sorts of men of fashion; some thrusting by the mob . . . others getting upon stalls; and all would hire places, if scaffolds could be built in a moment.

Crime and Punishment

This was innocent enough, but there was also much that was dark and vicious in the London of Queen Anne. It was the hey-day of the highwayman and the common footpad, along the roads leading out of the town and in the narrow alleys sloping to the river. Not long before Anne came to the throne, the area to the east of the Temple was 'Alsatia', the privileged sanctuary of criminals, where ordinary citizens hardly dared penetrate. Now this had been abolished and the area opened up, but the criminals had not left London – nor would they while law enforcement was in the hands of elected parish constables, often old and open to threats and bribes. Away on the north-west borders of London, where Marble Arch is today, the gallows stood at Tyburn, where 242 hangings took place within the reign of the Queen. If corruption had not been so rife the number might have been higher: as it was, the law was not administered impartially between rich and poor. The condemned highwayman Macheath, in John Gay's *Beggar's Opera* (1728), believed this:

Since laws were made for every degree,
To curb vice in others as well as me,
I wonder we ha'n't better company
Upon Tyburn Tree.
But gold from law can take out the sting;
And if rich men, like us, were to swing,
'Twould thin the land, such numbers to string
Upon Tyburn Tree.

It was risky to enter or leave London by night, for footpads lay in wait and the highwaymen were often in league with ostlers in the town, so that they knew where to expect easy prey travelling by horse or coach. Von Uffenbach came up from Richmond one evening in some trepidation:

> We set off for London quite late in the evening in considerable terror of being robbed. For the footpads know that people return to London very late, so the roads are very unsafe . . . One can feel no security even in the vicinity of the town . . . Such robberies take place at night in the town itself and even in the neighbourhood of St. James's Palace.

Robbery with violence was punished by hanging – a squalid ending to exploits that often enough brought little gain. Common criminals were taken in carts to Tyburn on the six annual execution days, though an occasional gentleman might make his last journey by coach. Misson shows how lightly some of them professed to regard their fate:

> He that is to be hanged . . . first takes care to get himself shaved and handsomely dressed, either in mourning or in the dress of a bridegroom . . .
>
> When his suit of clothes, or nightgown, his gloves, hat, periwig, nosegay, coffin, flannel dress for his corpse, and all those things are brought and prepared, the main point is taken care of, his mind is at peace . . . Generally he studies a speech, which he pronounces under the gallows, and gives in writing to the sheriff, desiring that it may be printed. Sometimes the girls dress in white, with great silk scarves, and carry baskets full of flowers and oranges, scattering these favours all the way they go.

Whether in the last desperate show on the road to Tyburn, or among the abusive and sweating watermen upon the river, or in the warmth of the coffee houses, or in the crowd jostling to see the crown jewels at the Tower, the London scene is set within the largest concentration of urban population in Europe. We may fancy that they were also the most pushing and vigorous large group to be found anywhere at that time, those ancestors of ours who lived out their short lives under the shadow of Paul's great dome, to the accompaniment of the racket of their narrow streets, yielding place on Sundays to a multitude of church bells overhead.

Britain in 1714

But the quiet countryside away from the capital was an equal participant in the great changes which had occurred since the Scottish James VI had become James I in England. The most important was that, under the sceptre of his great-granddaughter, England and Wales had joined with Scotland to form a single state. Developments on both sides of the Border had ensured that this union should provide the national energies with new fields of employment. By Anne's time, the long struggle between Crown and Parliament was over, so that both Englishmen and Scots were freed to spend their talents for more constructive objects. The religious conflict, too, was finished: in Scotland, the Presbyterian Kirk was established, while in England security for the Church establishment had been combined with some measure of toleration for the Protestant nonconformists. Prerogative courts had been brought to an end, and in both countries the national legal system stood intact.

While old conflicts had been settled, foundations had been laid for the new Great Britain of the coming age. The battle for economic freedom was largely won: merchant and manufacturer were no longer seriously impeded by the privileges of corporations, gilds, and other monopolist interests. Big strides had been made in industry; some small ones in agriculture, too. In England, and to a smaller extent in Scotland, a national bank provided backing for the state, while the English stock market made private capital more readily available. By Anne's reign, London was beginning to rival Amsterdam as the financial centre of Europe. Overseas, the foundations of empire had been laid, and Scottish enterprise was now joining in its development. In 1603 England had been of comparatively small account in the great affairs of Europe – and Scotland very much less. In 1714 Great Britain was one of the major European powers, its largest free-trade area, and the centre of a system of commerce that reached from the Thames and the Western Approaches to the Caribbean Sea and the harbours of North America.

EARLY HANOVERIAN BRITAIN

15

KINGDOM AND EMPIRE

When George in pudding time came o'er,
And moderate men looked big, Sir,

the Vicar of Bray turned his coat for the last time: the best part of the meal had come. The anonymous song of which he is the hero can be traced back as far as 1734, and it is very characteristic of the age of prosperity and practical compromises which followed the Hanoverian succession. The last years of Queen Anne's reign had been a time of feverish excitement, culminating in the dismissal of the moderate Harley only five days before the end. If Bolingbroke had supplanted his rival a little sooner, the Queen's death might have been the signal for a new civil war. As it was, he accepted James Edward's determined adherence to the old faith as a sufficient reason for inactivity on that momentous Sunday: "England," said Bolingbroke, "would as soon have a Turk as a Roman Catholic for King."

George I and II

The arrangements made by the Act of Settlement having been brought peacefully into force, a good deal turned upon what other qualifications besides the essential one of Protestantism the new line of British sovereigns might prove to possess. As the grandson of Elizabeth, daughter of James I, the first George had some share of Stuart blood; but the German three-quarters was clearly predominant. Having ruled as elector of Hanover with absolute powers since 1698, he had a strong interest in German politics, and at the age of 54 was disinclined to make a close study of the affairs of his new kingdom, except where foreign policy or the army or the safety and emoluments of his own position were concerned. A king who spoke chiefly French, who consoled himself with German mistresses while keeping his wife a lifelong prisoner in a remote Hanoverian castle, and who quarrelled furiously with his son and heir, would have had difficulty in achieving popularity, even if he had tried. He remained a remote and unloved figure, absorbed in diplomacy and dying after thirteen years on one of the visits to Hanover which were his greatest pleasure.

Since the Whigs were the party which had actively helped him to secure the throne, George I chose Whig ministers, among whom General Stanhope, a soldier with a sound knowledge of foreign affairs, became the most prominent. The crisis of a Jacobite rebellion was surmounted in 1715, as was also a financial crisis (the South Sea Bubble) six years later, at which juncture the leadership of the ministry passed to Robert Walpole, in whom the King now saw the 'trouble-shooter' he needed. The impeachment of Harley had been dropped (1717) and in 1723 Bolingbroke was allowed to return from exile, but the opposition to the government which he tried to build up consisted mainly of disgruntled Whigs rather than avowed Tory politicians. In any case, at George I's death, Walpole was able to ingratiate himself with his successor by inducing parliament to increase the Civil List for the support of the new sovereign from £700,000 to £800,000.

George II, who was destined to reign for a third of a century (1727–1760) resembled his father in his generally German outlook. But the courage he showed at Dettingen,[1] advancing on foot at the head of his army to drive the French back across the Main, made 'the little captain' for a time immensely popular. He spoke English fluently (though with a strong German accent), took a lively interest in the details of politics, played a small part in the foundation of the British Museum, and continued his father's

[1] See p. 274.

patronage of the German-born composer Handel. His consort, Caroline of Anspach, was in all matters of serious policy her husband's better half. Unfortunately, their quarrels with their eldest son, Frederick, meant that there was again a rival, younger court, and the early death of the Queen in 1737 weakened the steadying influence of Walpole on his royal master. Yet by 1745 'God Save The King' was a popular anthem, and by the end of the reign constitutional monarchy had become so firmly established that no successor could disregard the need for a working partnership between the king, his ministers, and what the second George was pleased to call "that damned House of Commons".

The King's Ministers

The government of the British people was taking a more modern shape. Important results followed from George I's discontinuance in 1717 of the practice of presiding at the meetings of his Cabinet ministers – though the change seems to have been made almost casually, in part to exclude his son from attendance as his interpreter. This gave more power to the ministry as a whole and in particular to its leading member, who now presided. He normally held the post of First Lord of the Treasury, with an official residence provided by George II for Sir Robert Walpole at 10 Downing Street. The fact that this position of greatest influence was held almost without a break by Walpole for twenty-one years and then for ten and a half by Henry Pelham means that between 1721 and 1754 something like the office of prime minister came gradually into existence. The name of 'prime minister', however, did not yet come into general use, and in at least two ways his position was still relatively weak. Firstly, he was chosen and dismissed by the king according to the royal likes and dislikes, without any necessary regard for the wishes of parliament or the people. Secondly, while in office he had only a limited control over his colleagues, since some of his fellow Cabinet ministers were chosen directly by the king, to whom they reported separately in his Closet on the business of their departments.

Departments is perhaps a misleading term, since there was no civil service as we understand it: such officials as the country had were provided as part of the royal household. Only the Treasury controlled any large body of personnel, namely the officers of the customs and excise. Of the other ministers, the two secretaries of state had by far the widest duties. They controlled foreign relations and military and naval movements according to a division between north and south, counting Hanover and (normally) Scotland in the north and Ireland and the colonies in the south; English domestic business, however, concerned them both equally. For all these duties the staff of the secretaries' office totalled twenty-six, including the caretaker. But the chronic shortage of staff to carry out decisions made it all the more useful to an ambitious minister to get his way quickly through direct access to the sovereign.

Though his position was in so many ways weaker than that of a modern premier, the head of the ministry already depended for the retention of his post upon his ability to equip himself with a stable majority in parliament. Throughout this period most active politicians called themselves Whigs, since that name implied loyalty to the new dynasty, and Tories were normally to be found in the ranks of the parliamentary Opposition. But there were also Opposition Whigs, so that the problem with which a Walpole or a Pelham was perpetually contending was how to collect enough votes, not for Whigs against Tories, but for his group of politicians against envious rival groups. Some of these votes came from holders of public offices, court appointments, and pensions from the Crown, who would automatically support whomsoever the King had chosen for his chief minister. Other votes were won by the careful distribution of all kinds of patronage at the minister's disposal. Army commands, judgeships, and bishoprics given to the nominees of powerful persons caused them to influence the votes of their friends and dependants in parliament; lesser favours might be bestowed within a constituency, so as to keep its MP on the right side. We read of Walpole, long before he became a minister, securing a commission for the nephew of an influential alderman, who "having through excess and the follies of youth reduced his estate would gladly if possible assume a career in the forces". This was at King's Lynn, which he represented for forty years; there would be similar requests for the use of government patronage in every borough. Enormous importance also attached to the uses which the king could be persuaded by the minister to make of his prerogative as the 'fountain of honour'. The first Georges were reluctant to create new peers, but there were promotions within the peerage and occasional vacancies in the Order of the Garter. Baronetcies and knighthoods helped to control lesser mortals; 38 KCBs owed their appointments to Walpole.[1]

A Policy of Moderation

But government was not all graft. In order to keep his majority, the king's minister had somehow to attract to his side a part of the independent members of the House of Commons. These were country gentlemen, or in some cases wealthy merchants, who prided themselves on accepting no favours from Court or ministry. By tradition they were always disposed to mistrust the government, and Opposition politicians of course did their best to feed that mistrust. The safest line for the minister to adopt was to devote his energies to management and the conciliation of individuals, and to raise as few contentious issues as possible.

Financial changes were to some extent unavoidable, and Walpole, who was chancellor of the exchequer as well as first lord of the treasury throughout his long ministry, was an expert financier. He organized a sinking fund for the national debt, and tried to simplify and improve the tariff. His Excise Bill of 1733 was a commonsense measure for placing the collection of duties on tobacco and wine in the hands of excisemen, then more efficient than the customs officers, and making it harder to evade duties by having them levied when the article was taken from the warehouse for use instead of when it was first landed. Yet he gave up in face of an agitation fomented by his enemies in parliament and the City of of London, saying "This dance will no farther go." A few years earlier he had given way to an agitation against the introduction of English-made copper coins in Ireland, although Sir Isaac Newton testified to their value, and a few years later he gave way in a third matter which had some financial repercussions, namely the Porteous riot in Edinburgh.[2]

[1] For the 'management' of Scotland, see p. 283.
[2] See p. 283.

Pelham, however, was faced by an urgent need for reform. For a whole generation nothing effective had been done to check the scandal of the cheap, home-distilled gin which had replaced the heavily taxed brandy of France and was being consumed at the rate of a gallon per head per annum, to the great detriment of health and morals. He was roused by Hogarth's 'Gin Lane'[1] and a work by Henry Fielding, novelist and London magistrate, *On the Causes of the Late Increase of Robbers* to pass the restrictive Gin Act of 1751. This was followed by Hardwicke's Marriage Act, which prevented runaway marriages by insisting on banns and a period of residence. Pelham also reformed the calendar, which was eleven days in arrears, though his brother, the duke of Newcastle, thought it imprudent to "stir matters that had long been quiet". But he gave way to conservative prejudice by withdrawing a proposal to naturalize foreign Protestants; and a reasonable but unpopular measure, enabling Jews to obtain naturalization by Private Act without using a Christian form of oath, was actually repealed after one year.

The independent Members were still more sensitive on questions of foreign policy. As staunch patriots, they were always ready to denounce any move which could be represented as "truckling to Hanover". As reluctant taxpayers, who knew that the Land Tax on their estates was likely to be quadrupled in time of war, they were always ready to criticize a forward policy as running unnecessary risks. The result was a quarter of a century of almost uninterrupted peace, until trade interests drove Walpole into war with Spain, one consequence of which was his fall from power in 1742. But though the struggle against Spain, and later France, continued until 1748, the policy of moderation, which Walpole inaugurated and Pelham did his best to continue, produced great results for the kingdom and empire.

Jacobitism

Perhaps the most obvious was the eventual failure of Jacobitism. James Edward, born as heir to the throne in 1688, and his more attractive son, Charles Edward, offered a standing threat to the

[1] See plate 23.

settlement made in 1714, especially in the Scottish Highlands, among the Catholic minority in northern England, and in North Wales. The Jacobites of the south remained an unknown quantity, but their notorious strength in Oxford suggests a following among High Churchmen elsewhere; and Mr Facing Bothways was a common type of politician. In the constant watch for the Pretender's agents, Catholic priests were for obvious reasons particularly suspect: at moments of excitement they risked imprisonment for life under a law of 1700 forbidding the celebration of Mass, and the Catholic laity could be prevented from leaving home or residing in London.

The rebellion of 1715, however, lacked the two essentials of good leadership and outside support. Even so, most of Scotland fell to James Edward's supporters and there was a small-scale rising of Catholics in north-west England, suppressed at Preston on November 13th. A battle fought the same day at Sheriffmuir in Perthshire was no more than a slight setback for the Jacobites, but when James Edward landed in Scotland the next month he brought no help from France to prevent his followers from being pressed back into the north. After he left again in February, a sufficient garrison was established in the Highlands to crush a second attempt in 1719, when a small force of Spaniards landed there and was joined by 2,000 Scots.

The Forty-Five was a much more serious affair than the Fifteen. The young prince, Charles Edward, who had seen action with the Spaniards in Italy when he was 14, proved an inspiring leader; his name still lives in northern song and story. Moreover, the British forces had just suffered a major defeat at Fontenoy in the Netherlands at the hands of the French, who were prepared to back the prince's expedition. He had only seven friends with him when he landed in the western Highlands in late July, but there were still some chieftains whose sense of loyalty to the Stuarts would cause them to disregard any odds, both for themselves and for the clansmen under their despotic control. Cameron of Lochiel was one of the first to join him, sending his 'tacksmen'

> to intimate to all the Camerons that, if they did not forthwith

go with them, they would instantly proceed to burn all their houses and hough their cattle.

Except for the castles of Edinburgh and Stirling and the garrison at Fort William, the rebels this time overran almost all Scotland and defeated two forces of regulars, in September at Prestonpans and in January at Falkirk. But the advance of 5,000 Highlanders through England from Carlisle to Derby, which the Prince entered on December 4th, 1745, while meeting with little resistance roused little support: almost the only recruits were a few hundred unemployed from Manchester. His Council of War therefore refused to press on to London, where he hoped to take advantage of the prevailing panic among the moneyed classes, or to adopt the Prince's alternative proposal of marching into Wales. The sequel was a retreat which (in spite of the success at Falkirk) was bound to end in failure, as the disheartened Highlanders were pursued into the north by George II's soldier son, the duke of Cumberland, with an army nearly twice as large which had the support of a train of artillery.

On the shelterless field of Culloden the royal guns did heavy execution among the clansmen, impatiently waiting for their chiefs to give the order, 'Claymore!' The rest of the battle – apart from the merciless cavalry pursuit at the end – followed the pattern of the Jacobite attack described by one of Cumberland's volunteer officers:

> Like wildcats their men came down in swarms upon our left wing . . . They began to cut and hack in their natural way without ceremony. When just near us and a fine mark, the king's men discharged a complete running fire that dropped them down as they came on.

Long before nightfall of this April day, the last battle to be fought on the soil of the island was over and the Prince a fugitive, who after six months in hiding among the mountains escaped to France and was quickly forgotten. As for his followers, about 1,200 were killed on or near the scene of action, and out of a total of 3,470 prisoners, which included women and children, 120 were executed and 936 transported to America or the West Indies; some prominent Jacobites were also punished by banishment. 'Butcher' Cumberland had made his father the first king whose writ ran unquestioned from one end of the island to the other, and a grateful parliament rewarded him with £25,000 a year for himself and his heirs. No modern regiment, however, includes Culloden among its battle honours.

Military measures were followed by political. Chiefs were deprived of all legal powers over their clansmen other than those of any ordinary landowner over his tenants;[1] a tacksman was now a principal tenant, not a kind of officer in a private army. For thirty years even the kilt and the bagpipes as well as the carrying of arms were banned because of their association with a militancy which had cost the Lowlands dear. The 250 miles of bridged roads, which had been constructed as a measure of pacification after the Fifteen, were now extended to 1,050 miles. Even more important was the impetus given to agricultural improvements, the woollen and linen industries, and Highland education by grants from the Commissioners for the Forfeited Estates, who until 1784 administered the revenues of the Jacobite exiles. Only 27 years after Culloden, Dr Johnson was to observe:

> There never was any change of national manners so quick, so great and so general as that which has operated in the Highlands by the last conquest and the subsequent laws.

This may therefore be an appropriate moment at which to take stock of the position in other parts of the king's dominions. In the Lowlands of Scotland, which then comprised about half its population, the fusion of the kingdoms showed earlier results. Though the woollen industry was among those which suffered at first from efficient English competition, the quantity of Scottish linen stamped for sale was quadrupled in the second quarter of the century. In 1755 the population of Glasgow was roughly twice what it had been when the Act of Union was passed. Edinburgh grew by only one-half, but in 1753 its first Improvement Act was passed; ten years later the decision to build the New Town with its spacious Georgian squares was presaged by an article in the *Scots Magazine*, citing 'the free intercourse with England' as the reason for an

[1] This was a breach of Article XX of the Treaty of Union.

increased love of society which was causing people of rank to winter in the northern capital.

Wales

Wales had no capital city, nor did the first half of the eighteenth century produce any great change in its traditional economy, except for an increase in the output of coal. But people experienced the beginnings of a cultural growth which in the long run made them larger contributors to the life of the kingdom as a whole. In spite of the full union with England under Henry VIII, their language as well as their remoteness had to a large extent cut off the Welsh from the cultural movements which were affecting England: even the 120 charity schools[1] set up after 1700 by the SPCK had only a limited impact. But from 1737 onwards a Welsh rector instituted a system of Circulating Schools to teach Bible-reading and the Catechism. These used Welsh in the Welsh-speaking districts and were open in the winter months, when adults could spare time from their work on the land, with the result that by 1760 fully a quarter of them had attended school and were able to read.

During the same period a trio of great Welsh preachers, headed by a layman, Howel Harris, spread a movement of religious revival through the Principality. While it almost immediately developed close relations with English Methodism,[2] its strength lay in a characteristic Welsh appeal to the emotions, for which their own language was the most acceptable medium. As in England, the revival soon burst the bonds of the Established Church. It helped to re-create a national tradition of poetry and music, and made the chapel-going community a central feature of Welsh life in the new industrial era.

Ireland: The Ulstermen

To contemporaries the British people seemed to be successfully combining the creation of unity within their island home with

[1] See p. 209.
[2] See p. 311.

the consolidation of their hold upon possessions overseas. In the case of Ireland, indeed, appearances were doubly deceptive. On the one hand, the Protestant Ascendancy, which even extended to the suppression of whatever Irish industry or commerce might rival Britain, kept the Catholic Irish in abject submission – there was no Jacobite rebellion in Ireland – without ever reconciling them to their lot. The future was foreshadowed only by the flight of the 'Wild Geese', the refugees who formed five regiments in French and five in Spanish service. On the other hand, the Ascendancy was based on a parliament in Dublin from which the Scottish Presbyterians of Ulster were rigidly excluded as non-Anglicans; until 1719 they were not even allowed to serve in the army or take any other post under the Crown. These Ulstermen developed the linen industry, in which the sister island did not feel endangered by rivalry, and made Belfast a centre for the importation of coal, linen yarn, and colonial goods from Scotland. But by mid-century about 50,000 had fled from religious inequality to New England, where they later made an important contribution to Washington's rebel army and to the political leadership of the new United States.

The Oceanic Trades

Meanwhile, the First British Empire was rapidly approaching its brief zenith, as the expansion of trade led to the expansion of territory. Under the first two Hanoverian kings the East India Company doubled both its imports and exports and substantially increased its annual dividend, although for most of this period it had no more than a toe-hold upon the territory of the sub-continent. A few hundred Englishmen and Scotsmen, residing in the 'factories' at Bombay, Madras, and Calcutta, organized the traffic ready for the annual visits of the Company's ships. But the break-up of the Mogul Empire confronted the British and other foreign traders with the problem of how to safeguard these valuable commercial interests in a country torn by civil war. In 1751 Robert Clive's capture and subsequent defence of Arcot marked the beginning of the forward policy which for two centuries was to present the British people with the greatest of all their opportunities.

From the commercial standpoint the East India Company's activities were rivalled in importance by those based on the plantation colonies of the West Indies and the North American mainland. Tobacco, dyestuffs, cotton, and (until the 1730s) sugar and rice were 'enumerated commodities' which could not legally be exported except through Britain, where the merchants of London, Bristol, Liverpool, and Glasgow made great fortunes from sales at home and abroad. Since these crops required much hard cultivation and the frequent breaking of new land in a hot climate, their profitability stimulated the demand for slaves from West Africa, where the Royal African Company maintained forts along a 1,100-mile stretch of the Guinea coast, at which native chiefs delivered about 30,000 men, women, and children captured in the interior for sale each season. Ships trading from British ports brought coarse cloth, trinkets, and rum; they then made the 'middle passage' to the plantation colonies, where they sold their second cargo, of slaves; and finally they carried the colonial produce home. Since the round trip took from nine to twelve months, the profits were not necessarily greater than those earned on shorter voyages within Europe; but it was a trade in which, at each of three stages, the British entrepreneur was in a stronger position than his customer. "The Negro Trade, and the natural consequences resulting from it, may be justly esteemed an inexhaustible Fund of Wealth and Naval Power to this Nation" was a sentiment fully representative of opinion at mid-century in both Bristol and Liverpool, where only hard-bitten sailormen had actually seen such 'natural consequences' as the high death-rate among the fettered victims making the middle passage in the slavers' holds.

The colonies in temperate climates played a different role in British trade. These were communities of farmers, foresters, and fishermen, who bought their manufactures in the home market, partly under pressure from much-resented laws requiring them to 'buy British', but chiefly because Britain was their natural source of supply. In return the home country bought ships, fish, and naval stores for her own ship-building, but in spite of the offer of bounties, timber, hemp, and tar continued to be procured mainly from the Baltic.

Development of the American Colonies

Nevertheless, the advantages gained at the peace of Utrecht were in several respects consolidated. Newfoundland was given its first governor in 1729, with a view to its conversion from a seasonal base for the fishing fleets to a colony of settlement. Four years later, a more ambitious settler colony was begun on the Spanish border under the name of Georgia. General James Edward Oglethorpe, a philanthropist of wide vision who had recently secured the release of debtors from appalling conditions in London prisons, raised a fund to make their emigration possible, together with a body of exiled Protestants from Germany, some Jews, and a party of Scottish Highlanders. He governed the colony in person and conducted a successful defence against the Spaniards, but it lay too far south to flourish under existing conditions until slaves were introduced and the attempt to employ white men as the labour force was abandoned.

Elsewhere, the American population of British or other white stock was increasing very fast, partly from immigration during the long period of peace, but chiefly because New England and the Middle Colonies offered favourable conditions for the rearing of large families. From about 340,000 in 1720 it rose to at least 1,200,000 in 1760. Others besides Oglethorpe concerned themselves with Britain's responsibility for its development. The idealist philosopher Berkeley spent three years in Rhode Island, inspired by the noble vision of his own verses:

Westward the course of empire takes its way,
The four first acts already past,
A fifth shall close the drama with the day,
The world's great effort is the last.

His hopes of establishing a massive educational foundation to serve the needs of the New World came to nothing. But Berkeley's aspirations are a reminder that the British had not yet forfeited the empire of the west.

Military Events in North America, 1739–56

On the contrary, the war which broke out in 1739 against Spain and broadened into a general European conflict, involving victory against the French at Dettingen and defeat at Fontenoy, also produced a forward movement in North America. In the year of the defeat the New England colonists captured Louisburg, the French stronghold at the mouth of the St Lawrence. To their intense indignation, the British Government returned it in exchange for Madras at the peace of Aix-la-Chapelle in 1748. But next year the establishment of a new British fortress at Halifax, Nova Scotia, by the president of the board of trade whose name it commemorates, prepared the way for the harsh expulsion of the French population from the province and its resettlement with New Englanders. This action, like the abortive attempts to oust the French from Fort Duquesne and their other new advanced posts in the region of the Great Lakes, prepared the way for the formal renewal of hostilities between Britain and France in 1756, when Frederick the Great of Prussia was our only ally against a seemingly invincible European coalition.

The Army and Navy

Since the Seven Years War, stretching beyond the period of this book, gave the British people for the time being an undisputed position as the leading world power – a very definite stage in their 'making' – this will be a convenient point at which to consider briefly the foundations already laid by the development of British military and naval resources under the first two Georges.

The army was an unpopular institution, still associated in the public mind with Cromwell's major-generals and the force which James II had placed on Hounslow Heath to overawe the capital. Its peace-time strength was therefore very small, about 18,000 men, rising to about four times as many in a prolonged period of war. It was recruited from volunteers among the poorest classes, with an admixture of forced entries from prisons and workhouses. The net pay was 6*d*. a day, with accommodation grudgingly provided in rural inns and discipline maintained by flogging and even crueller 'field punishments', under which the victims often died. Since in addition the regiments were almost entirely under the personal control of their colonel (by whose name they were usually known), with junior officers who had to buy their commissions, it seems surprising that they acquitted themselves well on the whole in the wars on the Continent. But a more efficient army, such as the Prussians at least possessed at this period, would probably have suppressed the Forty-Five rebellion more rapidly. It is also noteworthy that the British government habitually employed foreign mercenaries, not only to swell the forces available for its Continental campaigns but, in at least four critical years (1715, 1719, 1745, and 1756), to help garrison our own island.

In several respects, however, the army made marked progress. Its cumbrous organization, in which the secretary at war, ordnance board, and paymaster-general shared the management or mismanagement of campaigns which were planned and ordered by the higher authority of a secretary of state, benefited to some extent from the personal interest of George I and II. The duke of Cumberland, who became commander-in-chief at 25, though his career was to end in disgrace through his failure to defend Hanover in 1757, put down many military abuses and was "noted for a conscientious energy of administration . . . not common among the great personages of his time".[1] A great technical advance was the formation in 1727 of the Royal Artillery, which had its officers trained at Woolwich and promoted on merit; by the end of the new reign its strength exceeded 3,000 men, with cannon ranging up to 24-pound howitzers and a good reputation for efficiency. In the same period a Scots army doctor named John Pringle, who had served under Cumberland, made the treatment of the sick and wounded more scientific and transformed conditions in field hospitals.

The general spirit of the army was also improved. The Black Watch, a force of loyal Highlanders formed in 1729 to watch their rebellious compatriots, prepared the way for Pitt's Highland regiments, raised from among former rebels. The war of 1739 brought in some better volunteers through the offer of a three-year

[1] W. E. H. Lecky; *History of England in the Eighteenth Century*, II, 407.

engagement in place of enlistment for life. The war of 1756 was to see the reinstatement of the militia as an active reserve force, made up of local levies which were to be trained by the county gentry and called out to support the Regulars when invasion threatened.

The generation which first applauded the strains of 'Rule Britannia' could not be accused of distrusting the Royal Navy, which had never been seen as a danger to the national liberties. On the contrary, it was widely appreciated that the Navy was Britain's first line of defence against invasion by the great military powers of the Continent, making certain that "Britons never shall be slaves", and at the same time the protector of her seaborne trade, fulfilling the promise of the same song, "Thy cities shall with commerce shine". Nevertheless, the system of administration was chaotic, as in the army, and at the outbreak of war in 1739 only 80 out of 124 ships of the line were fit for service, as against 40 Spanish and 50 French. A still more surprising fact is that, in spite of four sets of technical changes to improve British naval architecture, the best British men-of-war continued to be less effective, ship for ship, than the best products of French and Spanish designers.

Able-bodied seamen were invited to enter the service of the Crown by a bonus of up to £5, but crews were collected mainly by the press-gang, which combed the sea-port towns and might even penetrate inland in search of its prey. The sailor's net pay was scarcely more than the soldier's, his living conditions were worse, and the discipline probably harsher. But the naval officer earned a more genuine respect from his men: both the King's Letter Boys, nominated by the Admiralty, and the far more numerous Captain's Servants, who were often family connections, came aboard at 12 or 13 and had to spend many arduous years before they could reach the higher commissioned ranks. Moreover, the hazards of the sea made a commander's skill clearly demonstrable. All the same, a more democratic generation cannot but wonder at the acceptance of a system by which, after sharing the same risks in battle, the admiral's share of any prize money earned by his fleet might be equal to that of 30,000 of his seamen.

All things considered, it is perhaps less surprising that the main campaigns of the war of 1739 began with a wholly disastrous large-scale attack on the Spanish West Indies, to which the initial capture of Portobello had seemed to point the way, than that by 1747, thanks to Anson and Hawke, "the enemy's fleets had been driven off the seas and their colonies exposed to our attacks".[1] This same Admiral Anson three years earlier had turned shame to glory in his voyage round the world, for which the authorities had provided him with landing parties of 259 Chelsea pensioners, none of whom survived the expedition, and sent him off after delays that warned the Spaniards and also ensured the worst weather at Cape Horn. He returned after three and three-quarter years, having lost five ships out of six but with captured treasure to the value of £600,000. Eight future admirals shared his hardships and his eventual triumph, which was a fitting prelude to the naval successes of the Seven Years War of 1756–63, won when Anson was First Lord of the Admiralty.

Climax of the Seven Years War

That war began with disasters for both Services, including the loss of Minorca, of forts in North America, and of our position in Germany. But it was the long list of reverses which made a change of political system at least for the time being inevitable. William Pitt, later earl of Chatham, had first made his name as a virulent opponent of Walpole and the King. He had been reluctantly admitted to the Government during the crisis of 1745–6, but – like another great war minister two centuries later – he was kept in the background by the regular politicians, such as Pelham and his brother and successor, the duke of Newcastle, as long as they dared. In the summer of 1757, however, after he had been dismissed from office by the King, "the popular cry without doors was violent in favour of Mr Pitt", and army and navy passed at last under the control of a great strategist.

The six regiments of British infantry which defeated the French cavalry at Minden; Wolfe's men scrambling up the path on to the heights to capture Quebec; the four ships of the line and three regiments which Pitt sent to support the conquest of Bengal, which

[1] B. Williams, *The Whig Supremacy 1714–1760*, p. 248.

Clive had initiated at Plassey – all these achieved memorable results. They were made possible by the boldness with which Pitt depleted the garrison of the island, relying upon a half-trained militia – the British people in arms – to defend it at need. But the need never arose, because the Navy justified Pitt's belief in its ability to prevent the French invasion which might have made 1759 something very different from a 'Year of Victories'. Two French fleets put to sea, but were decisively defeated off Portuguese Lagos and in the perilous waters of Quiberon Bay. When George III succeeded to his grandfather's throne in October 1760, the fall of Montreal had completed the conquest of Canada; the French possessions in West Africa, the West Indies, and India lay at Britain's mercy; and Clive was master of Bengal. A united British people looked eagerly to the future, and Jacobitism was at best a romantic memory.

16

THE CLASSES AND THE MASSES

THOSE first singers of 'Rule, Britannia', who were pictured in the last chapter, must be presumed to have seen a clear difference between realms of 'haughty tyrants' and the institutions of their own 'happy coast'. It would never have occurred to them to question the justice of the class structure upon which those institutions were firmly based. That structure was, indeed, less rigid than elsewhere, for in Britain it was comparatively easy for families to move both up and down in the social scale and parliament itself, the chosen instrument of class rule, was to some extent open (as we shall see) to outside influences. But broadly speaking, the Britain of those days was divided between what we may call 'the classes', which monopolized power, and the masses, which lived their lives within a framework of hard economic and social conditions imposed from above and virtually unalterable.

The Peerage and the House of Commons

The nobles as a class had an authority and prestige second only to that of the monarchy itself. With less than a quarter of its present-day membership, the House of Lords had as much legislative power as the House of Commons and in some ways greater influence. Peers provided nearly all the other members of Walpole's and Pelham's cabinets, and something like a quarter of their total number usually held appointments of some kind in the Government or at Court. Moreover, the upper house contained the great Whig dukes and other holders of the largest landed properties in the island, who were able to form their own political connection or group of supporters. Such a connection was made up of the nobleman's family and kinsfolk, his friends and would-be friends, and a multitude of hangers-on; when well led, it could often control appointments and other activities of the ministers. Even if such a nobleman was in opposition to the ministry of the moment, he still had much power. The sums which he spent during his annual residence at his principal country seat might affect the prosperity of a whole county, with a corresponding impact upon its political outlook. If his properties were judiciously scattered, as the duke of Newcastle's were, he might have the full or partial control of the election of a dozen MPs.

The House of Commons, with its 489 representatives of England, 24 of Wales, and 45 of Scotland, was required by a law of 1711 to be composed exclusively of substantial landowners. Though the law could be circumvented, landowners certainly predominated, for membership was deemed a high honour: a four- or five-month session was not oppressively long, and much of the business concerned uncontentious private Bills about land and roads and other matters of local interest. As we have already seen, the attitude of many MPs on questions of general policy was influenced by the receipt of ministerial or other favours, but they were in a position to weigh up the full statements of Opposition leaders, who no longer had to fear impeachment for their attacks on those in power. In any case, the fact that Walpole, Pelham, and Pitt the 'Great Commoner' all preferred to rule as members of the lower

Plate 24. *The Saloon, Houghton Hall.* The finest room in Robert Walpole's splendid Palladian mansion, which was built between 1722 and 1735; the furniture was designed by William Kent and the plaster work by Artari. The massive mahogany doors are 'so excellently hung that they open and close to the slightest touch' (J. H. Plumb, *Sir Robert Walpole: the King's Minister*, p. 84). (Cf. text pp. 288–9.)

Plate 25. *Tull's Seed Drill and Hoe.* Jethro Tull's two great innovations were first publicized in his *Horse-Hoeing Husbandry* (1st edition 1731; the 2nd, as here, 1733) – though he invented the drill as early as c. 1701. This replaced the ancient and wasteful method of broadcast sowing by planting in rows at a regular depth. The drill was horse-drawn and dropped the seeds from containers into grooves which it made in the soil, finally covering them with earth from other containers mounted on the machine. Once seeds were planted in lines, other machines could be brought to the land, working up or between the rows. Tull, therefore, introduced the horse-hoe to weed the growing crops – drawn by two horses and guided from the chair by a labourer who could slot down the six hoes to work at different depths. Neither invention was wholly original, and they were not capable by themselves of producing such a revolution as Tull himself supposed. Nevertheless, the 'Tullian system' exercised an increasing influence throughout the century. (Cf. text p. 304.)

Plate 26. *South Sea Bubble Playing Cards.* These are two specimens of the cards preserved in the library of Worcester College, Oxford – each holding up to ridicule the speculative follies of the time. Many Pennsylvania land sales were as little genuine as the whale-fishing schemes boosted in the City. (Cf. text pp. 297–8.)

Plate 24

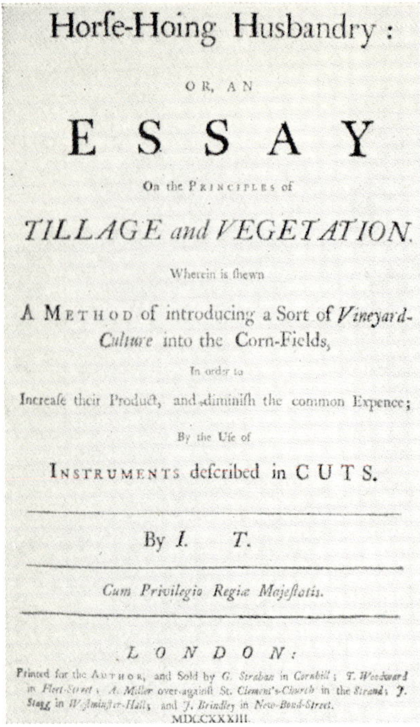

Horse-Hoing Husbandry:

OR, AN

ESSAY

On the PRINCIPLES of

TILLAGE and VEGETATION.

Wherein is shewn

A METHOD of introducing a Sort of *Vineyard-Culture* into the Corn-Fields,

In order to

Increase their Product, and diminish the common Expence;

By the Use of

INSTRUMENTS described in CUTS.

By *I.* *T.*

Cum Privilegio Regiæ Majestatis.

LONDON:

Printed for the AUTHOR, and Sold by *G. Strahan* in *Cornhill*; *T. Woodward* in *Fleet-Street*; *A. Millar* over-against St. *Clement's-Church* in the *Strand*; *J. Stagg* in *Westminster-Hall*; and *J. Brindley* in *New-Bond-Street*.
MDCCXXXIII.

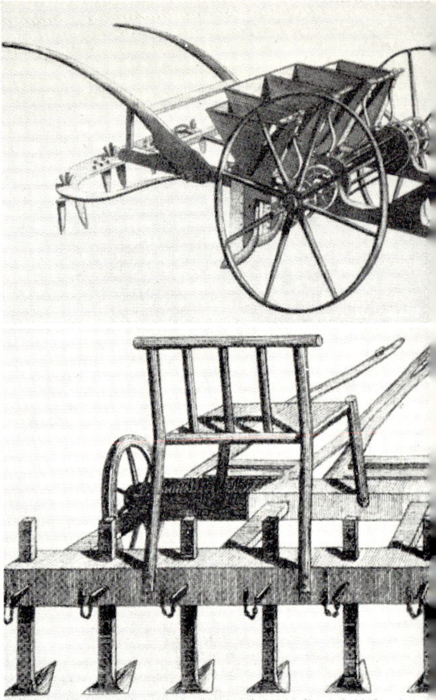

Plate 25

Plate 26

house is a reminder that here was the centre of the taxing authority of the nation and a representation of at least a limited national electorate.

Influence of the Electorate

The Septennial Act of 1716, under which the maximum interval between general elections was more than doubled (seven years instead of three), was a measure, passed during the aftermath of the Jacobite rebellion, which gave all the electors a reduced say in public affairs. They were in any case a small part of the nation, made up of individuals who were not always free to exercise their own judgment. The freeholders who chose the knights of the shire usually numbered several thousand, but those who were near the minimum qualification (the ownership of land worth £2 a year) were often tenants of other land and might have to defer to the opinions of those from whom they rented it. The number of voters in a borough varied enormously, but an average constituency would consist of a few scores of shopkeepers and other fairly substantial residents. The influence of the great landed families upon elections was very large. The individual voter could be beguiled by entertainment or hard cash, or the whole local community won over by the promise of new amenities – in one town a piped water supply, in another a new grammar school. Harsher methods could also be employed, such as the dispossession of recalcitrant tenants or the ruining of shops by the withdrawal of patronage.

But great families were often rivals for the control of the same body of voters, in which case they might come to an agreement to divide a two-member constituency between them or each to have control at alternate elections. Or the result might be a serious contest, in which the preferences of the voters would play some part. In 1754, for example, an ambitious politician named George Bubb Doddington spent £2,500 on the election at Bridgwater, which had returned him obediently for more than thirty years. But this time he was challenged by a political rival, the second Lord Egmont, who like Doddington had property in the neighbourhood. Doddington's diary tells the story:

April 11. I set out at four o'clock in the morning for Bridgwater, where, as I expected, I found things very disagreeably framed.

12. Lord Egmont came, with trumpets, noise, etc.

13. He and we walked the town: we found nothing unexpected, as far as we went.

14–16. Spent in the infamous and disagreeable compliance with the low habits of venal wretches.

17. Came on the election, which I lost by the injustice of the Returning Officer. The numbers were for Lord Egmont 119, for Mr Balch 114, for me 105. Of my good votes, 15 were rejected: 8 bad votes for Lord Egmont were received.

18. Left Bridgwater – for ever.

However, Doddington had another seat at his disposal at Weymouth, and at the beginning of the next reign he beat Lord Egmont (who was an Irish peer) by one year in achieving their common ambition – a seat in the British House of Lords, which would free him from any further direct dealings with 'venal wretches'.

More important than the occasional uncertainties attending the practice of bribery was the influence of public opinion when sufficiently aroused. Some constituencies were completely under control, some few were completely independent of influence, and there were always many marginal cases where the genuine feelings of the electors might turn the balance at an election. The fact that they felt strongly on some matters can be seen from the use made of the right of petitioning parliament. There were petitions presented against excise in 1733 and in favour of a Spanish war in 1739, when the City of London whipped up enthusiasm by employing sailors to display alleged specimens of loathsome food from the dietary they had experienced in Spanish dungeons. But the rise of the press provided a less cumbrous means of bringing public opinion to bear on parliament. Both Government and Opposition now had newspapers which were paid to ventilate their respective views. Bolingbroke's *Craftsman*, for instance, which he ran for about a decade after his return from exile, reached a circulation of more than 10,000 copies. Although parliamentary debates were still officially closed to reporters, such periodicals as the *Gentleman's*

Magazine often succeeded in reproducing them under a very thin disguise and were always eager to stir up the emotions of the reading public by satirizing politicians. The theatres also tried to join in, with the result that Walpole introduced the long-continued system of censorship by the Lord Chamberlain.

The Mob

The conduct of politics by the Classes was open intermittently to one more form of external pressure, that of the mob. It is significant that one of the first statutes under the new dynasty was the Riot Act, which made it a capital offence for twelve or more persons to 'remain and continue together' after one hour's warning to disperse had been publicly proclaimed by any magistrate. The immediate motive was the menace of Jacobite gatherings, but in the absence of any organized professional police force rioting was a possible resort for any political movement. In the case of the Excise Bill Walpole may, indeed, have yielded chiefly to the strength of the Opposition in the House, but the King's Speech at the close of the session referred explicitly to 'tumults and disorders that almost threatened the peace of the kingdom'. Another case in which mob violence had its way was the Porteous riot in Edinburgh in 1736. The captain of the city guard, which had killed four persons and injured others while keeping order at the execution of a highly popular smuggler, was seized from prison and lynched. When the local authorities shielded all those responsible, Walpole limited the pressure applied to the imposition of a £2,000 fine for the benefit of Porteous's widow, one of his reasons for giving way being the united opposition of the parliamentary representatives of Scotland.

'Management' of Scotland

Their tacit support for the rioters was particularly striking because in several respects the government normally had fuller control over the Scottish than over the English element in parliament. Though the entire peerage of Scotland could take part in the election of its 16 representatives for each parliament, they chose in strict accordance with a 'King's List' sent from London. The 30 MPs for Scottish shires were returned by a total electorate of about 2,700; the others by the town council of Edinburgh and by those of smaller burghs arranged in groups. While this made it necessary to have influence over several burghs in order to control one seat, there was often a landed family in a position to achieve this. In any case the holders of the seats, together with the gentry and most of the nobility who controlled or influenced elections (including the election of the King's List), were possessed of such limited means that it was easy for the arts of 'management' to be applied. Inside Scotland, there were civil posts ranging from judgeships to customs and excise appointments and (under the act of 1712) Crown nominations to about one-third of the livings in the established Presbyterian Church. Outside what was still a relatively poor country, diplomatic and colonial appointments were eagerly sought, and in the British Army of this period one colonelcy in five was granted to a Scotsman.

Local Government

On day-to-day local issues on both sides of the Border rioting was the chief weapon of the masses, as every justice of the peace was painfully aware. In turning our attention to this all-important official, we may notice at the outset that in social and economic matters he would have the automatic support of parliament, for most MPs were also JPs; also that the owner of a large property was usually included in the magistrates' bench, irrespective of his attitude in politics. In the absence of any civil service network of officials, they were virtually the only representatives of the central government in the countryside. Besides the conduct of trials and the sentencing of those whom they convicted of crime, JPs were responsible for whatever was done locally in matters of police (through the amateur parish constable) and pauperism, highways and health. In times of emergency, such as the Jacobite risings, they corresponded with the government about measures of repression and the raising of troops.

In general, the only check imposed upon the justices, acting singly or at petty sessions or the quarter sessions for the county, was the authority of the high-court judge, before whom persons of sufficient means could usually present an appeal case or state a grievance at assizes. Thus the country gentry, heads of the land-owning 'county families', had a legal authority which matched their undisputed social pre-eminence. The novels of Henry Fielding describe a rural world in which the word of a JP settles the fate of all lesser mortals: in doubtful cases an upper-class Jacobite might receive the benefit of the doubt, a lower-class poacher never.

About two hundred corporate towns were governed in accordance with the legal interpretation, usually on very narrow and restrictive lines, of their much-prized and often venerable charters. London was exceptional in that the freemen of the city, who elected the Common Council and aldermen, were numerous and active: indeed, they took the lead in many movements of protest directed against the government at nearby Westminster. But in most corporations power now rested with the mayor and the aldermen, co-opted or otherwise appointed from a little group of wealthy families. They drafted the by-laws, administered borough affairs of all kinds, from night-watchmen to street-cleansing (if any) and the conduct of markets, and automatically provided magistrates for the area. Thus the well-to-do middle class, made up of merchants, leading figures in the professions, and the principal retail tradesmen, had an entrenched position in the older towns. The unincorporated towns, which included urban centres of rapid recent growth such as Birmingham and Manchester, were placed under the legal authority of the county JPs. In practice, however, they enjoyed an atmosphere of greater freedom in trade, social life, and even religion (membership of corporations was in principle restricted to Anglican communicants), which often attracted the most enterprising type of business entrepreneur to reside and take the lead there.

The Wealthy Middle Classes

Since finance and commerce ranked higher than industry in public esteem, the most influential elements in the middle class were the London financiers and the thriving merchants of London and other major ports. The Lord Mayor of London was commonly rewarded with a baronetcy, and even the greatest of the Whig nobles, such as the dukes of Beaufort and Bedford, regarded the leading men in the Bank of England and the chartered companies as counting for something in politics and were not indisposed to marry their daughters to them. Eleven such marriages are in fact listed by Defoe in his *Complete English Gentleman*, a work left unpublished at the author's death in 1731. The wealthy clothier or ironmaster or mine-owner was likewise an important figure in the society of his own county, especially if the wealth was not of recent acquisition. But the new development which probably did most to weld the Classes together was the more rapid growth of the professions, fostered by a period of peace and prosperity.

The Professions

The clergy occupied a special position, since the bishops with their seats in the House of Lords, the deans and prebendaries of the richer cathedrals, and some other Church dignitaries owed their appointments to political influence and ranked with other important servants of the Crown. Stipends, however, were fantastically unequal, so that the status of the ordinary parochial clergy ranged from that of the richest livings, where the incumbent was on a level with the squire, to that of a multitude of ill-paid vicarages and curacies, which the average tradesman would not envy. More than half the benefices in England had revenues of less than £1 a week. Relations between bishop and parson were often embittered by a political gulf: the former were mostly loyal to the Whig ministry which appointed them, the latter were chosen by their local squire and were mainly High Churchmen, bitterly resentful of Whig toleration of dissenters and ready to welcome the Pretender the moment he abandoned his faith. Quarrels in the ecclesiastical parliament known as Convocation were so fierce in 1717, and again in 1741, that its meetings were suspended for more than a century. Yet with the rise in the value of his tithe the economic position of the parson was slowly improving, so that by mid-century a good many villages had seen the parsonage rebuilt on an ampler scale to accommodate a younger son of the squire, who took Holy Orders as a sedater but still respectable alternative to a commission in the armed forces.

University dons and the headmasters and ushers of the few public and many grammar schools were also clergymen. But the schools under Church control had a serious rival in the dissenting academies, which appealed to many other parents besides dissenters because their curriculum included modern languages and other useful subjects, which played no part in the traditional form of secondary education. Schoolmasters, however, whatever their religious complexion, were not yet a prominent element in the professional middle class. Its advance is to be traced chiefly in the growth of two professions, each of which had one element in direct contact with the heads of society. A flourishing practice at the bar in London (or Edinburgh) was a recognized avenue by which young men of great ability could make their way into the world of national politics. The solicitors or attorneys of provincial towns, however, remained part of the local business community whose growth they served. The same distinction may be made between the fashionable physician, who had probably attended a university, and the apothecary who prescribed for the ailments of the humbler classes. In social standing the surgeon, who until 1745 belonged to an undifferentiated Company of Barber Surgeons, came nearer to the apothecary.

Nevertheless the growth of medical science, which was a feature of this period, was laying the foundations for the eventual attainment of an unassailable professional status. The brothers William and John Hunter, who brought their advanced knowledge of anatomy from Scotland to London just before the middle of the century; James Lind, whose *Treatise of Scurvy* made possible improvements in the health of the Navy to match those already inaugurated by John Pringle in the Army; and yet a fifth Scotsman, William Smellie, who revolutionized the practice of midwifery – men like these gave value to the specialized hospitals which were now being established by charitable individuals. In 1751 London possessed a smallpox hospital, a lying-in hospital, and an institution (St Luke's) for the kindlier treatment of the insane. By the same date the Edinburgh medical school, originally an offshoot of Dutch

Leyden, was turning out properly trained doctors by the score to establish their profession all over the kingdom and empire.

The professions included that of the writer, though the struggling existence of Dr Johnson in his youth, as recorded by Boswell, reminds us that the ill-paid and despised journalist was a much more representative figure than the occasional society notable of the type of the poet, Alexander Pope. Native painters and sculptors, however, enjoyed a greater vogue than at any earlier time in modern history. At the close of George II's reign the movement was already under way which led to the foundation of the fashionable Royal Academy, with Sir Joshua Reynolds as its first president. But the most characteristic artist was surely William Hogarth. He had served a humble apprenticeship to engraving and knew at first hand the hideous London underworld which he placed on imperishable record in 'A Rake's Progress', 'Industry and Idleness', 'Four Stages of Cruelty', and other famous series. But his most whimsical satire was reserved for a brief trip to France, in 1747:

'Twas at the gate of Calais, Hogarth tells,
Where sad despair and famine always dwells.

Design of Buildings and Furniture

The rising prosperity which ministered to national complacency gave new scope for architecture and many subordinate crafts. Such mansions as Stowe Palace and Walpole's Houghton Hall were marvels of spacious design and lavish decoration, as an early visitor to Houghton reported in the winter of 1731:

> The finishing of the inside is, I think, a pattern for all great houses that may hereafter be built: the vast quantity of mahogany, all the doors, window-shutters, best staircase, etc., being entirely of that wood; the finest chimneys of statuary and other fine marbles; the ceilings in the modern taste by Italians, painted by Mr Kent, and finely gilt; the furniture of the richest tapestry, etc.; the pictures hung on Genoa velvet and damask; this one article is the price of a good house, for in one drawing-room there are to the value of three thousand pounds; in short,

> the whole expense of this place must be a prodigious sum, and, I think, all done in a fine taste.

The guest was also shown the lay-out proposed by the King's Gardener for the plantations which were to surround the 40 acres of gardens set in the 700 acres of the park:

> They are to be plumps[1] and avenues to go quite round the park pale, and to make straight and oblique lines of a mile or two in length, as the situation of the country admits of. This design will be about 12 miles in circumference.

But the early Georgian streets and squares of London, Bath, and other towns gave opportunities to architects of merely local reputation. Moreover, their influence was carried further by books of designs, which enabled the harmonious proportions of Georgian country houses to be transmitted by the builders to farm-houses and other homes of very modest pretensions. The same is true of furniture. The grandest houses sometimes had pieces specially designed for them by their architect; otherwise their furniture came from the best London craftsmen, some of whom were artists rather than mere technical experts. But a book such as Chippendale's *Gentleman and Cabinet-Maker's Director*, first published in 1754, enabled humbler cabinet makers to produce graceful work at more moderate prices. Thus a considerable section of the middle class lived in elegant as well as comfortable surroundings.

Farmers and Tradespeople

As we descend in the social scale, it becomes relevant to notice an analysis made by Gregory King in 1688, according to which farmers (including 'freeholders of the lesser sort') were then three times as numerous as all the superior classes put together. Half a century later the small freeholders had become noticeably fewer, but 'John Bull', the prosperous rustic type first heard of in Anne's reign[2], was still clearly pictured as the representative Englishman. With him we may group the tradesmen of the towns, from owners of workshops and minor manufacturing enterprises to shopkeepers

[1] Clusters (*O.E.D.*)
[2] See p. 210.

employing no more than an assistant or two, who sold their wares retail to the farmers who came to town on market days. This class as a whole throve in quiet times. Many of its members belonged to the Protestant sects which the accession of the Hanoverian line confirmed in their right to freedom of worship; others became active later on among the Methodist lay preachers. In worldly matters, too, they were not placed too low to be able to benefit widely from a system of government which opposed no insuperable barriers to the rise of the industrious and thrifty from very humble levels. James Cook, the Cleveland labourer's son and future explorer, who charted the St Lawrence for the expedition which captured Quebec, and George Whitefield, who at 15 was a pot-boy in the inn his widowed mother kept at Gloucester and at 30 an evangelist of nation-wide influence, are two examples of the career open to talent.

The position of a tenant-farmer or small shop-keeper was not, however, comparable with that of the masses; though closely dependent upon the goodwill of his landlord or his customers, he was still likely to be a person with some modest resources to cushion him against adversity. What about the multitude of those whose labour was their only stock-in-trade? In their case, the most important criterion was skill.

Skilled and Unskilled Workers

In the towns, the man who had served a full legal apprenticeship of seven years, or who in some quicker way had obtained a thorough knowledge of a handicraft, was favourably situated. Even if there was insufficient employment in his trade in one neighbourhood, he had a reasonable prospect of finding a new master in another, so long as he did not appear likely to become a burden on the poor rates. In the country likewise, a man who had above-average skill in some kind of farm work could earn tolerable wages. Whole-time farm labourers were becoming more in demand, and in any case there were scraps of land and miscellaneous uses of the common which a useful man could count on for eking out part-time employment.

The rise of friendly societies among those workers who could afford to make a small weekly payment into a fund for security in sickness and old age was an important feature of this period. So was the first emergence of trade unions, which often grew out of friendly societies. Those in the West of England woollen industry were described by the employers to parliament in 1718 as

> riotous and tumultuous clubs and societies of workmen, who hinder labourers in the woollen manufactures from working therein except they have such exorbitant prices as the clubs prescribe.

Altogether, at least a dozen trades are known to have had some such organization at some time during the first half of the century. Most of them were on a local basis, so far as our information goes, but workers with special skills, such as woolcombers and millwrights, certainly tried to maintain the same standards for their employment in different parts of the country. In the case of tailoring, a typical metropolitan handicraft, the masters claimed in 1721 that in London and Westminster the 'combination to raise their wages and leave off working an hour sooner than they used to do' had 7,000 members: the fact that tailors in both Cambridge and Sheffield were in action at the same juncture is presumably more than a coincidence.

In the woollen industry, tailoring, and other trades, the unions were put down by law. They survived, however, partly as an underground movement, to reappear with increased force in the age of machine industry. They came into existence because of the increasing gulf between master and man. But their existence is also evidence of the ability of skilled workers to some extent to assert their claims against their masters.

But the unskilled workers and their families were almost certainly the largest of all social groupings. At best, they would have to accept a lower wage than skill could command, and to perform their humble task, when required, for longer than the normal twelve-hour day – because they had no bargaining power. At worst, there must have been some cottagers in nearly every village, whose homes (one room up and one down, with the floor and, in some parts of the country, even the walls made of beaten earth) were the source of chronic ill-health, who had little use of the commons, and whose entire family went hungry all the year round, except during the short period of harvest work and harvest bounty. In the towns, the worst situated must often have suffered still greater privations, since it was easier for the larger community to ignore their plight or to suppose comfortably that the unemployed (or the chronically under-employed) could always find work if they tried. The death-rate in London is believed to have exceeded the birth-rate, especially in the two decades when the poor could drown their sorrows in cheap gin, so that its rising population of two-thirds of a million or more was recruited by a steady flow of immigrants from the countryside, destined to die early in their turn. Though Bristol, with perhaps 30,000 inhabitants, and the other towns were all much smaller than the capital, life in the crowded alleys of their poorest quarters was probably no more salubrious.

Such conditions were of course only endured because effective resistance was impracticable. Mention has already been made of one or two instances of mob violence based on political prejudice, which it was particularly easy to arouse in London. On one occasion the theatre proprietors were even prevented by violence from employing French actors. But it was very different when the motive for rioting was economic and no upper-class agitator was likely to be at work behind the scenes. Although it was still possible to appeal to the JPs at quarter sessions to fix wage-rates under the Elizabethan statute, such appeals were only rarely successful. In general, the accepted function of the magistrate in town and country was to preserve the king's peace, which meant that in periods of dearth, when the poor rioted for cheap bread, they were suppressed if necessary by the reading of the Riot Act proclamation, the calling in of troops, and subsequent hangings.

Administration of the Poor Law

However, England and Wales – though not Scotland – was one of the very few European countries which had a nation-wide system of poor relief in operation at this time. In years of bad harvests and high prices, such as 1740 and 1756, even the regular wage-earner might have to fall back on the rates for a small subsidy to tide him over his troubles. It was not usual for an unskilled labourer to accumulate any savings; he would spend at once, mainly no doubt in the ale-house, anything he received beyond what covered his customary minimum requirements – it was better spent than stolen, and there were no savings banks to put it in. Even in good years the poor law was the inevitable refuge of the orphaned, crippled, sick, and aged poor; of everybody who could not find work; and of those who did not intend to look if they could live without it. The analysis in 1688, referred to above, estimated that more than one million persons, or nearly one-fifth of the population, were in occasional receipt of alms, which came mainly from the parish.

The distribution of relief was entrusted to the amateur, reluctant overseers of the poor in each of 15,000 parishes, acting under the often cursory supervision of the justices of the peace. The task was bound to be inefficiently discharged, but unfortunately the law directly encouraged the natural tendency to watch only the interests of the single parish for which the overseers were responsible. An Elizabethan statute was often invoked to prevent the building of new cottages, which might house additional poor families (or house the existing families better), unless the unthinkable amount of four acres of ground was attached to each. An even stronger defence against newcomers was provided by the settlement laws of 1662 and 1697, under which they could be turned out (normally, within 40 days of their arrival) on the supposition that they might eventually become a burden on the rates, unless they arrived with a certificate from their original parish undertaking in that case to receive them back or pay for their support. In the eyes of many generations of poor people these must have been among the most important laws in the statute book, but no overall picture is left to show their effectiveness. "Everything goes to show that the law did not interfere appreciably with the mobility of the single man who was looking for work," writes one modern authority.[1] It certainly did not impose any serious check on the movements of criminal and semi-criminal elements: Dick Turpin's 'place of settlement' was presumably his native village near

[1] Sir John Clapham: *Concise Economic History of Britain to 1750*, p. 304.

Saffron Walden – which was nowhere near his haunts on the Great North Road! But it is impossible to say how many more families would have moved to London or to some other nearby town or even to the scattered rural industries, and found permanent employment there, if their natural dread of the unknown had not been fortified by these known legal obstacles.

The system of relief within parishes was extremely harsh in its treatment of orphaned and otherwise uncared-for infants. Boys who survived were apprenticed to the humblest trades, the girls usually to domestic service, and no great trouble was taken to see that they were taught anything in return for seven years labour or that they received sufficient board and clothing. But many of them did not live to be apprentices: some figures available for London show that three-quarters of the children in the charge of metropolitan parishes were dead before the age of five. A second category which fared ill, but whose members were not always so innocent of offence as the infant poor, was the 'vagrant', a term which a JP could apply at his discretion to almost any non-resident brought before him without visible honest means of support. He or she was to be whipped 'till bloody', then placed in a House of Correction or driven immediately out of the parish. The rest of the poor were usually relieved by the provision of a weekly pittance in their own homes or in a local almshouse. But an Act of 1723 enabled parishes to require paupers of every kind, able-bodied and sick, young and old, even sane and insane, to reside and, if capable, labour in a workhouse. In spite of this economy measure, the cost of poor relief was approximately doubled in the first half of the eighteenth century, which encouraged many ratepayers in the belief that the overseers pandered to the laziness and luxurious tea-drinking habits of their charges.

An Age of Barbarism

As the last sentence suggests, this was in many respects a callous age. Cruel sports, such as bull-baiting and cock-fighting, continued to be the delight of every section of society. Conditions at the great public schools were in many respects harder than in a modern prison, and soldiers had sometimes to be called in to suppress schoolboy rebellions. At the other end of the scale, this was the period when the first climbing-boys – doubtless pauper apprentices to the art of chimney-sweeping – were forced to crawl up inside the twisting chimney-stacks of great houses. It contains the last cases in which a wife was burnt to death for the murder of her husband and a man who refused to plead guilty or not guilty, so as to save his possessions for his heirs, was crushed by the *peine forte et dure*. Whippings at the tail of a cart drawn through the streets were too frequent to arouse much interest, but public executions were still a widely attended and hilarious spectacle, as they had been in the London of Queen Anne. The crowd seems often to have been even more merciless than the law. A newspaper records, for instance, an episode at Tring as late as 1751, where an old couple, accused of witchcraft by a local publican, were subjected by the mob to the ancient trial by water, after which "the old woman . . . almost choked with mud, expired in a few moments, being kicked and beat with sticks even after she was dead".

An Age of Philanthropy

But the existence of such horrors, which the press brings more vividly before our eyes than the similar misdeeds of earlier centuries, must not blind us to the fact that this age of peace and growing national unity was also notable for philanthropic developments. The scientific advances in medicine, already mentioned, would scarcely have been possible without the hospitals, which in almost every case owed their origin to the generosity of individuals such as Thomas Guy, the London bookseller who built the hospital which bears his name and three wards of St Thomas's as well. Under the first two Georges the number of metropolitan hospitals of all kinds increased from 2 to 11; those in the provinces, Scotland, and Ireland, from 1 to 22. The work which Oglethorpe initiated on behalf of friendless debtors, who might even starve in prison if they could not pay the gaoler for their keep, was matched by that of Coram, who established the Foundling Hospital in 1739 for the heartlessly abandoned infants of the capital.

The movement which attracted the widest patronage, however,

was that which the Society for the Promotion of Christian Knowledge had launched in 1699 for the provision of charity schools. This reached its zenith at the end of George I's reign, when there were about 1,400 such schools, with an average of 20–30 pupils. In London and the larger towns they received part of their support through annual charity sermons in the churches, attended by children in their bluecoat or greycoat uniform, and they included some prominent residential institutions. Since the subscribers were mainly the local tradespeople, the curriculum often combined the inculcation of sound Church principles through Bible-reading and the Catechism with manual activities such as spinning and knitting, designed to inure the children to a life of toil; writing and arithmetic were sometimes discouraged as likely to lead to too much independence. The smaller the population of a neighbourhood, the more likely it was, however, to leave its primary education to private ventures such as dame's schools or classes taught by the more energetic clergy or their wives. But the number of newspapers which came into existence, both in London and the provinces, and the extent to which their contents became known among the masses, suggests that the proportion who could at least read was increasing fairly fast.

Thus the state of primary education, though there are no statistics, seems to represent some advance in civilization. So does the rapid spread from 1739 onwards of the Methodist movement, which (as we shall see in our final chapter) was primarily concerned to save souls, but in so doing imprinted new standards of self-respect upon some of the most degraded elements of the population. In 1760 the British people as a whole were almost certainly less barbarous than their grandparents had been. Moreover, poor as the masses undoubtedly were, they were rather better off than their counterparts in any other of the major European countries, where Britain's exceptional opportunities of economic growth were lacking.

17

ECONOMIC GROWTH

THE absorbing interest in trade, which had so much to do with imperial developments at this time, was likewise a main factor in the internal history of the kingdom. It is significant that the first ministry of George I's reign, in which Lord Stanhope conducted a brilliant foreign policy, was overthrown by a trading disaster. This was the South Sea Bubble, the bursting of which in September 1720 opened the way for the long ministry of Walpole.

The South Sea Bubble

The South Sea Company had been incorporated in 1711 to conduct whatever trade might be conceded to British subjects in Spanish South America. Under the treaty of Utrecht this consisted of the Asiento for supplying 4,800 slaves a year and the admission of an annual trading ship of not more than 500 tons; no large-scale commerce resulted. But the Company, which had taken over a block of the National Debt at its foundation, offered in 1720 to take over all the rest that could be made available, to a nominal value of £31,000,000. The terms were that the Company should pay £7,000,000 for the privilege and reduce the interest required from the government to 4 per cent, recouping themselves by their ability to exchange Debt holdings for South Sea stock. Their readiness to increase their capital by so large an amount suggested that the prospects of the Company must be exceptionally brilliant, so there was a prodigious boom in South Sea shares. In a few months they rose from 150 to 1,060, carrying other stocks up with them. Then confidence wavered, the 'bubble' was pricked, and thousands of speculators were ruined,

Since various members of the government and the royal entourage had accepted shares at nominal prices as an inducement to favour the scheme, which the ministry had conspicuously failed to check, the political result was to bring back Walpole and his brother-in-law, Lord Townshend, who had quarrelled with Stanhope and left his government four years before. Lord Stanhope died of apoplexy; the South Sea Company subsided into a minor financial organization, continuing as such even after the termination of the Asiento in 1750; and the Bubble Act (originally directed by the Company against rival concerns) was retained for more than a century to hinder the formation of joint stock companies by requiring them to go to the expense of obtaining a charter.

Availability of Capital

Nevertheless, this was a period in which British financial resources in general were more effectively developed. The Bank of England provided an increasingly helpful source of credit for business, both through its notes, which circulated as an addition to the gold and silver coin of the realm, and through its loans to companies and the merchants of the metropolis. London also contained by 1750 a score or so of private banks, which issued their own bank notes and discounted bills of exchange. In the provinces, however, banking services were still provided mainly by prosperous merchants with wide connections, who not only arranged to transfer large payments by bills drawn on London and other centres, but also found much of the capital requirements for industry.

The typical business was pre-eminently a family concern. The spirit of the age favoured individual enterprise, even in foreign trade: only the East India and Hudson's Bay Companies, which traded over exceptional distances, continued the old corporate organization successfully. But there was a noticeable pooling of resources in the modern way for purposes which furthered every enterprise – the maritime insurance business based on Lloyd's coffee house; the fire and life insurance companies; and the activities of jobbers and brokers in Change Alley, which prepared the way for the London stock exchange.

Overseas Trade

Popular beliefs about the importance of a demonstrably favourable balance of trade caused political pamphleteers and others to watch the relationship between import and export values. Between 1714 and 1760 Custom House figures showed a rise in the former from £5,792,000 to £8,948,000 and in the latter from £7,696,000 to £14,694,000: thus recorded imports increased by only one-half, while recorded exports very nearly doubled. The real import totals were considerably larger. Tea, spirits, wine, tobacco, lace, silk, and printed calicoes were smuggled in all round the coast, directly from France or Holland and also through many vantage points in the Channel Islands, Ireland, and the Isle of Man. By 1759 the standard rate of duty was 25 per cent plus numerous special charges: in the case of tea, there is fairly good evidence that the quantity smuggled was twice as big as that which passed the customs. Some commodities were smuggled in the opposite direction, especially wool and woollen yarn, of which the export was forbidden: it paid English graziers to send supplies as far as the Orkneys in order that they might be surreptitiously shipped back to France or the Low Countries. After taking all this into account, we may still conclude that the net trade balance was still very much in Britain's favour, though less so than the official figures suggest.

Another important trade factor was the much increased activity of British shipping, on which the Navigation Acts policy had had a big cumulative effect. Up to one-third of the total merchant fleet was built in the American colonies, where timber was plentiful, yet by 1750 English tonnage reckoned separately was 40 per cent greater than in 1714. Over the whole period since the Revolution the proportion of English to foreign tonnage outward bound from English ports had risen from 2:1 to 10:1. This development had its disadvantages: freight costs were often higher than on the Dutch ships, which were more skilfully adapted to the needs of the various carrying trades; and in wartime many cargoes had to be transferred to foreign bottoms to avoid possible capture. But a mercantile marine which already exceeded 600,000 tons was an important asset to the invisible balance of trade – and one which would be increasingly valuable when the visible balance began to turn against Britain.

A striking feature of the foreign trade of this period was that it passed through a multitude of ports. London, indeed, enjoyed an overwhelming superiority. Its 25 docks offered unrivalled facilities for handling goods; it had traditional export connections and was the prime market for the disposal of imports; and most of the bigger vessels were built in Thames-side yards. But by the end of the 1750s Bristol, which had long been the second-largest port in Britain, was being overtaken by Liverpool, its rival both in the slave trade and the trade with Ireland. Moreover, the various other ports round the south and east coasts of England which have retained their vigour into the twentieth century, from Newcastle to Plymouth, were at that time supplemented by a score of smaller ones, from Whitby to Penzance, each of which then sent its ships abroad from harbours which now shelter only trawlers and pleasure-craft. The Welsh coal and iron trade was also calling into existence new developments at both Swansea and Neath, while in the north-west the same trades for a time made Whitehaven one of the most flourishing of English ports.

The Scots, too, were increasingly active at sea. In the 1750s the first acts were passed for deepening the Clyde below Glasgow and for extending Edinburgh's trade outlet at Leith. But as early as 1735 the estuary of the Clyde, with 67 sea-going vessels, had established the lead over the east coast ports which it has since retained. Linen and coal were exported from both coasts, but Glasgow obtained a decisive advantage from the importation of tobacco from the colonies, which was sold throughout the kingdom and also re-exported to France and other countries. By mid-century the city had a class of wealthy 'tobacco lords' and two banks which could finance exports, while a humbler body of "shopkeepers and mechanics or successful pedlars occupied large warerooms full of manufactures of all sorts, to furnish a cargo to Virginia".

Just at this time one of the many Scottish immigrants to London, the writer John Campbell, summed up the importance of the overseas trade in the following terms:

The interest and commerce of the British Empire are so inseparably united that they may very well be considered as one and the same. For commerce is that tie, by which the several and even the most distant parts of this empire are connected and kept together, so as to be rendered parts of the same whole, and to receive not only countenance and protection but warmth and nourishment from the vital parts of our government, of which, if I may be indulged so figurative an expression, our monarchy is the head and our liberty the soul.

Internal Trade and Communications

It was not only foreign trade which depended for its prosperity upon access to the sea. Goods were conveyed to the nearest port, however small its quay and however precarious the protection from storm and wind, for conveyance to other ports in Britain giving access to their ultimate destinations inland. Even such mobile articles as Scottish cattle were often brought round by sea to Norfolk to be fattened for the London market. The coasting trade as a whole was a bigger thing than all the overseas trade of the island; indeed, its convenience was one excuse for the deficiency in other forms of communication, as compared for instance with early-eighteenth-century France.

A bird flying over Britain at this time would have seen a great deal of movement on horseback: farmers to market, squires and their ladies paying calls, postboys conveying letters from town to town, the occasional highwayman lurking on the edge of the woods or the common, and even travellers on long journeys to and from the metropolis or Bath or a regional capital, such as York or Exeter. No rider would be seriously impeded by the state of the roads, except in periods of flood or storm, and the same would be true of the multitudes of poorer folk who trudged long distances on foot. A bird would also have been familiar with the sight of strings of pack-horses, each with its two panniers, and of herds and flocks, including even flocks of geese, walking or waddling along to nearby market or distant fair: they were driven by preference along bridle-paths and grassy tracks, where narrow stone bridges may still mark what was once a much-trodden pack-horse road.

But a bird's-eye view would have disclosed remarkably little wheeled traffic, judged by any modern standard. Farm carts seldom carried their loads farther than the local market-place, and in the fields they were still often replaced or supplemented by the use of sledges. Over long distances carriers' wagons and stage wagons – hauled all the way by a single team – the smaller four-horse stage-coaches, and even the six-horsed coach of the great nobleman, were rarely tempted to exceed a walking-pace, since until after mid-century the deficiencies of the road surface were not mitigated by any effective springs. By that time, indeed, a number of stretches of the most important thoroughfares had been made into turnpikes: that is to say, the responsibility for their proper upkeep had been transferred from the parishes through which they ran to a body of local trustees, empowered to levy fixed charges for their use at turnpike gates; about four hundred road Acts of different kinds were passed between 1700 and 1750. But it still took up to a fortnight to reach London from Edinburgh or Glasgow (no Sunday travel), six days from Newcastle, four and a half from Manchester, and two from Birmingham. These are times for coaches: the traveller by post-chaise could cover the same distance a little faster at much greater cost.

The widespread distribution of heavy goods by road was obviously impracticable. Coal, needed increasingly both for domestic and industrial purposes; stone, brick, and timber for the expansion of the towns; corn, potatoes, and dairy produce to feed the townspeople; the inward flow of raw materials and the outward flow of finished goods, on which any big concentration of industry must be based – all these required a more efficient system of transportation. Later generations found a better answer in the canals, the macadamized high-roads, and then the railways: but the age with which we are now concerned made a start through the 'inland navigations'.

Mention has already been made of the pioneer work done by Yarranton in the reign of Charles II towards making rivers navigable. But the first such 'navigation' of importance was that of the Aire and Calder, made at the turn of the century to serve the woollen towns of the West Riding. A spate of similar undertakings followed, especially in the north of England, where the Trent and

Derwent were improved to help the development of Nottingham and Derby; the Mersey and Irwell, to strengthen communications between Liverpool and Manchester; the Weaver, to open up the salt-pans round Northwich; and finally the Douglas and the Sankey, for moving the coal from Wigan and St Helens. The last of these, the Sankey 'navigation' of 1755, involved so much modification of the river-bed that it may with equal justice be acclaimed as the first of the new canals.

In the meantime, the internal trade of the island seems to have expanded as fast as its commerce with the outside world. There was a marked increase in the number of shops even in the smaller provincial towns, which showed that the gentry and rising middle class almost everywhere now provided sufficient custom for well-stocked establishments of a kind that had previously been confined to London and a few other fashionable centres. The available statistical evidence indicates that in the vicinity of London and other large towns, and also in progressive rural areas like east Lancashire, the earnings of skilled workers rose more than the cost of living, so in these humbler circles too there was at least a little more spending-power than before. The food and clothing of their families might be partly home-produced, but we know that the consumption of sugar increased six-fold and that the drinking of tea was becoming a universal habit; we may also reasonably infer growing sales of household gear and decorative items for the home and person from the stalls at market or fair, where the labourer usually spent some of his pay.

Agriculture

In early Hanoverian Britain the key producer was still the farmer. Agriculture fulfilled a threefold function: by feeding the population; by providing a large part of its industrial raw materials, such as wool, hides, and tallow; and in most years by yielding a surplus of corn to swell Britain's exports. The land, as organized by hard-headed country squires with an increasing proportion of large farmers as their chief subordinates, is believed to have given employment to fully half of the working population. Its management still suffered, however, from the handicap of open-field cultivation, which in the early eighteenth century affected about 50 per cent of the English arable acreage. Enclosure through application to parliament, very rare before 1720, averaged a little more than three acts a year in the next two decades and ten a year in 1741–60. The area involved was small, probably less than 400,000 acres (as compared with 5,000,000 acres in the next half-century), but the impact on the corn-growing counties of the east and east midlands was already considerable. Only such enclosed land provided a continuous stretch of arable large enough to repay proper drainage, if it was wet, or elbow-room for experimenting with new crops or methods of cultivation.[1]

The novelties introduced in this period had their main effects later on. In 1731 Jethro Tull's *Horse-Hoeing Husbandry* advocated the sowing of best quality seed in the most economical way by drills and the improvement of the crop by frequent use of the hoe, which could pass easily between the regular rows produced by drilling. Tull believed that his method would make manuring superfluous: this was more true of turnips than of the wheat in which he was chiefly interested, and in any case his example caught on very slowly. Walpole's former colleague, Lord Townshend, was able to command a larger following for the practices of his Norfolk estate, which drew chiefly on Dutch methods; these had already been introduced to a good many English counties by small-scale pioneers. 'Turnip' Townshend created a vogue for growing roots, which transformed the problem of winter feed for cattle. Reviving the use of marl to enrich the sandy soil, he made Norfolk famous for its four-course rotation – two grain crops alternating with turnips and clover. Its adoption automatically increased productivity by roughly one-third through the abolition of the fallow year, as it gradually made headway against rural conservatism. But Townshend died in 1738, only eight years after he retired from politics to interest himself in agriculture at Raynham.

Except in seasons of dearth, the Corn Bounty Act encouraged exportation, which reached its maximum between 1732 and 1766. At the latter date corn prices on the home market were no higher than at George I's accession, though a more refined popular taste demanded an increased proportion of wheat flour to produce a

[1] See Appendix I, 14.

whiter loaf. Thus Britain provided her own cereals, even after some slight rise in the standard of living, together with a considerable margin for export. The position as regards animal husbandry was less satisfactory, in spite of the larger supplies of fodder available and the steady intake of beef cattle from Scotland. Cattle plague and sheep rot were the most obvious and frequent handicaps. In so far as the average weight of carcasses sold at Smithfield market (said to have been a quarter of the sales for the whole country) showed an increase, this may have been due less to better practices in stock-feeding than to the availability for slaughter of large oxen, which were being replaced as draught-animals by horses.

As for the industrial consumption of agricultural products, Britain continued to provide for her own needs. When disease reduced the flocks, so that mutton fat became scarce, the homes of the poorer classes went short of soap and also of tallow candles – which perhaps made the dirt less noticeable. So also, when corn was diverted to the distilleries to make cheap gin, starch was in short supply, becoming plentiful again after the Gin Act of 1751. In the same way, the tanneries, which were largely concentrated in London because of Smithfield market, suffered from the incidence of cattle plague, when footwear, saddlery, and the workman's unhygienic leather jerkin became expensive and scarce. Above all, a whole series of people, from shepherd to clothier, depended for their living upon a variable crop of native wool, either the short fleeces shorn in open-field villages and moorland settlements all up and down the island, or the scarcer, heavier, long-wool fleeces of the Cotswolds, Romney Marsh, and a few other favoured districts.

The Textile Industries

For the woollen industry was still king: though prices were low, output was increasing by about 8 per cent per decade. Between 1720 and 1750 the value of exports rose from £3,000,000 to £4,000,000, a third of them being sent to North America. At home and overseas, the West of England supplied broadcloth for the upper classes and Yorkshire the cheaper stuff for the masses, while many other districts had their own speciality, such as the Norfolk worsteds. In 1733 John Kay, a Lancashire man in charge of a woollen manufactory at Colchester, invented the 'fly shuttle', which for the first time enabled a single weaver to pass the shuttle to and fro on a width of cloth which exceeded the span of his own arms. Although this made it possible for the weaver to earn more – at any rate in the first instance – its adoption was held up for a generation or longer (except to some extent in the West Riding) by the conservatism natural to workers in an industry which had flourished by traditional methods for so long. Instead of technical progress, what they welcomed was a measure like the Calico Act of 1721, which followed up an earlier ban on the importation of printed cottons by forbidding the use of this popular type of cotton material even when it had been made in England, on account of "the great detriment of the woollen and silk manufactures of this kingdom".

Silk was not regarded as a dangerous rival to wool, partly because of its limited usefulness and durability and still more because the manufacture was fully developed in France and Italy, which were also the sources of the raw material. Therefore the remarkable achievement of Thomas Lombe, who in 1719 erected at Derby a factory for throwing high-quality organzine silk, for which the design had been filched by his brother John in north Italy, aroused no hostility. Lombe's waterdriven mill, with its 22,586 inter-connected wheels and 300 workers, made a fortune for its owner and soon had half a dozen imitators, at Macclesfield and elsewhere. But the rate of expansion was not sufficient to affect the weaving and finishing processes.

The case was very different with the comparatively new manufacture of cotton, of which the products were cheap, washable, and adapted to many uses. Imports of the raw material, through Liverpool to east Lancashire and adjoining districts, rose from an annual average of 1,000,000 lb in the reign of Anne to twice as much in the 1740s; by then the fly shuttle was beginning to be adopted and experiments were in progress with machinery for spinning. On the home market the trade was restricted by the Calico Act to fustians, made of cotton and flax; but exports were unrestricted and in 1740–60 increased nearly eightfold. Thus the way was already prepared for the new staple which was destined to end the age-long supremacy of the woollen trade.

Coal and Iron

Apart from wool, the raw materials for industry which were most readily available in Hanoverian Britain were the minerals – coal, iron, copper, lead, tin, and the alloy, brass; Newcastle coal and Cornish copper were important exports. Coal-mining derived the principal benefit from the Newcomen engine,[1] because its extravagance in the use of coal was no drawback. By 1718 the 'fire engine' had reached Tyneside, where eight years later a clerical visitor from the south records its performance in some detail:

> From Chester-le-Street we go about half a mile to the left, where is a very large fire engine for draining the coal pits there. The boiler holds eighty hogsheads.
>
> The fire stove consumes five fothers[2] or sixty bushels of coal in twenty-four hours.
>
> The brass barrel or cylinder is nine feet long. Its diameter two feet four inches.
>
> Thickness of the brass - one inch and a half. From the surface of the ground to the bottom of the water is twenty-four fathoms or forty-eight yards.
>
> The water in the pit is two yards deep. From the surface of the water to the drift or level where the engine forces it out is twelve fathoms.
>
> It discharges two hundred and fifty hogsheads in one hour; it strikes (as they term it) or makes a discharge fourteen times in one minute.

Pits were becoming a common sight in Staffordshire, east Lancashire, and parts of South Wales, as well as in additional areas of the Scottish Lowlands; but the new workings were mostly small and total production, estimated at 2,500,000 tons in 1700, is unlikely to have been more than doubled by mid-century. One reason was the difficulty of distribution beyond the limits of the rivers, including their improvements; another was the long delay in the

[1] See p. 235.
[2] Loads (*O.E.D.*)

successful application of coal to the fuel needs of the iron and steel industry.

The ironmasters depended on charcoal for heating the ore in the blast-furnace, which produced the pig-iron for castings; and again for refining the pig into the bar-iron which they sold to the smith for forge work; it was also required for the cementation process by which small quantities of bar-iron could be converted into steel. Thus the smith was the only iron-worker who habitually employed coke. Each of the other three processes was rendered increasingly expensive by the scarcity of woodland, which was driving the industry from ancient haunts like the Weald to remoter areas such as the upper valley of the Severn, where the coppice wood for charcoal-making was still reasonably plentiful. It was at Coalbrookdale in this region that Abraham Darby had learnt how to use coke from high-grade coal to make a rather rough quality of pig-iron for firebacks, pipes and pans, and other not too ambitious castings.[1]

His method did not find many immediate imitators – whether from lack of knowledge or inclination it is hard to say. But by the middle of the century his son, Abraham Darby II, with a more carefully selected coal for his coke and a more powerful blast to intensify the furnace-heat, began to supply a quality of pig-iron adequate for the needs of nailers, chain-makers, and even locksmiths. Coke-burning blast-furnaces then began to increase in numbers, even before the Seven Years War encouraged their development through the big demand for the casting of cannon. Meanwhile, in 1748 a new kind of steel began to be made in Sheffield by Benjamin Huntsman, a former clockmaker, who devised a method of converting bar-iron into steel in small crucibles made of a special heat-resisting clay; the heat was applied in a coke furnace. This was superior to anything previously available for razors, edged tools, and watch-springs; but the quantity produced was very small, and the high-grade bar-iron required as raw material was itself imported from Sweden. The great days of the British iron and steel industry still lay ahead.

[1] See p. 238.

A Society on the Eve of Great Changes

Looking back, it is easy for us to picture the subjects of the first two Georges as thrusting forward eagerly towards the large-scale, power-driven industries which lay just around the corner. Both the textile and the iron industries included some large units, where a big labour-force was employed by a single capitalist and might even work under one roof. Specialization had been carried very far in some cases, particularly in the metal industries. As regards inventiveness, a writer on trade in the 1750s could make the following claim:

> Few countries equal, perhaps none excel the English in the numbers and contrivance of their machines to abridge labour . . . At Birmingham, Wolverhampton, Sheffield and other manufacturing places almost every master manufacturer hath a new invention of his own, and is daily improving on those of others.

Because of its importance for the future, our attention is naturally caught by such a town as Birmingham, with its modern outlook. It already described itself in the language of sales promotion as

> famous all over the world for the rare choice and invention of all sorts of wares and curiosities in iron, steel, brass, etc., admired as well for their cheapness as their peculiar beauty of workmanship.

Many of its most distinguished citizens were self-made men such as John Baskerville, an ex-footman who introduced the art of japanning to the town in 1740 and began his type-casting there, prior to his appointment as university printer at Cambridge. A still more representative figure was John Taylor, once a journeyman, whom trade rivals later nicknamed 'the Esquire'; his speciality was gilding with brass and plating of smallware. In 1755 a visitor to his workshops found that he employed 500 persons in the manufacture of buttons and snuff-boxes alone, and that altogether no fewer than 70 processes were being carried out by distinct groups of workers. Taylor became one of the founders of what is now Lloyd's Bank, and left a fortune of £200,000.

Nevertheless, the truth is that at the death of George II the great majority of his subjects still pursued much the same daily routine as their forefathers had done. On the verge of their momentous expansion in numbers, the people of the island were being fed by largely customary methods of farming, which usually left some margin for export. London and the older industrial centres, such as the clothing towns, continued to base manufacture upon traditional craftsmanship aimed at familiar markets. Human muscle, the horse, the water-wheel, and the sail remained the sources of power upon which civilization contentedly rested. In our final chapter we will look through the eyes of contemporaries at a society seemingly so remote from our own, which nevertheless directly prepared the way for the making of modern Britain.

18

THE BRITISH PEOPLE AS SEEN BY DEFOE AND WESLEY

APART from the overlapping between their lives, these two famous men might appear to have very little in common. The author of *Robinson Crusoe* died in London in 1731 at the age of 70, a rather mysterious figure, who had made his way by turns as trader, journalist, political agent, and novelist. Only his astonishing imaginative genius uplifts the character of this man on the make, habitually untruthful and an expert 'double-crosser'. In 1731 John Wesley was an Oxford college tutor in his late twenties, a clergyman like all his colleagues, but unlike most of them in the strictness with which he practised his religion. Seven years later his conversion – a sudden strengthening of his faith by a henceforth unshakeable conviction that his sins were conquered and forgiven – led to the mission in which he sought to spread conversion and consequent sanctity of life. With the help of his brother Charles (the great hymn-writer), a handful of other clergymen, and a large body of lay preachers, John Wesley set going a tremendous revival movement, which by the time of his death in 1791 was taking permanent shape in the new Methodist Church. At the end of George II's reign he was already a national figure, with organized societies of earnest followers in many parts of the kingdom and in Ireland: in London, for instance, he could record "three-and-twenty hundred and fifty members: few of whom we could discern to be triflers".

What the 'Tour' and the 'Journal' Describe

As observers of early Hanoverian Britain, however, these two men are equally deserving of attention, for Defoe's *Tour thro' the Whole Island of Great Britain*, published in 1724–6, and the *Journal* which Wesley began to keep in 1735 share a number of valuable features. Each is the work of an author who combined a wide intellectual curiosity with a gift for easy writing. Thus Defoe's prodigious total output of at least 150 volumes is classified by his biographers under seven main heads. As for the mere 32 volumes of Wesley's prose works, they are of course primarily theological, but they bear witness also to a close interest in politics, literature, education, philanthropy, and even science. Again, both the *Tour* and the *Journal* are the work of men who concerned themselves with the daily lives of people outside the charmed circle of upper-class society, where most of the surviving memoirs, diaries, and letter collections for this period originate. Defoe was the son of a Nonconformist London butcher; he had been in wholesale trade himself and shared the interests of his class. Wesley, a clergyman's son educated at Charterhouse and Christ Church, Oxford, had friends and associates in every walk of life, but two decades after he began his mission writes revealingly: "If I might choose, I should still (as I have done hitherto) preach the Gospel to the poor."

Finally, each of the books we are about to examine is the work of a man who, though his activities were inevitably centred upon the capital, wrote extensively about his experiences all over Britain. London indeed, was still growing with astonishing rapidity: but we must be content to picture the impetus it had received in Anne's reign continuing under her successors – more squares and stately streets in the West End, more wealth in City counting-houses, more ships in the Pool, more workers drifting in from the countryside, more squalor in the crowded alleys of the East End and the South Bank. What we are now concerned with is the light which these authors can shed upon conditions in every part of the united island.

Defoe may have done some of the travelling he purports to record as late as 1723, though he draws mainly upon recollections of journeys made in rather earlier years. What matters most, however, is that he had been in almost every district at least three times and brought his earlier impressions up to date with the skill of an expert journalist, especially as regards economic and social changes, with which he was closely in touch. As for Wesley's *Journal*, it is based on notes made day by day during his incessant travels about the country and edited by him for publication in short sections, which usually appeared about half a dozen years after the events described. Since Wesley's object was to record the spread of his mission, the references to secular events are scattered and episodic; but he can never be suspected, as Defoe may sometimes be, of conducting propaganda in favour of the places he visits.

Possibilities of Travel

One feature of the society depicted in these books is its mobility. Apart from the settlement laws,[1] to which it is difficult to trace any reference, people (and goods) are seen to move freely throughout the island without any kind of legal hindrance, while the physical hindrances are represented as serious but no longer insuperable. Indeed, Defoe's professed reason for writing was his belief that a popular guide book was needed, and the correctness of his judgment was proved by the fact that his work passed through eight editions in the following half-century.

In 1726 the second volume of the *Tour* supplied readers with a long and encouraging appendix, mainly devoted to an account of the turnpiked roads and rebuilt bridges in the neighbourhood of London and among the midland clays. On the Watling Street, for instance,

> there are wonderful improvements made and making, which no traveller can miss the observation of, especially if he knew the condition these ways were formerly in.

Twelve road Bills were reported to be before Parliament, and Defoe looked forward to a time when

> travelling and carriage of goods will be much more easy both to man and horse than ever it was since the Romans lost this island.

That time did not come very quickly. More than thirty years later, Wesley travelled the selfsame Watling Street in the face of a March wind.

[1] See pp. 201, 293.

> It was hard work to sit our horses. The rain continued all the way to Dunstable, where we exchanged the main road for the fields, which, having just been ploughed, were deep enough.

On the Great North Road, too, after a snowfall, his servant reported that travelling was impossible, to which his reply was, "At least we can walk twenty miles a day, with our horses in our hands." The *Journal* adds, "So in the name of God we set out." Perhaps the most valid conclusion to be drawn from the record of Wesley's movements about the country, in which he habitually rode as much as fifty miles a day between preaching engagements, is that a man of determination was seldom impeded seriously if he travelled light.

Visits to Wales and Scotland

This does not apply only to England. Defoe's *Tour* includes a brief account of an exploration of Wales, which he completed in spite of his having entered the Principality in the region of the Black Mountains,

> a country looking so full of horror that we thought to have given over the enterprise . . . But after a day or two conversing thus with rocks and mountains, our guide brought us down into a most agreeable vale, opening to the south.

Persevering, he found that Swansea already had

> a very great trade for coals and culmn[1] . . . so that one sometimes sees a hundred sail of ships at a time loading coals here.

After visiting Wrexham, with its great sales of Welsh flannel, "by which the poor are very profitably employed", Defoe emerged eventually at Shrewsbury, where "They speak all English in the town, but on a market-day you would think you were in Wales." Wesley made his first preaching visit to Wales from Bristol in October 1739. By 1760 he had been there eighteen times, including his passages to and from Ireland, and although he had frequently to preach through an interpreter, he shared with George White-

[1] Anthracite-slack made up into balls (*O.E.D.*)

field and native evangelists the credit for a great awakening there.

Defoe gave considerable space in his third volume to Scotland, where he faithfully reported on the decaying east coast harbours as well as Glasgow, which he calls approvingly "a city of business; here is the face of trade, as well foreign as home trade." He noticed that the former was already profiting from the adaptability of the Scot to emigrant life.

> So many more of the Scots servants, which go over to Virginia, settle and thrive there than of the English . . . that if it goes on for many years more, Virginia may be rather called a Scots than an English plantation.

Wesley did not enter Scotland until April 1751, when he rode over the border in a thick mist via Berwick. He was agreeably surprised by the material prosperity of the Lowlands – "all things good, cheap, in great abundance, and remarkably well dressed" – though Edinburgh was noted as "one of the dirtiest cities I had ever seen, not excepting Cologne in Germany". Later in the same decade he paid two visits to Glasgow, where he observed:

> Nothing is wanting but more trade (which would naturally bring more people) to make a great part of Scotland in no way inferior to the best counties in England.

Carriage of Goods by Water

The growth of trade being Defoe's principal interest, he has much to say about inland navigations, even as far south as the Kennet and the Tone, and repeatedly notices their usefulness to the northern counties of England, not only for the carriage of "every sort of heavy or bulky goods", but even for some highly specialized provision trades.

> 'Tis calculated that there is about four thousand ton of Cheshire cheese only, brought down the Trent every year from those parts of England to Gainsborough and Hull.

Weighing up the people of Glasgow, he even foresaw the day when "the rising greatness of their commerce" would lead to the digging of a Forth – Clyde canal. Wesley, on the other hand, was not specially concerned about matters of trade, in spite of the fact that his mission was directed very largely to the neglected population in areas of rapid economic growth, such as the coalfields, the Black Country, and the neighbourhood of the great ports. The rising port of Liverpool, for example, drew the attention of both men. Defoe has much to say about the "new navigation of the Rivers Mersey, the Weaver, and the Dane", and describes in detail the

> large basin or wet dock . . . made at an immense charge, so that the ships lie, as in a mill-pond, with the utmost safety and convenience.

But when Wesley went there in 1755 to consider its importance for his work, he was satisfied to note without further explanation:

> Two-thirds of the town has been added within these forty years. If it continue to increase in the same proportion, in forty years more it will nearly equal Bristol.

A Peaceful Society: Jacobitism

A second feature of the new age, which partly explains the relative ease of movement for men and goods, was the peaceful and law-abiding character of British life as compared with the life of earlier ages and many contemporary régimes on the Continent. The two Jacobite rebellions form an important exception, but only a minority of the population lived in the areas affected and there was no continuous unrest. Defoe, writing within a decade of the Fifteen, mentions it only once in more than two volumes on England – a passing reference to "the late bloody action with the northern rebels" at Preston, where "they seem to have a kind of remembrance of things upon them still". Wesley, on the other hand, records a direct contact with the events of the Forty-Five, for he visited Newcastle that year during the anxious month of September, when an advance party of rebels came within 17 miles of its walls and he "cried mightily to God to send His Majesty King George help from His holy place". He also preached to the 15,000 troops, including many Germans, encamped in readiness on Newcastle Moor – and pointed doubtless to the courageous behaviour of Methodist soldiers on the fields of Dettingen and Fontenoy, of which he transcribed the reports into the *Journal.* Ten years later, however, he makes his last, passing reference to the Jacobites: "They profit nothing; for more and more people 'fear God and honour the King'."

Limits of Mob Violence

The king's peace was also liable to intermittent disturbance by mob rioting. Possibly for reasons of propaganda, Defoe's allusions to this subject are remarkably few. Charlton in Kent is roundly denounced by him for the "yearly collected rabble of mad-people" at its fair, where the mob takes liberties which would justify suppressing the institution. Otherwise, it is chiefly Coventry that incurs his censure, on account of its election riots, continuing for several weeks, in which "the inhabitants, enraged at one another, met and fought a pitched battle in the middle of the street". Wesley, however, in the first twenty years of his mission, records violent interruptions at no fewer than thirty places from one end of England to the other – though none in Scotland, in spite of what he calls the "national shyness and stubbornness". He always wore the dress of his profession, was gifted with a strong voice and an authoritative manner, and made it his rule "always to look a mob in the face". Yet he was exposed to a series of ordeals which differed only in length from the well-known occasion in the Black Country in October 1743, when rival mobs held him at their mercy for five hours on end and "To attempt speaking was vain, for the noise on every side was like the roaring of the sea".

Such persistent disturbances shed a sombre light upon the prejudices of the age, but in order to form a balanced picture of British life it must be taken into account that Wesley's position was exceptional. A clergyman who directed his mission to the most savage elements in the population, and who attracted huge crowds by outdoor sermons, hymn-singing, and spectacular mass conversions, seemed to represent a serious challenge to the established authorities. The enthusiasm which his mission aroused called to mind the politico-religious strife of the previous century, which had been allayed with such difficulty. The forces of law and order were therefore in many cases hostile rather than powerless: rumours were spread that he was a Jacobite agent or at best a Catholic priest in disguise, fellow-clergymen egged on the mob to drive him out of their parishes, and prejudiced magistrates on some occasions refused to intervene on his behalf.

But Wesley's *Journal* also testifies to the existence of many magistrates who kept excellent order. In Bristol, at a time when his activities had all the excitement of novelty, rioters were brought up promptly at quarter sessions, where

> the Mayor cut them all short, saying, "What Mr Wesley is, is nothing to you: I will have no rioting in this city."

At St Ives, too, where a mob had pulled down the Methodist meeting-house "for joy that Admiral Matthews had beat the Spaniards", on their re-assembling

> the Mayor came without delay, and read the Proclamation against riots: upon which, after many oaths and imprecations, they thought proper to disperse.

And whether the Riot Act was invoked or not, the *Journal* again and again records later visits of Wesley to the same places without any recurrence of trouble: even in the Black Country, by 1755 "the success overpays the labour".

Growth of Charitableness

If we are right in picturing an increasingly peaceable society, its peace may well be related to an increase in charitableness. Defoe described educational institutions and hospitals together with churches and country houses, as objects of merely historical interest to the traveller, except at Winchester, where the misappropriation of an ancient hospital foundation provokes him to exclaim: "'Tis a thing worthy of complaint when public charities, designed for the relief of the poor, are embezzled and depredated by the rich." In general, however, he sees the 'relief of the poor' in terms of their employment by the rich under the guidance of a sagacious parliament. Thus he applauds the Calico Act of 1721, as a result of which

> the stuff trade revived incredibly, and the manufacturers assured me that there was not in all the eastern and middle part of Norfolk any hand unemployed, if they would work; and that the very children after four or five years of age could every one earn their own bread.

He noted the employment of four-year-olds with equal approval among the poorer families in other woollen districts. Even when he for once sounds a note of genuine compassion, in describing a chance encounter with the family of a Derbyshire lead-miner living in a cave on 8*d*. a day, he adds the moralizing comment that their dwelling did not

> look like the dirt and nastiness of the miserable cottages of the poor, though many of them spend more in strong drink than this poor woman had to maintain five children with.

At a rather later date, Wesley's very strong concern for the welfare of the poor connects to some extent with his special intellectual interests. He was the author of a *Primitive Physic*, which ran through twenty printings between 1747 and 1781, and the enthusiastic purchaser of an electrical apparatus (1756), from which, he says, "hundreds, perhaps thousands, received unspeakable good". Accordingly, as early as December 1746 he opened a rudimentary dispensary in London; in its first year this provided medicine for 400 persons, a quarter of them regular recipients, at a cost of £40. Again, he was not content with founding two schools in Bristol and charity schools in connection with his work in London and earlier in Oxford. He wrote a whole series of school text-books and spent much time (and money) on the publication of a Christian Library in fifty volumes, thus helping to make education and culture available at different levels.

What is most striking, however, is the number and variety of the forms of help which he devised. While the Bristol colliers had their school, the centre of Wesley's activities at Newcastle was his 'orphan-house'. At Bristol, too, in the heavy frost of January 1740, he made three collections in a single week, "by which we were enabled to feed a hundred, sometimes a hundred and fifty a day, of those whom we found to need it most". When his new Methodist societies became fully organized, he appointed regular officials to distribute whatever alms the members could make available, adding the noteworthy injunction:

> If you cannot relieve, do not grieve, the poor . . . Put yourself in the place of every poor man, and deal with him as you would God should deal with you.

Mention must also be made of two special experiments he tried successfully in London. During a four months period of acute unemployment, he supplied twelve of his own members who were destitute with someone to teach them to card and spin cotton. "The design answered: they were employed and maintained with very little more than the produce of their own labour." A little later on, he got together a lending-stock of £50, from which 255 persons were relieved in a period of one and a half years: his rule was, "To lend only twenty shillings at once, which is repaid weekly within three months."

These details seem to show that charity was gaining ground, and that its spirit was not confined to a few persons of rank and substance. They also indicate clearly the terribly narrow margin of resources within which many of the people to whom Wesley ministered had to live. He even describes a visit to the sick "in their cells underground, others in their garrets", commenting that he "found not one of them unemployed who was able to crawl about the room."

Economic Expansion

Yet in their different ways both the writers we have been following leave the impression that they felt strongly aware of belonging to a great nation and one which was still advancing. At the very beginning of his book, what Defoe promises his readers is "a description of the most flourishing and opulent country in the world", and one for which

> the face of things so often alters, and the situation of affairs in the great British Empire gives such new turns, even to nature itself, that there is matter of new observation every day presented to the traveller's eye.

London to him is the most wonderful of all capital cities, not only in itself but because of its all-pervading economic influence. "London is in general supplied with all its provisions from the whole body of the nation." Again, for better or worse, "The neighbourhood of London sucks the vitals of trade in this island to itself": even a Buckinghamshire brass foundry owes its financial troubles to involvement with the City.

> They turned it into what they call a Bubble, brought it to Exchange Alley, set it a stock-jobbing in the days of our South Sea madness, and brought it up to be sold at one hundred pounds per share, whose intrinsic worth was perhaps ten pounds, 'till with the fall of all those things together, it fell to nothing again.

At the same time, however, Defoe extolled the expansion he saw almost everywhere in the provinces, with which we are here more closely concerned. He visited the centres of the woollen industry when it was approaching its peak. In Norfolk, he found

> a face of diligence spread over the whole country; the vast manufactures carried on (in chief) by the Norwich weavers employ all the country round in spinning for them.

He was even more impressed by the growth of the manufacture in the south-west, as for instance at Frome in Somerset, whose population at the present day is less than 12,000.

> Its trade is wholly clothing . . . and, if we may believe common fame, there are above ten thousand people in Frome now more than lived in it twenty years ago, and yet it was a considerable town then too.

As for the other textiles, he called Lombe's silk-mill at Derby "a curiosity in trade" and wondered "whether it answers the expense". But he remarked upon linen as "a principal merchandise" among Scottish exports to the colonies, and was fully alive to the growth of the cotton industry.

> The Manchester trade we all know; and all that are concerned in it know that it is, as all our other manufactures are, very much

> increased within these thirty or forty years especially beyond what it was before.

What is still more striking is the emphasis which Defoe lays upon the prospects for the north, viewed as a whole.

> The northern part is much larger than the southern, now Scotland is united . . . The country south by Trent is the richest by far and most populous, occasioned chiefly by the city of London and the commerce of the Thames; as for the cities of Bristol, Exeter, and Norwich, which are large and very populous, and in some things drive a prodigious trade, as well in merchandise as manufacture, we shall find them matched, if not outdone, by the growing towns of Liverpool, Hull, Leeds, Newcastle, and Manchester, and the cities of Edinburgh and Glasgow.

Wesley was concerned with moral rather than economic progress. Among the Cornish, for example, his ministry is held to have been responsible for the final disappearance of the hideous practice of inducing shipwrecks, to which Defoe may be taken to allude when he calls them "a fierce and ravenous people". Wesley refers directly to his efforts to put down smuggling or (as he calls it in another coastal community) "robbing the King, selling or buying run goods", and also the taking of bribes at elections, which was rife in a county notorious for its tiny parliamentary boroughs. The pleasure he took in his later visits to Cornwall suggests that his followers set their neighbours a higher standard in these respects. In general there is no doubt that he taught the Methodists to put method and conscience into their daily work as well as into their religious exercises, and that they tended as a group to go up in the world in consequence. But he seldom recorded their increase in prosperity, and if he did so, it was with misgiving. Revisiting his congregation in Bristol, where he had preached his first open-air sermon to the rough crowd assembled in a brickyard, he observes:

> As many of them increase in worldly goods, the great danger I apprehend now is their relapsing into the spirit of the world; and then their religion is but a dream.

A Self-confident People

Yet Wesley's other-worldliness did not prevent him from sharing with Defoe a kind of patriotic exultation over Britain's rise to power among the nations. Defoe makes a visit to the Norfolk residence of Admiral Russell an occasion for telling his readers that the battle of La Hogue "so broke the heart of the naval power of France that they have not fully recovered it to this day". Wesley likewise, on the eve of the Seven Years War, dismisses the dilapidated condition of Pendennis Castle in Cornwall with the complacent reflection, "Our wooden castles are sufficient." Then, when the Year of Victories had justified his confidence in the Royal Navy, he concludes his account of the Day of General Thanksgiving without a trace of irony in the following terms:

> This is indeed a Christian holiday, a 'rejoicing unto the Lord'. The next day came the news that Sir Edward Hawke had dispersed the French fleet.

Providence was seen to have watched over the fortunes of an expanding Britain, even among the shoals of Quiberon Bay.

Less than a year later, Wesley's *Journal* mournfully records: "King George was gathered to his fathers. When will England have a better prince?" The new king in his first speech from the throne said that he 'gloried in the name of Britain'. Neither the youthful George III, nor the peers and faithful Commons to whom he spoke, nor certainly the ordinary citizens of his united kingdom could guess at the tremendous changes then gathering momentum, for which the first two Hanoverian reigns had prepared the way. But perhaps Defoe had caught a glimpse of the future when he wrote:

> No description of Great Britain can be what we call a finished account, as no clothes can be made to fit a growing child.

APPENDIX I

Social History in the Reports of Foreign Visitors

1. *Andrea Trevasino, Venetian ambassador to the court of Henry VII, has been identified as the originator of* A RELATION OF THE ISLAND OF ENGLAND. *The following passage gives a lively impression of English society, and makes an agreeable allusion to the Scots.*

The English are for the most part, both men and women of all ages, handsome and well proportioned; though not quite so much so, in my opinion, as it had been asserted to me before Your Magnificence sent me to that kingdom. I have understood from persons acquainted with these countries that the Scots are much handsomer; and that the English are great lovers of themselves and of everything belonging to them. They think that there are no other men than themselves and no other world but England. Whenever they see a handsome foreigner, they say that 'he looks like an Englishman' and that 'it is a great pity that he should not be an Englishman'; and when they partake of any delicacy with a foreigner, they ask him 'whether such a thing is made in *their* country.'

They take great pleasure in having a quantity of excellent victuals, and also in remaining a long time at table, being very sparing of wine when they drink it at their own expense. And this it is said they do in order to induce their other English guests to drink wine in moderation also; not considering it any inconvenience for three or four persons to drink out of the same cup. Few people keep wine in their own houses, but buy it for the most part at a tavern; and when they mean to drink a great deal, they go to the tavern, and this is done not only by the men but by ladies of distinction. The deficiency of wine, however, is amply supplied by the abundance of ale and beer, to the use of which these people are become so habituated that, at an entertainment where there is plenty of wine, they will drink them in preference to it and in great quantities.

2. *The same observer describes the third – and to foreigners most remote – of the peoples of the island, in accordance with the injunction in his commission of June 12th, 1497, 'to be diligent and careful in giving the Republic news of those parts, so that it may be acquainted with everything'.*

Wales is bounded by rivers and is very mountainous. The inhabitants attend to agriculture only so far as is necessary for their subsistence. They take great delight in large herds of cattle, and most of them live upon the produce of their dairies. They do not dwell together in large towns, but separately, in the country. There are, however, some barons who have fortified castles. The Welsh people are generally supposed to have been the original inhabitants of the island, and they themselves say, and it is also believed by the English, that they are descended from the Trojans; and they all consider themselves to be gentlemen, and call each other "Cosaio", a word in their language which bears that meaning; nor would they on any account intermarry with the English, of whom they are the most mortal enemies. Their language is different from both the English and the Scotch.

Wales was formerly a separate kingdom, but they were reduced to a dominion of the English. They may now, however, be said to have recovered their former independence, for the most wise and fortunate Henry the Seventh is a Welshman.

3. *Stephen Perlin, a French ecclesiastic who lived in England in the reign of Mary Tudor, published his* DESCRIPTION OF ENGLAND AND SCOTLAND *in Paris in 1558. It is full of vivid detail.*

The English in general are cheerful and great lovers of music, for there is no church, however small, but has musical service performed in it. They are likewise great drunkards; for if an Englishman would treat you, he will say in his language, *vis dring a quarta rim gasquim oim hespaignol, oim malvoysi*; that is, will you drink a quart of Gascon wine, another of Spanish, and another of Malmsey. In drinking or eating they will say to you above an hundred times, *drind iou*, which is, I am going to drink to you; and you should answer them in their language, *iplaigiu*, which means, I pledge you.

In this country all the shops of every trade are open, like those of the barbers in France, and have many glass windows, as well below as above in the chambers. In the windows, as well in cities as villages, are plenty of flowers, and at the taverns plenty of hay upon their wooden floors, and many cushions of tapestry, on which travellers seat themselves. They consume great quantities of beer, strong and small, and do not drink out of glasses, but from earthen pots with silver handles and covers, and this even in houses of persons of middling fortune; for as to the poor, the covers of their pots are only pewter, and in some places, such as villages, their pots for beer are made only of wood.

4. *Perlin also visited Scotland, which he viewed as the country of the Auld Alliance with France.*

Scotland is a kingdom beyond England, and is very cold and septentrional. With respect to habitable lands, it may be styled small, that is to say, there is much bad and wild uncultivated land; the country is likewise small with respect to the size of its cities and villages.

This country, although it is in a bad neighbourhood, being near a haughty, treacherous, and proud enemy, has nevertheless sustained itself in a manly sort by the means and assistance of the most noble King of France, who has many times let the English know what were the consequences of the anger of so great a monarch.

One thing I find reprehensible among the Scotch, which is, that it is difficult to obtain a lodging from them. If you say to an ordinary sort of man in Scotch, *Guede gueduit goud maistre praie qui mi longini*, which is to say in our language, Good evening, master, I pray you to give me a lodging; they will answer you haughtily in their tongue, *est est no bet*, which is to say, there is no bed; and will not vouchsafe to lodge you, unless they can expect a considerable recompense. . . .

They carry bucklers like the English, and use the bow, and in other respects live like them, except that they are not so great dealers and tradesmen, and have not, as everyone knows, such weighty purses.

5. *Mario Savorgnano, Count of Belgrade, shows us London as it looked to a citizen of Venice on a short visit in August, 1531.*

London is the capital of the kingdom and the residence of the ambassadors and merchants; it is a very notable city situated on the Thames. This river is convenient for trade, embellishing the city, and rendering it cheerful, and over it is a very large stone bridge.

London contains many houses on both sides of the river, and two large churches of extreme beauty, in one of which the present King's father is buried. In various parts of the city there are many palaces of divers citizens and merchants, but the larger ones and the most superb are on the river . . .

The population of London is immense and comprises many artificers. The houses are in very great number but ugly, and half the materials of wood, nor are the streets wide. In short, a very rich, populous, and mercantile city, but not beautiful.

6. *The visit to London in 1592 of Frederick, later Duke of Wurttemberg, was a more formal affair, which was carefully recorded by his private secretary, Jacob Rathgeb, and is even alluded to by Shakespeare in* THE MERRY WIVES OF WINDSOR *(Act IV, Scene 5, 'the duke de Jamany').*

London is a large, excellent, and mighty city of business, and the most important in the whole kingdom; most of the inhabitants are employed in buying and selling merchandise and trading in almost every corner of the world, since the river is most useful and convenient for this purpose, considering that ships from France, the Netherlands, Sweden, Denmark, Hamburg, and other kingdoms come almost up to the city, to which they convey goods and receive and take away others in exchange.

It is a very populous city, so that one can scarcely pass along the streets on account of the throng.

The inhabitants are magnificently apparelled, and are extremely proud and overbearing; and because the greater part, especially the tradespeople, seldom go into other countries, but always remain in their houses in the city attending to their business, they care little for foreigners, but scoff and laugh at them; and moreover one dare not oppose them, else the streetboys and apprentices collect together in immense crowds and strike to the right and left unmercifully without regard to person; and because they are the strongest, one is obliged to put up with the insult as well as the injury.

7. *Emanuel van Meteren was a merchant from Antwerp who served as Dutch consul in London from 1583 to 1612. His opinion of the English is recorded in his* HISTORY OF THE NETHERLANDS.

The people are not so laborious and industrious as the Netherlanders or French . . . the most toilsome, difficult, and skilful works are chiefly performed by foreigners. They have a great many sheep which bear fine wool, of which for these two hundred years they have learnt to make fine cloth. They keep many lazy servants, and also many wild animals for their pleasure, rather than trouble themselves to cultivate the land. The island which they inhabit is very large, and abounds with fish; they have likewise the best harbours in Christendom. They are also rich in ships; nevertheless they do not catch as many fish as they require, so that they are obliged to buy more from their neighbours; but they do catch a great quantity of herrings . . .

The English dress in elegant, light, and costly garments, but they are very inconstant and desirous of novelties, changing their fashions every year, both men and women . . .

The English language is broken German, mixed with French and British terms and words and pronunciation, from which they have also gained a lighter pronunciation, not speaking out of the heart as the Germans, but only prattling with the tongue.

8. *The travels of Cosmo III, Grand Duke of Tuscany, were written up by Count Lorenzo Magalotti, a noted savant who corresponded with Newton. The two Italians toured southern England in 1669.*

By the convenience of its seas and navigable rivers England is abundantly supplied with whatever it does not produce within itself. It has no want of iron, lead, tin, and wool of peculiar fineness, which is exported into other countries at a great profit.

The face of the country throughout the kingdom is, for the most part, an undulating plain, interspersed with pleasant hills. . . .

From this abundance of all things arises in the English nation that contemptuous disposition which it entertains towards other countries, thinking them unprovided with the advantages which it finds in its own; and on this account the common people treat foreigners with little respect and even with haughtiness, and are scarcely induced to relax by any act of civility whatever that is shown to them on the part of the latter. Nor does their natural insolence terminate here; it was manifested to a much greater extent in the effort made of late years to overthrow the royal authority, making England the theatre of revolution and of deplorable spectacles . . .

It is a common custom with the lower order of people after dinner and at public houses, when they are transacting business of any kind, to take tobacco and smoke, so that there does not pass a day in which the artisans do not indulge themselves in going to the public houses, which are exceedingly numerous, neglecting their work, however urgent it may be; hence it is that the French make fortunes in London, for, being more attentive to their business, they sell their manufactures at a lower price than the English, who would fain derive the same profits as other artisans, however little they work.

9. *Jorevin de Rocheford's* DESCRIPTION OF ENGLAND AND IRELAND *was published in Paris in 1672. It includes an account of one of the leading industrial towns, which then rarely attracted the interest of foreign visitors.*

Newcastle is a sea-port frequented by all the nations of the world, on account of the quantity and goodness of the sea-coal loaded there, digged from the mines in the environs of that great town; as also lead, and very fine tin; insomuch that it is one of the most mercantile places in the kingdom . . .

I went to see the great market-place, than which there is not a handsomer or larger in England. Here is the town-hall, one of the finest buildings I saw in my travels; the architecture of its staircase deserves admiration; and its clock is ornamented with several figures. Under this great edifice is the Exchange, where the merchants assemble to treat in matters of commerce, in a great hall sustained by many columns, having one opening to the quay and the other towards the market-place. This part of the town is the chief habitation of the richest merchants of Newcastle, which is, without dispute, one of the richest and largest towns in the kingdom. The lesser part of the town, called Gateshead, to go into which you must pass over a large stone bridge, covered with houses and shops, is inhabited by divers manufacturers, employed in making cloth and worsted stockings, which are here very cheap; wherefore they are sent all over Europe, even to Paris. They are esteemed for the fineness of their wool and the excellence of their workmanship.

One may go down the river at every ebb by means of little boats, to see its mouth, the great port where vessels are loaded with coal; where also one may see a quantity of salt made from sea-water, which is boiled with fire made from this coal. All along the banks of the river, quite to Newcastle, are many fine houses . . .

10. LETTERS ON THE ENGLISH AND THE FRENCH *by B. L. de Muralt, a Swiss pietist who had served as an officer in the French Army, was first published at Zurich a year or two after his visit to England in 1693–4. An English translation appeared in London in 1726.*

I pass to the merchants. They seem to me different from other merchants in several respects: they have neither the passion of the French for hoarding, nor the niggardliness of the Dutch in economizing. They have well furnished houses and keep a good table . . . and undoubtedly it is this sumptuous way of living which obliges them to sell dear, as they do; accustomed to large expenditure, they disdain small profits. Something more remarkable, and which I think distinguishes them further from other merchants, is that in many cases, when they have acquired a fortune, they give up trade and turn themselves into country gentlemen. That is to say, there are people among them who know how to stop and enjoy their labours.

English workmen have acquired a big reputation in the world, and in some respects with reason: they excel in clockmaking, in woodwork, in saddlery, tools of all kinds, and several other things which I cannot at the moment recall. There are also instances in which their reputation is undeserved: their steel products, for instance, are nothing much, though they make a lot of them and sell them very dear. Their worth comes from the tempering, which is very good; for the rest, you would find a lot of work misplaced and badly finished. In general, for all these trifles, these little nipes[1] more curious than essential, they are excelled by the French, and their best masters come to them from Paris. The reason for the want of smartness in what is made in this country is apparently the lack of taste in the English in trinkets and their being too easily able to pay well for everything they buy. Most of them judge a piece of work by the price put on it: obviously the workman, since he has no difficulty in giving satisfaction and can make money easily, will be little concerned in applying himself to his trade and will not excel in it.

[1] fragments, bits (*O.E.D.*)

11. *François Maximilien Misson was a French Protestant who fled to England in 1688. His Memoirs, based on nine years residence, consist of short articles on different aspects of English life; first published at The Hague in 1698, they were translated into English by John Ozell in 1719.*

Bath. This town takes its name from the baths for which it is famous. Several in Switzerland and Germany are called Baden for the same reason. In winter Bath makes a very melancholy appearance; but during the months of May, June, July, and August there is a concourse of genteel company that peoples, enriches, and adorns it; at that time provisions and lodgings grow dear. Thousands go thither to pass away a few weeks, without heeding either the baths or the waters, but only to divert themselves with good company. They have music, gaming, public walks, balls, and a little fair every day.

Islington. A large village, half a league from London, where you drink waters that do you neither good nor harm, provided you don't take too much of them. There is gaming, walking, dancing; and a man may spend an hour there agreeably enough. It is not much flocked to by people of quality.

Tunbridge is a borough upon the Medway, in the county of Kent, famous for its mineral waters. The pretence of these waters brings together vast numbers of people, of both sexes, that are in very good health, and come there only to play and divert themselves. They go in the same manner to Bath, Epsom, Richmond, Acton, etc.

12. *Zacharias Conrad von Uffenbach, a student and bibliophile from Frankfort, came to England with his brother at the age of 26, intending to settle at Oxford. The final entries in his diary indicate some of the reasons why he returned home in November, 1710.*

We had still much to see in England; but did not care to spend a winter in the country, partly because of the unhealthy climate, partly because of the disturbances consequent on a change of ministers: nor would we stay longer, for fear of a rough passage.

4 Nov., in the morning we set out in a coach hired for £5. We dined at Brentwood; found Chelmsford in the ferment of an election; the mob shouting Child! Child! (the Tory candidate's name) and pelting us for lukewarmness in this cause.

5 Nov., in the morning we set out at 6 for Colchester, where we bought a barrel of oysters for 5*s*. . . . and reached Harwich at 4.30; where we put up at the Rotterdam. Foul winds kept us here 6 days; nothing to see, nothing to

do, poor fare, and a terribly long bill. Every day we spent 30*s*. a head, and should have starved, but for our barrel of oysters. The captain was in league with the landlord.

10 Nov., we saw a true English, or rather devilish, sport. Some lords, waiting for the packet-boat, had promised two sailors a crown, if they would strip to their trousers and fight with fists. Their faces were running with blood, and their bodies were as blue as an apron. Whenever they wanted to give over, the spectators tossed them a shilling, to keep them to it. This is a common pastime of passengers.

11 Nov., at 6 a.m. we put to sea; as we passed the fort in the dark, the guard fired at us: after sailing about a quarter of an hour we ran aground, and did not get off for half an hour.

12 Nov., nothing to eat but some old ship's biscuit, for which we had to pay dear; it was night before we landed at Helvoetsluys.

13. *Pehr Kalm, a Swedish naturalist and friend of Linnaeus, made a closer study of England than he intended. Having crossed the North Sea at the start of an official mission to examine the natural resources of America, he was kept waiting from February 6th to August 5th, 1748, for a vessel to carry him farther. To pass the time he cast a highly expert eye over the agriculture then practised in the neighbourhood of London.*

The farmers of Middlesex lay out all the ground which they have only and solely as meadow . . . As they live near London they buy and carry home from thence all their manure . . . A farmer in these parts commonly has no more servants than one single man. He wins all his meadows in the summer with day labourers. In the beginning of May there come from Ireland over to England a very large number of Irishmen, who go and hire themselves out everywhere to the farmers. The whole of this part of England which lies immediately north and east of London carries on nearly all its haymaking and harvest work with only this people, who remain there the whole summer, leaving their own dwellings at home in Ireland to the care of their wives and children; but towards autumn, after the haytime and harvest are past, they return home with the money which they have been able to earn.

In the same way as the Irishmen seek their food and income on this side in the summer, so it is the case with those from Wales. They earn their money also on this side of England in Kent, for towards the haymaking season the folk come from thence in very large numbers down to the country parts of Kent to work for wages; but with this difference that, instead of only men coming as from Ireland, there come mostly only women and girls from Wales, all well, cleanly, and very neatly clad. These perform nearly all the summer cropping in Kent, both of hay and grain. They also take down and pluck off the hops. They remake the hop gardens. They gather the various kinds of beautiful fruits which Kent produces.

14. *Kalm, as might be expected, was an advocate of enclosure.*

Around Little Gaddesden and on all Chiltern land every farmer more or less had his own severalties which he afterwards divided into small enclosures by hedges. There was one enclosure sown with wheat, another with barley, turnips, peas, oats, sainfoin, clover, trifolium, tares, potatoes, or whatever he wished.

While the fields were lying fallow, he could sow it with turnips, feed sheep on it, and afterwards plough down the remaining bitten turnips, and have thereby a much greater advantage than if he had left it fallow. In short, he could in a thousand ways improve his property and earn money.

On the other hand, here about Ivinghoe, where the common fields are everywhere in use, no hedges are seen. Nor are there here any peas or kinds of grass sown as fodder . . . Nor had they any turnip land to feed sheep upon. Therefore they were deprived of the advantage of getting to sell any fat sheep or other cattle, etc. The reason they gave for all this was that their arable was common field and thus came to lie every other year fallow, when one commoner had always to accommodate his crops to the others . . .

On the common land no one has freedom to enclose his strips, without a special permission and Act of Parliament.

15. *Finally and unforgettably, Kalm shows London to us in its rural setting.*

In the morning of February 28th I went out into the country to a place named Woodford, 10 miles from London, in Essex. The prospect of the country between London and Woodford, where we now travelled, was mostly level or only in small hills. The whole way there is nothing else but a succession of beautiful houses, fertile arable fields and verdant meadows. At every house there was commonly a garden full of various beautiful trees.

The whole of the land was divided into enclosures, which were all surrounded by hedges of all kinds of planted trees . . . In some places, especially nearer to London, there were high earth-banks cast up, about 4 feet high, instead of hedges round the fields . . . The beautiful appearance of the country must altogether be ascribed to industry and labour. It resembles one continuous pleasure-garden, from the many living hedges there are everywhere.

London's many towers appeared in the distance. However clear the air may be, there seems always to be a fog-like cloud standing over the town, which comes from the coal-smoke which ascends in abundance from the innumerable fireplaces, where fires are continually burning. The roads are full of travellers, on foot and on horseback, in wagons and carts, journeying in both directions, so that one often has as it were to steer through them. In some places the Thames appears in the distance with many ships and vessels sailing up and down.

APPENDIX II

References for Source Quotations

Chapter 1

p. 1 *Anglica Historia* (quoted in J. D. Mackie, *The Earlier Tudors,* p. 27).
p. 6 *Calendar of State Papers, Venetian* (quoted in *Cambridge Economic History of Europe*, IV 74).
p. 7 SEBASTIAN FRANCK: *Germaniae Chronicon* (quoted in *Cambridge Economic History of Europe*, IV 25).
p. 7 Statement of 1576 (quoted in *Cambridge Economic History of Europe,* IV 30).
p. 10 RICHARD CAREW: *Survey of Cornwall,* published in 1602 (quoted in A. L. Rowse, *Expansion of Elizabethan England,* p. 34).
p. 12 *History of Henry the Seventh*, 1622.
p. 13 ibid.

Chapter 2

p. 16 SIR JOHN HAYWARD: *Annals of the First Four Years of Queen Elizabeth* (C. R. N. Routh, *They Saw It Happen 1485–1688*, p. 63).
p. 16 Scene at Tilbury, August 8th, 1588 (quoted in J. E. Neale, *Queen Elizabeth*, p. 297).
p. 16 *King Richard II*, III. ii. 59.
p. 17 Act for the Confirmation of Henry VII (G. R. Elton, *The Tudor Constitution*, p. 4; *English Historical Documents,* general editor D. C. Douglas, V 445).
p. 20 *The Life of Cardinal Wolsey* (*They Saw It Happen*, p. 16; *E.H.D.*, V 738).
p. 21 Elton, p. 344; J. R. Tanner, *Tudor Constitutional Documents*, p. 41.
p. 21 Elton, p. 355; Tanner, p. 47.
p. 22 SIR SIMONDS D'EWES' *Journal*, November 30, 1601 (quoted in J. B. Black, *Reign of Elizabeth,* p. 194; Neale, p. 383).
p. 23 *Letters and Papers, Henry VIII*, xi, No. 892 (Tanner, p. 217).
p. 23 SIR THOMAS SMITH: *De Republica Anglorum* (Elton, p. 164; Tanner, p. 284).
p. 25 *Acts of the Privy Council*, edited by J. R. Dasent, viii, 33 (Elton, p. 110; Tanner, p. 233).
p. 28 D'EWES' *Journal*, February 28, 1593 (Elton, p. 313; Tanner, p. 572).
p. 30 *De Republica Anglorum*, Book 2, c. 19 (Elton, p. 457; Tanner, p. 456).
p. 30 LEWIS GLYN COTHI (quoted in Rowse, p. 47).
p. 32 ROBERT LINDSAY OF PITSCOTTIE: *History and Chronicles of Scotland,* I, 307.

p. 35 Memorial to the Earl of Essex, Historical Manuscripts Commission, Salisbury Papers, viii, 146 (quoted in Rowse, p. 7).

Chapter 3

p. 37 Tanner, p. 57.
p. 40 Elton, p. 404; Tanner, p. 171.
p. 41 SIR PHILIP SIDNEY: *Arcadia* (quoted in Elton, *England under the Tudors*, p. 440).
p. 42 *Penguin Book of Elizabethan Verse*, p. 214.
p. 44 *King Richard II*, II. i. 61 and 43.
p. 46 *Moriae Encomium*, published in Paris, 1511 (quoted in G. M. Trevelyan, *English Social History*, 1946 edition, p. 101).
p. 48 Tanner, p. 94; *E.H.D.* V 811.
p. 49 FOXE'S *Book of Martyrs*, edited by G. A. Williamson, p. 311.
p. 50 *Works* (ed. R. Warwick Bond) II, 210 – 'Euphues' Glass for Europe'.
p. 50 Quoted in Walter Ralegh, 'Essay on the English Voyages of the Sixteenth Century' (Hakluyt Society Publications, Extra Series, 1905, XII 31).
p. 50 Act Against Reconciliation to Rome (Tanner, p. 152).
p. 51 quoted in S. T. Bindoff, *Tudor England*, p. 229.
p. 52 Injunctions of 1554 (H. Gee and W. J. Hardy, *Documents Illustrative of English Church History*, p. 383).
p. 53 *The Schoolmaster*, edited by W. A. Wright, p. 201; (*E.H.D.*, V 1048).
p. 53 THOMAS ELYOT: *The Book Named the Governor*, 1531 (Everyman edition, p. 18).
p. 54 *Memorials of Father Augustine Baker*, p. 16 (Publications of the Catholic Record Society, Vol. 33).
p. 57 'one of archbishop James Beaton's familiars', quoted in J. D. Mackie, *History of Scotland*, p. 151.
p. 58 JOHN KNOX: *History of the Reformation in Scotland*, edited by W. C. Dickinson, II 7.

Chapter 4

p. 64 quoted in J. Winny, *The Elizabethan Voyages*, p. 26.
p. 69 R. HAKLUYT: *Principal Navigations* (Everyman), VI 35.
p. 71 quoted in J. H. Froude, *English Seamen in the Sixteenth Century* (Longman's Silver Library, p. 228).
p. 72 quoted in D. Mathew, *The Naval Heritage*, p. 4.
p. 76 quoted in C. Morris, *The Tudors* p. 19.
p. 77 'Report of the Azores Fight' (Hakluyt, V 9).
p. 77 HAKLUYT, VIII 311.

Chapter 5

p. 83 Penguin edition, translated by P. Turner, p. 46.

p. 83 *Catechism*, edited by J. Ayre, p. 434 (quoted in W. K. Jordan, *Philanthropy in England,* p. 64).
p. 83 *Certain causes . . . wherein is showed the decay of England only by the great multitude of sheep*, Early English Text Society (quoted in Mackie, *Earlier Tudors,* p. 457; *E.H.D.* V 948).
p. 84 A. E. Bland, P. A. Brown, and R. H. Tawney: *English Economic History Select Documents*, p. 248.
p. 84 *Five Hundred Points of Good Husbandry*, edited by J. Tregaskis, p. 135.
p. 85 A prayer used by reformers (quoted in Sir John Clapham, *Short Economic History of Britain to 1750*, p. 204).
p. 86 edited by F. Furnivall, I 241.
p. 86 *A Discourse of the Common Weal of This Realm of England*, edited by E. Lamond, p. 19; *E.H.D.*, V 950.
p. 87 *State Papers Domestic, Edward VI*, IV No. 33 (quoted in A. F. Pollard, *England Under Protector Somerset*, p. 232).
p. 87 *Tudor and Stuart Proclamations* I No. 1042 (quoted in E. Lipson, *Economic History of England*, I 161).
p. 88 *A Caveat of Warning for Common Cursitors vulgarly called Vagabonds* (Early English Text Society edition, p. 19).
p. 88 Beggars Act (Tanner, p. 477; *E.H.D.*, V 1026).
p. 91 Section XV (Bland, Brown, and Tawney, p. 329; Tanner, p. 505).
p. 91 Section XI (Bland, Brown, and Tawney, p. 328; Tanner, p. 503).
p. 92 W. C. Dickinson: *A Source Book of Scottish History*, II 7.
p. 93 *Register of the Privy Council of Scotland* (edited by J. H. Burton), Vol. I (1545–1569), p. 114.

Chapter 6

p. 95 quoted in W. T. Maccaffrey, *Exeter 1540–1640*, p. 161.
p. 96 *State Papers Domestic, 1619–1623*, p. 271 (quoted in Lipson, III 53).
p. 100 edited by R. H. Tawney, p. 249.
p. 101 *H. M. C. Salisbury*, I 165 (quoted in Rowse, *England of Elizabeth*, p. 140).
p. 102 Tanner, p. 106; Bland, Brown and Tawney, p. 289.
p. 103 G. Unwin: *Industrial Organization in the Sixteenth and Seventeenth Centuries*, p. 43.

Chapter 7

p. 108 DRAYTON: *Complete Works* (edited by R. Hooper, 1876).
p. 108 *Penguin Book of Elizabethan Verse*, pp. 246 and 214.
p. 109 Act I, Scene 2; Act III, Scene 2.
p. 109 p. 66b (edition of 1769).
p. 110 W. HARRISON: *Description of England* (edited by F. J. Furnivall, 1877), I 341.
p. 110 W. CAMDEN: *Britain* (translated by Philemon Holland, 1637), p. 245.

p. 110 Harrison, I 141.
p. 110 *Penguin Book of Elizabethan Verse*, p. 159.
p. 111 Camden, p. 601.
p. 111 Harrison, I 153 and I 150.
p. 111 *Penguin Book of Elizabethan Verse*, p. 252.
p. 111 *Works*, III 17 and 3.
p. 112 Harrison, I 258 and 260.
p. 112 Camden, p. 675.
p. 113 ibid., pp. 641, 581, 567.
p. 113 Harrison, I 345.
p. 113 Camden, pp. 306 and 358.
p. 113 STOW: *Survey of London* (Everyman's Library), p. 134.
p. 114 Harrison, II 68.
p. 114 *Poly-Olbion* (R. Hooper edition, 1876), III 204 and 207.
p. 114 Camden, pp. 810 and 608.
p. 115 ibid., p. 556.
p. 115 J. VOWELL *alias* HOOKER: *Description of the City of Exeter* (1919) Part 2, p. 30.
p. 116 Stow, pp. 115 and 116.
p. 116 ibid., p. 161.
p. 117 Act I, Scene 4.
p. 117 Stow, p. 15.
p. 117 ibid., pp. 343 and 18.
p. 118 W. K. Jordan: *Charities of Rural England 1480–1660*, p. 43.
p. 118 Stow, p. 270.
p. 118 Camden, p. 414.
p. 118 Stow, pp. 359, 86, 87, 86.
pp. 119–20 ibid., pp. 25 and 494.
p. 121 Harrison, I 144.
p. 121 Act I, Scene 4.
p. 121 *Penguin Book of Elizabethan Verse*, p. 101.
p. 122 Act IV, Scene 7.
p. 122 *Patient Grissil*, Act II, Scene 1.
p. 122 Harrison, II 128.
p. 123 *History of Greater Britain* (1892 edition), pp. 48, 50, and 49.
p. 123 Camden (Scottish section), p. 39.
p. 123 ibid. (Scottish section), p. 18.
p. 124 Harrison, II 151; I 142; and II 130.
p. 125 Major, pp. 31 and 29.
p. 125 Camden (Scottish section), pp. 14 and 23.
pp. 125–6 Major, pp. 28, 29, and 41.

Chapter 8

p. 128 quoted in J. D. Mackie, *History of Scotland* (Penguin), p. 193.
p. 131 Speech in Star Chamber, June 20th, 1616 (G. W. Prothero, *Statutes and Constitutional Documents 1558–1625*, p. 399).

p. 131 Charles I's speech before his execution (quoted in G. M. Trevelyan, *England Under the Stuarts*, Penguin edition, p. 277).
p. 134 quoted in Trevelyan, p. 74.
p. 134 DR. ROGER MANWARING, July 4th, 1627 (quoted in J. R. Tanner, *English Constitutional Conflicts of the 17th Century 1603–1689*, p. 21; Prothero, p. 438; J. P. Kenyon, *The Stuart Constitution 1603–1688*, p. 15).
p. 136 December 18th, 1621, Commons Journal I 668 (Prothero, p. 313; Kenyon, p. 47).
p. 137 *Selections from Clarendon*, World's Classics edition, p. 95.
p. 137 J. Rushworth: *Historical Collections* (1682), i. 607 (quoted in Tanner, p. 64).
p. 138 Reply to Commons Address, March 15th, 1626 (S. R. Gardiner, *Constitutional Documents of the Puritan Revolution*, p. 3).
p. 138 Rushworth, i. 562 (quoted in Tanner, p. 63).
p. 139 SIR BENJAMIN RUDYERD, 1628: Rushworth, i. 552 (quoted in Tanner, p. 61).
p. 142 Protestation of March 2nd, 1629 (Gardiner, p. 83, Kenyon, p. 85).
p. 142 D. Masson: *Life of John Milton* (1859–80) i. 644 (quoted in Tanner, p. 70).
p. 144 quoted in Tanner, p. 71.
p. 144 First Speech as President of the Council of the North, December 30th, 1628, quoted in Lord Birkenhead, *Strafford*, p. 138.
p. 144 Letter of September 1633 (*Works*, Oxford 1857, VI 310).
p. 146 quoted in Mackie, p. 209.

Chapter 9

p. 148 quoted in Mackie, p. 211.
p. 150 quoted in C. Hill: *Century of Revolution 1603–1714*, p. 125.
p. 153 noted under September 3rd in JOHN DORNEY: *A Brief Relation of the Siege of Gloucester* (1643).
p. 155 Section I, Gardiner, p. 268; Kenyon, p. 264.
p. 155 quoted in Wedgwood, p. 327.
p. 158 Prayer-meeting at Windsor Castle, May 1st, 1648 (Kenyon, p. 318).
p. 158 quoted in Sir Charles Firth, *Oliver Cromwell*, p. 260.
p. 159 'Horatian Ode upon Cromwell's Return from Ireland' (Palgrave's *Golden Treasury*, No. 65).
p. 160 quoted in Trevelyan, p. 269.
p. 160 ibid., p. 270, footnote 1.
p. 160 quoted in Hill, p. 133.
p. 162 entry for May 2nd, 1660.
p. 164 Masson iii 525 (quoted in Tanner, p. 136).
p. 165 Corporation Act, XII (G. B. Adams and H. M. Stevens, *Select Documents of English Constitutional History*, p. 427).
p. 165 Thanksgiving 'For restoring Publick Peace at Home' (*Book of Common Prayer*: Prayers and Thanksgivings upon Several Occasions).

p. 167 quoted in G. S. Pryde, *A New History of Scotland*, II 17.
p. 167 quoted in Mackie, p. 227.
p. 168 ibid., p. 229.
p. 168 *History of My Own Times*, edited by O. Airy, I 109.

Chapter 10

p. 170 quoted in Macaulay's *History of England* (Everyman edition), II 208.
p. 171 *Selections from Clarendon* (World's Classics), pp. 384 and 382.
p. 176 OLIVER HEYWOOD: *Diaries*, II 285 (quoted in Tanner, *Conflicts*, p. 245).
p. 178 Declaration of Rights: E. N. Williams, *The 18th Century Constitution*, p. 27.
p. 180 quoted in Pryde, II 45.
p. 181 C. Grant Robinson: *Select Statutes, Cases, and Documents*, p. 132.
p. 183 Letter of GEORGE HOLMES, November 16th, 1689 (*E.H.D.* VIII 754).
p. 192 Wilkins: *Political Ballads*, II 113 (quoted in Trevelyan p. 495).

Chapter 11

p. 195 Section III (Grant Robertson, p. 62).
p. 198 SIR JOHN RERESBY, *Memoirs* (1875), under the year 1668.
p. 198 ibid.–1670.
p. 198 ibid.–1671.
p. 199 ibid.–1674.
p. 199 ibid.–1684.
p. 199 ibid.–1671.
p. 200 ibid.–1670.
p. 200 H.M.C., Fifth Report, Appendix i, 375 (quoted in Hill, p. 273).
p. 200 *Reasons of the Decay of the Clothing Trade*, p. 2 (quoted in Lipson, III 326).
p. 201 quoted in Hill, p. 268.
p. 201 ibid.
p. 202 ROGER NORTH: *A Discourse of the Poor*, p. 76 (quoted in Lipson, III 466).
p. 202 *Selections from Clarendon* (World's Classics), p. 451.
p. 203 quoted in E. Victor Morgan, *A History of Money* (Penguin), p. 133.
p. 204 *The Journeys of Celia Fiennes*, edited by C. Morris, p. 85.
p. 204 ibid., p. 96.
p. 204 ibid., p. 132.
p. 205 quoted in P. Mantoux, *Industrial Revolution in the 18th Century* (1964 edition), p. 122.
p. 206 Poor Book of Westbury-on-Trym (quoted in D. Marshall, *The English Poor in the 18th Century*, pp. 125 and 264 – note 67).
p. 207 JOHN CARY: *An Essay Towards Regulating the Trade*, p. 158 (quoted in Lipson, III 475).
p. 208 J. AUBREY: *Brief Lives*, edited by A. Clark, ii 329 (quoted in G. N. Clark, *Later Stuarts*, p. 393).

p. 210 *The History of John Bull* (quoted in J. McCarthy, *The Reign of Queen Anne*, pp. 512–13).

Chapter 12

p. 211 THOMAS MUN: *England's Treasure by Foreign Trade*, p. 5 (facsimile reprint of first edition, 1927).
p. 212 'Memorandum' on commerce, quoted in Sir John Clapham, *Concise Economic History of Britain*, p. 279.
p. 214 WILLIAM PENN: *Account of the Province of Pennsylvania* (1681), p. 2.
p. 214 ibid., p. 2.
p. 216 quoted in M. Ashley *Life in Stuart England*, p. 168.
p. 217 COTTON MATHER: *Magnalia Christi Americana* (quoted ibid., p. 169).
p. 217 quoted in R. B. Nye and J. E. Morpurgo: *A History of the United States*, I 78.
p. 221 Margaret Verney: *Memoirs of the Verney Family* (1894), IV, c. 5
p. 222 *House of Commons Journals*, XIII 783 (quoted in Lipson, III 288).
p. 222 Scottish Historical Society's edition, p. 448 (quoted in *A Source Book of Scottish History*, edited by W. C. Dickinson and G. Donaldson, III 306).
p. 223 ibid., p. 331.
p. 224 ibid., p. 383.
p. 224 ROBERT BAILLIE (quoted in Pryde, II 30).

Chapter 13

p. 225 *An Anatomy of the World*: The First Anniversary, line 205.
p. 225 BACON: *Novum Organum*, Book I, Aphorism iii.
p. 225 quoted in A. E. E. Mckenzie, *The Major Achievements of Science*, I 82.
p. 225 *Novum Organum*, Book I Aphorism lxxxi.
pp. 225–6 Letter to Lord Salisbury (quoted in McKenzie, I 84).
p. 226 quoted in Hill, p. 94.
p. 226 *De Magnete*, Book VI, c. 3.
p. 227 *The Circulation of the Blood* – the dedication (Everyman Library).
p. 228 quoted in J. D. Bernal, *Science in History*, p. 317.
p. 228 facsimile edition, 1938 (*Early Science in Oxford*, Vol. 13).
p. 228 quoted in Bernal, p. 320.
p. 229 *New Experiments Physico-Mechanical Touching the Spring of the Air and its Effects* (1660), p. 7.
p. 229 ibid., p. 22.
p. 229 *Diary* – May 7th, 1662.
p. 230 *Micrographia* (1665), Observation 1.
p. 230 ibid., Observation 2.
p. 230 ibid., Observation 54.
p. 230 ibid., Observation 1.
p. 230 Book IV, section 8, c. V.
p. 231 Book I, section 21.
p. 231 Book IV, c. V, section 1.

p. 231 HALLEY: *Ode to Newton* – preface to *Mathematical Principles.*
p. 232 *Mathematical Principles* – Laws of Motion III.
p. 232 ibid.
p. 233 quoted in E. N. DA C. Andrade, *Sir Isaac Newton*, p. 58.
p. 234 R. NORTH: *Lives of the Norths* (*E.H.D.* VIII 484).
p. 234 quoted in McKenzie, I 44.
p. 234 *Naval Minutes*, edited by J. R. Tanner (*E.H.D.*,) VIII 483.)
p. 235 Reprinted in No. 51, *Journal of Royal Institute of Cornwall* (1913),
p. 25 The dedication.
p. 235 M. TRIEWALD: *Short Description*, translated by R. Jenkins (quoted in *History of Technology*, IV 174).
p. 236 Hume Brown: *Early Travellers in Scotland*, p. 116 (*A Source Book of Scottish History*, III 314).
p. 237 SIR W. BRERETON: *Travels in Holland, England, Scotland, and Ireland*, published by the Chetham Society, I 88 (quoted in J. U. Nef, *The Rise of the British Coal Industry*, I 176).
p. 237 CELIA FIENNES (edited by C. Morris), p. 224.
p. 237 p. 9.
p. 238 Petition in B.M. Add. MSS, quoted in M. W. Flinn, *Men of Iron*, p. 4.
p. 238 *Metallum Martis*, p. 4.
p. 239 'probably written about 1775' (T. S. Ashton, *Iron and Steel in the Industrial Revolution*, p. 249; Mantoux, p. 290).
p. 239 quoted in G. Donaldson, *Edinburgh History of Scotland*, III 395.
p. 240 quoted in Lord Ernle, *English Farming Past and Present*, p. 135.
p. 240 quoted in Hill, p. 201.
p. 241 quoted ibid., p. 151.
p. 241 *Memoirs*, under the year 1677.

Chapter 14

p. 242 *Travels of Conrad von Uffenbach*, translated and edited by W. H. Quarrell and M. Mare as *London in 1710*, p. 32.
p. 242 M. MISSON: *Memoirs and Observations in his Travels over England* (1719) p. 177.
p. 242 quoted in R. J. Mitchell and M. D. R. Leys, *A History of London Life* (Penguin), p. 171.
p. 243 Von Uffenbach, p. 34.
p. 243 ibid., p. 15.
p. 243 Misson, p. 21.
p. 243 Von Uffenbach, p. 16.
p. 244 N. WARD (EDWARD WARD), *The London Spy* (Cassell edition) Book VII, p. 117.
p. 244 Misson, p. 11.
p. 245 Ward, p. 41.
p. 245 JOHN MACKY: *A Journey through England* (1714), p. 193.
p. 245 Misson, p. 318.
p. 246 Von Uffenbach, p. 56.

p. 247 Macky, p. 118.
p. 247 Act II, Scene 1 – first lines.
p. 247 Misson, p. 206.
p. 247 Ward, p. 280.
p. 249 Von Uffenbach, p. 73.
p. 249 EDWARD HATTON: *A New View of London* (1708), II 629.
pp. 249–50 Misson, p. 80.
p. 250 ibid., p. 134.
p. 251 Macky, p. 198.
p. 252 Ward, pp. 80 and 79.
p. 252 Von Uffenbach, p. 32.
p. 252 Misson, p. 320.
p. 252 Von Uffenbach, p. 40.
p. 252 Ward, pp. 198 and 189.
p. 252 ibid., p. 196.
p. 252 Act V, Scene 1 – first lines.
p. 254 Macky, p. 112.
p. 254 Ward, p. 116.
p. 254 Misson, quoted in J. Ashton, *Social Life in the Reign of Queen Anne*, p. 370.
p. 255 Ward, p. 27.
p. 255 J. VANBRUGH: *The Provoked Wife*, Act III, Scene 2.
p. 255 Misson – quoted in Ashton, p. 164.
p. 256 Misson, p. 219.
p. 256 quoted in Ashton p. 257.
p. 257 Von Uffenbach, p. 48.
p. 257 ibid., p. 59.
pp. 257–8 Misson, pp. 306 and 304.
p. 258 Act III, Scene 13. Air 27.
p. 259 Von Uffenbach, p. 156.
p. 259 Misson – quoted in Ashton, p. 408.

Chapter 15

p. 261 *British Musical Miscellany* (1734), i (*New National Song Book*, edited by D. McMahon, p. 19).
p. 264 letter to Walpole, February 21, 1704 (quoted in J. H. Plumb, *Sir Robert Walpole*, I 60).
p. 265 JOHN, LORD HERVEY: *Some Materials towards Memoirs of the Reign of George II*, I 162 (quoted in Plumb, II 269).
p. 265 quoted in W. E. H. Lecky, *History of England in the Eighteenth Century*, I 334.
p. 267 quoted in J. Prebble, Culloden, p. 53.
p. 268 quoted in K. Tommasson and F. Bust *Battles of the '45*, p. 177.
p. 269 *Journey to the Western Islands of Scotland*, edited by E. J. Thomas, p. 68.

p. 272 anonymous essay of 1749, quoted in C. E. Carrington, *The British Overseas*, p. 286.
p. 273 'America or the Muse's Refuge', original version dated February 10th, 1726 (*Works*, edited by A. A. Luce and T. E. Jessop, VII 370).
p. 277 JAMES, EARL WALDEGRAVE: *Memoirs from 1754 to 1758* (quoted in B. Williams, *The Whig Supremacy*, p. 352).

Chapter 16

p. 282 Diary of GEORGE BUBB DODDNGTON (*E.H.D.* X 185).
p. 283 HERVEY: I 203–4 (quoted in Plumb, II 282).
p. 288 Letter of Sir Thomas Robinson to Lord Carlisle (Historical Manuscripts Commission, *E.H.D.*, X 539).
p. 288 quoted in *Works of Hogarth*, edited with descriptions by John Trusler, I 33.
p. 291 House of Commons Journals, XVIII 715 (quoted in Lipson, III 393).
p. 291 F. W. Galton: *Select Documents: The Tailoring Trade*, pp. 1–4.
p. 295 quoted from 'a contemporary newspaper' in J. H. Whiteley, *Wesley's England*, p. 75.

Chapter 17

p. 300 Autobiography of ALEXANDER CARLYLE (*E.H.D.*, X 671).
p. 301 *The Present State of Europe*, 1750, p. 504 (*E.H.D.*, X 851).
p. 306 preamble, quoted in E. Lipson, *History of the English Woollen and Worsted Industries*, p. 97.
p. 307 letter of the chaplain to the 2nd earl of Oxford (*E.H.D.*, X 476).
p. 309 JOSIAH TUCKER: *Instructions for Travellers*, 1757, p. 20 (quoted in Lipson, III 54).
p. 309 'Prospect of Birmingham in 1730' – engraving in the Birmingham Public Library (cited by H. Heaton, *Johnson's England*, I 235).

Chapter 18

p. 311 *Journal of John Wesley*, January 28th, 1760 (IV 364 in the Standard Edition, edited by Nehemiah Curnock, from which all quotations are made).
p. 312 *Journal*, November 17th, 1759 (IV 358).
p. 313 DEFOE's *Tour thro' the Whole Island of Great Britain*, II, 124 (quotations are from the Everyman edition, except for Scotland, which it omits).
p. 313 *Tour*, II 127 – future prospects.
p. 314 *Journal*, March 6th, 1758 (IV 254) – Watling Street; February 18th, 1747 (III 279) – Great North Road.
p. 314 *Tour*, II 54, 55, 75 – Wales.
p. 315 *Tour* (complete edition) ii 751, 781 – Scotland.
p. 315 *Journal*, April 24th and 25th, 1751 (III 522, 523).
p. 315 *Journal*, June 4th, 1757 (IV 217)
p. 315 *Tour*, II, 208, 141 – river trade.

p. 315 *Tour* (complete edition), iv 137 – Glasgow.
p. 316 *Tour*, II 258 – Liverpool.
p. 316 *Journal*, April 14th, 1755 (IV 112).
p. 316 *Tour*, II 268 – Preston.
pp. 316–17 *Journal*, September 29th, 1745. The references to Dettingen are at III 115 and 155 (entries for February 1st and December 3rd, 1744); to Fontenoy at III 216 and 226 (entries for October 26th and December 2nd, 1745).
p. 317 *Journal*, April 2nd, 1755.
p. 317 *Tour*, I 97 – Charlton, I 83 – Coventry.
p. 317 *Journal*, June 7th, 1757 (IV 218) – Scottish character.
p. 317 *Journal*, August 6th, 1746 (III 250) – facing mobs.
p. 317 *Journal*, October 20th, 1743 (III 99).
p. 318 *Journal*, April 2nd, 1740 (II 340) – Bristol; April 5th and 12th, 1744 (II 127, 131) – St. Ives; April 5th, 1755 (IV 109) – Black Country.
p. 318 *Tour*, I 187 – Winchester.
p. 319 *Tour*, I 62 – Norfolk; II 163 – Derbyshire cave-dwellers.
p. 319 *Journal*, November 9th, 1756 (IV 191) – electrical apparatus.
pp. 319–20 *Journal*, January 21st, 1740 (II 333) – Bristol; June 4th, 1747 (III 301) – poor stewards; November 25th, 1740 (II 404) – spinning taught; January 17th, 1748 (III 329) – lending-stock; February 9–10th, 1753 (IV 52) – conditions in sickness.
p. 320–1 *Tour*, I 1–2 – the great British Empire; I 59 – provisioning of London.
p. 321 *Tour*, I 59, 43, 299 – London; I 61, 280 – woollen industry; II 156 – silk.
p. 321 *Tour* (complete edition), iii 747 – linen.
p. 321 *Tour*, II 261 – cotton.
p. 322 *Tour*, II 140 – the North; II 244 – the Cornish.
p. 322 *Journal*, June 16th, 1757 (IV 220) – Sunderland. See also June 23rd, 1759 (IV 325) and for Cornwall, July 25th, 1753 (IV 76) and September 21st, 1762 (IV 530).
p. 322 *Journal*, July 1st, 1747 (III 305) – elections; October 17th, 1760 (IV 417) – Bristol.
p. 323 *Tour*, I 75 – La Hogue.
p. 323 *Journal*, September 3rd, 1755 (IV 132) – Pendennis castle.
p. 323 *Journal*, November 29th, 1759 (IV 361) – Public Thanksgiving.
p. 323 *Journal*, October 25th, 1760 (IV 417) – death of George II.
p. 323 *Tour*, I 4 – a growing child.

APPENDIX III

Book List

1. INTRODUCTORY
2. THE TUDOR STATE

Introductory

C. MORRIS, *The Tudors* (Batsford).

J. HURSTFIELD, *The Elizabethan Nation* (B.B.C.) – introduces the period.

K. GARVIN (ed.), *The Great Tudors* (Nicholson & Watson) – forty very short Lives.

Authorities

G.R. ELTON, *England under the Tudors* (Methuen): cc. I and XIV.

S. T. BINDOFF, *Tudor England* (Penguin Books): cc. 2 and 7.

J. D. MACKIE, *The Earlier Tudors* (O.U.P.): c. I – the new monarchy.

A. NICOLL, *The Elizabethans* (C.U.P.): pp. 3–12 – on Elizabeth.

3. RENAISSANCE AND REFORMATION

Introductory

G. W. O. WOODWARD, *Reformation and Resurgence 1485–1603* (Blandford): cc. 5–8.

F. E. HALLIDAY, *An Illustrated Cultural History of England* (Thames and Hudson): cc. 7 and 8 – an attractive brief presentation of the arts.

Authorities

V. DE S. PINTO, *The English Renaissance* (Cresset).

D. HARRISON, *Tudor England* (Cassell): Vol. II, pp. 149–79 – the Elizabethan Renaissance.

H. MORRIS, *Elizabethan Literature* (O.U.P.): cc. I, VI, and IX.

F. M. POWICKE, *The Reformation in England* (O.U.P.).

A. C. DICKENS, *The English Reformation* (Batsford).

New Cambridge Modern History (C.U.P.): Vol. II, c. 7 – G. R. Elton on the Reformation in England.

4. THE SEAFARERS

Introductory

R. R. SELLMAN, *The Elizabethan Seamen* (Methuen).

J. HAMPDEN (ed.), *Richard Hakluyt – Voyages and Documents* (World's Classics, O.U.P.) – selection of texts.

Authorities

J. A. WILLIAMSON, *The Age of Drake* (Black).

A. L. ROWSE, *The Expansion of Elizabethan England* (Macmillan): cc. 5–7.

E. G. R. TAYLOR, *Tudor Geography, 1485–1583* (Methuen).

5. THE RURAL SCENE
6. INDUSTRIAL GROWTH

Introductory

P. WILLIAMS, *Life in Tudor England* (Batsford): cc. I–III.

L. F. SALZMAN, *England in Tudor Times* (O.U.P.): cc. II–IV.

G. W. O. WOODWARD, op. cit.: c. 11.

Authorities

J. THIRSK, *Tudor Enclosures* (Routledge).

A. L. ROWSE, *The England of Elizabeth* (Macmillan): cc. III and IV.

G. R. ELTON, op. cit.: c. IX.

G. D. OWEN, *Elizabethan Wales* (U. of Wales Press): cc. 1 and 3.

J. D. MACKIE, op. cit.: c. II, on the face of England, and c. XIII, on economic development.

J. B. BLACK, *The Reign of Elizabeth* (O.U.P.): pp. 211–38.

7. SHAKESPEARE'S ENGLAND

Introductory

A. H. DODD, *Life in Elizabethan England* (Batsford).

M. ST CLARE BYRNE, *Elizabethan Life in Town and Country* (Methuen).

Authorities

J. DOVER WILSON, *Life in Shakespeare's England* (Penguin Books): cc. II, IV, and V.

H. C. DARBY, *An Historical Geography of England Before A.D. 1800* (C.U.P.): c. X.

G. M. TREVELYAN, *English Social History* (Longmans): cc. VI and VII.

J. E. NEALE, *Essays in Elizabethan History* (Cape): No. 2.

8. KING AND PARLIAMENT, 1603–1640

Introductory

G. E. AYLMER, *The Struggle for the Constitution 1603–1689* (Blandford): cc. 2 and 3.

CHARLES FIRTH, *Oliver Cromwell* (Putnam): cc. I and II.

Authorities

C. HILL, *The Century of Revolution 1603–1714* (Nelson): c. 4.

M. ASHLEY, *England in the Seventeenth Century* (Penguin Books): cc. I–V.

G. M. TREVELYAN, *England under the Stuarts* (Methuen): cc. I–VI – an old-fashioned but thrilling presentation.

R. H. TAWNEY, *Business and Politics in the Reign of James I* (C.U.P.): c. VII.

L. STONE, *The Crisis of the Aristocracy 1558–1641* (Longmans): cc. I (sections v and vi) and XIV.

9. THE CLASH OF ARMS

Introductory

F. W. JESSUP, *Background to the English Civil War* (Pergamon): pp. 54–155.

A. H. WOOLRYCH, *Battles of the English Civil War* (Batsford).

R. R. SELLMAN, *Civil War and Commonwealth* (Methuen).

Authorities

C. V. WEDGWOOD, *The King's War 1641–7* (Collins).

C. HILL, *Puritanism and Revolution* (Secker & Warburg): cc. 1, 6, and 10.

C. V. WEDGWOOD, *Truth and Opinion* (Collins): pp. 222–48 – the common man in the Civil War.

H. N. BRAILSFORD, *The Levellers and the English Revolution* (Stanford U.P.): cc. XV, XXI, XXVII, and XXXIV.

H. R. TREVOR-ROPER, *Religion, the Reformation and Social Change* (Macmillan): c. 8 – on Scottish aspects.

10. THE SETTLEMENT

Introductory

D. L. FARMER, *Britain and the Stuarts* (Bell): c. 6.

R. W. HARRIS, *England in the Eighteenth Century 1689–1793* (Blandford): cc. 3 and 5.

Authorities

G. M. TREVELYAN, *The English Revolution* (Home University Library, O.U.P.): cc. V–VII.

C. HILL, *Century of Revolution:* cc. 14 and 18.

G. M. TREVELYAN, *England under Queen Anne* (Longmans): Vol. II, cc. X–XIV, and Vol. III, c. XVII.

G. N. CLARK, *The Later Stuarts* (O.U.P.): c. X – on Scotland.

11. THE GROWTH OF PERSONAL LIBERTY

Introductory

R. J. MITCHELL and M. D. R. LEYS, *History of the English People* (Longmans): Book III, c. V.

G. N. CLARK, *Three Aspects of Stuart England* (O.U.P.): c. 3 – a lecture given in Canada.

Authorities

D. OGG, *England in the Reign of Charles II* (O.U.P.): Vol. II, c. XIV – on the liberty of the subject.

R. H. TAWNEY, *Religion and the Rise of Capitalism* (Murray): c. III, section iii.

C. WILSON, *England's Apprenticeship 1603–1763* (Longmans): cc. 1, 6, and 11.

G. M. TREVELYAN, *English Social History* (Longmans): c. IX.

12. THE BRITISH OVERSEAS

Introductory

R. DAVIS, *A Commercial Revolution* (Historical Association Pamphlet No. G.64).
C. WILSON, *Mercantilism* (Historical Association Pamphlet No. G. 37).

Authorities

C. E. CARRINGTON, *The British Overseas* (C.U.P.): c. I.
LORD ELTON, *Imperial Commonwealth* (Collins): pp. 36–110.
G. N. CLARK, *The Wealth of England from 1496 to 1760* (Home University Library, O.U.P.): cc. IV and V.
G. DONALDSON, *The Scots Overseas* (Hale): c. 3.

13. SCIENTIFIC AND TECHNICAL ADVANCES

Introductory

A. E. E. MCKENZIE, *The Major Achievements of Science* (C.U.P.): Vol. I, cc. 3–7.
P. MOORE, *Isaac Newton* (Black).

Authorities

H. BUTTERFIELD, *Origins of Modern Science* (Bell).
A. R. HALL, *The Making of Modern Science* (Leicester U.P.)
J. G. CROWTHER, *Francis Bacon* (Cresset): Part I – his scientific activities.
C. HILL, *Intellectual Origins of the English Revolution* (O.U.P.): c. II – on science and medicine in London.
C. SINGER *et al.* (ed.), *A History of Technology* (O.U.P.): Vol. IV, pp. 168–79 – on the steam-engine.

14. LONDON IN THE REIGN OF QUEEN ANNE

Introductory

R. J. MITCHELL and M. D. R. LEYS, *A History of London Life* (Penguin Books): cc. 7–9.
J. MCCARTHY, *The Reign of Queen Anne* (Chatto & Windus): c. XII.

Authorities

T. F. REDDAWAY, *The Rebuilding of London after the Great Fire* (Arnold).
M. ASHLEY, *Life in Stuart England* (Batsford): cc. V, VII, and VIII.
A. S. TURBERVILLE (ed.), *Johnson's England* (O.U.P.): Vol. I, c. VII – a fascinating account by M. D. George of London in Dr Johnson's time, much of which is relevant also to the beginning of the century.
G. M. TREVELYAN, *English Social History* (Longmans): pp. 330–38.
E. M. CARUS-WILSON (ed.), *Essays in Economic History* (Arnold): Vol. II, pp. 197–207 – F. J. Fisher on the development of London as a centre of conspicuous consumption, 1500–1700.

15. KINGDOM AND EMPIRE

Introductory

D. D. LINDSAY and D. S. WASHINGTON, *A Portrait of Britain 1688–1851* (O.U.P.): cc. 5–7.

R. W. HARRIS, op. cit.: cc. 6 and 7.

Authorities

B. WILLIAMS, *The Whig Supremacy 1714–1760* (O.U.P.): cc. II, VIII, and X.

W. E. H. LECKY, *History of England in the Eighteenth Century* (Longmans): Vol. I, c. II, and Vol. II, cc. V and VI – old but still of great interest.

K. TOMASSON and F. BUIST, *Battles of the '45* (Batsford): c. 7 – Culloden.

C. GRANT ROBERTSON, *Chatham and the British Empire* (E.U.P.): c. II – The Great Ministry.

16. THE CLASSES AND THE MASSES

Introductory

R. J. MITCHELL and M. D. R. LEYS, *History of the English People* (Longmans): Book IV, c. I – entitled 'A Landscape with Figures'; this covers a long period in an unusual way.

A. S. TURBERVILLE, *English Men and Manners in the Eighteenth Century* (O.U.P.): c. III – 'The Social Scene'.

Authorities

J. H. PLUMB, *England in the Eighteenth Century* (Penguin Books): Part I, cc. 1, 4, and 5.

G D. H. COLE and R. POSTGATE, *The British People 1746 – 1946* (Methuen): cc. VI and VII.

New Cambridge Modern History (C.U.P.): Vol. VII, c. XI – by W. R. Brock.

M. G. JONES, *The Charity School Movement in the XVIIIth Century* (C.U.P.): cc. I (1); II (1); III (2); V (1); VI (on Scotland); VIII (on Wales).

17. ECONOMIC GROWTH

Introductory

T. K. DERRY, *A Short Economic History of Britain* (O.U.P.): Part 1, c .12.

D. D. LINDSAY and D. S. WASHINGTON, op. cit.: c. 4.

Authorities

C. WILSON, *England's Apprenticeship: 1603–1763* (Longmans): cc. 12–15.

A. S. TURBERVILLE (ed.), *Johnson's England* (O.U.P.): Vol. I, cc. IX and X – surveys of industry and agriculture from the 1720s onwards, by H. Heaton and C. S. Orwin respectively.

A. REDFORD, *The Economic History of England 1760–1860* (Longmans): c.l.

T. S. ASHTON, *Iron and Steel in the Industrial Revolution* (Manchester U.P.): cc. I and II.

T. S. ASHTON, *The Industrial Revolution* (Home University Library, O.U.P.): c. II – 'The Earlier Forms of Industry'.

18. THE BRITISH PEOPLE AS SEEN BY DEFOE AND WESLEY

Introductory

M. D. GEORGE, *England in Transition* (Penguin Books): cc. 2 and 3.

D. MARSHALL, *John Wesley* (O.U.P.)

Authorities

G. D. H. COLE, *Persons and Periods* (Penguin Books): pp. 7–38 – on Defoe and his *Tour*.

G. M. TREVELYAN, *English Social History*: c. X – Defoe's England.

J. W. BRADY, *England: Before and After Wesley* (Hodder and Stoughton): cc. X–XIV.

R. F. WEARMOUTH, *Methodism and the Common People in the Eighteenth Century* (Epworth Press): Section 2, cc. II and III, and Section 3, c. I.

INDEX

Numbers in italics refer to Illustrations

APPENDIX IV

Comparative Table of Events

(pp. 362–9)

MAIN EVENTS (foreign events italicized)	LEGISLATION	SOCIAL AND ECONOMIC	SCOTLAND, IRELAND, AND UNIFICATION	THE BRITISH OVERSEAS	PUBLICATIONS
1480					
1485 HENRY VII 1487 Special court established ('Star Chamber') 1487 Lambert Simnel defeated and captured	1489 Act for justices of the peace				
1490					
1492 Columbus discovers America 1492 Treaty of Etaples 1494 *Transoceanic world divided by Spain and Portugal*		c. 1496 First English blast-furnace 1496 Magnus Intercursus	1494 Poynings' law		
1497–8 Vasco da Gama's voyage to India 1499 Perkin Warbeck executed			1497 Cornish rebellion	1497 Cabot discovered Newfoundland	
1500					
1509 HENRY VIII			1502 Marriage of James IV and Margaret Tudor		
1510					
1513 Battle of the Spurs 1513 *Machiavelli's* Prince written			1513 Battle of Flodden		
1517 Luther at Wittenberg		1517 Wolsey's Commission on Enclosures			1516 More: *Utopia*
1519–22 *First voyage round the world*					
1520					
1520 Meeting at Field of Cloth of Gold					1521 Major: *History of Greater Britain* 1523 Fitzherbert: *Book of Husbandry*
1529–36 Reformation Parliament			1528 Patrick Hamilton burnt		

1531 *Death of Zwingli*

1534–40 Ascendancy of Thomas Cromwell
1535 Execution of More
1536 Dissolution of monasteries begun
1536 Pilgrimage of Grace
1536 Calvin's Institutes

1533 Act of Appeals
1534 Act of Supremacy

1531 Act against Beggars

1534 Council in the Marches of Wales fully established

1536, 1543 Laws incorporating Wales with England
1536 Council of the North fully established

1538 English Bible placed in churches

1540

1545 *Silver mined at Potosi*

1547 EDWARD VI

1549 House of Commons first sat in St. Stephen's Chapel
1549 Religious revolt in Devon and Cornwall

1544 Debasement of coinage begun

1547 Chantries Act

1549 Ket's rebellion against enclosures

1542 Battle of Solway Moss
1543 Title of 'King of Ireland' assumed

1547 Knox's Reformation preaching begun
1547 Battle of Pinkie

1549 Cranmer's first Prayer Book

1550

1550 Somerset loses power to Northumberland

1553 MARY I
1553 Revolt on behalf of Lady Jane Grey
1554 Wyatt's rebellion
1554 Reconciliation to Rome
1555 Burning of Latimer and Ridley

1558 Loss of Calais
1558 ELIZABETH I

1559 Acts of Supremacy and Uniformity

1554–60 Regency of Mary of Lorraine in Scotland

1557 Lords of Congregation signed first Covenant

1559 Final return of Knox to Scotland

1553–4 Voyage of Chancellor and Willoughby

1555 Muscovy Company founded

1557 Tusser: *Hundred Good Points*

MAIN EVENTS (foreign events italicized)	LEGISLATION	SOCIAL AND ECONOMIC	SCOTLAND, IRELAND, AND UNIFICATION	THE BRITISH OVERSEAS	PUBLICATIONS
1560					
		1561 Recoinage	1560 Treaty of Edinburgh 1561 Mary's return to Scotland		
1562–98 *Wars of Religion in France* 1563 Thirty-Nine Articles		1563 Statute of Artificers		1562–8 Hawkins's slave-trading voyages	1563 Foxe: *Book of Martyrs*
			1567 Murder of Darnley 1567 Regency established for James VI		1566 Gilbert: *Discourse on Cathay*
1568 *Revolt of the Netherlands against Spain* 1569 Rising of the Northern Earls.		1568 Mines Royal and Mineral and Battery Works established	1568 Mary fled to England		
1570					
1570 Excommunication of Elizabeth					1572 Wilson: *Discourse on Usury*
				1576–8 Frobisher's search for N.W. Passage 1577–80 Drake's circum-navigation	1577 Holinshed: *Chronicles* 1578 Lyly: *Euphues: the Anatomy of Wit* 1579 Saxton: *Atlas of England and Wales*
1580					
	1581 Increased fine for non-attendance at church			1583 Gilbert's voyage to Newfoundland	
1584 *Assassination of William the Silent* 1584 Bond of Association				1584, 1587 Attempted colonization of 'Virginia' 1585–7 N.W. voyages of Davis	1586 Camden: *Britannia*
1587 Drake's raid on Cadiz 1587 Execution of Mary Queen of Scots 1588 Armada		1589 Lee's invention of stocking-frame			1589 Hakluyt: *Voyages* (1st edition) 1589 Spenser: *Faerie Queene* (Books 1–3)
1590					
		c. 1590 First English slitting-mill		1592 Levant Company founded	1591–1600 Shakespeare: historical plays 1594 Hooker: *Laws of*

1600	1603 JAMES I 1604 Peace with Spain 1604 Hampton Court Conference 1605 Gunpowder Plot		1601 First cancellations of monopolies	1608 Calvin's Case 1609 Plantation of Ulster	1600 East India Company founded 1607 Virginia colonized	1600 Gilbert: *De Magnete* 1600 Shakespeare: *Merchant of Venice* 1600 Dekker: *Shoemaker's Holiday*
1610	1618–48 *Thirty Years War*					1611 Authorized Version of the Bible
1620	1621 House of Commons Protestation 1623 Spanish marriage project 1625 CHARLES I 1628 Assassination of Buckingham 1628 *Surrender of Huguenots at La Rochelle* 1629–40 Period of Prerogative Rule	1628 Petition of Right	1624 Statute of Monopolies	1621 Five Articles of Perth	1620 Voyage of *Mayflower* 1625 Barbados colonized 1629 First settlement of Nova Scotia	1620 Bacon: *Novum Organum* 1622 Bacon: *History of Henry the Seventh* 1622 Drayton: *Poly-Olbion* 1628 Harvey: *De Motu Cordis* 1629 First settlement of Nova Scotia
1630	1633 Laud archbishop of Canterbury 1635–7 Case of Ship-Money 1639 1st Bishops' War		1634 Agreement for drainage of fens	1633 Wentworth lord deputy of Ireland 1638 National Covenant signed		

MAIN EVENTS (foreign events italicized)	LEGISLATION	SOCIAL AND ECONOMIC	SCOTLAND, IRELAND, AND UNIFICATION	THE BRITISH OVERSEAS	PUBLICATIONS
1640					
1640 2nd Bishops' War 1640 Meeting of Long Parliament				1640 Fort constructed at Madras	
1641 Execution of Strafford 1641 Grand Remonstrance 1642–6 1st Civil War 1642 Battle of Edgehill	1641 Triennial Act 1641 Act for Abolition of Star Chamber		1641–9 Irish Revolt		
1643 Solemn League and Covenant		1643 Excise introduced			
1644 Battle of Marston Moor 1645 Battle of Naseby					1644 Milton: *Areopagitica*
1648 2nd Civil War 1649 COMMONWEALTH		1649 Leveller movement at its height	1648 Battle of Preston 1649–50 Reconquest of Ireland		
1650					
			1650–1 Charles II king in Scotland 1650 Battle of Dunbar		
1652–4 1st Dutch War 1652 Assembly of Saints 1653 PROTECTORATE	1653 Instrument of Government		1651 Battle of Worcester 1652–60 Scotland united with England	1651 Navigation law	
1655–6 Rule of Major-Generals				1655 Capture of Jamaica	1656 Harrington: *Oceana*
1658 Capture of Dunkirk 1658 Death of Oliver Cromwell		1659 The Rota Club			
1660					
1660 Declaration of Breda 1660 CHARLES II 1661–79 Cavalier Parliament 1661–1715 *Louis XIV's personal rule in France*	1661–5 Clarendon Code		1661 Act Rescissory	1660 Navigation Act	
		1662 Settlement law 1662 Charter of Royal Society 1663 First turnpike Act		1662 Bombay acquired from Portugal	
1664–7 2nd Dutch War	1664 Triennial Act			1664 Fort James acquired (Gambia)	

1667 Fall of Clarendon					1667 Milton:
1670					
1670 Treaty of Dover 1672–4 3rd Dutch War 1674–8 Danby in office	1673, 1678 Test Acts	1671 First game law 1672 Stop of the Exchequer 1673 Corn Bounty established		1670 Hudson's Bay Company founded 1672 Royal African Company founded	1675 Wycherley: *Country Wife*
1678 Popish Plot 1679–81 Exclusion Parliaments	1679 Habeas Corpus Amendment Act		1679 Battles of Drumclog and Bothwell Brig		1678 Bunyan: *Pilgrim's Progress*
1680					
1683 Rye-house Plot 1685–8 JAMES II 1685 Monmouth's rebellion 1685 *Revocation of the Edict of Nantes* 1687, 1688 Declarations of Indulgence			1681–6 The 'Killing Time'	1681 Pennsylvania established	1681 Dryden: *Absalom and Achitophel* 1685–92 Locke: *Letters on Toleration* 1687 Newton: *Principia*
1689 WILLIAM III AND MARY II 1689–97 French War	1689 Mutiny and Toleration Acts; Bill of Rights		1689 Battles of Killiecrankie and Dunkeld		
1690					
1690 French victory at Beachy Head 1692 Anglo-Dutch victory at La Hogue		1692 Land Tax	1690 Battle of the Boyne 1691 Treaty of Limerick 1692 Glencoe massacre		
1694 WILLIAM III 1697 Treaty of Ryswick	1694 Triennial Act 1697 Civil List Act	1694 Bank of England founded 1695 Censorship lapsed 1696 Recoinage 1697 Settlement law modified 1698 Savery's engine patented 1699 Charity schools introduced		1698–1700 Scottish Darien expeditions	
1700					
1701 Death of ex-king James II 1702 ANNE 1702–13 French War	1701 Act of Settlement				

MAIN EVENTS (foreign events italicized)	LEGISLATION	SOCIAL AND ECONOMIC	SCOTLAND, IRELAND, AND UNIFICATION	THE BRITISH OVERSEAS	PUBLICATIONS
1704–9 Victories of Marlborough			1704 Act of Security	1704 Capture of Gibraltar	1704 Newton: *Optics*
1707 Union of parliaments			1706–7 Treaty of Union accepted		
		c. 1709 First coke-smelting of iron		1708 Capture of Minorca	1709–12 Steele and Addison: *Tatler* and *Spectator*
1710					
1710–14 Tories in power	1711 Occasional Conformity Act 1712 Patronage Act (for Scotland)	1710 Wren's rebuilding of St. Paul's completed 1712 Newcomen engine		1711 South Sea Company founded	1711 Swift: *On the Conduct of the Allies* 1712 Arbuthnot: *History of John Bull*
1713 Treaty of Utrecht 1714 GEORGE I 1715 Jacobite rebellion	1715 Riot Act 1716 Septennial Act		1715 Battle of Sheriffmuir	1713 Possession of Newfoundland and Nova Scotia confirmed by treaty	
		1719 Lombe's silk-mill	1719 Spanish landing defeated at Glenshiel		1719 Defoe: *Robinson Crusoe*
1720					
1721–42 Walpole in office		1720 South Sea Bubble 1721 Calico Act 1723 Act for erection of workhouses			1724–6 Defoe: *Tour*
1727 GEORGE II		1726 Act against trade unions of woollen workers	1726–33 Wade's Highland roads built	1729 First governor of Newfoundland	1726 Swift: *Gulliver's Travels* 1726 *The Craftsman* 1728 Gay: *Beggar's Opera*
1730					
1733 Excise Bill		1730–8 Townshend active as agriculturist 1733 Kay's fly-shuttle		1733 Colonization of Georgia	1731 *The Gentleman's Magazine* 1733 Tull: *Horse-Hoeing Husbandry*
1737 Death of Queen Caro-		1737 Welsh Circulating	1736 Porteous Riot		

1739–48 War against Spain (and, later, France)	1739 Foundling Hospital established 1739 Methodist open-air preaching began			c. 1739 Wesley: *Journal*
1740				
1740–4 Anson's voyage round the world 1740–8 *War of the Austrian Succession*				
1743 Victory over French at Dettingen 1744–54 Pelham in office 1745 Defeat by French at Fontenoy 1745–6 Jacobite rebellion				
		1746 Battle of Culloden 1747 Heritable jurisdictions abolished		1747 Wesley: *Primitive Physic*
1748 Treaty of Aix-la-Chapelle	1748 Huntsman's crucible steel			
			1749 Halifax, N.S., founded	
1750				
	1751 Gin Act 1752 Reform of the Calendar 1752 Hardwicke's Marriage Act	1752 Commissioners for Forfeited Estates established	1751 Clive's defence of Arcot	1751 Fielding: *Increase of Robbers*
				1754 Lind: *Treatise on Scurvy* 1754 Chippendale: *Cabinet Maker's Director*
	1755 Sankey 'navigation'			
1756–63 Seven Years War 1757 Pitt in power			1757 Battle of Plassey	
1759 Year of Victories			1759 Wolfe's victory at Quebec	
1760				
1760 Death of George II				

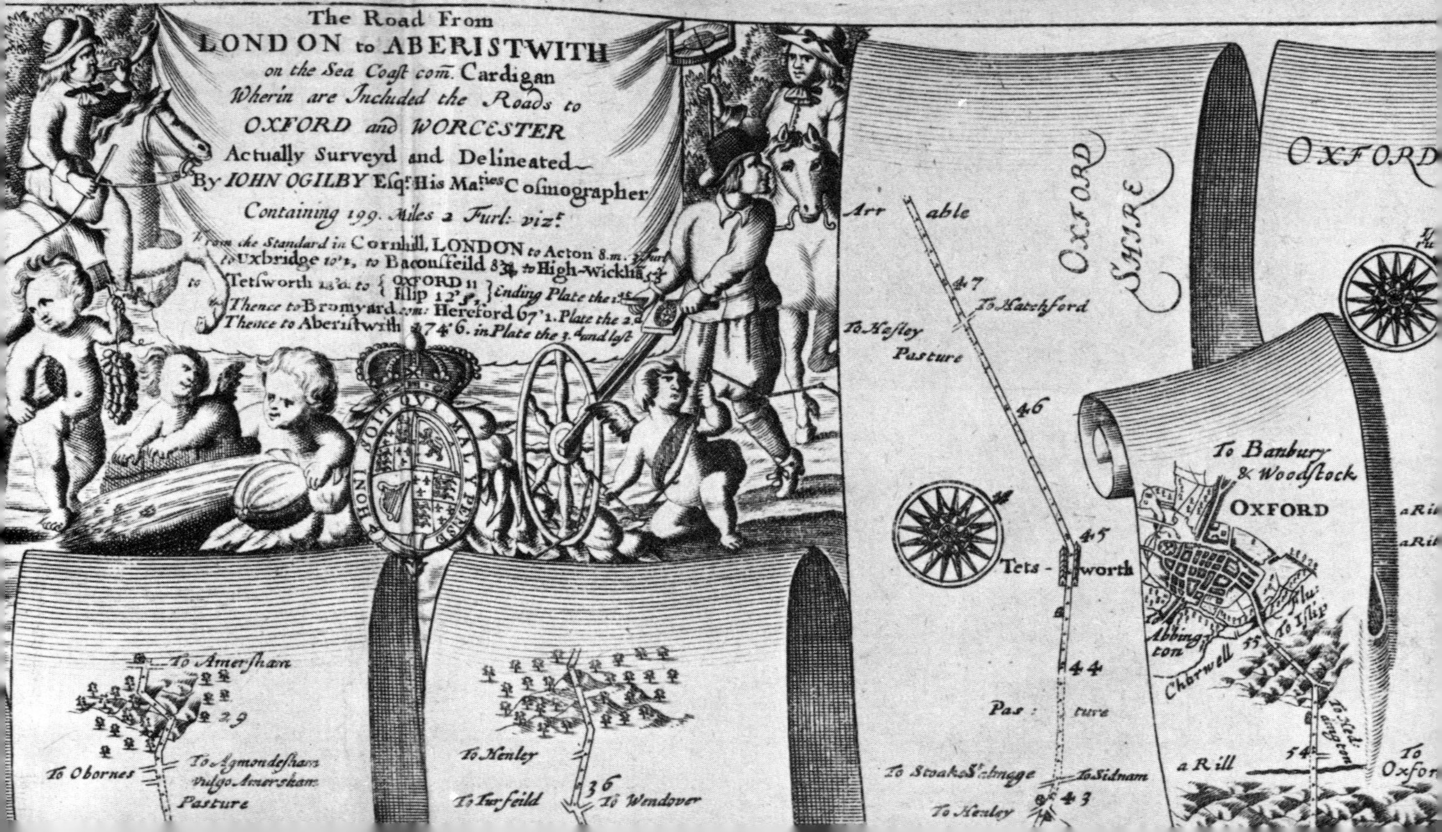
The Road From
LONDON to ABERISTWITH
on the Sea Coast com. Cardigan
Wherin are Included the Roads to
OXFORD and WORCESTER
Actually Surveyd and Delineated
By IOHN OGILBY Esqr. His Maties Cosmographer
Containing 199. Miles 2 Furl. vizt.
From the Standard in Cornhill, LONDON to Acton 8.m. 3 furl. to Uxbridge 10.1, to Baconsfeild 8.3, to High-Wickham
to Tetsworth 13.6. to { OXFORD 11 / Islip 12.5 } Ending Plate the 1st.
Thence to Bromyard com: Hereford 67.1. Plate the 2d.
Thence to Aberistwith 47.6. in Plate the 3d and last
HONI SOIT QVI MAL Y PENSE
OXFORD SHIRE
OXFORD
Arr able
To Hatchford
To Hasley
Pasture
Tets worth
Pas ture
To Stoake Talmage
To Sidnam
To Henley
To Banbury & Woodstock
OXFORD
Abbington
Cherwell
To Islip
To Hedington
a Rill
To Oxford
To Amersham
To Agmondesham vulgo Amersham
To Obornes
Pasture
To Henley
To Turfeild
To Wendover
47
46
45
44
43
36
29
55
54